Grundlagen der Kommunikation und Kognition
Foundations of Communication and Cognition

Herausgeber/Editors
Roland Posner, Georg Meggle

Signs, Search and Communication

Semiotic Aspects of Artificial Intelligence

Edited by
René J. Jorna
Barend van Heusden
Roland Posner

Walter de Gruyter · Berlin · New York
1993

♾ Gedruckt auf säurefreiem Papier, das die US-ANSI-Norm über Haltbarkeit erfüllt.

Printed on acid-free paper which falls within the guidelines of the ANSI to ensure permanence and durability.

Die Deutsche Bibliothek — CIP-Einheitsaufnahme

Signs, search and communication : semiotic aspects of artificial intelligence / ed. by René J. Jorna ... — Berlin ; New York : de Gruyter, 1993
(Grundlagen der Kommunikation und Kognition)
ISBN 3-11-013658-9
NE: Jorna, René J. [Hrsg.]

Printed in Germany
Druck: Arthur Colllignon GmbH, Berlin
Buchbinderische Verarbeitung: Lüderitz & Bauer-GmbH, Berlin

Foreword

This volume contains a selection of papers presented at the conference: Expert Systems, Culture and Semiotics. The conference was held in Groningen in December 12-15, 1990 and was jointly organized by the Faculty of Management and Organization and the Faculty of Arts of the University of Groningen with the cooperation of the Royal Dutch Academy of Sciences (de Koninklijke Nederlandse Academie voor Wetenschappen), the International Association for Semiotic Studies (IASS) and the Nederlandse Vereniging voor Semiotiek (NVvS).

A companion volume containing another selection of papers presented at the Groningen conference is published at the DSSW Press in Leiden. It is entitled: *The expert sign: Semiotics of culture and expertise*, and is edited by L.J. Slikkerveer, B. van Heusden, R.J. Jorna & G. van den Broek.

We express our sincere thanks to Marijke Wubbolts and Wilna Mittendorp, who typed and corrected the manuscripts, and to Henny Wever, who drew all the (sometimes difficult) figures.

Groningen, August 15, 1992

R.J. JORNA, B. VAN HEUSDEN & R. POSNER

Contents

III Communication with Expert Systems

Signs, search and communication: Towards an empirical future for semiotics

R.J. JORNA & B. VAN HEUSDEN (Groningen)

1. Semiotics

From the point of view of Artificial Intelligence (A.I.) the time has come to establish a scientific field or discipline related to communication and interaction based on signs, that is to say symbols, signals, icons, etc. However, such a field already exists, it is called semiotics, but it is not as well known as it should be. This situation has to be regretted for two reasons. In the first place because several elements of this field can easily be applied to A.I. research, e.g., theory fragments from the works of Leibniz, Peirce, Morris, Hjelmslev, Goodman and Eco. In the second place there remains an explicit need for a theory of communication and interaction between natural and artificial intelligent systems. The communication between humans and between humans and computers is often realized with the help of highly sophisticated signs and other communication structures. In this introduction we will discuss the role of semiotics (§1), the relation between signs, information processing and cognitive science (§2), the issue of communication (§3 and §4) and, finally, the contents of the contributions in this volume (§5).

Posner has demarcated the field of semiotics in the very first issue of the Zeitschrift für Semiotik (1979), as follows:

(1) Semiotics studies all sorts of sign processes in the communication and the exchange of information between humans, between humans and other organisms and inside organisms in general.

In this definition there is no reference to the concepts and latest results of the study of human cognition and computer systems. Moreover, there is no mention of the fact that the processing of information is considered to involve symbol systems, symbol manipulation, computation and (mental) representations. For that reason we proposed a slightly adjusted definition (Jorna, 1990).

(2) Semiotics is the study of all sorts of sign or symbol process in the communication and the exchange of knowledge, in the sense of data, between and inside information processing systems, such as humans, other organisms and machines.

Definition (2) has the advantage that it takes into account the conception of sophisticated modern computers as well as humans as symbol manipulating devices (Newell, 1990). Moreover, it includes the growing importance of, and interest in, man-machine interfaces (Card, Moran & Newell, 1983; Mulder & v/d Veer, 1988).

The forthcoming Handbook of Semiotics by Posner, Sebeok & Robering (1993), includes the latest research efforts on semiotics and classifies the study of signs in relation to such areas as endosemiosis, zoosemiosis, phytosemiosis, anthroposemiosis and machinesemiosis. Semiosis is equivalent with sign (or symbol) *processing* and represents the object level. Semiotics represents the meta level and studies signs, sign *structures* and sign *processing*.

Nöth (1985) provides an extensive overview of all sorts of interpretations of semiotics and confronts the broad definitions (1) and (2) with a narrow definition, in which semiotics is restricted to the field of anthroposemiotics. Within this field, criteria such as cultural determination (which opposes nature and culture), systematicity of signs (which focuses on the structure of sign systems) and intentionality (which means that only signs produced with the intention to communicate are relevant to study) are formulated. These criteria further restrict the applicability of semiotics.

Semiotics is not undisputed in the general domain of research. It is said to lack internal consistency due to competing theories; there are too many philosophical perspectives; it lacks an object of study accepted by all researchers; there is no outspoken research program nor a balanced methodological instrument, empirical or theoretical. This qualification is stimulating and fruitful as well as frustrating and embarrassing.

Another interesting discussion arises concerning the question whether semiotics is a field of study or a scientific discipline (Posner, 1988). Should semiotics be compared with, for example, physics or with, for example, women's liberation? According to Posner:

> ... it is possible to decide the problem of whether a given set of activities should be considered a discipline on the basis of a few questions: (1) Are these recurring activities? If so, they are a field. (2) Is the field used to earn one's living? If so, it is work. (3) Is the work assigned to a specific group of persons? If so, it is a profession. (4) Is the profession taught in an institution? If so, it is a discipline. (p. 166-167)

Besides the professional perspective Posner also puts forward an epistemological point of view on disciplines. For this purpose several criteria in terms of questions are formulated. For example, does the study concern itself with a specific domain of objects, or are the propositions coherent enough to form a doctrine or, stronger, a theory, or does the field have a history? A closer look at the history of the sciences reveals that many of the before mentioned criteria have been used to demarcate a scientific discipline. Posner concludes with the statement:

> A field of studies is a scientific discipline if and only if it has (a1) a fixed domain of objects that is studied in its totality, as well as (a2) a specific value-free perspective, (a3) methods that are repeatedly applicable, (a4) a theory that can be falsified, and (a5) means of presentation that are intersubjectively comprehensible, and if its borders are determined with respect to either (b1) the homogeneity of its domain, or (b2) the unity of its perspective, or (b3) the central role of one of its methods, or (b4) a core theory, or (b5) a dominant means of presentation. (Posner, 1988, p. 178).

According to this high standard, semiotics is not a scientific discipline, but neither are cognitive science, artificial intelligence or management science. The problem for semiotics is that although there is a domain of objects (a1), i.e., signs in all their various manifestations, together with means of presentation that are intersubjectively comprehensible (a5), there is no specific value-free perspective (a2), nor repeatedly applicable methods (a3) nor a theory that can be falsified (a4).

There are some arguments concerning the coherence of a fixed domain of objects (a1). We may question whether words, icons and pictures fall under the same heading, i.e., that of signs. Of course, in a sense, this certainly is the case. On the other hand linguists want to reserve the study of words (in a language) as a separate field, whereas media scholars (*vis a vis* painting, sculpture, film and other pictorial material) do not equate pictures with language. Several attempts have been made to establish a terminology that unites all manifestations of signs (Goodman, 1981; Hjelmslev, 1963). However, there is no definite conclusion concerning the results. We will return to this point below.

The above characterization of semiotics precisely points to its defects. It can be argued that from a philosophical viewpoint unification will be very difficult; i.e., how should the hermeneutic tradition in semiotics be combined with the logical and analytical tradition? More concretely, how can we realize a combination of the philosophy of Russell, Carnap or Morris with the philosophy of Gadamer or Heidegger? Put more extremely, how should we combine scientific research and its philosophical foundations with the perspective of scholarship, literature, i.e., the exegesis of texts and aesthetics? Several semioticians (see: Nöth, 1985) have attempted to construct semiotics on the basis of both traditions. Unfortunately, the results of these attempts do not easily fit together. The same situation, however, holds for mainstream philosophy.

At the beginning we asserted that a scientific field or discipline concerned with communication and interaction based on signs is relevant at present for A.I. and related fields. The reason for claiming this, is that the state of the art in cognitive science and computer science is such that semiotics can offer valuable contributions to artificial intelligence, human-computer-interaction and communication theory. This volume is a testimony of that belief. Another illustration can be found in the work of Newell & Simon, who are still working on the foundations of artificial intelligence.

Newell & Simon go as far as to say that symbols and search are the core concepts in computer science, cognitive science and artificial intelligence. These concepts can be compared to other basic concepts in other fields or disciplines, such as cells in biology, tectonic plates in geology, atoms and quanta in physics and so on. If one holds the position that the physical symbol systems hypothesis in relation with empirical research on symbols and search form the cornerstone of artificial intelligence, one should go one step further and express the belief that the basis of artificial intelligence is semiotic in nature. The recognition of this nature paves the way for more thorough semiotic analyses concerning signs, codes, icons, intentions, rationality and communication. Some of these analyses are included in this volume.

2. Symbols in artificial intelligence and cognitive science

The title of this introductory chapter is more than just a paraphrase of the 1976 Turing Award address by Newell & Simon: Computer Science as Empirical Inquiry: Symbols and Search. The issue, here, is not a discussion about the importance of computer science. This has been done elsewhere and much better (Newell, 1990; Posner, 1989). The reference in the title is to the basic terms "empirical", "symbols" (or in semiotic terms: "signs") and "search". These three terms in combination with "communication" form the core of this book and almost every article in this volume discusses one or more of these terms in a substantial way.

One may wonder why Newell & Simon never broached semiotics in their work, while what they were doing is on the one hand of great importance for semiotics, but on the other hand neglects results from semiotics, such as the discussion about symbols (Peirce or Goodman) or the relation between syntax, semantics and pragmatics (Morris or Posner).

The fundamental thesis in Newell & Simon's Turing Address is the physical symbol systems hypothesis. It claims that intelligent systems which exhibit rational behaviour show their intelligence by manipulating symbols internally in their system. "Symbol" is used as a primitive term equivalent in meaning with sign or even code. The manipulation consists in performing operations on these symbols such as deletion, creation, direction, duplication and so on. The addition "physical" refers to the fact that every symbol has a material carrier. This can be an electronic pattern in computers or a neurological pattern in humans. This implies that, although intelligent systems are different in their physical make up, they can still be equivalent on a functional level. Apart from that, it is the symbolic assertion that is challenged in recent work on connectionism (Bechtl & Abrahamson, 1991).

Besides the manipulation of symbols, the sequence of the operations on symbols also forms a cornerstone of computer science and cognitive science. In these terms thinking and problem solving can be conceived to be the path through an enormous space of symbol structures with the goal to reach a final state. This is equivalent to reaching a solution for a problem. The way one takes or foresees a route through this problem space can be called reasoning, or in terms of symbol structures, the search through a universe of symbols. In earlier days when we did not have computers, the only way to investigate thinking and problem solving was to study logic and inference making which was only a theoretical and abstract matter. Now that we have computers we can simulate symbol processing and symbol manipulation on these computers and compare the results in intelligent behaviour with the performances of human intelligence. This possibility turns theoretical science into empirical science which means that symbols and search can be studied within empirical inquiry.

3. Human-Computer-Interaction (the user interface)

Today, it is still not the case that we communicate with computers in the same way we communicate with humans. No adequate natural language interfaces are available and the ones that have been developed cannot deal with ambiguity, intentions, completely different frames of reference, i.e., with pragmatics in general. Communication involves three fundamental aspects: content, form or presentation, and action. In the user-interface a language metaphor (content and form) as well as a world metaphor (action) are mixed (Mulder, Lamain & Passchier, 1992). The first implies syntax, semantics and pragmatics, the second manipulation and action. Both aspects of interfacing are hardly elaborated and sometimes not even realized.

This arrear is not only due to limitations in hardware and software, but mainly to the fact that communication involves other then merely technological aspects. Shneiderman (1987), one of the founding fathers of man-machine communication, puts it as follows:

> The central problem for psychologists, human factors professionals, and computer scientists is to develop adequate theories and models of human behaviour with interactive systems. Traditional psychological theories must be extended and refined to accommodate the complex human learning, memory, and problem solving required in these applications. Useful goals include descriptive taxonomies, explanatory theories, or predictive models (p. 78-79).

It is symptomatic for the relation between cognitive science, human computer interaction and semiotics to note that Shneiderman nowhere mentions the possible role of a science of signs in this discussion.

Before 1980 the user interface was considered to be a non-issue in the software environment. Computers seemed to consist of heaps of iron and electronics and programming languages and the people that developed this material were the same as those who worked with it. Today, however, in the software environment things are getting more and more complex, because developer and user are not necessarily one and the same person anymore. Developers have ideas about what is easy or difficult to understand, with which the users do not always agree. This is one of the reasons why the problem of the user interface has come up. Another reason for the growing interest in the user interface is the availability of several styles of interaction and forms of presentation on the screen within one software package. The problem, here, is which style to choose in which situation.

The manipulation of objects and the performance of actions on computers is in the end always done by using expressions, models or icons on the screen. There is no more agreement about the use of these forms on the screen than there is on interaction styles. In this respect one issue, mainly present in the form of an implicit assumption, should have our special attention. The use of icons seems to become the standard way of communication in screen presentation, because icons are supposed to be signs that appear to have natural resemblance. The meaning of icons, in the form of pictures of, for example, record files, waste baskets or telephones is supposed to be immediately clear. These icons do not seem to need explicit interpretation. None of these statements is accepted without debate.

A very special relationship exists between semiotics, linguistics and the study of pictures or icons. The issue boils down to the question of whether linguistics is an area inside semiotics or an area next to semiotics. The first position implies that an answer should be given to the question under which heading do verbal, oral, visual and auditive signs come together. The second position must answer the question in what sense verbal and oral signs are so special that they have to be studied separately. The two positions emphasize both generality and particularity.

In general the terms "language", "alphabet", "character", "syntax" and "grammar" are indicative of verbal signs. However, there are attempts to also apply these terms to visual signs, such as icons, pictures, figures or images (Arnheim, 1968; Goodman, 1984; Saint-Martin, 1990). For example, Lotman (1973) says the following about language: "By language, we mean any system of communication which uses signs arranged in a particular way." (p. 34). According to Chomsky a language is defined by its alphabet and its grammatical sentences. This makes the case for interpreting visual signs and marks as constituting an alphabet, syntax, etc. very weak.

According to Saint-Martin (1990), the attempt to formulate a semiotics of visual languages was abandoned in the 1970s. It proved impossible to define the basic elements and rules of concatenation in visual domains. Nevertheless, in her book, Saint-Martin is once again trying to formulate a semiotics of visual language. Although she does not mention them, there are at least two good reasons why renewed attention for visual signs and symbols is very important. In the first place, the instruments by which humans can communicate with each other are not restricted primarily to words. Of course, humans have always communicated with pictures, sculptures, paintings, and so on, but today we are able to make icons, pictures and models in the same amount of time and with less effort than when we produced a whole page of text in the past. Any systematicity in this is welcome, but what we should really want is an alphabet and a syntax of visual signs. An alphabet and a syntax guarantee unambiguity, systematicity and productivity. In the second place much individual task support is nowadays organized in interaction with very powerful computers. The future may be that all human-computer-interaction is only performed with icons and pictures, which are not tested on coherence and meaningfulness, but are randomly generated by software developers who have their own view on the reality of tasks and users. Therefore, it is much better to previously constitute a visual language. A semiotics of visual language may help to realize this undertaking.

Saint-Martin formulates syntactic rules to describe visual messages as can be found in painting, sculpture and movements. As already indicated, she does not include screens and other visual media in her analysis, but integrating these elements should not cause many problems. As a starting point for a semiotics of visual languages, she mainly uses Lewin's topological psychology. Visual language has to do with the experience of space, which is different from the experience of temporal order. This contrasts visual signs with verbal signs. According to her, "topological models allow us to think of the visual-spatial field as a field of forces or dynamic tensions that are in a state of continual change". (Saint-Martin, 1990, p. xii). The basic question here is, and she quotes Marin:

> Are there, [for example], in painting elements equivalent to phonemes, to distinctive traits which do not have meaning in themselves but are, in some way the constituents of meanings that the units of the first level obtain by the integration of their constitutive elements? (Saint-Martin, 1990, p. 3)

In order to realize a visual language the characteristics of the elements have to be established, just as is the case with verbal language elements of which the characteristics are that the elements have to be simple, autonomous, isolated, independent and that they should form a finite set. Although Saint-Martin (1990, p. 5) makes a proposal for such a basic element: "the coloreme", which she defines as the zone of the visual linguistic field correlated to the centration of the eyes which is constituted by a mass of energetic matter presenting a given set of visual variables, she does not end up with an unambiguous set of elements of a visual language.

We predict that in the next ten years the call for an alphabet and a syntax of visual elements will become louder and several articles in this volume anticipate this need. Therefore, there is a growing need for semiotic analysis. There is no common standard for screen signs and screen presentations available yet. Visual sign production and processing is so important for communication that it should not develop randomly.

4. Aspects and levels of communication

The discussion about user interfaces takes for granted that to a certain degree users *communicate* with computers. In a very extreme sense this assumption has been challenged by Dennett (1978).

> Do we communicate with computers in Fortran? Fortran seems to be a language; it has a grammar, a vocabulary, a semantics. The transactions in Fortran between man and machine are often viewed as cases of man communicating with machine, but such transactions are pale copies of human verbal communication precisely because the Gricean conditions for non-natural meaning have been bypassed. There is no room for them to apply. Achieving one's end in transmitting a bit of Fortran to the machine does not hinge on getting the machine to recognize one's intentions. This does not mean that all communications with computers in the future will have this shortcoming (or strength, depending on your purposes), but just that we do not now communicate, in the strong (Gricean) sense, with computers. (p. 280)

The strong (Gricean) sense of communication is totally based on first and higher order intentions. Grice (1957) has stated that two persons, A and B, are communicating if A by uttering a sentence intends B to give a certain answer or to do something. Furthermore, B has to recognize the intention of A and finally has the intention to fulfil the intention of A. According to Dennett this is something computers cannot do (yet); computers do not have intentions, although some people may assert that computers can fulfil intentions (of humans).

There are three possible roads leading to a treatment of the problem raised by Grice and Dennett. The first one is to analyze the conceptual basis of intentions, expectations and beliefs in relation to semiotics. In part III of this volume several authors take this road. The second road is to develop more powerful computer systems which gradually give us the impression that computers interpret the intentions of users and try to understand meaningful expressions. Very sophisticated decision support systems and knowledge systems form large steps on this road (Jorna & Simons, 1992). The third road is to analyze communication in terms of tasks, users and cognition. The last road, for example, is taken by Waern (1989), who distinguishes different aspects and levels of communication in the relation between humans and computers.

The starting point for Waern's ideas about communication is that computers should intelligently support users in accomplishing their tasks, such as designing, writing, advising, diagnosing or computing. This can only be realized if one takes into account the cognitive aspects of users, the division of tasks, the lay-out and signs in displays and the strategies users apply in executing a task.

In order to establish a certain classification in these aspects, Waern combines different levels of communication with the different stages in the development of computer systems. She takes for granted that in the future only computer supported or computer governed tasks will appear in institutions. The three forms she distinguishes are a) human-human communication, b) human-computer communication and c) metacommunication. A fourth form can easily be added: d) computer-computer communication.

Human-human communication in this respect concerns the tuning of two models of the task. The first is the user's (or expert's) model of the task, whereas the second is the designer's model of the task. Both models have to be adjusted such that a designer has a very thorough idea of the nature and the execution of the task. In order to accomplish this tuning, designer and user have to discuss, explain and understand each other's perspectives. Designer-user communication is a special case of the normal human-human communication, with the restriction that the two participants want to reach the same goal.

Human-computer communication implies that a computer assists a user in performing a task. We do not normally communicate with our car or our bike, but in the case of a computer which can be instructed and will give responses to a human being, it is important that user and computer share a certain level of understanding. This is the case if a computer program is constructed so that it supports and interprets conceptions of the task by the user. Effective and elegant human-computer interaction is the result of the implementation of the tuned task in the computer combined with a distinction in different levels of expertise. This enables novices, semi-experts and experts to gain support for their task level.

On top of human-computer communication we can situate metacommunication. The main concern is not the task support and the intelligent interaction between user and machine itself, but it is mainly directed towards help and instruction facilities.

> Metacommunication is used to inform the user about such aspects of the communication that are not self-explanatory. A new user must be informed of how to start the system and how to stop it, and every user can then and when need information about the system's facilities and the appropriate ways to invoke them. (Waern, 1989, p. 137)

Metacommunication also may be an aspect of human-human communication, but normally this distinction of levels is not made.

Computer-computer communication can range from very low level transmission of data to high level connections between different sorts of programs and computers. In the first case we are talking, for example, about the connection between a personal computer and mainframe by means of a modulator-demodulator (modem), the second case could refer to chains of knowledge systems in which solutions from the first system have to be interpreted before they are suitable for being used in a second system. No human being is involved.

One should not say that the discussion about computer-computer communication is only a matter of bits. Of course this is basically true, but the same could be said for human-human communication which only consists in puffs of air or light waves. The complexity of computer-computer communication may be illustrated by the fact that for more than twenty years a very complicated discussion has been going on concerning the standardization of codes for hardware and software configurations.

At right angles to the levels of communication different aspects of communication can be discerned, such as physical, lexical, syntactic and semantic aspects. Physical aspects concern the response time, the display mode and several input devices such as the keyboard or speech. Syntactic and semantic aspects not only refer to denotation and connotation of terms, but also to signs used in communication. Semantic aspects concern meaning, interpretation, understanding, or what in semiotics is called signification, but also communication styles, such as natural language, direct manipulation, menu selection or command language. We will not go into details of all these aspects, because several issues are dealt with in the chapters of this volume (see also: Waern, 1989).

Although we mainly discussed the third road in this section, the three roads should come together in the end. Conceptual analysis of intentions, expectations and beliefs is part of human-human communication and human-computer communication and should, in fact, precede it. The development of sophisticated decision support systems and knowledge systems may not only give us the impression that computers interpret intentions, beliefs and meanings of users, but it also could turn out to be the case that computers really understand and assist humans.

5. Presentation of the contents of the chapters (authors)

This volume is divided into three parts. The first part is about signs and representations, the second part about reasoning and search and the third part about communication and interaction between and with expert or knowledge systems. Taking the presence of expertise in artificial and natural intelligent systems for granted, at least four areas of scientific and practical interest can be discerned in this mixed field of signs, communication and expert systems or knowledge system.

If we arrange the areas into (descriptions of) levels of organization of semiotic structures or configurations and order the levels from low to high, the first level is concerned with the study of signs, i.e., signals, symbols, icons, maps and models as such. Structural in the sense of syntactic and semantic aspects are at the focus of interest here. The second level is one level of description higher, that is to say, is concerned with integrated symbol structures in the sense of information processing systems. This level is directly connected to the main research topic in artificial intelligence: the study and simulation of thinking and problem solving. The third level is again one level of description higher and is directed towards the study of the interaction and communication of intelligent systems, be it humans in organizations, computers in networks or humans and computers in handling tasks. There is even a fourth level of description in which the environment of interacting systems is taken into account. This level deals with what is normally called organizational and cultural issues. This level is not discussed in this volume (see however: Slikkerveer, van Heusden, Jorna & van den Broek, 1992).

The idea of levels of organization has its counterpart in cognitive science. In discussing levels of information processing, Newell (1990) distinguishes a biological, a cognitive, a rational and a social band. The distinctions are based on the dimension of time. Compared with our division, the study of signs and the study of symbol structures fall under the cognitive band, and the study of the interaction of intelligent systems can be equated with the rational band, whereas the study of organizations falls under the social band. The biological level has no counterpart in our hierarchy.

Furthermore, "organization" needs some qualification. Organization can be a regulating principle, for example, in the organization of cognition. Organization in this sense can be found everywhere in various manifestations. However, an organization can also be an object in reality. What we mean with cultural and organizational issues concerns itself with organizations as companies and institutions.

As we said before, several perspectives on the contributions are possible. This implies that more than one structure could be realized. One possible structure consists in distinguishing between 1) the internal structure of signs and 2) the use of signs. If we arrange the authors according to this structure we find:

The internal structure of signs:

1. The internal structure of and relations between signs, symbols and other communication structures: Barth, Luger & Stern, v/d Lubbe & Backer, Pelc, Meunier, Posner
2. The generation of signs, that is to say the issue of semiogenesis: Müller, Pelc
3. The problem of common sense. Is there a common code which expresses common sense and takes into account its flexibility? Visser, Rastier

The use of signs:

4. The real world and its description in signs (symbols): Müller, Silverman, Pelc, Braga, Meunier, Peschl
5. The role of the human-computer-interface: Silverman, Chignell, Vogelenzang & de Vuyst, Posner
6. The context of cognitive systems and their flexibility: Marostica, Silverman, Visser, v/d Lubbe & Backer
7. The concrete issue of communication and cooperation (tuning, time and dialogics): Müller, Barth, Michon, Chignell, Luger & Stern, Peschl, Posner

This structure can be used within the overall structure of the book. The contributions of the authors will be discussed in the perspective of the three parts of the book.

The contributions of Pelc, Santaella Braga, Barth, Meunier and Peschl together form the first part of this volume. This part is called: Signs and Representations.

Pelc discusses semiosis, cognition and interpretation from the perspective of the Polish school of logic and epistemology. He emphasizes a pragmatic approach towards semiotic problems, which means that semiosis, cognition and interpretation are conceived as activities. Semiosis refers to the activity of using signs, cognition to the activity of cognizing something and interpretation to the activity of arriving at an understanding of signs. In all three cases the subject of the activities is as important as the activities themselves. Including the objects of the activities, this means that semiotics can be conceived as a triad consisting of subject, object and activity. Each element has certain peculiarities, but, more important, several relations between the elements can be conceived. This also implies relations between semiosis, interpretation and cognition. Several of these relations are discussed by Pelc, such as sign-type and sign-token compared to thought-type and thought-token, meaning versus thought, meaning versus cognitive act and, finally, expression versus truth and reference. He ends his contribution with the intriguing insight that the relation between the organization of speech and the organization of language is as problematic as the relation between the organization of language and the organization of mind. In both cases language as an abstract product has a structure, whereas the structure of mind and speech has to be derived a posteriori from our (mental) activities.

Santaella Braga examines Peirce's theory of perception. According to Peirce cognition presupposes perception, but unlike present theories of perception which are dyadic, Peirce's theory is triadic. Dyadic means that the only important distinction in perception is that in the one who perceives and that which is perceived. Peirce, who supposed that strong traces of the old Cartesian division in subject and object are responsible for dyadic theories, introduces the notion of a dynamic object, that "frees his semiosis from the snares of idealism without at the same time incurring the risk of falling into a naive realism". The perceptive triad in the Peircean theory consists of a percept, a percipuum and the perceptive judgement. A percipuum as the new element is "the percept as it is immediately interpreted in the perceptual judgement". It is not the objective reality in the form of the percept nor the sign interpreting act of human cognition. Santaella Braga ends her contribution with a suggestion for a three-level gradation of the percipuum.

Barth's overall perspective is on systems of logical forms in human cognition and language. According to her, logic and semiotics are constituents of cognitive science. The main goal in her contribution is to conceptually analyze why asymmetrical binary relations are so problematic in certain philosophical circles. The main issue for Barth is not the logical problems involved here, but to show that conceptual mistakes also are the product of some line of reasoning. Conceptual mistakes are not arbitrary or random, they may also be systematic. The way to analyze mistakes is not only to concentrate on (wrong) inferences, but also to take an empirical point of view in logic. The reason for this, according to Barth, is that "together with the theologians and the mathematicians, most people in my own field, logic, are philosophically the last of the Mohicans - theologians, mathematicians and most logicians are the last pure and strict rationalists. Chomskyan linguists follow suit." Barth tries to develop a new scheme of fundamental categories in which disagreement, misunderstanding and conflict play an important role. She argues that cognitive science (and semiotics) should not (only) rest on rationalism and should not disregard discussion, communication, asymmetry and disagreement.

Meunier goes into the details of the A.I. debate in relation to the following question. What does it mean for a non-natural system to have representations and to exhibit, what external observers may call, intelligent behaviour? In a more semiotic perspective this question is phrased as: "can a semiotic system be non-conceptual and still be adequate for knowledge representation?" Meunier then discusses various suggestions from modern philosophy, from Locke and Peirce to Frege and Goodman, and cognitive psychology, e.g., Newell & Simon, to deal with this question. This leads Meunier to the conclusion that the starting question boils down to "what semiotic primitives and their carriers are powerful enough to enable meaning and intelligence". But not only semiotics primitives, but also conceptual structure and formalization is important and Meunier deals with the subsymbolic position in recent connectionism in order to show that one does not easily circumvent the issue of semiotic (or symbolic) primitives.

Peschl does not take for granted the symbolic approach which is present in much of A.I. and cognitive science today. His focus is on the problem of meaning, but he tries an alternative route in explaining this phenomenon. Therefore, he introduces the context of neuro-epistemology, which includes neuro-science, computer science and epistemology. Peschl rejects the traditional approach that says that a symbol has meaning in itself. Fundamental in this approach is the fact that the environment is mapped into the symbols in the representational system, be it natural or artificial. The problems with this approach is that information is lost - as a consequence of modelling -, that the direct contact between organism and environment is lost, and that the direction of mapping is only one way, from outside to inside. According to Peschl these problems cannot be mastered within the traditional approach and therefore neurally based solutions, such as developed in connectionism and in Parallel Distributed Processing models, are necessary. Adopting this approach also makes it possible to incorporate learning.

The contributions of Van der Lubbe & Backer, Marostica, Luger & Stern, Silverman and Visser together form the second part of this volume. The second part is called: Search and Reasoning in Expert Systems (or Knowledge Systems).

Van der Lubbe & Backer discuss the close relationship between induction, deduction and abduction. These three types of inference constitute the human reasoning process. Induction and deduction are very well known in logic, mathematics and computer science, but this is not the case for abduction. It is also very well known that humans are not very skilled in using induction and deduction. It appears that humans mostly use abductive processes in reasoning. Abduction is defined as the situation in which "on the basis of a rule and conclusion the fact is inferred in the form of a hypothesis". For example, from the conclusion that these apples are red and the general rule that all the apples from the box are red, the hypothesis (fact) is formulated that these apples are from the box. Van der Lubbe & Backer combine the types of inference with the characteristic aspect of human reasoning, namely that we are able to draw conclusions on the basis of uncertain information. If we should take expert systems seriously in that they to a certain degree also make inferences and reason, it is almost a necessity that expert systems can draw "valid" conclusions given uncertain data. One way to deal with uncertainty is to work with certainty factors. Van der Lubbe & Backer discuss certainty factors in combination with induction, abduction and deduction.

Marostica continues the discussion about abduction started by Van der Lubbe & Backer. She calls abduction the creative process and tries to answer the intriguing question: where do hypotheses come from? In Peircean terms this means the question what type of sign abduction is. In the problem solving literature, search is mostly connected to induction, and only sometimes to deduction. Using the state space terminology Marostica concludes that abduction does not fit into the schemes of quantitative induction and deduction. Abduction, according to Marostica, implies illumination, a sort of creative process, not (yet) included in logical reasoning schemes. Abduction employs qualitative procedures and these procedures are not mechanical. Marostica classifies abduction and problem solving as types of explanation, but "abduction is the process that creates the model or basic search pattern to be used in creating the goal state."

Luger & Stern start with the generalization that expert systems are becoming more and more successful in supporting human problem solving. This also holds for abductive problem solving, for example in diagnosis or error detection. According to Luger & Stern the basic idea is that expert systems embody symbol processing architectures which in most cases mean production systems. These architectures are essentially semiotic. Important in discussing these architectures is also the distinction in levels of description. However, the current generation of expert systems has several limitations. They are brittle, lack deep reasoning, have weak explanation facilities, do not have common sense and lack learning potential. Luger & Stern conclude that more emphasis on deductive reasoning patterns is not a successful road to take. Instead they propose and developed "a sign-based account of abductive explanation which offers significant advantages over the current entailment-based account". This forces one, however, to reexamine the "rationalistic" epistemological foundation of expert systems and problem solving.

Silverman emphasizes an interesting dimension of the common practice of expert systems. Normally expert systems are meant to support and assist users. For that reason knowledge or domain expertise is implemented in a knowledge base. According to Silverman an expert system should not only be an assistant, but also a critic. Therefore, he makes an important conceptual distinction in judgement and knowledge. If one wants to build intelligent systems in the sense of semiotic machines this means that one is describing the guidance in the interaction between man and machine. Intelligence for an expert system means advice, analysis and help, whereas an expert system that gives critique is a system that provides deep knowledge. An expert system then judges whether the level of expertise of a user is adequate to solve a problem. If an expert system has the impression that a human expert suffers from biases, the system offers remedies to overcome these prejudices. To implement this, it is necessary, according to Silverman, to complete knowledge engineering with "critic engineering". This also could result in a better understanding of the task processing and might lead to a generic task theory.

Visser expects that it will be almost impossible for A.I. to model or to formalize common sense. The fact is, however, that common sense is one of the key success factors in human reasoning. The reason for this problematic situation is that A.I. is based mainly on linguistics and logic and not on natural language in combination with psychology. Visser defends the position that intelligence consists of knowing plus acting, flexibility and common sense. This means that the "naive physics" program in A.I. will not lead to success in general. Special aspects of this program, however, might be covered which could mean that humans unlearn certain skills they once had. This could result in a disastrous loss of flexibility.

Posner, Müller, Michon, Vogelenzang & de Vuyst, Rastier and Chignell form the third part of this volume. This last part is about communication in relation to expert systems and is called Communication with Expert Systems.

Posner starts his contribution with a joke about teachers as teaching machines and students as learning machines. The intention of this joke is to explain that it is quite a job to fulfil all conditions of communication. Whether artificial systems will communicate, depends on their ability to respond to questions, to sustain a dialogue and to jointly set goals. All this means that A.I. has to endorse that communication "involves beliefs, intentions to make others believe, intentions to modify beliefs and intentions to make communication partners act". Posner then shows how basic concepts of an intensional logic can be used to define the central objects of semiotics, that is to say, signs. He produces a hierarchy of sign types, in consecutive order: signal, indicator, expression and gesture. This hierarchy is followed by levels of reflection up to communicating and then by the conditions of communicating. Posner also tries to bridge the gap between causal and semantic relations, for example in the phrase $I(b, E(f) \rightarrow E(e))$, to read as: a person (b) intends that putting a cup of yogurt in the freezer (E(f)) will cause the yogurt to get frozen (E(e)). Phrases like this can be easily expanded. Posner concludes his article with the remark that implementing belief systems into computers is one step, but that training for computers to communicate is another.

Müller discusses adaptation and coordination. Adaptation means on-line learning, whereas coordination involves distributed reasoning. The interesting question with which Müller starts his contribution is how do two strange persons in a strange environment develop communication. This is the question of semiogenesis, that is to say how do signs evolve or emerge and how does the semiotic relation between two intelligent agents originate? Müller formulates the question as follows: "Under what conditions is a "bootstrap semiogenesis", the self-organized generation of a common code, possible? Which assumptions and internal mechanisms of these strangers are necessary in order to reach a "common ground"?" To answer this question Müller uses the theory of parallel distributed processing. This implies a discussion of the underlying theory of neural networks and its possibility to enable self-organization. Self-organization is governed by genetic algorithms, a powerful class of adaptive methods. The whole approach implies machine learning in hybrid architectures. This architecture is called a DSS, not a Decision Support System, but a Dynamic

Semiotic System, in which signs are transient states between complex systems.

Michon starts his contribution with a discussion about time. He asks questions like what the discriminative stimulus for time is; what the function of a sense of time is and what processes are involved. One of his conclusions is that "time appears as a "property" of patterns of information in the real world which we call objects and events. There is no useful way of distinguishing between this latter aspect and the other properties of information, such as size, intensity or locus." The issue of time seems adventitious in relation to expert systems, but Michon argues that if we do not know what we mean by time and if we do not know what part of the information processing architecture is involved in processing time we are not able to achieve realistic communication between natural and artificial intelligent systems. Empirical research shows that the timing and tuning of interaction is decisive for successful communication. For that reason it is necessary to implement a sense of time in artificial systems. As an illustration of his ideas about timing and tuning, Michon discusses the GIDS-project. GIDS stands for Generic Intelligent Driver Support and is meant to support the intentions and capabilities of individual drivers.

Vogelenzang & de Vuyst evaluate natural language interfaces. Until now the development of these interfaces has been very difficult, not only from a technological point of view, but also from a linguistic point of view. Vogelenzang & de Vuyst strive to generate criteria in order to judge the relative performance of natural language interfaces. These criteria should incorporate syntactic, semantic and pragmatic aspects of language communication. For example, an adequate natural language interface should handle, among others, grammaticality checking, complex clause embedding, ellipses and anaphoric reference and inference. Vogelenzang & de Vuyst mainly discuss the method developed for testing the linguistic capabilities of a natural language interface.

The contribution of *Rastier* concentrates on the linguistic analysis of expert texts. For that reason Rastier coins a new term "linguistic ergonomics". The important goal of linguistic ergonomics is to embrace the starting points of ergonomics, that is to say: work towards objectives, be practical and take advantage of multidisciplinary outcomes. According to Rastier mainstream linguistics has been concentrated too much on an idealized image of language. Rastier advocates a more ergonomic approach towards texts in which the task, the task structure and the cognitive aspects of the human expert are included. As an example of this approach, he deals with two interviews conducted during a long term research project with the French rail road company.

Chignell goes into the details of cooperative human machine reasoning. In discussing the WIMP model (windows, icons, mice and pull-down menus) Chignell concludes that this model "does not address the fundamental issues of communication in the computer interface". What is needed, is a conceptual model, a model that is more task oriented and task dependent. A closer look at interface modelling reveals that an interface consists of several layers. The WIMP-model is at the physical level, whereas the model proposed by Chignell is at the conceptual level. This model, the NERD model, consists of Navigation, Evaluation, Refinement and Demonstration. At a third layer we can then discern a task model, but Chignell does not discuss this last issue in greater detail. The hierarchy of layers in which the physical layer is above the conceptual layer which is above the task layer also implies that the normal development of technology should be restructured. This means, for example, that the WIMP-model is the last step in the development and not the first step.

6. Conclusion

On one side there is an age-old field called semiotics, consisting of several philosophical perspectives, theoretical approaches and methodologies. At present this field is rapidly growing and is in continuous development (Andersen, 1990; Saint-Martin, 1990). Semiotics promises to be fruitful, yet at the same time it may be somewhat frightening for some researchers because of the breadth of its scope. On the other side there exists a very young field called A.I. concerned with expert systems or knowledge systems and asking for theoretical support with respect to questions regarding representation, signs, knowledge and communication. These two fields observe each other with mistrusting eyes. Aren't the newcomers rediscovering the wheel? Will philosophical speculation impede rapid success in applied research? The conference on "Expert Systems, Culture and Semiotics" proved that reciprocal distrust is not justified. The discussion on larger semiotic issues in the restricted context of A.I. can bring both fields together. It forces researchers in both fields to realize the impact of their ideas and technologies. Clearly a meeting ground exists, and it is: an empirical science of signs or semiotics. That this science has to be empirical is very important, because it means that hypotheses have to be formulated, that testing is a major issue and that the observation of data goes together with theoretical speculation. Only on this basis will the empirically and technically oriented A.I. community fruitfully work together with the more philosophically oriented semioticians. This volume (together with its companion (Slikkerveer, van Heusden, Jorna & van den Broek, 1992)) is an attempt to establish such a empirical science of signs.

References

Andersen, P.B. (1990). *A Theory of Computer Semiotics*. Cambridge: Cambridge University Press.

Arnheim, R. (1969). *Visual Thinking*. Berkeley: UCLA Press.

Dennett, D.C. (1978). *Brainstorms*. Brighton, Sussex: The Harvester Press.

Bechtl, W. & A. Abrahamson. (1991). *Connectionism and the Mind*. Oxford: Basil Blackwell.

Card, S.K., T.P. Moran & A. Newell (1983). *The Psychology of Human-Computer Interaction*. Hillsdale: Lawrence Erlbaum Associates.

Goodman, N. (1981). *Languages of Art*. Brighton, Sussex: The Harvester Press. (Second Edition)

Goodman, N. (1984). *Of Mind and Other Matters*. Cambridge: Harvard University Press.

Grice, H.P. (1957). Meaning, *Philosophical Review, 66*.

Hjelmslev, L. (1963). *Prolegomena to a Theory of Language*. Madison: University of Wisconson Press.

Jorna, R.J. (1990). *Knowledge Representation and Symbols in the Mind*. Tübingen: Stauffenberg Verlag.

Jorna, R.J. & J.L. Simons (Eds.) (1992). *Kennis in organisaties*. Muiderberg: Coutinho.

Lotman, I. (1973). *La Structure du Texte Artistique*. Paris: NRF.

Mulder, G & G. van der Veer (Eds.)(1988). *Human-Computer Interaction: Psychonomic Aspects*. Berlin: Springer Verlag.

Mulder, G., W. Lamain & P. Passchier (1992). De mens-machine interface. in: R.J. Jorna & J.L. Simons (Eds.) *Kennis in organisaties*. Muiderberg: Coutinho.

Nöth, W. (1985) *Handbuch der Semiotik*. Stuttgart: Metzler.

Newell, A. (1990). *Unified theories of cognition*. Cambridge, Massachusetts: Harvard University Press.

Posner, M.I. (Ed.) (1989). *Foundations of Cognitive Science*. Cambridge, Massachusetts: The MIT Press.

Posner, R. (1979). Introduction, *Zeitschrift für Semiotik, 1*: 1-5.

Posner, R. (1988). What is an Academic Discipline, in: R. Claussen & R. Daube-Schackat (Eds.). *Gedankenzeichen: Festschrift für Klaus Oehler*. Tübingen: Stauffenberg.

Posner, R. & T. Sebeok & K. Robering (Eds.) (1993). *Semiotics: A Handbook on the Sign-Theoretic Foundations of Nature and Culture.* Berlin and New York: Walter de Gruyter.

Saint-Martin, F. (1990). *Semiotics of Visual Language.* Indiana: Indiana University Press.

Shneiderman, B. (1987) *Designing the User Interface. Strategies for Effective Human-Computer Interaction.* Reading: Addison Wesley.

Slikkerveer, L.J., B. van Heusden, R.J. Jorna & G. van den Broek (Eds.)(1992). *The Expert Sign: Semiotics of Culture and Expertise.* Leiden: DSSW Press.

Waern, Y. (1989). *Cognitive aspects of computer supported tasks.* New York: John Wiley & Sons.

I

Signs and Representations

Semiosis, cognition, interpretation

J. PELC (Warsaw)

1. Semiosis, cognition and interpretation as activities

The terms in the title of this paper - "semiosis", "cognition" and "interpretation" - may be seen as referring either to certain activities, actions or processes, or to the products thereof. The distinction between activities and their products is due to Kazimierz Twardowski (1866-1938), founder of a Polish philosophical school known as the Lvov-Warsaw School, and is used by many of his pupils and followers.

In what follows the terms "semiosis", "cognition" and interpretation" will refer to the respective *activities*, namely the term "semiosis" - to the activity of using signs; "cognition" - to the activity of cognizing something; and "interpretation" - to the activity of arriving at an understanding of signs.

Every activity, every action has its *agent*, that is to say a person or group of persons or, generally, beings, endowed with consciousness. Such an activity agent pursues an *objective* of this activity, an event intended by the agent. The activity of an agent also has its *result*, that is its effects: intended and unintended, predicted and unforeseen, central and incidental. In his activity the agent uses certain *means*, i.e., ways or *methods*, among them acts which are intermediate objectives on the way to the final goal of the activity. The agent acts in a specific *situation* and under specific *subjective conditions*. He uses a suitable *apparatus* serving to operate on the material of action, and especially on the *stuff*, or this part of the material from which the *product* of the action will arise (Kotarbiński, 1965).

Evidently, by treating semiosis, cognition and interpretation as activities I adopt the pragmatic approach to problems I wish to discuss here. I owe this pragmatic attitude to my university teachers - Tadeusz Kotarbiński, author of *Traktat o dobrej robocie* (Kotarbiński, 1965), a pioneering and classical work in praxiology; and Kazimierz Ajdukiewicz, author of *Pragmatic Logic* (Ajdukiewicz, 1974); both Kotarbiński and Ajdukiewicz were pupils of Twardowski.

2. The subject of semiosis, cognition, and interpretation

What are the theoretical consequences of opting for the pragmatic concepts of semiosis, cognition and interpretation? The answer to this question appears simple.

The analysis of semiosic activities - the sending, receiving and processing of signs - cannot overlook the *subjects* of these activities: the senders and receivers interpreting signs, participants of communication processes. In analyzing the activity of cognition - and not its product in the form of a state of knowledge understood, for example, as the sum total of sentences regarded as true, those that are true, and the well-substantiated ones - as opposed to cognizance, one cannot disregard the subject of this activity. Likewise, the analysis of the activity of interpretation - as contrasted with its product in the form of this or that interpretation understood, for example, as a sentence or sentences being one of the possible translations of the interpreted text - cannot be carried out without considering the interpreter as the executor of this activity. Each of the mentioned activities also has their object.

On the other hand, this focus on the activities of semiosis, cognition and interpretation by no means leaves out of consideration the *products* of each of these activities, nor does it stand in the way of abstracting the product out of the process of its production and then analyzing the relations of this product (e.g., the meaning of a sign) to other entities such as the referent of this sign and its extension. The fact of the activities of semiosis, cognition and interpretation - and hence also, implicitly, the experiences of their agent - being taken into account does not doom the analysis to gnoseological, and especially ontological subjectivism denying the objective existence of the object of cognition. Nor does it force one to ascribe psychic character to non-psychic objects, events and phenomena. Finally, it does not lead to the rejection of the opinion of most logicians whereby the basic semantic concepts are those of reference, truth, satisfaction, set and model.

In pronouncing ourselves in favour of the pragmatic approach to semiosis, cognition and interpretation, we are motivated by the obvious fact that for each of these activities to take place there must be an agent endowed with a psyche and an object. I will conclude this part of my contribution with this memorable, albeit unoriginal, statement: there are no signs outside the use thereof, there is no sign use without sign interpretation, and there is no sign interpretation without a cognizing subject.

3. Relations between semiosis, cognition, interpretation and inference

The next question is: Why do I include side by side in my considerations these particular three concepts of semiosis, cognition and interpretation? The answer is trivial. *Semiosis* consists in sending, processing and receiving signs. In order to be able to *use* some object, event, property or phenomenon *as a sign*, I must first of all establish cognitive contact with it; for example I must see an inscription, hear a sound sequence, or imagine that I am perceiving them. But this is just the preliminary step. Even if pure perception were possible, and I doubt it is, then it would not in itself suffice to use the perceived thing in the capacity of the sign. It is not enough to see or hear A, or to be convinced that one perceives this A; one must perceive this A as such-and-such an object, event, property or phenomenon, and hence, applying conceptualization, single it out from the environment and recognize it as belonging to a certain system: sometimes as part of a certain whole, sometimes as an element of a certain set, and in other cases still as a link in a chronological sequence, etc. A number of problems come into the picture here - such as the distinction between observational and theoretical terms, or between direct and indirect cognition - problems I cannot go into here. Let me just declare that I do not think either purely observational terms or purely direct cognition are possible.

Once I have recognized the perceived or imagined object, or, more generally, entity A as such-and-such, I have merely satisfied the necessary condition for using this entity as a sign. As we know, each *sign A is a sign of something*, a sign of some B different from A. The *assignment* of the equivalent B to this A requires that the person doing the assigning sees a *basis* justifying the occurrence of a *sign relation* between A and B. Such a basis may be, for example, a similarity between A and B in regard of C of which similarity the interpreter is conscious, with this similarity not necessarily existing objectively: it suffices for the interpreter to be convinced that it exists and that this entitles him to *infer* that A is a sign of B, and, further, that B takes place or has such and such properties. In another case, the basis for assigning a B to this A may be a correspondence rule R belonging to the system S of which A is an element, or at least the fact that the interpreter is convinced that A is an element of system S and that this system includes the rule R. In still other instances, the interpreter feels justified in making the A/B assignment by the fact of a causal relationship between A and B or B and A, either actual or merely imagined.

As we see, in the act, activity or process of *semiosis* the subject of this semiosis *thinks*, that is to say becomes aware that it is so and so; in particular, he *believes* that it is so and so and derives certain sentences from others, i.e., *makes inferences*. According to many psychologists, thinking is connected with speech, if only silent speech. The reverse relationship is obvious. The relation between believing, or *judgement*, and *proposition* is seen as consisting in the fact that the latter is the *content* of the former, and at the same time also the *meaning of a sentence* expressing this judgement. In turn, the *concept content* is the *meaning* of the relevant *nominal expression*. Thinking and believing together with their component, conceptual apprehension, and also inferring are all included in the category of *indirect cognition* activities. Hence, activities of indirect cognition are present in the semiosis process. Also present in this process are *perceiving*, *retrieving* and *imagining* - activities included by some cognitive psychologists in *direct cognition*. However, even the most direct of these activities - perceiving - contains an admixture of retrieved judgements and complements of representations originating in imagining. Thus, even in what is called direct cognition there are elements of indirect cognition.

We now know that the process of *interpreting sign* A consists in performing *cognitive activities*. But is the converse true? Does the *activity of cognizing* some entity E always include the element of *interpreting* this E? If I were to concede this is not always so, I would be doing it out of consideration for, firstly, all those who maintain that one kind of cognition is revelation, the object of which may be something incomprehensible by nature and hence not subject to interpretation *ex definitione* and secondly for those who make a distinction between direct and indirect cognition and include perceiving in the former category, claiming that it consists in a single cognitive leap, namely in coming into contact with the perception data without interpreting them. Incidentally, those who distinguish between direct and indirect cognition probably do not always remember that the adjectives "direct" and "indirect" are of typological character and hence gradable; thus, perceiving should be regarded not as strictly direct but only as more direct or less indirect than, say, reasoning. In any case, whenever the cognition of A leads to the cognition of B different from A, that is whenever we have an obvious case of indirect cognition, there occurs an interpretation of this A.

The process of *semiosis* consists of a succession of *cognitive activities* and acts, among which *sign interpretation* plays an important role. In the course of sign interpretation I make various kinds of *inferences*. Sometimes I infer deductively on the basis of premisses establishing: the occurrence of a sign, the fact that it is an element of a specific semiotic system, and the fact that this and this interpretation rule applies in this particular case - arriving at a conclusion as to what this sign means and what it refers to. In other cases I apply inductive-probabilistic explanation. This happens, for example, when interpreting an indication, index, symptom or syndrome. I put forward and verify hypotheses about the semiosic and semiotic properties of a sign. Typical *premisses* in most of these *interpretative inferences* are sentences asserting the occurrence of a certain semiotic event, namely something which we intend to treat as a sign token, a sentence asserting that this token has such and such a structure, a sentence asserting that this sign belongs to a specific semiotic system, and a sentence - following from the previous one - asserting that in this case such and such an interpretative rule applies, giving also the content of this rule. In making inferences I have to take into account not only these premisses but also the *rules* of the performed *inference*. These premisses and rules are sentences which I accept as true; I must therefore first *understand* these sentences. And I arrive at the understanding of these sentences by performing the activity of interpreting these sentences. As can be seen, the process of interpreting signs is intertwined with the process of inferring. An important element in both these processes is *accepting a sentence as true*, for which it is necessary to understand this sentence. This is not a process running along a *circulus vitiosus* since I understand some of the sentences involved in it by bringing up to date the previously acquired knowledge about their meaning; in such cases I do not need to undertake the activity of interpreting them. The accepting of a sentence as true and the understanding of a sign are pragmatic relations. Although it sometimes happens that an interpreter accepts as true a sentence that in fact is not true, the very activity of accepting a sentence as true requires that he has at his disposal a notion of *truth*, which is a semantic notion. In using the vocabulary of a certain language he must also make use of the property of *referring*, and hence also of the notion of truth. The distinction between a sign token and a sign as a type would be extremely difficult if we were to abandon the notion of truth; and the distinction between metalanguage and object language would be downright impossible without the notions of reference and truth. I thus find it hard to share the reservations and even hostility of some authors (Jackendoff, 1986), proponents of the so called *conceptual semantics*, towards the notion of truth as a relation between a statement and reality, towards the notion of truth in a model, and towards the set-theoretical approach to the notion of reference, and to accept the objections other authors (Lakoff, 1986), arguing for *cognitive semantics* and the so called *experimentalist cognition* have to the *objectivist conception of meaning* as something determined by the relationship between symbols and external objects in the world. I also do not see the *world-oriented theories of meaning* (Barwise, 1986) and the approach of logic to semantic problems (Jackendoff, 1986) as traditional, and the views of cognitive semantics proponents as nontraditional. I do not give the word "traditional" a pejorative or positive meaning here. Using it descriptively, one may argue whether semantics of Fregean type is or is not more traditional than cognitive semantics, or rather its different variants falling back on the concepts of *lingua mentalis*, *universal grammar* and on the classical *science of definition*. I believe that the roots of both these semantic doctrines reach down through Medieval soil to sources in Antiquity. Finally, I am reluctant to accept the division of semantic views into the logical on the one hand and the linguistic, psychological and those embraced by researchers in cognitive science on the other. Being a pupil of Polish logicians and philosophers, it never crossed my mind that semantics - or, more generally, semiotics - might be "uncognitive"; the expression "uncognitive semantics" contains, as far as I am concerned, a *contradictio in adiecto*, while "cognitive semantics" is a pleonastic expression, for can there be any other semantics? More than 60 years ago Kotarbiński defined the meaning of a sentence in terms of the pragmatic relation of expression of the speaker's thoughts by the sentence used by him, expression of this thought in respect to content, while for Ajdukiewicz meaning was the way, defined in certain respects, in which an expression is understood. I suspect that the accusation against logicians that they ignore the pragmatic, and especially the psychological aspects of language are sometimes the result of exaggeration characteristic of polemical fervour, while the opinion that linguists and psychologists show little concern for truth and reference springs from the naive view that language and thought serve to propound both truth and falsity and that, accordingly, there is no need to give truth too prominent a place in semantic considerations. Bear in mind, though, that to be able to lie one must know what the truth is. And to be able to qualify certain utterances as true in the given circumstances of sign use and other utterances as straying from the truth we must have concepts of truth and of reference. Let me add that these concepts must be defined properly, that is with sufficient precision, and must be tools adapted for performing specific research tasks.

4. Semiotic ecumenism

I hereby declare that I do not consider myself an adherent of any of the camps, rather inaccurately characterized in the polemical publications of the last two decades. Thus, I belong neither to the camp of traditional logic of the Frege-Russell type, nor to the "possible-worlds-truth-and-reference-semantics" sect (Van Fraassen, 1986: 205), nor to the autonomy semantics party, nor to the subjective semantics faction, nor to the objective semantics party, nor am I in favour of the decompositional or semantic networks or meaning postulate approaches, or of mental spaces (Fauconnier, 1985), or procedural intensionalism (Wilks, 1986). This does not mean however that

I regard all these various scientific positions as unsound. On the contrary, I see certain correct views in each of these approaches, and I often fail to perceive the fundamental and unreconcilable differences between them stressed so much by proponents of almost every one of their number. I try to maintain a neutral stance and from this position encourage others to embark on semiotic ecumenism - a critical ecumenism which does not turn a blind eye to theoretical drawbacks and differences, but is aware of difficulties and defects as well as of the advantages of the various semiotic theories, and realizes whether and how to overcome these difficulties, remove or limit drawbacks and reconcile differences.

I will discuss only a few of the relevant problems.

5. Sign-token and thought-token versus sign-type and thought-type

The first problem is connected with the distinction between *sign-token* and *sign-type* on the one hand, and *thought-token* and *thought-type* on the other. Wishing to adopt a pragmatic approach to semantic problems, and especially to the theory of meaning of ordinary language expressions, we should find a way leading from (a) the token of the thought experienced at such and such a time and place by the sender or receiver of this and this sign-token in connection with the use by this sender or receiver of this particular sign-token to (b) the thought-type connected with the relevant sign-type as belonging to a specific semiotic system, i.e., the thought-type of an arbitrary user of this sign. One is tempted to treat an expression-token as an individual concrete physical object. But then the expression-type - or, more generally, sign-type - would be a set of all and only those tokens created. And here we have the question: In regard to which property of the tokens is the set created? Not in regard to their visual or acoustic appearance because one would like, say, the word "house" in various inflections, set in various types, and pronounced in voices of various pitch and colour to belong to the same word-type. Another problem concerns the concept of thought-token: what kind of physical, perceptual properties is it supposed to have? Experience tells us that by the occurrence of "the same" word one means an event consisting in: (a) the occurrence of a graphic or acoustic object which does not differ "too much" (in a rather vague way) from a certain standard, differ in regard to certain perceptual properties like shape or sound that are not defined precisely in the given language, but (b) on the condition that each of these tokens means "the same" as other tokens. Likewise in the case of thought-tokens: I include them in the same thoughttype in respect to their shared content, the additional difficulty here being the empirical identification of an individual token of a single thought. The conclusion from these observations is pessimistic: the treatment of a signtype Z as a set of all and only those tokens $Z_1, Z_2, ..., Z_n$ which are created in regard to their physical properties, will be of little help. The situation is still worse when we decide to treat a thought-type T as a set of all and only those tokens T_1 , $T_2, ...$, T_n created with their content left out of account. And defining a thought-type T in regard to its content, while sign-type Z is defined in regard to, among other things, its meaning, eliminates the possibility of defining sign meaning with the concepts of sign-type and thought-type. It is this kind of disappointment experienced on the road from the concept of thought to the concept of meaning that probably prompted many researchers to look for help in detectivistic inquiries into truth and reference.

6. Symbol and symbolic representation

The term *symbol* has enjoyed and still enjoys a tremendous career in cognitive semantics and artificial intelligence speculations. As is well known, "symbol" is a polysemic term. In order to use it properly one must be aware of the discussed distinction between *symbol-token* and *symbol-type* and of the problems this distinction causes. The symbols inscribed on a typewriter or computer keyboard are symbol-tokens. The sign activity of the writer or a chance touch of a key (as by a cat) causes the relevant symbol-tokens appear on paper or on screen. If we refer to the relation between a symbol on the keyboard and the corresponding symbol on paper as the relation of *representation*, then we must distinguish between this relation and the one between each such symbol and the relevant symbol-type. The former relation occurs between symbol-tokens belonging to the same symbol-type, i.e., between individual objects, whereas the latter occurs between an individual object and a relevant abstract entity. But of what kind and between what is the relation whose members are a string of ordinary language expressions on the one hand and their *translation* in the form of a sequence of "Mentalese" language, or *lingua mentalis* if one prefers the old terminology, or sequences of internal computational representations if one favours new terminology - on the other? Expressions of ordinary language which we are translating into Mentalese may be regarded as symboltypes. The question arises, however, whether each of them *represents* the relevant Mentalese "expression" or whether it *refers* to its equivalent in the way a metalanguage expression refers to its equivalent in object language. And another question: Does this referred Mentalese expression indeed occur in the reference relation in the role of symbol (symbol-token or symbol-sign) or does it assume this role only within a further relation, namely in respect to some extra-linguistic reality, the fragments of which are referred to by the individual "expressions" of the Mentalese language, and indirectly by the relevant expressions of ordinary language? What is striking in this distinction is the polysemy of the term "*symbolic representation*" and the fact that it is overused in semantic considerations. One may also wonder whether it is true that "symbolic processes can only be brought into contact with other symbolic processes" (Wilks, 1986: 228), whatever "to bring [two symbolic processes] into contact" might mean.

7. Meaning versus thought

The speculations of many cognitive semanticians and specialists in artificial intelligence are a land in which metaphor, personification and hypostasis reign supreme. The blame for this lies with several words which are being used in different meanings and without definitions. Among them are "symbol", "representation", "structure", "thought", "mental level", "cognitive level", "objective content", "meaning" and "language."

As we know, the concept of *meaning* is fundamental in semantics. We also know there are many different theories of meaning. Expressions like "the locus of meaning", "meaning in the mind of the speaker", "meaning in the world", "the meaning of a sentence or text [identified] with its truth conditions" or "with an intrinsically meaningful mental representation of the 'logical form'" (Barwise, 1986: 23), "level of meaningful representation" (Fauconnier, 1986: 61), "meaning in natural language is an information structure that is mentally encoded by human beings" (Jackendoff, 1986: 81) - are all indicative of this polysemy. Questions like: "How can the individual mind grasp sense?" or "Is meaning primarily a psychological or logical notion?" must remain unanswered until it is made clear what the questioning person understands by "meaning." For similar reasons one cannot either accept or reject the assertion that "meaning is totally unrelated to truth and reference"; and formulations of this kind are frequent in semantic texts. Also for this and yet another reason one cannot accept or reject the claim that "meaning is independent of *individual minds*" (Santambrogio & Violi, 1986: 5), for we do not know in what sense it is "independent" and what is an individual mind. On the other hand, all those willing to accept my motto that "there are no signs outside the use thereof" and those concerned with the meaning of signs and not, for example, with the objective of some activity or the value of some state of affairs - for this is how the words "meaning" and "sense" are also being understood at times - all those will probably agree that in order to use something as a sign of something else, i.e., as a *meaningful* entity, one must *think* that so and so when this sign serves to express a judgement or supposition, or else to represent in one's mind some object when the sign is a name of a concrete thing, or grasp something conceptually in the case of abstract signs. There is no sign use without thinking. In this sense the meaning of an expression is not independent of an individual interpreter; on the other hand it is not identical with the individual thought of each user of this expression, experienced whenever this expression is used. And it is in this sense that it is independent of the individual interpreter.

8. Definition and analysis of meaning versus cognitive act

To explain what an expression of a given language means one can, for example, formulate a nominal *definition*. The classical structure of this explicit equivalence definition, clearly formulated, consists of the *definiendum*, a definitional connective, and the *definiens* in which there occurs an expression denoting the kind - i.e., the superior extension - and also an expression limiting this extension to the level of species, i.e., the extension of the definiendum. The fundamental idea in this Ancient doctrine is the *translation* of the explicated word into suitably ordered *definitionally equivalent* components. This well tried way of analyzing meaning gave rise to theories such as the *theory of semantic networks* and especially of the *decomposition of meaning into semantic primitives*, sometimes referred to as *semantic markers*. The *theory of meaning postulates* is a variant of the analytical definition, sometimes contrary to the intention of its proponents, while the *theory of prototypes* or the *theory of meaning schemes* called *frame systems* makes use of rules of partial defining and of properties of stipulating and synthetic definition.

Ever since the earliest times, the ambitions of the defining person drove this person to claiming that the particular analysis of meaning given in his definition is a standard which cannot be deviated from. In Antiquity, for example, it was insisted that the proper extension of the definiendum is to be carved out not from just any terms with an extension superior to that of the definiendum, but from a term denoting the closest species, or *genus proximum*, and this not with the use of one of many terms limiting this extension in the desired manner, but with a term denoting a species-related difference, or *differentia specifica*. Thus, for example, man had to be defined as an intelligent creature, and could not be defined as a featherless biped mammal with flat fingernails. These claims were eventually joined by the conviction that these singularly correct semantic primitives are *universal* in all languages. From this it was only a small step to the claim that these primitives owe their universal linguistic character to the *structure of the human mind*, namely to a one-to-one correspondence with elements of mental language. The fact remains, however, that various authors propose various lists of those *semantic primitives*. And this is just all right since the analysis of the meaning of expressions ought to be guided by the particular research or practical (e.g., technical) task this analysis is to serve. This does not support the hypothesis of universality of these elements or of the existence of a single short list of *image schemes* according to which experiences are supposed to be structured prior to and independently of any concepts (Lakoff, 1986: 140; Johnson, 1987). It seems that the diversity of our behaviour, including also linguistic behaviour, in very similar or analogous situations - an example of which are the various ways of defining the same expression - is evidence of the elastic nature of the human cognitive apparatus, and of the fact that its arsenal of cognitive categories is rich, variegated and dynamic: depending on the needs, the choice of cognitive forms and tools changes, and these tools moreover undergo such adaptive changes as circumstances demand; these circumstances including in particular the object of cognition, the goal of cognition and the capabilities of the cognizing subject.

9. Meaning of expressions versus truth and reference

The analysis of *meanings* performed by cognitive semanticians involves operations of defining expressions, as well as the creation of types, prototypes, standards and schemes, and also procedures connected with these operations, and accordingly must rest on the concepts of *truth* and *reference*. These concepts are indispensable in formulating a definition with an equivalence relation between its various parts, and also in constructing an ideal type featuring properties given prominence in some set of objects. Cognitive semantics also makes use of the concept of *set*, even if it ostensibly rejects it. It turns up in the concept of linguistic system, in several concepts of meaning expressions, and in the concept of denotation, to mention but a few. Even if many expressions of ordinary language, e.g., the word "game", do not have extensions in the form of a set of elements classified as belonging to it, based on satisfying sufficient and necessary conditions, there are other expressions that have this kind of extension, e.g., the word "hexagon" or the expression "X's son-in-law." If biologists have found that in the animal and vegetable worlds the so called natural kinds are not sets in the set-theoretical sense, then their observation concerns not only the nature of organisms but also the correctness of the systematics of these organisms. It may be that an unsuitable network of concepts was superimposed over animate nature, this leading to an unnatural classification and ordering of organisms. It is thus wrong to say that there do not exist sets of animals or plants in nature; rather, one should say that the kinds and species were distinguished in such a way that not all of the individuals grouped in a kind satisfy specific necessary and sufficient conditions. Hence there are also no grounds to the claim that reality is not "structured in such a way that [it] can be modelled by set-theoretical models" (Lakoff, 1986: 123). Such modelling is always possible, although probably not always useful. And even if the set-theoretical approach to some domain of reality were to disappoint some researchers in some respect, this would not mean that we should abandon this approach in all research procedures, in semantics in particular. It proved useful in many analyses in language theory, not as the only one, admittedly, but as one of many possible ones.

One must bear in mind here that semantic theories described by their critics as objectivistic, e.g., "The symbolic theory of meaning: Arbitrary symbols can be made meaningful in one and only one way: by being associated with things in the world (where the world is taken as having a structure independent of the mental processes of any beings)" (Lakoff, 1986: 119) - these theories, contrary to charges by their opponents, by no means ignore the role of imaginative factors in creating concepts, or the role of conceptual apparatus in forming an image of the world. For example Ajdukiewicz (1978: 67-89) sees empirical cognition as dependent not only on the world that is being cognized but also on the language the cognizing subject is using. Davidson bases his theory of meaning not only on Tarski's theory of truth but also on the theory of action, i.e., of the behaviour of an agent guided by intentions. On the other hand, however, the reduction of the understanding of a sentence to the knowledge of its truth conditions, or identifying it with meanings of ordinary language expressions, fails in many cases, e.g., in intensional contexts. It is this observation - that the concepts of truth and reference are indispensable in activities of sign interpretation, i.e., in semiosis, but that they do not suffice to carry out these activities - that prompts one to advocate semiotic ecumenism in which *truth* theory and *reference theory* as well as *pragmatic* (i.e., also psychological and sociological) *theories of sign use* will occupy side by side the places they deserve.

10. Organization of speech, structure of language, structure of mind

The expression "sign use" requires the mention of an important distinction connected with the sign-token - sign-type relation discussed here, namely the distinction between *speech* and *language* and also, within speech alone, the distinction between individual acts of speech and systems of acts of speech as a system different from language. The *semiosic activities* developing in time, are *organized* in some way. Also organized are *cognitive* and, more generally, *mental activities*. *Language*, on the other hand, being an *abstract product*, has a *structure*. We attempt to reconstruct the structure of the mind *a posteriori*, namely on the basis of the organization of speech activities and mental functions. There is much to suggest that there are important analogies between language structure and mind structure. We try to verify this hypothesis with, among other things, methods worked out in computer and artificial intelligence science, keeping in mind that it is not the human brain that is simulating the operation of a computer, but that it is in fact the computer that simulates human thought on the basis of the knowledge about the organization of semiosic activities and the structure of the semiotic system.

References

Ajdukiewicz, K. (1978). *The Scientific World Perspective and Other Essays 1931-1963*. Ed. Jerzy Giedymin. Dordrecht: D. Reidel, pp. 67-89.

Barwise, J. (1986). "On the circumstantial relation between meaning and content." *VS-Versus, 44/45*, pp. 23-39.

Barwise, J. & Perry, J. (1983). *Situations and Attitudes*, Cambridge, Mass: MIT Press.

Davidson, D. (1982). *Essays on Action and Events*. Oxford: Clarendon Press.

Fauconnier, G. (1985). *Mental Spaces*. Cambridge, Mass.: MIT Press.

Jackendoff, R. (1983). *Semantics and Cognition*. Cambridge, Mass.: MIT Press.

Jackendoff, R. (1986). "Conceptual semantics", *VS-Versus, 44/45*, pp. 81-97.

Johnson, M. (1987). *The Body in the Mind: Bodily Basis of Reason and Imagination*. Chicago: Chicago University Press.

Johnson-Laird, P.N. (1983). *Mental Models: Towards a Cognitive Science of Language, Inference and Consciousness*. Cambridge: Cambridge Univ., Press. Cambridge, Mass.: Harvard Univ. Press.

Johnson-Laird, P.N. (1986). "How is meaning mentally represented?" *VS-Versus, 44/45*, pp. 99-118.

Kotarbiński, T. (1965). *Praxiology: An Introduction to the Sciences of Efficient Action*. Transl. from the Polish by. O. Wojtasiewicz. Oxford/Warszawa: Pergamon Press PWN-Polish Scientific Publishers.
Lakoff, G. (1986). "Cognitive semantics." *VS-Versus, 44/45*, pp. 119-154.
Lakoff, G. (1987). *Women, Fire, and Dangerous Things: What Categories Reveal About the Mind*. Chicago: Chicago Univ. Press.,
Santambrogio M. & Violi, P. (1986). "Introduction." *VS-Versus, 44/45*, pp. 3-22.
Wilks, Y. (1986). "Reference and its role in computational Models of Mental representations." *VS-Versus, 44/45*, pp. 221-237.

A triadic theory of perception

L. SANTAELLA BRAGA (São Paulo)

1. Introduction to Peirce's theory of perception

As it is well acknowledged, the importance of the role which is performed by perception in the processes of cognition does not need to be emphasized. For Charles S. Peirce, there is no possible cognition that does not presuppose perception: "The elements of every concept enter into logical thought at the gate of perception and make their exit at the gate of purposive action; and whatever cannot show its passports at both those gates is to be arrested as unauthorized by reason" (CP 5.212). Due to this basic and irreplaceable function of perception in logic and cognition, Peirce came to develop a theory of perception which is as original as the whole of his system of logic considered as semiotic. The main scope of this paper is to point out the coherence of Peirce's theory of perception so that the paper may function as a hint of the importance for bringing his theory into dialogue with modern cognitive science.

Until today, near the end of the twentieth century, all theories of perception known to us are diadic. Indeed, in the case of perception, it is difficult to reject the evident duality between the one who perceives and that which is perceived. Thus the very title of this work obliges me to begin it with a question. In what measure is the Peircean theory of perception an advance in relation to the past and to what degree is it still original?

The retrospective view proposed by the question has already been covered in a precious study by R.J. Bernstein (1964), and I shall begin with a quotation which synthesizes with great clarity the tangled nature of the question. Bernstein tells us that in his papers of 1868[1]

> Peirce dramatically attacked Cartesianism, which he took to be the cancer of modern philosophy. He sought to demolish in one fell swoop the interrelated motifs which make up Cartesianism: the ontological duality of mind and body; the subjective individualism implicit in the ultimate appeal to direct personal verification; the method of universal doubt which was supposed to lead us to infallible truths; the doctrine that language and signs are an external disguise for thought; the doctrine that vagueness is

> unreal and that the philosophic endeavour is one of knowing clearly and distinctly a completely determinate reality; and most fundamentally, the doctrine that we can break out of the miasma of our language or system of signs and have direct intuitive knowledge of objects. It is this last claim that Peirce took to be the heart of Cartesianism and the central dogma of modern philosophy. (p. 165-166)

Peirce's vehement opposition to Descartes did not simply arise from nowhere. Indeed, it was possible only because Peirce already had an alternative in mind. At first sight this anti-Cartesian alternative would seem to bring him very close to a Hegelian viewpoint and to the more sophisticated forms of idealism. But one of the most profound Peircean insights is that the idealists had lost an essential aspect which the traditional empiricists had always attempted to redeem: "the fact that through perception a world which is not of our own making or a creature of the Absolute is forced upon us" (Bernstein 1964, 167). However, to take account of this compulsive element in perception, the empiricists ingenuously took as given that which is in the outside world. How then may one accommodate on the one hand the unquestionable idealist thesis that percepts, images or sense data must not be confused with perceptive judgements which, in any case, are essentially similar to judgements of any other sort, and on the other hand the empiricist thesis that there is a compulsive ingredient in judgements of perception? How may we find a *via media* between these two opposed paths? "We shall see that it is the irreducibility of Secondness in perception and action that is the key to Peirce's attempt to find a *via media* between rationalism and empiricism, idealism and naive realism." (Bernstein 1964, 167)

After this look back into the past, Bernstein's study moves on to the twentieth century and tries to recontextualize Peirce's position in the confrontation with the contemporary intellectual environment. Once more, Bernstein confirms in this context the up-to-date-ness of the Peircean theory, together with its degree of originality:

> ... the "new" philosophic climate is characterized by a contextualist approach in which the dominant epistemological "unit" is no longer discrete sense data or simple phenomenalistic reports, but conceptual frameworks and language games within which our perceptual data are to be analyzed and understood. A new linguistic relativism has emerged which bears a very strong resemblance to "old" idealism. It is mainly idealism fractured, because instead of one all-encompassing monistic system, there are many systems, conceptual schemes or language games. The terminology and emphasis of "this way of words" is new, but many of the arguments have their prototypes in the writings of the idealists.
>
> The shortcomings of this new variety of idealism are not so much in what it says, but in what it *omits*. (...) No matter how much we emphasize the

> ways in which our conception of the world is determined by the conceptual schemes that we employ and insist that we can never hope to escape from these schemes to know reality in-itself, we must take account of the compulsion, stubbornness, bruteness and facticity which is so much a part of our encounters with the world. It is the attempt to reconcile opposing insights that is the distinctive feature of Peirce's theory of perception, and this attempt is characteristic of his entire philosophic outlook. (p. 168-169)

The Peircean theory of perception was not constructed all at one go. It happened rather otherwise: Peirce came up against numerous impasses due to the conflicting aspects of perception itself. These conflicts were worked out over a period of many years, so that it is possible to have a clear view of the way in which the impasses were gradually overcome only through a more general knowledge of Peirce's work. Any attempt to understand his theory of perception on the basis of isolated fragments draws one unavoidably into apparently insoluble contradictions, and leads to the sensation that the theory is no more than an ill-stitched patchwork of unrelated pieces. In my opinion, any attempt to grasp the idea of perception in Peirce which is based on a fragmentary vision of his work will end up in this unsatisfactory situation. Without undervaluing the importance of some of the existing bibliography about Peirce's theory of perception such as Pape (1981), Almender (1980, 1970), Ransdell (1979), Thompson (1963), I put emphasis on Bernstein's work because it is for me the most lucid and coherent overview of the paths followed by Peirce and the results which he obtained with regard to perception.

It is not the purpose of this study to enter in minute detail into the historical development of Peirce's theory of perception. The idea is to call attention to the fact that, in presupposing the question of perception, the notion of dynamic object frees Peircean semiosis from the snares of idealism without at the same time incurring the risk of falling into a naive realism. In this respect I shall restrict myself to pointing out the most fundamental aspects of perception with the intention of accentuating its interdependence with the object of the sign. If, on the one side, the insertion of perception in the logical diagram of semiosis helps to clarify the notion of object of the sign, on the other side the reading of perception in the light of the semiotic trivium helps to clarify perception itself.

2. Object and perception

There can be no doubt that, for Peirce, the object of the sign is always semiotic in nature. Although perception may constitute a gateway by which knowledge may enter, we are never in a situation in which body and mind are immediately conferred upon an object which can be taken as the originating object of semiosis:

> ...it is easy to see that the object of the sign, that to which it virtually at least professes to be applicable, can itself only be a sign. For example, the object of an ordinary proposition is a generalization from a group of perceptual facts. It represents those facts. These perceptual facts are themselves abstract representatives, through we know not precisely what intermediaries, of the percepts themselves, and these are themselves viewed, and are - if the judgement has any truth - representations, primarily impressions of sense, ultimately of a dark underlying something, which cannot be specified without its manifesting itself as a sign of something below. There is, we think and reasonably think, a limit to this, an ultimate reality, like a zero of temperature. But in the nature of things, it can only be approached; it can only be represented. The immediate object which any sign seeks to represent is itself a sign. (MS 599, 35-36, apud Johansen 1985, 231-232)

Yet Peirce lays great emphasis on the dominance of the category of secondness (factual interaction) in perception. In his own words:

> As to the direct object of perception, the percept, it is true that it does not possess fully developed reality; but it is the very existing thing itself, independent of and exterior to the mind. For to say that *it exists*, means only that it reacts. Now the percept forces itself upon me, in spite of all direct effort to dismiss it. So, it satisfies the definition of an *existent*. It is independent of the mind in as much as its characters do not depend upon my will to have them so and so. But that it is only known in its relation to my organs is obvious enough. That in no wise contradicts the independence of it, unless one were nominalist enough to deny that independent objects can be members of pairs of which pairs something is true. For a relation is nothing but a fact concerning a set of objects. That the percept is *exterior* to the mind; since, making due allowance for different points of view, another observer, or photographic camera will show the same thing. (L. 427, 20-21, apud Johansen 1985, 228-229)

It is hardly difficult to see how Peirce reconciles the two apparently opposed sides at the intersection of object and perception. To do this, two points may be dwelt upon: first, that although the object never constitutes a naked datum, immediately present, in view of the fact that it is always possible to go on dividing it interminably into layers of percepts,

> this does not mean that the object as existent does not exert an influence; in other words, the infinite series of supposed immediate objects have the same infinity as a line drawn upon a piece of paper, i.e., it can be divided into an infinite number of points (at least in the imagination). Second, even if it is possible to push the analysis of the object indefinitely, this does not

mean that it is impossible to make true statements about something at a given level." (Johansen 1985, 232)

Peirce gives us an excellent example of this in one of his works (8.187), starting out from the printed page which the supposed reader has before him. Peirce affirms that the reader really perceives that very page, 10 inches from his eyes, while another reader behind him will see the same object, though each will see it from a different angle and each sees the real object not in its entirety but only as it is related to his or her literal and tropical viewpoint. Thus it is true to say that two people are reading the same page, even though its sub-atomic structure is constantly undergoing modification and the readers' angle of vision is not the same. And so Peirce was able to postulate that "the immediate object of thought in a true judgement is real" (8.17).

Here, it should be noted, is the embryo of the Peircean position regarding the relationship between thought and reality, and his consequent conception of truth, worked out in detail in his *Pragmatism*. This is not, however, the purpose of this study; let us return to the question of perception and some aspects which have not so far been raised.

I have up to now pointed to what is more properly the epistemological problem built into the notion of the dynamic object in its presupposition in perception. In brief: the perception always has a mediatory function in the apprehension of the dynamic object; to this object we can only have access by way of layers of percepts which undergo indefinite displacement. In spite of this fact, the dynamic object exerts a force over whatever representation or presentation of it we may have. To cast further light on this, we must here open a parenthesis.

3. The perceptive triad

With a view to reconciling and integrating into a coherent and logical process the duality intrinsic to the ingredients of perception, Peirce arrives at a dialectic position, a triadic scheme (as if it could be otherwise) which determines three and not just two ingredients in each and every perception: percept, percipuum, and the perceptive judgement. The ingredients are interdependent but irreducible, which allows them to be analytically isolated for examination of their respective characteristics.

When we perceive something, we are alerted to an essential duality, in which there is something which lies outside us and which is presented to us, and which cannot be diminished or exhausted by the act of perception. To perceive is to perceive something external to ourselves. But we can say nothing of that which is external to ourselves except through the mediation of a perceptive judgement. To that which is outside us, Peirce gives the name of percept; that which tells us what we perceive is the perceptive judgement. And the percipuum? The following quotation makes clear the position of each element:

> We know nothing about the percept otherwise than by the testimony of the perceptual judgement, excepting that we feel the blow of it, the reaction of it against us, and we see the contents of it arranged into an object, in its totality, - excepting also, of course, what the psychologists are able to make out inferentially. But the moment we fix our minds upon it and *think* the least thing about the percept, it is the perceptual judgement that tells us what we so "perceive". For this and other reasons, I propose to consider the percept as it is immediately interpreted in the perceptual judgement, under the name of the "percipuum". (7.643)

As may now be seen, the introduction of the term *percipuum* is not merely a sophistication in terminology. If we apply the network of semiosis to the ingredients of perception, it becomes evident that the percept fulfils the logical role of the dynamic object, the percipuum performs the task of the immediate object, and the judgement of perception acts as the sign-interpretant.

In detail: there is an element of compulsion, of insistence in perception; an entirely irrational insistence which corresponds to the stubbornness with which the percept resists generalization in its singularity and compels our attention to itself. It is something outside ourselves, beyond our control. We may, for example, turn our head and close our eyes to avoid a dazzling source of light. Yet the light remains, it insists, and is ready to invade us once again the moment we turn our head back. The percept is simply this element of insistence, something outside ourselves which we cannot avoid due to the plain fact of our being equipped with sensors which display their sensitivity on being exposed to the myriad impulses from "out there". Stubborn, these impulses do not submit to modification by our will or our imagination. Yet the percept professes nothing. It does nothing whatever beyond compelling our attention, and that quite blindly. It is not guided by reason. But as soon as it reaches our senses it is immediately converted into the percipuum, that is, the percept as it presents itself to the person of the perceiver. It is the percept as it appears to us, translated into form and in accordance with the limits imposed upon it by our sensors.

Thus the percipuum is forced upon us, and is located below the level of our deliberation and self-control. The percipuum arises within us and continues to flow within us. As soon as it arises, however, it is swept up and absorbed in the meshes of the interpretative schemes with which we are endowed: the judgements of perception. Thus Peirce says that we only perceive what we are equipped to interpret. Here again the interpretative schemes lie only relatively within our control. We have no control over the mental operations involved in the formation of a perceptive judgement.

In brief review: the percept presents itself, in the form of a percipuum, to that which perceives; this percipuum is immediately captured in the general schemes of interpretative processes. Thus there is always an element of generality in the judgements of perception, while the percept is a *hic et nunc*, singular and unrepeatable. The guiding principles and habits which regulate the formation of judgements of perception bring the singularity of the percept to conform, to be governed by the generality of the perceptual schemes.

Even so, if we wish for a more faithful view of Peirce's panorama of perception, two further matters demand illumination. Let us see the first one.

4. Gradations of the percipuum

The percipuum (the immediate object of the perception, the percept as it appears to the perceiver) displays itself to the perceiver in a three-level gradation which corresponds to Peirce's three categories.

1. As a vague and ill-defined feeling which looms monadically in the consciousness of the perceiver and wraps it in a twilight of imprecision; a qualitative immediacy between haze and clarity which finds resonance among artists and poets; a mere *tonus* of porous and defenceless consciousness which dilates and dissolves, absorbed in the mingled alchemies between the percept and the senses. This ingredient is a constant in any percipuum. What is variable is its intensity, which may range from the imperceptible to the billows of a diffuse infinity, no beginning, no end, a capsule of uncommitted feeling which we usually call the "poetic state", and which may overwhelm us at any moment, be it in the elevator or by the sea. Nothing can regulate the straightforwardness of this state. Only chance can call it up, for it is born of the rightness of the encounter, the conjunction of a particular percept and a particular state of mind, both coming together in the coagulation of the right moment. This has the savour of eternity to it; thus its non-attachment in time and space.

2. As a reaction to an external impulse which breaks brutally into the feeling, interrupting the flux of consciousness; a reaction to the unexpected or the excessive, which characterizes the percipuum as defensive, resisting the blow with equal and opposite force. These are the states of perceptive surprise, in the *hic et nunc* of the conflict. When very intense, these states bring about an effect of disturbance, of jumbled feelings, of imbalance of the body and a cloud cast on the spirit. When they are deeply undesirable,

they cause a shudder of aversion to course through the body and leave the dry metallic taste of fear in the mouth. But these are extreme cases. Reaction too is a constant ingredient of the percipuum and, in most cases, takes on the forms of automatism. It is not always that percepts thus brutally command our attention. In general, though they demand attention, they come to us more mildly, or, rather, predictably and without alarm.

3. As governed by the guiding principles of the habits of perception. These guiding principles, in themselves true conducts, bring the percipuum into conformity with the general regulatory schemes of perceptive action, which itself flows into an interpretation or signification conferred by perceptive judgement. And this tells us something of what is perceived.

These three levels of the percipuum are interdependent and constant. One or another may vary in its degree of dominance, but in greater or lesser proportion all three are always present. While the third level results in an interpretation of the percept held within the continuity of the mental processes, the first and second levels are pre-interpretative. The non-attachment, the fragility, the simplicity of the consciousness at the first level, and its amalgam between percept and feelings, do not admit the characteristic discrimination of the second level, much less the mediation of habit which is characteristic of the third. The second level already corresponds to the break between ego and non-ego, the boundary-mark between the insistence of what lies outside us and the force for resistance which lies within. Thus we come to the second question of the two which I noted earlier as in need of elucidation. What sort of judgement is the perceptive judgement? Here it is that we find, among other things, what Bernstein mentions as being the greatest novelty of Peirce's theory of perception in relation to the contexts of past and even present ones. But this is a matter for another paper, which for the time being must await its moment.

Note

1. *Questions Concerning Certain Faculties Claimed For Man* (5.213-5.263), *Some Consequences of Four Incapacities* (5.264-5.317), and *Grounds of Validity of the Laws of Logic: Further Consequences of Four Incapacities* (5.318-5.357). In this sequence the papers also appear in *W.II*, p. 193-272.

References

Almender, Robert F.(1970). Peirce's Theory of Perception. In: *Transactions of the Charles S. Peirce Society*, Spring, vol.VI, no.2, 99-110. Republished in *The Philosophy of Charles S.Peirce: A Critical Introduction*. Totowa, New Jersey: Rowman and Littlefield, 137-147.

Bernstein, Richard J. (1964). Peirce's Theory of Perception. In: E.C. Moore and R.S.Robin (eds.), *Studies in the Philosophy of Charles Sanders Peirce*. Amherst: The University of Massachusetts Press, 165-189.

Johansen, J.Dines (1985). Prolegomena to a Semiotic Theory of Text Interpretation, *Semiotica*, 57-3/4, 225-288.

Pape, Helmut (1981). On a connection between Peirce's theory of perception and his theory of indexical identification. In: *Proceedings of the C.S. Peirce Bicentennial International Congress*, K.L. Ketner et al. (eds.). Lubbock: Texas Tech Press, 233-238.

Peirce, C.S. (1931-1966). *Collected Papers*, C. Hartshorne, P. Weiss and A.W. Burks (eds.). Cambridge, MA: Harvard University Press. MS refers to Peirce's unpublished manuscripts as numbered and paginated by the Institute for Studies in Pragmaticism, Texas Tech University, Lubbock, Texas. W II refers to *Writings of Charles S. Peirce, A chronological edition* vol.II, E.C. Moore (ed.), Bloomington: Indiana Press.

Ransdell, J. (1979). The Epistemic Function of Iconicity in Perception, *Peirce Studies*. Lubbock, Texas: Institute for Studies in Pragmaticism, 51-66.

Thompson, Manley (1963). Pragmatism and Perceptual Judgements. In: *The Pragmatic Philosophy of C.S.Peirce*. The University of Chicago Press, 202-212.

Systems of logical representation and inference: An empiricist approach to cognitive science

E.M. Barth (Groningen)

1. Case study: the Master Premiss

In this paper I shall give a connected analytical presentation of some ideas and theories that I have been working on, and from, for a long time. They are concerned with the variety of systems of logical forms in human cognition and language, or, in a more modern vernacular, with the variety of types of logic-relevant "representation", or "logical representation", for short.[1]

I shall assume that semiotics and logic (and parts of linguistics) are constituents (though not the only ones) of cognitive science.

As a warm-up, I would like to present a certain "case study" of logic-relevant representation. The case concerned has had scientific implications as well as political consequences, and it has offered mankind enormous problems of (mutual or self-) understanding. Or, better, of misunderstanding, better still: of *adequate translation*, in the sense of re-representation of what is written or said.

A variety of historical representational forms with their attached inference forms are still with us today, embedded in so-called "natural languages". What I would like to do here is to highlight some of those problems and the cognitive import of the some types of representation and logic (inference) offered as their solution. I start with a case that is particularly clear.

This is the specific problem of representing non-symmetrical relations, and of doing this in a way that allows for safe and efficient methods of drawing inferences that may be regarded as "valid" on the basis of ones representations. I shall present a survey of 4 attitudes to non-symmetrical relations: that of Immanuel Kant, that of traditional European metaphysics, that of Friedrich Engels, and that of modern philosophy of science.

Traditional metaphysicians, Immanuel Kant and Friedrich Engels may seems rather strange bedfellows, but they all started out from what we may call the Master Premiss concerning asymmetric relations, social or otherwise. This is the following - invalid - principle:

The Master Premiss:

> *The hypothesis that asymmetrical binary relations - social or otherwise - are real leads to contradiction, in at least the following three senses:*
> *(a) it generates the Great-and-Small in Plato's ontology and logic,*
> *(b) it is in conflict with the ontology of substance and accident,*
> *(c) it leads to the acceptance of* **quaternio terminorum** *in syllogistic formal logic, which is a fallacy in that logic.*

You will agree that since all *direction* involves asymmetry and all *movement* involves direction, the category **Movement** involves and presupposes the category **Asymmetry**. The German idealist metaphysician Günther Jacoby wrote, years after WW II, in 1955:

> "Movement contradicts itself."

He continued as follows:

> "There is none. It only exists for the gnoseology of a frog perspective. For the bird perspective, in the time-world, nothing is in movement or at rest."[2]

The first sentence is not specific to idealism. The industrialist and materialist Friedrich Engels said the same. In his counter-attack on Dühring Engels wrote:

> "Movement itself is a contradiction."[3]

So on the connection between movement and contradiction the other-worldly metaphysician Jacoby and the revolutionary materialist Engels agree.

But from this common conviction they drew diametrically different conclusions. This has covered up the problems at stake. You will allow that the Marx-Engels outlook on movement and on change in general has, or has had, great political-cognitive importance.

I shall put their arguments in schematic form, and I add two other competing arguments as well, that of Kant and that of modern philosophy of science (at least before quantum mechanics).

I. Kant 1770, 1783

(K1) The hypothesis that there are real [social or physical] asymmetric relations leads to contradiction *(The Master Premiss)*

(K2) Contradictions must be avoided *(second premiss)*

(K3) Ergo, such relations [whether social or physical] are not real, do not characterize the thing-in-itself *(conclusion)*

II. Engels 1878
(E1) *(The Master Premiss)*
(E2) Movement is real [hence at least some asymmetric relations must be ontologically fundamental] *(second premiss)*
(E3) Ergo, representations of reality that do justice to it will necessarily be contradictory *(conclusion)*

III. Traditional metaphysics
(TM1) *(The Master Premiss)*
(TM2) Movement and asymmetrical relations [whether social or physical] are not real *(second premiss)*
(TM3) Ergo, there is no necessity for contradictions *(conclusion)*

IV. Modern logic and (philosophy of) science
(ML1) Movement is real, i.e., Engels' **second premiss** (E2) is true *(first premiss)*
(ML2) But the Master Premiss is false with respect to the representational forms of modern logic *(second premiss)*
(ML3) Ergo, the traditional metaphysicians' **conclusion** (M3) is true *(first conclusion)*
(ML4) Ergo, as a principle of representation Kant's **second premiss**, (K2), is sound *(second conclusion)*

The category of **contradiction** as seen by Marx and Engels was systematically tied up with **dichotomization**, with **restriction to binary relations** and **with restriction to holistic relations**. I cannot go into that here.

So, as P.T. Geach said, "logic matters" - or, the differences between logically relevant representational forms matter a great deal.

2. Empiricism - except in cognitive science?

From a methodological point of view, the remarkable fact to notice here is that most linguists and most logicians, whether as mathematicians or as philosophers, do nothing to elucidate such questions as these - questions of logical representation and of interpretation and understanding, and of misunderstanding. Why is that? I have become convinced that the answer is this:

The received philosophy of cognition generally, including the science we call logic, is "in dire straits", namely in an almost reactionary conceptual state: together with the theologians and the mathematicians, most people in my own field, logic, philosophically are the last of the Mowhikans - theologians, mathematicians and most logicians are the last pure and strict rationalists. Chomskyan linguists follow suit. Everywhere else, strict philosophical rationalism has had to give way, in questions of method, to some amount of empiricism.

At the cradle of cognitive science undertaken as a joint effort it is important that this be clearly understood. There are, in our time, three kinds of eye-opener that something is fundamentally amiss:

first, there is the fact that *physics*, which is an empirical science, utilizes representational forms that are *fundamentally different* from those representational forms that linguists, as students of so-called "natural languages", "ordinary languages", or "Language", for short, and the logicians who associate mainly with them, are familiar with;[4]

second, there is the sad predicament of automatic translation;

third, there is the urgency of *political argumentation*, and the total lack of help offered by professional logicians.

If cognitive science does not yet aspire to the status of a field with a potential for assistance to interpersonal argumentation, at least it cannot - given its ties with the computer sciences - bypass the problem of Automatic Translation.

This requires a clear and full recognition of the variety of basic cognitive categories (a) in time, (b) among the fields of human cognitive endeavour.

3. Non-adiabatic logic

Contemplate these fact for some time, and I think you will admit that various forms of philosophical emancipation *re* human cognition are now required:

(1) in the philosophy of cognition and of "rationality", as well as in semiotics, in fact in cognitive science quite generally, we need to eliminate from our philosophizing and theorizing the idea of "the Reasoning mind". In other words, in Connectionism as well as in Artificial Intelligence the philosophy and science of human cognition should now be extracted from the grip of the old conception of (logical or other) Reasoning as a kind of process that, by real definition, takes place in a communicational vacuum, shielded from the heat of the battle. *Human Reasoning should no longer be conceived at the outset as a process*[5] *that is impenetrable from the outside as long as it is going on - we shall have, at long last, to drop the assumption of logical processes as "adiabatic"* (if I may be allowed to speak metaphorically and borrow a term from thermodynamics);

(2) methodologically: emancipation from the idea of computationalism as the only true methodical basis is required;

(3) and in systematical logic, from deductivism and computationalism alike, wherever these outlooks are taken as the only permissible ones.

4. Summing up

First, there is a need for *empiricist approaches and empirical methodological components* of logic as a science, in particular of empiricist components of the study of *logical* representation, which I take to be a part of logical semiotics as a science, logic and mathematics being the two last refuges of pure rationalism, in the strict philosophical sense.

What should now be taken seriously is the need for attempting a thorough mapping of the various logics of other minds than one's own. This is compatible with the outlook that a "pathological" approach has a great analytical value, but it would also be compatible with the view, which is sometimes voiced, that no "exotic" logic is worse than any other logic - a view to which I do not subscribe. I say this in order to avoid being misunderstood on this point.

Second, in addition to computational philosophy there is also a need for *non-computational approaches* to logic, to logical semiotics, and to cognitive science in general. The present, strictly computational methodology in large parts of cognitive science should be supplemented with what my sometime student Robert Cuperus - with reference to Oliver Sacks - in his Master's Thesis calls the *pathological approach*. This is the approach we all know so well from medical science, and which Sacks suggests as a systematic complement to computationalism: What can go *wrong*? What did go wrong?

In medicine these questions which play an important role in the growth of understanding of what *bodily health* consists in, that is to say: in what it *means* to "go right". It is an approach that has been missing from logic, methodology and philosophy of science, to the detriment of all these fields of inquiry. In logic, in logical semiotics, and in semantics of all kinds, to adopt a pathological methodological approach means to take the categories ***mis*understanding** and ***dis*agreement** as absolutely fundamental, not merely (as Aristotle would call it) as "essentially privative concepts" deriving from "really fundamental" categories **understanding** and **agreement**. Notice that one cannot meaningfully say here that in order to have some idea what it is to "go wrong", one must first have an idea what it is to "go right"; for as far as misunderstanding and disagreement are concerned that retort may as well be turned the other way round. (After all, we are not prepared to let an etymological analysis of inherited words decide our scientific vocabulary.)

Summing up: all this indicates that there is a general philosophical need for - speaking metaphorically - a "non-adiabatic outlook", in all of these areas of inquiry: cognitive and linguistic representation, political understanding, automatic translation, and - last but not least - logic. Though contemporary logic, like Newtonian mechanics, breaks with its Aristotelian predecessor in quite fundamental ways, even in our century the science of logic has remained in the "adiabatic" state in which mechanics was first conceived and presented, i.e., unaffected by the existence of diathermic (non-adiabatic) energetic processes.[6]

Thermodynamics, however, has long since fought its way into recognition, not only from a practical but from a philosophical point of view as well, and contains an adiabatic as well as a more complex diathermic level.[7] The need for a logical counterpart to the latter can no longer be disregarded, and the same holds of cognitive science generally.[8] That this possibility is more than a chimaera is amply demonstrated by the *communicational* or *dialogical* set-up of logic, the closest candidate for further conceptual and theoretical innovation in this direction (next Section).[9]

If the "non-adiabatic thermodynamics" metaphor is rejected, then call the required counterpart: "pathological approaches to logical representation and inference".[10] Why pathological?

5. Fundamental categories

A number of category switches that can be studied in the dialogical form of formal logic clearly inaugurate a break with the adiabatical philosophy of logic:

> from the category *Truth* to the category *Disagreement*;
> from *Validity* to *Conflict*;
> from the category *Understanding* to *Misunderstanding* as the fundamental category;

Also:

> from *theoretical properties* to *theoretical ordered couples and n-tuples,* as in the step from the conceptual category *Premiss* to the ordered pair <*concessions, thesis*>, or, better,
> to: <*instantaneous concessions, instantaneous thesis*>;

Also:

> from the class of so-called "truth values", {**Truth, Falsity**}, to the class of non-adiabatic values {**Agreed, Not-agreed**}.

Then there are the ideas and technical concepts of *empirical approaches to comparative logic and comparative logical representation.* They are less visibly "non-adiabatic", perhaps, but are no less so than the ones we just mentioned:

- the idea of human logical category construction as a *problem-solving activity*, taking place *within a certain (sub)culture*;
- and in fact the very idea of an "adiabatic" origin of certain solutions, certain conceptual structures, or representational forms;
- the assumption of *initial non-distinction* of many presently distinct categories;
- the analytical principle of *imaginal functional compensation* (*in* a system of logical representation), for the absence of categories present in another system.

6. Imaginal Functional Compensation (IFC)

I shall quite briefly illustrate the use of this analytical principle, thereby returning to a problem I have dealt with earlier, but without having isolated and given names to this and other principles of comparative analysis. Take the well-known restriction on logical representation consisting in the assumption that predication is to be understood as essentially and necessarily monadic. On historico-empirical grounds - written historical testimonies - we may say that very many human beings seem to have imposed this idea upon themselves as a very deeply lying principle of cognition. Very deeply lying indeed, for it is reflected in the Noun Phrase/Verb Phrase sentence constitution of so-called "ordinary language". Every analytical philosopher is familiar with the results of the change wrought by Frege and Peirce in the theory of logical representation in this respect.

What is not generally understood by anyone, is that before that change in the theory of logical representation took place, mankind had invented certain forms of what *we,* in hindsight, may characterize as *imaginal compensation* for this restriction. Left to itself, the restriction to monadic predication makes it impossible logically to account for the relatedness of things in this world. Reflective minds have tried to solve the logico-intellectual problem of representing relatedness in other manners (a sub-problem of which is the problem of representing non-symmetrical relations). In other words, they have tried to *compensate* for this lack of our direct - predicative - representation of relatedness. One has sought compensation in at least two quite different manners, which are exotic to most of us here, I suppose:

1. The first is the representational technique of representing relatedness in connection with negation, i.e., by giving pride of place in the theory of negation to what we may call *relative negations* (in particular, to contrariety and contradiction; subcontrariety never was all that popular). This representational technique, however, renders all relatedness as symmetrical.
2. The second method is that of representing (binary) relatedness as a ratio of two essences, as in the "romantic" understanding of differential quotients in the Calculus. The structural link is with the aboriginal category of Polarity; the (fixed) infinitesimals *dx* and *dy* are taken as "polar opposites" and hence as each others "contradictions".

By employing these cognitive patterns in non-trivial thinking one could, not entirely without justification, feel that one did follow modes of thought that allowed one to account for the obvious connectedness of things, even though ordinary predication was taken to be a unary phenomenon. That those cognitive patterns were not optimal for the purpose of developing a theory of logical inference is another matter, albeit a serious one. We may call the first of these two compensatory phenomena *negational relatedness* or *relatedness via relative negations* and the second *essential relatedness* or *relatedness via infinitesimal quotients*.

The said principle of logico-semiotical analysis might also be called "*The Durkheim-Beth Principle*", on account of a perspective on human attempts at constructing modes of thought that may be found both in Durkheim's *Les formes élémentaires de la vie religieuse* (1912) and in Beth's *Aspects of Modern Logic* (1970, pp. 131ff). The principle concerns the forms of reasoning and discourse that are current in a certain period in a certain (sub)culture. It should on no account be called simply a principle of *cognitive* compensation; for that would falsely suggest that systems that are at all comparable as to intended functioning are also logically equivalent.

It is not yet possible systematically to distinguish the representational forms in the language that a certain person inherits, and what he/she does with it, and to it, from what the same or another person writes about the representational forms he/she believes it to be.

Consider the logico-intellectual problem of constructing logico-linguistic categories that can carry out a certain representational function **f**. This may, but need not be, the function of representing a certain experiential feature. "Experiential" should here be taken in a wide sense, to include also the introspective experience of (ones own, or communicated) ideas, their connections and characteristics. For example, **f** may be the function of representing the obvious relatedness of many things and ideas, or the ratios between them; or that of representing some binary relations between things, or between ideas, as non-symmetrical (non-convertible); or that of representing relations as sometimes more-than-binary; or of some properties as more fundamental than other ones.

Our analysis requires some new language. I shall employ the following terminology:

By "presumably logical representation" I shall understand cognition or verbalization by means of representational structures that, in the imagination of the user and/or of those who recommend their use, support the drawing of inferences in a somehow "valid" manner. Let r(S_i, R, **f**) stand for: "In the representational system S_i, category/principle R is called upon in presumably logical representations with the function **f**", or "(presumably logical) **f**-functional representation".[11]

Let S_1 and S_2 be different systems of presumably logical representation, human or artificial. Let S_1 contain or presuppose the use of a representational category/principle R, cognitive or linguistic, and let R be incompatible with some category/ principle or set of such, R^*, that is called upon in S_2-based **f**-functional representation:

$$S_1: R \qquad S_2: R^*, \quad \text{with } r(S_2, R^*, \mathbf{f})$$

Shortcomings, if any, of R will include restrictions enforced by R. The (unstarred) letter "R" and the letter "C" introduced below are chosen as abbreviations of "restrictive" and "compensatory".

Now what may happen if some other S_1-principle, C, that does not belong to S_2, is added to the latter system? Let us speak of users of a representational system S_i as S_i-based minds.

> DEF. 1. A category/principle C of S_1 offers S_1-based minds, from the point of view of an S_2-based mind, some **imaginal f-functional compensation** for conceptual shortcomings of S_1-category/principle R as compared to some R^* as a means of **f**-functional **representation,** *iff* C, when added to S_2 or any other system containing not R but R^*, would be superfluous for the purpose of **f**-functional representation (or, **f**-superfluous).

We shall also say:[12]

> DEF. 2. As seen from the point of view of an S_2-based mind, an S_1-category or principle C offers to S_1-based minds an **imaginal f-functional compensation for the absence in S1 of R^*,** less restrictive or otherwise more adequate than some S_1-category/principle R, *iff* (same condition as above).

We may also say that R and C together form an **imaginal f-equivalent** **(IE^f) in S_1 to R^* in S_2**. This may be defined in terms of imaginal **f**-functional compensation:

> **DEF. 3.** $<R_i, C_i, S_1> \;_{\text{-IE}}^{f}\; <R_i^*, S_2>$ *iff* C_i, from the point of view of an S_2-based mind, in combination with R_i offers to S_1-based minds some imaginal **f**-functional compensation for the absence of R^*_i in S_1.

Specific functional superfluousness in our sense should not be confused with the logical superfluousness of logically derivable principles, or of definable categories. An S_i-derivable/definable axiom/term is logically superfluous and will be **f**-superfluous in S_i for all **representational functions f** that are catered for by that representational system. In the definitions above we are, however, systematically concerned with one function, or a limited number of functions, **f**. We shall have to keep the notion of *representational f-superfluousness in S_2* to some extent an open notion; in any case it is a notion of great efficacy in the comparative understanding of human logics, and of their differing representational bases.

Can the **f**-superfluousness of C be defined in operational terms? Let us use the expression "inferential opacity" in connection with those representational forms whose set of logical rules do not suffice to furnish expressions of these forms with an interactional meaning. For the empirical study of human logics I would then suggest the following:

Heuristic principle:

> Let a category/principle C, taken from a categorial system S_1, be conjoined to system S_2. If this cannot be done without an increase in the dialogical and inferential opacity of S_2, then it is reasonable to assume
> *a.* that C is functionally **f**-superfluous with respect to S_2;
> *b.* that C mainly/primarily/essentially functions in S_1 as an imaginal functional compensation for the reliance upon some functionally inadequate category/principle R in S_1.

This last assumption (b) seems reasonable even when there is no way in which we could *prove* that C is not independent of the categories and principles of S_2 and could be added to S_2 without risk of contradiction.

I do not offer this as an inductive principle of justification, but rather as a heuristic principle, one that should lead us to the *discovery* of that restriction that is implicit in, and enforced by, R, and for which C offers imaginal compensation.

7. Awareness of IFC, and a thesis of (Partial) Commensurability: Case studies

In this section I shall sketch some conspicuous cases which take us toward one general *methodological principle* for comparative empirical logic - that of *awareness of* the phenomenon of imaginal/symbolic functional compensation. Taken together with certain other principles (not discussed here), these cases amount to an inductive defense of a thesis of commensurability - a thesis of partial commensurability, at least, of intellectual paradigms; and one that I want to defend against what has become the received opinion.[13] The "partial" is put in here merely for reasons of hedging. No hypothesis of the limitation of the degree of commensurability is implied.

In each of these case studies the compared terms will be or include (subsets of) logic systems in the narrower sense, with certain additions. I shall refer to three such systems of logic- relevant representation, outlined in such a way as to be functionally comparable: the Aristotelian system, including all general categories and principles with a bearing on logic-relevant representation that are recommended in his oeuvre; the Neoplatonic-Fichtean system[14] of logic in the narrower sense (NPF) - invalid, in our opinion - with the addition of the "romantic" reading of the Infinitesimal Calculus[15] that went with it: NPF+; and the "Modern" system, here defined as some post-Fregean system of inference/dialogue rules with the addition of Weierstrass' non-infinitesimalist reading of the Calculus.

Case 1

NPF+		**Modern**	
R_1:	restriction to monadic predication: *S is P*	R_1^*:	polyadic predication: $F(s_1, ..., s_n)$
C_1:	negation as a relative notion: the relation *contrad (A, B)* [Aristotle: also *contrary (A, B), subcontrary (A, B)*]		(negation can therefore be restricted to unary negation: *not p*)

Notice, in connection with our discussion of the Master Premiss above, that this compensation for the restriction to monadic predication - an emphasis in the Aristotelian system on the three dyadic relations contradiction, contrariety and subcontrariety - remains safely within the traditional set of *symmetrical categories*.

Case 2

NPF+		**Modern**	
R_2:	particularly strong emphasis on symmetric relations, as expressed by the symmetrical *is*: *If S is P, then P is S*	R_2^*:	due emphasis on non-symmetric relations: vector analysis; ordered couples and n-tuples; *F(a, b)* not interchangeable with *F(b, a)*
C_2:	polarity, with "+" and "-" ("positive" and "negative")		(polarity can be discarded as a category *of logic*, and the +/- vernacular as well)

Case 3

Aristotle; NPF^+		**Modern**	
R_3:	restriction to exclusive disjunction: *B aut C*	R_3^*:	inclusive disjunction (veljunction): $p \vee q$
C_3:	potentiality, potency: *A is potentially ("en puissance") B and C*		(potentiality can be discarded as a category of logic)
	(The *potential* genus, with conjunction of species.)[16]		Notice that $(p \vee q) = (p \text{ aut } q) \vee (p \,\&\, q)$

Case 4

Post-Aristotelian tradition		**Modern**	
R_4:	restriction to lateral symmetries: *congruence*, *equiformity*, *equality*, *identity, heredity, parentage,*[17] *reproduction, similarity, species and genera*: the traditional	R_4^*:	lateral asymmetry and vector algebra; enantiomorphy

	Similarity Set of logical categories
C_4:	vertical asymmetry: hierarchical logical order, represented by the *graded copula (is)*

Case 5

NPF^{+}		**Modern dynamics and its mathematics**	
R_5^{*}:	the physics and metaphysics of potent - 'infinitesimals'; the romantic understanding of the Calculus[18]	R_5:	restriction to finite magnitudes ▲ *x*, ▲ *y* and their ratios; Weierstrass' def. of *limit.* (Hence no emphasis on hierarchical logical order and vertical asymmetry
		C_5:	*The lateralization of the world picture*

Case 5 can just as well be put like this:

Dynamics of the Naturphilosophie:			
R_5':	restriction to C_4 (no vector analysis)	$R_5^{\prime *} = R_5$	
C_5':	powerful infinitesimals (cf. C_3, the *potential* genus)		

Case 6

Aristotle		**Modern**
R_6 =	R_1: restriction to monadic predication with	$R_6^{*} = R_1^{*}$: polyadic predication

	simple (non-iterated) quantification: *Every A is B, No A is B, Some A is (not) B*	
C_6:	hierarchical connectedness of individual objects (and of species) through participation in a (potential) *genus*	C_6 can be discarded - lateral connectedness of individuals: *The Lateralization of formal logic*

The Lateralization of formal logic took place as a consequence of "The Mechanization of the World Picture", as Maier, and later Dijksterhuis, called it (Case 5).[19]

Case 7

Pre-Darwinian logic		**Darwin**
R_7:	restriction to the Similarity Set	R_7^*: *variation* as a "positive", non-privative, category,[20] hence one that transcends the Symmetry Set

(no imaginal compensation; or perhaps one should say:)

C_7: *Identity - the summum (potential) genus -* as representative of the fullness of Being[21]

8. Automatic translation: the need for a Projective Logic and Semantics

The Master Premiss. Directly or indirectly, the case studies that we have briefly sketched all bear upon the Master Premiss concerning non-symmetrical relations. In a sense, even the introduction of Variation as a category of thought does - for Darwinian Variation cannot be understood by people who, like Friedrich Engels, assume the Master Premiss, with its presupposition of restriction to the Symmetry Set. This is one example of the problems of understanding, and hence also of automatic translation, that one has to learn to conquer.

Allow me to mention, as a finish, some points of considerable importance that are directly related to what I have been talking about.

Phases of cognitive operation. The distinction between "adiabatic" and "non-adiabatic" logical and other "rational" processes may also be formulated in terms of a distinction between *phases of logical operation.* Some observed representational forms will not only be determined by the category set that the thinker/speaker is familiar with - is programmed with, one might say; but also by one of the two (or more) *phases of cognitive operation* that we may distinguish in human cognition, and this sometimes leads to differences that are not easily explained in other ways. One has to brace oneself for this phenomenon. Does the thinker or author in question focus on what we may call the social-solipsist, or Laboratory, phase of cognition, or does he/she rather operate in (or with respect to) the communicative, or Arena, phase of cognitive activity? Much to the detriment of analytic work, these different phases of operation are not usually distinguished and brought to bear upon formal analysis.

The phase-dependency of "theories of Truth". Any thinking person's "truth theory" will also depend on the operation phase he/she has in mind. This of course goes for the semiotic theoretician or logician, too. The step from {**Truth, Falsity**} to {**Agreed, Not-agreed**} corresponds to a shift in phase interest from Laboratory to Arena.

For a Projective logic and semantics. There clearly is a need for a representational analogy - syntactic as well as semantic - to projective geometry. Such a projective logical linguistics should be erected on the basis of a new, empirical component of the science of logic, based on empirical studies of varieties of logic-relevant representation and of the logical rules that have been associated with them.[22]

Our study of imaginal functional compensation, and of imaginal functional equivalence, may be taken as a necessary step in this direction. It seems unlikely in the extreme that there can be success in automatic translation until we master the rules of some such projective syntax and projective semantics. For full success in automatic translation it will be necessary also to study the non-projectible properties of systems of logical representation.

Notes

1. A number of examples will be discussed in Sections 2 and 7.

2. G. Jacoby, *Allgemeine Ontologie der Wirklichkeit, II,* p. 611.

3. F. Engels, *Herr Eugen Dührings Umwälzung der Wissenschaft,* Leipzig 1886 [1978], p. 110.

4. We have mentioned asymmetry. I shall not here go into another, equally important inspiration that general logic might pick up from physics: the distinction of of identity concepts in modern physics (Bose-Einstein statistics); but let me quote the beginning of a paper by Maria Luisa Dalla Chiara: "It is largely recognized that physics has represented an important source of suggestions in the historical development of mathematics and, in more recent times even of logic" ('Some Foundational Problems in Mathematics Suggested by Physics', *Synthese 62* (1985), 303-315, p. 303). "[S]ome problems suggested by the physical properties of bosons [] seem to put in question some fundamental logical and mathematical concepts regarding, for instance, the notions of *individual, identity, cardinal* and *ordinal number"* (op. cit., 307).

5. Or set of various process types.

6. Even so, mathematical or "rational" mechanics has its uses, in particular it has an interesting meta-systematic value. Exactly the same holds of present one-role or no-role logic, "adiabatic", logic, whether deductive or computational.

7. Barring logic (and continental metaphysics), where thermodynamics and its philosophy seem to have had no influence.

8. Is the call in some A.I. circles for a "Distributive Artificial Intelligence", D.A.I., to some extent inspired by a general philosophy which is related to what is here called a Non-Adiabatic outlook on methodological problems?

9. Lorenzen ca. 1959. Cf. P. Lorenzen & K. Lorenz, *Dialogische Logik,* Darmstadt 1978; compare papers by Hintikka on "game-theoretical *semantics*" from ca. 1970. E.M. Barth & E.C.W. Krabbe, *From Axiom to Dialogue*, Berlin 1982. Empirical-logical problems are set out in this light in: E.M. Barth, *The Logic of the Articles in Traditional Philosophy,* Dordrecht/Boston 1974.

10. Compare here: E.W. Beth's Semantical-Tableau method, on which the dialogical methods are historically based; cf. (Barth and Krabbe 1982).

11. A distinction between *categories* and *principles* here would seem to be premature.

12. When R of S1 and R^{*} of S_2 seem to be called upon for representation with the same function **f** they may be called "representationally competing categories/principles". If the variable "R" may take "the empty principle" as a value, then every category/principle of any system will have at least one representationally competing category/principle in any other system. These definitions might be rephrased in terms of "competing categories/principles of representation".

13. The discussion about (in)commensurability, the revision of logic, the plurality of logics, and the possibility of real conflicts, as far as written in French or English, is reviewed in Paul Gochet, *Ascent to Truth - A Critical Examination of Quine's*

Philosophy, Munich/Vienna 1986. Gochet refers to P. Destouches-Février, *La structure des théories physiques,* Paris 1951; S. Haack, *Deviant Logic*, Cambridge, 1974; and to M.L. Dalla Chiara, "The Relevance of Quantum Logic" (forthcoming). Another contribution to this discussion, published in Dutch, is found in my *Evaluaties* (Assen, The Netherlands, 1972). I regret having overlooked the earlier paper by P. Février in my own discussion, in the said publication, of the status and plurality of logics.

14. Cf. Leonard Nelson, *Progress and Regress in Philosophy, Collected Works, Vol. VII.*

15. For its history, see C. B. Boyer, *The History of the Calculus and Its Conceptual Development,* New York, 1959.

16. I have discussed this on p. 417ff. of *The Logic of the Articles in Traditional Philosophy,* Reidel, Dordrecht, 1974.

17. "In other words, all *likeness* was originally represented as *kinship*" (F.M. Cornford, *From Religion to Philosophy - A Study in the Origins of Western Speculation,* 1957 (1912), p. 86).

18. For the philosophy of the romantic understanding of the "infinitesimal calculus" in spite of Berkeley's criticism, see Hermann Cohen, *Das Prinzip der Infinitesimalmethode und seine Geschichte. Ein Kapitel zur Grundlegung der Erkenntniskritik,* Berlin 1883; also the following testimony by Friedrich Engels: "Die Sache ist so Sonneklar, dass man sich wirklich nicht genug wundern kann, wie die Mathematiker so hartnäckig darauf bestehen, sie zu mystifizieren. Aber dass kommt von der vereinseitigten Denkweise der Herren. dy/dx resolut und ohne Umschweife = 0/0 zu setzen, will ihnen nicht in den Schädel. Und doch ist es klar, dass dy/dx erst dann der **reine** Ausdruck eines an x und y vorgegangenen Prozesses sein kann, wenn von den *Quanta* x und y auch die letzte Spur verschwunden, nur der Ausdruck des an Ihnen vorgehenden Veränderungsprozesses **ohne alle Quantität** geblieben ist" (letter from Engels to Marx of 18 August 1881, *Karl Marx - Friedrich Engels Werke*, vol. *35*, Berlin 1967; p. 23).

19. A. Maier, *Die Mechanisierung des Weltbildes,* Leipzig 1938; E. J. Dijksterhuis, *De mechanisering van het wereldbeeld,* Amsterdam 1950, transl. *The Mechanization of the World Picture,* Oxford 1969. On chronological as well as systematical grounds it is possible to draw the conclusion that the category of direction (or, as Russell said, of the *sense*) of a relation, and the category of order among related individuals, owe their presence in contemporary academic logic to the development of vector algebra. Ernest Nagel drew the same conclusion in "The Formation of Modern Conceptions of Formal Logic in the Development of Geometry", *Osiris 7* (1939), 142-224. Cf. Maria Luisa Dalla Chiara, quoted above in n. 4.

20. I owe this shrewd insight to a paper by R.C. Lewontin, "Darwin's Revolution", *New York Review* June 16, 1983, 21-27.

21. See last note.

22. Discussed in two earlier papers by the present author: "Two-Phase Epistemology and Models for Dialogue Logic", *Philosophica 35* (1985), 69-88; "Waiting for Godot. On attitudes towards artefacts vs. entities, as related to different phases of operation in cognition', *Epistemologia XIV* (1991), 77-104.

Semiotic primitives and conceptual representation of knowledge

J.G. MEUNIER (Montréal)

1. Introduction

From a philosophical point of view, one of the most important contributions of artificial intelligence (A.I.) has been to revive the ancient philosophical thesis that all knowledge of reality depends on some pre-existing cognitive structures. Indeed, most non-empiricist philosophical theories of knowledge have postulated some preliminary form of cognitive structure in order to explain the complexity of the integration process that serves to generate ideas or concepts from elementary perceptual data and account for the reasoning process that relates and joins ideas among themselves. A.I. has elaborated systems that were accorded to some type of a priori knowledge representation whose function it was to ensure a causal link in the behaviour of machines.

> Any mechanically embodied process with at least a claim for intelligence will be comprised of a particular configuration of ingredients that a) we, as external observers naturally take to represent a propositional account of the knowledge that the overall process exhibits, and b) independent of such external semantic attribution, has a formal causal and essential role in engendering the behaviour that manifests that knowledge. (Smith, 1982, p. 2)

This central thesis remains the object of considerable debate. As Mylopoulos and Delgrande have argued, even if the representation of knowledge content is necessary for the construction of an A.I. system, we remain uncertain as to the exact role of this representation: "It is difficult to pinpoint exactly what knowledge representation is, does or promises to do." (Mylopoulos and Delgrande 1986, p. 2)

Aware of the foundational difficulties inherent in the knowledge representation thesis, A.I. has preferred to approach the problem primarily in terms of a greater formalisation. In classical A.I. models, this formalisation was conceived in strict symbolic terms (Newell and Simon, 1976; Pylyshyn, 1986; Fodor, 1976; Johnson-Laird, 1988; Haugeland, 1986).

> What do we mean by "description"? We do not mean to suggest that our descriptions must be made of concatenations of ordinary language words. ... Rather the simplest kind of description is a structure in which some features of a situation are represented by single (primitive) symbols with the relations between those features being represented by other symbols or by others features explaining the way in which the description is put together. (Minsky & Papert, 1973, p. 11)

More specifically, the problem of symbolic description has itself been interpreted in terms of a symbolic language. Originally, this symbolic representation took the form of more or less directed graphs where the information was stocked in an atomic and relational fashion (Quillian, 1968; Schank, 1972; Wilks, 1975; Winograd, 1972; Rumelhart, 1975). Later on, under the influence of logical grammar (Montague, 1973) and of psycholinguistics (Anderson, 1976, 1983; Fodor, 1976), the representational form was organised in a more systematic fashion. Researchers such as Hendrix (1977), Schubert (1975), Hayes (1979), Goldstein and Roberts (1979), Lehnert (1979), Levesque (1984), Shapiro (1979), Sowa (1984, 1991) gave to these representations a more logical and propositional form. Naturally these logical representations were studied, compared and criticised (Woods, 1975, 1986; Brachman, 1979; Hayes, 1979). Modifications of various type where given, among them: the introduction of operator types (Brachman and Fikes, 1983; Levesque, 1984, Desclées, 1987). For many theorists, the logical form of a symbolic representation was and remains the only valid working hypothesis.

In actual systems, the formalism adopted is often akin to a "pidgin propositional language", that is, it is often not very rigorous and does not always follow all the rules of classical logical languages. But it nonetheless retains their main characteristics: it is always submitted to some form of syntactic and inferential rules that one intends to be based as much as possible on a logical model. They are thus slightly less strict from the semantic point of view. And on the whole, these systems seek to constitute a symbolic language that is atomic, productive, inferential, and interpretable. For many theoreticians, these properties are essential to any representational system that is to be useful in the understanding of cognitive behaviour whether this behaviour be natural or artificial. These properties overlap what in linguistic terms is said to be the syntax and the semantics of a language.

Many researchers, however, have refused to define a language of cognitive representation in strict logical and conceptual terms. The most radical opposition comes from the connectionist school. Their micro-cognitive approach to knowledge representation rejects the symbolic thesis because of its inherent limitations in explaining the complexity of the learning and processing of information.

> The subsymbolic paradigm challenges both the syntactic and semantic role of language in formal cognitive models. (Smolensky, 1988, p. 4)

More profoundly though, the classical logical representation always contains some implicit conceptual postulate that is not readily acceptable as an adequate explanation of a given knowledge representation:

> Formal cognitive models have taken their structure from the syntax of formal languages, and their content from the semantics of natural language. The mind has been taken to be a machine for formal symbol manipulation, and the symbols manipulated have assumed essentially the same semantics as words of English (Smolensky, 1988, p. 4)

They have proposed instead a sub-symbolic approach to knowledge representation. Though their proposition is somewhat radical, it does not alleviate the semiotic and conceptual dimensions: even with the sub-symbolic we are still in the domain of the symbolic; this fact is well noted by Lycan:

> "If subsymbols are still representors manipulated according to precise rules, they are still symbols, expressing concepts in any traditional sense of those terms. (Lycan, 1988, p. 43)

As many others studies have shown, (cf. Smythe, 1990; Jorna 1990a, 1990b; Goschke, 1990), the symbolist or the connectionist models seem unable to circumvent the semiotic dimension of representation. These dimensions are constantly engaged in representation, interpretation, information and signal processes. So, the question we would like to raise here is the following one: can a semiotic system be non-conceptual and still be adequate for knowledge representation?

2. The semiotic and the cognitive

Surprising as it may seem to many, the problem of a cognitive representation is a semiotic one; in fact it has been in one manner or another the concern of most semiotic theories. If one goes back to the origin of semiotics, one will find there an important preoccupation with the representational problem, one which will be conceived in its cognitive dimension.

> A sign is something that shows itself to the senses, but also beyond itself shows something to the mind. (Augustin, 40, *De dialectica*, V, 11-12; my translation).

For Locke, signs are the media by which the world is presented to the mind. They are, he tells us, ideas themselves. Locke writes:

> For since the things the mind contemplates are none of them, besides itself, present to the understanding, it is necessary that something else, as a sign or representation of the thing it considers, should be present to it: and these are *ideas*. (Locke, 1690; book IV, chap. XXI).

This dimension is more evident still in Peirce:

> A sign or *representamen* is something which stands to somebody, for something in some respect or capacity. It addresses somebody, that is, creates in the mind of that person an equivalent sign or perhaps a more developed sign. (Peirce 1931, Vol 2; p. 228)

The classical formula that a sign substitutes for a thing is in fact a metonymic formula insofar as it holds that a sign is something an *agent* must use in order to refer to another thing. In other words, a representation is the name given to a complex structure of signs that stand for something else for a given interpreter. For many researchers, what has made this semiotic question more difficult is the linguistic turn it has taken from Saussure on (see Harman, 1979). Indeed most of the traditional semiotic theories have been modelled on the basis of linguistic theories. Hence the semiotic systems derived from these theories implicitly or explicitly deployed components that were to be understood in terms of "grammar", "words", "concepts" and "sentences", "texts" and even of linguistic "meaning", etc. For example, pictures and paintings became texts, had sentences and bore specific lexical meaning. This transposition of linguistic concepts however has not been without technical difficulties.

But in its more recent history, general semiotics has reoriented itself by studying signs not exclusively as systems but as the result of action undertaken or related to interpretive agents. It has thus stressed the processing of signs, or in more classical terms: "the process of semiosis", rather than the structure of signs in and of themselves.

These same semiotic theories then studied signs, signals, symbols and indices, but only to the extent that the agent active in their processing was taken into account. The attribution of signification to a given entity is always the result of an operation which is external to the signifying object itself. The support of this operation, that is to say the operator who effectuates these operations is what is termed *a semiotic agent*.

This conceptual transformation of semiotics enabled it to realise that it was closely related to the contemporary information theory which treats the causal relation between a sign and what it signifies and the consequent interpretation it receives by a cognitive agent. As Dretske (1988) states, the informational theory regarding this relation is merely a repetition of the theory of natural signs. He observes:

> talking about information is a third way of talking about the fundamentally important relation of indication or natural meaning. (Dretske, 1988, p. 58)

From the perspective of natural signification living organisms are considered as agents within a localised process of semiosis, that is to say they are agents exhibiting a specific type of behaviour in relation to objects or events insofar as they attribute to them new signification. This process of semiosis is evident just as much in the processing of information by electronic agents as in the most elementary living organisms and is certainly evident in the processes of intellection and comprehension of superior organisms.

On the basis of this model, an axon can be said to be interpreting information when, confronted with chemical molecules, it either accepts or rejects them thus reacting to the fact that these entities bear (or do not bear) specific information. Even animals said to be "evolved" possess their own procedures which clearly bear witness to this very complex type of information processing. In this way information is considered as a signal which circulates within the sensory sphere of the organism and which is immediately accessible to it. However, in more complex organisms such as humans and animals, the information is correspondingly more complex; it is also stored and handled differently. The information taken in does not directly associate a given signal with a reaction. There is always a certain lapse-time between signal reception and reaction; as a result, the organism-agent, on the basis of the received information, produces a specific representation. From this perspective the question of representation is central.

Modern theories of representation conceive of the mind as having access to systems of internal representations:

> Mental states are characterized by their being assertions of the specific content of internal representations and mental processes characterised by how such internal representations are obtained and how they interact. (Marr, 1982, p. 7)

One of the semioticians who has always defended the relation between semiotics and agents is Sebeok. For him, not only does this relation imply an agent but it also implies a communicative relation between agents. According to Sebeok:

> Semiotics [...] can be informally defined as the science that studies all possible varieties of signs, and the rules governing their generation and production, transmission and exchange, reception and interpretation. Concisely put, semiotics has two complementary and interdependent aspects: communication and signification. (Sebeok, 1976, p. 23)

Of course this perspective introduces certain conceptual changes into semiotics: it is no longer the sign as such that is of primary interest but rather the process of semiosis, that is to say, the act by which a semiotic agent processes particular signs, signals, or symbols. Broadening the conceptual framework of investigation in this way entails a shift in our understanding of what a representation is. Moreover it compels us to reevaluate our understanding of the classical properties of symbolic systems such as their atomicity, their productivity, their inferentiality and their interpretativity. Of interest as well is how a possible reconceptualization of symbolic systems will affect our understanding of many basic related concepts such as "units of information", "gnosons", "micro-units", "semiotic primitives" or even "atomic symbols", all together a configuration of terms that, taken together, designate the essential constituents that a cognitive system should possess.

In order to understand better what function these so called "primitives" have in a representation we will first need to reflect on what it means for a physical entity to become a semiotic entity or symbol within a representational and informational system and also what it means for these entities to receive a conceptual structure.

3. The character of semiotic carriers

At first glance, semiotic primitives may seem somewhat abstract or of dubious ontological status. But for cognitive scientists, the basic symbols in a representational system cannot be an esoteric, evanescent and abstract entity. It must above all be a physical reality. Even when Newell and Simon talk about artificial intelligence in terms of manipulation of physical symbols, they are really referring to physical entities of one type or another. They write:

> A physical symbol system consists of a set of entities, called symbols, which are physical patterns that can occur as components of another type of entity called an expression (or symbol structure). (Newell and Simon 1976, p. 40)

For semiotics this is a classical thesis: a symbol is always realized in some physical 'stuff' of some sort or another. But one must also be aware that it is not the physicality of an object itself that renders this same object semiotically pertinent. Having a physical support of some sort is only a necessary condition, not a sufficient one in order for an object to become a semiotic entity. In fact, a number of conditions comes into play in order for a physical object to become a semiotic one, conditions that are in fact extrinsic to the object. A physical carrier acquires a semiotic character when it becomes the argument of an interpretive function within a system. This semiotic character or property is not something which belongs intrinsically to the "genes" of the carrier. As medieval logicians said, it is a secondary property. More precisely, for some object, becoming semiotic depends on the function it occupies with respect to the interpreting system to which it is related. The semiotic dimension of a carrier is not an autonomous entity that blooms in the wild. It exists only in relation to some agent that gives it a role, that is an interpretive function. All semiotic theories from Aristotle through Peirce, and up to Carnap and Morris, called upon an interpreter which, if it is of the higher type as is the case with animals and humans, has cognitive abilities. A rock, a coloured piece of linen, a protein, an electric current are only what they are, wherever they are. In and of themselves, they are never semiotics entities. However relative to an interpretive system, they can become significant carriers and in this way become: a buoy, a flag, a neurotransmitter, a signal, etc.[1]

The relation to an interpretive agent directs us to the identification in a carrier of properties that are related to this interpretive function. Indeed a carrier which presents itself as a physical object is usually comprised of an infinity of properties. For example, the carrier that is an ink mark can be more or less black, thick, elongated, compact, round, etc. It has molecular width, chemical characteristics such as being acidic or alkaline. It may have a form, a length, an orientation and so forth, ad infinitum. If we take an electric current as a carrier passing through a copper or aluminium wire, it may be negative or positive, have different voltages and amperage rates, etc. The number of such properties, one may surmise, is infinite. In a specific description of a carrier, these properties will be represented by descriptors or predicates. For example, one could say that one carrier is *red* and made of *plastic*, and that another one is *1500 watts* and *5 amperes*.

But not all of these properties are pertinent to the semiotic function in which a carrier may be engaged. Only a few of these properties may be needed for such a role. We call the property type that is engaged in this semiotic function the (semiotic) character or feature of a carrier. And a carrier, be it electric, mechanical or chemical, plays a semiotic role if and only if one or more of such features is present. One finds here what a classical semiotic tradition termed "pertinent marks" and what cognitive theories call the distinct "features" of an input. From the point of view of a cognitive theory, the characters of a carrier are necessarily the smallest units an agent is capable of sensing, in other words, the smallest features that a being is capable of detecting, recognising, and identifying.

A classical example of this concept can be found in the description of phonemes in functional linguistics. A phoneme is a sound (carrier) produced by humans, but it presents a certain number of characteristics called "pertinent features". In French, there exists a sound carrier that offers an infinity of properties but for a French speaker only the one presenting a specific set features of will be recognised as a 'd'. In the visual system of certain organisms, for instance, cones and rods are not sensitive to the carrier as such - a beam of light, for example - but only to a specific set of its characteristics, for example, its luminous intensity, its chromaticity or its angle of incidence. Even if a light beam possesses a certain temperature, the eye as a perceptual system is insensitive to it.

Thus it is not the fact that an object or an event is being physically realized that makes this object or event a semiotic one.[2] The vocabulary of some cognitive theories is often ambiguous in this regard. According to these, to interpret seems to be equated with physical realisation. What within a given system constitutes a semiotic unit is not the carrier itself, but each of the characteristics of this carrier. Moreover an interpreting agent does not process carriers as such. If he can be said to process something, it is less in the sense of "factory" production (i.e., the physical transformation of goods and products) but more in the sense that in accordance with his own constitution he effectuates a set of operations or reactions related to the characteristics of the carrier itself. Meaningfulness in this context implies an idiosyncratic action by the interpretive agent.

4. Semiotic primitives and conceptual structure

Because the characteristic features of a carrier constitute the foundational dimension of their semiotic function, and because these features are often designated by specific predicates in the models serving to describe them, one will often attach to them conceptual structures of one form or another. Indeed, when one tries to identify some specific character of an objet one will usually use a predicate or configuration thereof, such as "red", "thick", "long", "heavy", "big", "alkaline", etc. In doing so, it becomes quite natural to think that because all the names used in the meta-language of the description carry some underlying concept, this conceptual structure can be applied to the primitives of the system that is described. This tendency is so strong that various theories of representation have given to their semiotic primitives some sort of conceptual interpretation. In fact this thesis has been formally integrated into many symbolic representational theories developed in A.I. More so, many specific programming languages have been built as to manipulate concepts as objects (object oriented language). Thus, it is not surprising that every constituent of a representation of knowledge is said to be a concept. For instance, the symbolic primitives in the "frame", "plan", "scenario" and "semantic net" models usually portray each primitive as a distinct concept. For example, in the case of a word such as "dog", one can associate a concept, an idea or some other type of mental representation.

> Conceptual entity is anything about which information can be given that is anything about which one can know. (Schubert et al., 1979, p. 122).

A typical example is to be found in the following semantic net illustration from Collins and Quillian (1969):

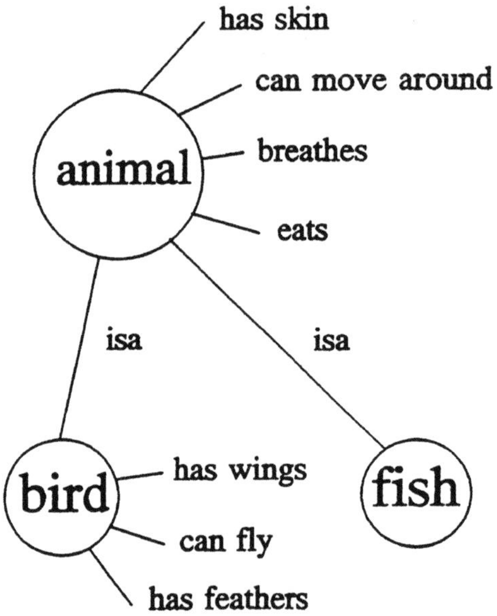

Figure 1: Nodes and links in a semantic net

Here the nodes are strictly identified as concepts and each node denotes an individual object or event or some relation among them:

> It seems fairly clear what frames mean: A frame instance denotes an individual, and each slot denotes a relationship which may hold between

> that individual and some other. [...] It seems that frames are simply an alternative syntax for expressing relationships between individuals, i.e., predicate logic. (Hayes, 1980, p. 48)

> Nodes in the (semantic) net represent concepts of entities, attributes, events and states. (Sowa 1991, p. 1)

This idea of ascribing to each primitive of a semiotic or representational system a conceptual structure of some sort is not new. It belongs to the traditional occidental philosophies where mental operations or thought processes are often said to be conceptual.

This thesis culminates in Hegel, who stated that mind processes are essentially conceptual. And it has migrated even in logic with the analytic philosophical interpretation of Fregean semantics according to whom, one recalls, a symbolic expression in a logical language always presents a sense and a reference (Sinn and Bedeutung). For strictly technical reasons, Frege distinguished between these two dimensions, identifiable by the semantic analysis of a symbolic expression such as would be the case with the artificial languages of arithmetic and logic. This thesis has also been applied to natural language expressions. The analytic philosophical tradition has long recognised the fecundity of this application. In the case of natural language expressions, one would try to discover what it would mean for a natural language predicate or a proper noun to have a sense and a reference. According to Frege's original theory, the sense of a logical predicate was treated in terms of a concept (Begriff) and the reference of a predicate in terms of objects or classes of objects. One would then naturally translate the notion of sense of a natural language predicate into terms of concept and the notion of reference into terms of object or relations between objects. For example in either a logical formula such as *"∀x (MEN x -> MORTAL x)"*, or in an English sentence such as *"All men are mortal"*, one would naturally attribute to the predicates, and to either the constants or the common nouns of these formulae, a conceptual structure of some sort. According to the same logic, the next step (a step that many theories of semantics, A.I. and cognition have taken) involves the assumption that all basic expressions contained in a symbolic system do indeed represent some sort of concept.

More problematic still is the fact that Frege's notion of concept has often become confounded with other theories of concept. In fact the debate about the conceptual structures of semiotic primitives becomes unavoidably complicated by the very range of current definitions of "concept". The logical Fregean position identifies a concept with the sense of a predicate in logical language, the latter being understood in terms of a function. A second definition identifies a concept with the semantic meaning or the sense of a natural language expression. A third one identifies a concept with the representational or psychological reality in a cognitive agent. A fourth definition identifies concept with the traditional philosophical notion of idea. However, as many philosophers (see Ryle, 1932) have argued, these definitions are essentially quite different; they do not assume the same criterion of identity and do not rely on the same theoretical paradigm.

According to Frege's logical definition the notion of concept bears a strict technical meaning: a concept is understood in terms of *function*; as such it is related to the "unsaturated part" of a propositional formula.

> A concept is a function whose value is always a truth value. [...] Thus we see how closely that what is called a concept in logic is connected with what we call a function. (Frege, 1952, p. 30)

On the semantical level, a concept is governed by a definitive set of necessary and sufficient criteria that determines whether or not an objet falls under it.

> A definition of a concept (of a possible predicate) must be complete; it must unambiguously determine, as regard any object, whether or not it falls under the concept (wether or not the predicate is truly assertible of it). Thus there must not be any object as regards which the definition leaves in doubts wether it falls under the concept; though for us men, with our defective knowledge, the question may not always be decidable. We may express this metaphorically as follows: the concept must have a sharp boundary. (Frege, 1952, p. 56)

According to Church (1951), a concept is related to the *sense* or *interpretation function* that is associated with the predicate part of a logical formula. So either in the Fregean or the Churchian sense, there is no concept associated with the argument of the predicate, that is to say, the constant, not the variable. For instance, in a logical formula, such as *John is a student*, a concept would only be attached to the "student" predicate.

In consequence, this means that although some basic constituents of a semiotic system are to be linked to concepts it must also be clear that this conceptual structure is to be understood in the line of a functional entity, and not as an idea, nor an image nor even an abstract class of some sort. Thus, it is in no way a representational or a psychological entity. It is more of an abstract relation. Frege himself has often insisted on the necessary distinction between the conceptual dimension of the predicate (its Sinn) and its representational dimension (Vorstellung). The latter represents the cognitive and often subjective dimension of the predicate. Frege's concept is quite distinct from the psychological and traditional definition of the notion of concept which is often synonymous with representation, conscious knowledge, and classification processes (Anderson, J.A., 1986) or even with fuzziness and typicality (Rosch, 1973) and hierarchical structure, etc. This does not mean that in a cognitive agent these dimensions are absent. It only means that these aspect are not to be confused with this technical sense of the Fregean concept. It would be like identifying a function with its implementation, or its formulation in a language or in algorithms, or its storing in the memory.

It is also important to note that the logical notion of concept cannot easily be equated with the idea of natural language meaning. If in logical languages the concept ascribed to a predicate can be defined as its "mode of presentation" or its denotation, that is to a say as a certain formal function associated with it, it does not follow that it can be identical with the lexical or semantic meaning of a term in a natural language. For instance, in the logical formulae given above, the predicate "men" can be given a technical conceptual sense (i.e., a function that allows it to denote something in the universe of discourse). But despite appearances, it is not true that the common noun *Men* has as its meaning the same concept as the predicate "men". In the linguistic literature on semantics, it has often been observed that even if two common nouns had the same conditions of denotation (i.e., the same sense or even the same truth conditions), it would not follow that the denotative meaning corresponds to the lexical meaning for this natural language. In the European tradition of semantics, far more so than in the American, the meaning of words is determined in part by "truth conditions" of the words, but also by the differential position with respect to the entire lexicon. For instance, the English word "man" would be studied not only in veridical terms but also as a carrier of meaning by virtue of its difference in the whole of the lexicon such as for example opposed to the terms *women, child, animal* and even *robot*. As one can see in the following sentences:

God created man.
She married a young man not a child.
Last week General Motors has fired a man and replaced it by a robot.

The conceptual structure of a natural language expression contains more dimensions than the strict truth conditions one can associate with it by means of a narrow redefinition in the form of a predicate language.

Finally, the Fregean notion of *concept* cannot be immediately identified with the traditional notion of idea such as Locke's or even a more contemporary one such as Husserl's. With these philosophers, the notion of concept has a much broader sense than the strict technical one it has in Frege. For instance, the concept that underlies the term "man" in classical philosophy cannot be identified with the concept that underlies the predicate "man" in a specific technical formula; the former concept assumes a transcendental category, while the latter is restricted to the dimension of a technical function.

What we have wished to make clear in the preceding pages is that considerable care is needed in order to decide whether a semiotic primitive should or should not receive a conceptual interpretation. All depends on how the concept of "concept" is defined. The thesis that we wish to defend here is that for every semiotic primitive there is not necessarily a corresponding concept in the psychological, linguistic, and philosophical sense of the word, that is to say there is not necessarily a corresponding "idea", a "mental image", a "noema", etc. We will attempt to demonstrate that a representational system can have primitives without these entities being "conceptually" meaningful in the latter sense. However this absence does not prevent these same primitives from participating in a well structured representational system nor from having a functional meaning within it.

There exist numerous semiotic systems containing primitives for which it is impossible to associate directly some ideational, psychological or linguistic "concept". Consider, for example, the phoneme in a natural language. A phoneme is a sound that plays a role in the semiotic system of a natural language. As a carrier, this sound presents itself to a listener with a specific set of characters. Only a subset of these characters associates a sound with a certain phoneme. Phonemics is not acoustics. But it is impossible for a speaker to associate with each of the basic characters or phonemic semiotic primitives an idea, a linguistic meaning, much less a mental image of some sort. It is only by means of their association, not to mention their composition, that the whole set of features succeeds in forming a phoneme. In isolation from one another, these characters lack any ideational dimension whatsoever. This however does not prevent to play a role in the semiotic system.

Even in the case of a single phoneme considered in itself as a whole primitive at a particular level of analysis (phonological), it is difficult to think of how we can associate with it any lexical, ideational or psychological concept. What idea, or image or " lexical concept" could one possibly associate with the phoneme B? One cannot ascribe a "concept" to the phoneme B as one can to the word "bubble".

In the case of visual language (painting or sculpture) colours, form, texture, directionality, orientation, etc., all constitute semiotic primitives, but in no way can one associate with each of these individual semiotic constituents a psychological or ideational concept. Only in a popular language one could say that red signifies love or yellow designates jealousy. In a traffic light, it is not the red, or the green colour that by themselves designate some concept or idea. In order to trigger the behaviour of stopping or going, the lights have to be of a certain *luminous density, form,* be placed in a *specific position,* be of a *certain height, orientation* and their *sequence of alternation* must be correct. What is decoded by a driver is the structured set of these "non-conceptual" primitives. One could not understand the meaning of a single red light, isolated from any other, laying in the middle of a sidewalk or a park.

Numerous other examples could be invoked to illustrate the same point. Consider a note of music which is constituted by sound vibrations having a tone, a pitch, etc. It is impossible to associate with each of these characters, as well as with the note as a whole, an ideational or lexical concept. Even for a whole melody this type of conceptual association remains inconceivable. Beethoven's Moonlight Sonata is in no way a linguistic or ideational description of the moonlight.

On the basis of the preceding remarks, it appears that primitives in a particular semiotic system may participate in a meaningful system, but without having attached to them a conceptual structure either of the linguistic, ideational or the psychological sort. Does this entail that these semiotic primitives do not have some *sense* (Sinn) associated with them in the Fregean acceptation of this term? In order to answer this question, one has to recall certain classical concepts of Frege's semantic and semiotic theories. As mentioned above, the concept of "concept" in the Fregean tradition has to be understood in a strict technical sense, that is to say, as having associated with it a function by which it can denote something in the universe of discourse and can also participate in the composition of the meaning of propositional formulae. It is in this way that the sense (Sinn) of the predicate is defined. However, for the formal and logical semiotic tradition, the Sinn or sense of semiotic primitives is discussed in terms other than that of concept. Indeed Peirce and Morris defined certain sign functions that resembled somewhat Frege's distinction. They distinguished for a sign the *interpretant* of the sign and the *object* of the sign. This interpretant, which is not the interpreter, is also not the psychological, ideational and lexical concept that can be associated with some types of signs. It may be so in the cases of certain conventional signs of natural language, and mainly in the case of the predicate of such languages, but it need not to be so in other types of semiotic systems. All signs necessarily have an interpretant, but this interpretant can not necessarily be equated with a linguistic, ideational or psychological concept.

Even with natural languages, semiotics is careful not to identify the interpretant with a concept in the sense we have defined it here. This is why Carnap, for instance, in order to avoid the ambiguity of the term concept, preferred talking in terms of intension, that is, of an interpretation function that can be attached to each semiotic primitive of a logical language. This allows the models to be associated with syncategorematic expressions such as: "and", "or", "not", "all", "it is possible", etc.; an intensional function without having attached to them a lexical, ideational or psychological concept.

Consequently, one can see that semiotic systems do not necessarily associate with each of their constituents a linguistic, ideational, or a psychological concept. This does not prevent these primitives from having a role in the constitution of a particular signification that, for a user, will be realised only when the semiotic form has attained a certain degree of complexity. It is therefore not absolutely necessary that there exist for each semiotic primitive a specific concept. However, it is essential that all formants participate in some way or another (and not necessarily in a compositional manner[3] in the general constitution of meaning that any system necessarily expresses. Otherwise the carrier will only exist as a kind of noise and as a consequence will have no relation whatever to meaning. It seems to us an abusive interpretation of the Fregean notion of "Sinn" to translate it always in terms of ideational, psychological or linguistic concepts.

Finally, one often forgets that a psychological concept is not a thing but the result of an operation. Conceptualization in the ordinary sense of the word does not produce objects, i.e., "concepts". It is essentially a cognitive process realised by an interpreting agent. In this way, a semiotic constituent can never be strictly associated with a concept. This association is only possible if made by an agent who conceptualizes on the basis of an interaction with a semiotic primitive. It is not surprising then that this process of conceptualizations is not on the agent's part a continuous cognitive one. Not all semiotic primitives require that the agent associate a concept with them. This usually happens only at a higher level of cognition. Many meaningful processes are active only at "subconceptual" or, as Hofstadter (1985) calls them, "subcognitive" levels. If it were otherwise, we would have to deny to animals cognitive operations because it would be difficult to accept that an animal associates conceptualizations at every stage of its cognitive behaviour. The same would have to be said of much of human behaviour.

One can then understand how a representational system can realise the semiotic functions that are proper to it without postulating that at every level of organization there is necessarily some psychological or linguistic concept associated with it. This does not mean, however, that compositionality of meaning has disappeared. It only means that compositionality must be based on something other than a conceptual structure. For the semiotic tradition this is not problematic, but for the analytical tradition on the other hand it is indeed a delicate problem.

5. Conceptual structure and formalization in semiotic systems

As an illustration of this problematic situation, we might mention the connectionist position that has developed a subsymbolic model of representation that is opposed to the classical symbolic languages (Rumelhart and McClelland, 1987; Feldman and Ballard, 1982; Smolensky, 1988):

> The name "subsymbolic paradigm" is intended to suggest cognitive descriptions built up of **constituents** of the symbols used in the symbolic paradigm; these fine grained constituents might be called subsymbols. Entities that are typically represented in the symbolic paradigm by a large number of **subsymbols.** (Smolensky, 1988, p. 45)

Logical languages, such as those developed in classical semiotics, were indeed among the first systems used to formalise representations. In these languages, one would always include a basic vocabulary that presents the basic set of semiotic primitives. Often, interpretation would associate a conceptual structure with these primitives. For instance, one could say that such and such a symbol serves to designate individuals and that other symbols are used to designate classes of individuals and so forth. It is precisely to this model that the connectionist thesis is opposed.

The connectionist models are complex and we shall not offer a summary of them here. However we can turn our attention to the ways in which the basic constituents of these models are formalised and see how the conceptual question is dealt with. These systems are built upon various interactive systems. There is a level called the basic processing level on which there is to be found a set of detectors whose function it is to react to a set of specific input features. Each input enters these processing units with a specific weight. The formalisation of these basic processing units is effected by means of a linear algebraic language with its own vectors and matrices. For instance, the description of a set of inputs will then be defined as the set of *pertinent characters* or features of the input $c_1....c_n$. That is to say, a processing unit has built in specific detectors of input features (for instance heat, colour, frequencies, etc.). Hence the description of a set of input characters or features at time t will take the form of the following matrix:

$$\left|\begin{array}{c|c} C_1 & + \\ C_2 & - \\ C_3 & + \\ C_n & + \end{array}\right|$$

In order to understand this process more precisely, the list or matrix needs to be interpreted carefully: in this matrix, the + and - represent the presence or absence of the chosen features. This is why the specific matrix can be translated in terms of a vector built out of 0's and 1's such as for example[4]:

vector $v_1 = (1,0,1,1)$

or in matrix form as:

V_1	a_{11}......	a_{1n}
	:	:

So, for a specific set of input features, we then have the vector v_1 with the values a_{11}, ..., a_{1n}

> The vectors chosen are often values of fine grained features of the inputs and outputs, based on some preexisting theoretical analysis of the domain. (Smolensky, 1987, p. 7)

Now because this vectorial representation is numerical and said to be "fine grained", one is lead to conclude that there are no semiotic primitives nor a conceptual structure supporting them. Let us look more closely at this claim. We must analyze more carefully the real nature of a vectorial representation. Indeed, if we properly understand what a vector represents we must see that each value in the vector corresponds in fact to an entry variable given *implicitly* on the top of the column. In this way, the real description o the vector should be:

P	f_1......	f_n
V_1	a_{11}......	a_{1n}
	:	:

where 'f' indicates which features are measured and has the value a_{11}, ..., a_{1n}. P indicates the nature of what is in the matrix (for instance the score, the results, etc.) What this vectorial notation indicates in fact is that for each scalar value the value of P for the feature f_i is a_{ij}.

If we take, for example, in conformity with the connectionist model, four processing units, v_1, v_2, v_3, v_4, we could then represent in the following matrix the scores for the various possible inputs these units share. For example: The score P of each of the processing units, v_1, v_2, v_3, v_4, for input features #1, #2, #3 and #4 could look like this:

at TIME t

ME t

Score	feature 1	feature 2	feature 3	feature 4
v_1	.5	.3	.4	.1
v_2	.0	.4	.9	.0
v_3	.5	.7	.3	.9
v_4	.2	.1	.0	.1

Now seen in this way, a matrix, and each of its constituents, is indeed far from being a conceptual structure understood as having either an ideational, linguistic or a psychological sense. As Smolensky says, it is a "fine grained" representation. It is not possible to associate with each entry an ideational, linguistic or psychosocial "meaning". Each entry in the matrix represents, in fact, a complex bit of information. Interpreted in this way, a matrix could be seen as subsymbolic. But is this picture complete?

Let us look at it from another perspective. Is there still not lingering in this representation some conceptual structure as understood in the logical sense? If we analyze this matrix carefully, we could translate it directly into a logical language. In order to do this one would have to read the scores in the matrix P as an extensional definition of a functional expression that involves two arguments (V_i, S_i). The horizontal lines would be equivalent to a predicate of identity (=) with the values a_{mn}. The vertical lines would be equivalent to expressions and conjunctions. So each entry of this matrix is part of an implicit proposition that can be translated in the following way:

$$P\ (v_1, f_1) = a_{11}$$

that is to say, it would express the proposition that, for instance:

The Score of V_1 at feature 1 = .5

All the other scores could be read in the same way. In fact, the entire matrix could then be understood as a *conjunction* of many such propositions. The whole translated matrix could be read as

$$P(v_1, f_1) = a_{11} \& P(v_2, f_1) = a_{12}, \ldots \& P(v_n, f_n) = a_{mn}$$

In other words, a matrix can be translated into a propositional language[5], and as such, these two formalizations can be considered homomorphic. For each entry in the matrix there are corresponding sentences in a propositional language[6].

Now, what could we say about the subsymbolic or a-conceptual thesis? If we are right, we would have to conclude that the representation is still a propositional representation although imbedded in a new physical carrier and expressed in a vectorial language. So the model would still be "symbolic" or more precisely propositional. But would it still be conceptual? In the strict Fregean sense we would have to say yes, for each proposition includes a predicate and therefore has an underlying concept and is liable to a functional interpretation. But would it have an ideational, psychological or linguistic meaning? Here we would have to say no. For despite appearances, each feature and entry in the matrix is not to be understood as forming an ideational, psychological or linguistic concept. Each entry in a matrix in fact corresponds not necessarily to a concept, but to a *part* of an entire proposition, such as:

"The Score of V_1 at feature 1 = .5"

And this proposition is not in the strict sense a concept.

Thus a vector and each of its symbols cannot be understood as expressing a concept in the ideational, linguistic or psychological sense. It is a proposition. And a sentence like

$$P(v_1, f_1) = a_{11}$$

includes many symbols that are not in the strict sense *concepts*. It describes a state of affairs in the processing unit, a state of affairs that by definition cannot necessarily be a "conceptual structure" of the machine or the brain of which this processing unit is a part.

Now, if we wish to translate a whole matrix into linguistic form, then each matrix, as said above, could be seen as a conjunction of this type of sentences. But in the linguistic and semiotic theories a conjunction or concatenation of sentences does not form a concept as such but rather something more complex called a *text* or a *narration*. In logic, a set of sentences or formulae does not form concepts but a *demonstration* or *proof*. So in analyzing a matrix not as a concept but as something more complex, say analog to a text or to a narrative structure or a proof, we are saying something important.

Indeed, on the semantic level, each entry - that is to say each proposition - in a vector is related to the other not by necessity, or by some logical rule, but by some other principle. Occasionally this relation can be based on logical inferences but most of the time it will be grounded on pure occurrence or association. When in a logical language the sentence P is stated and is conjoined with another one, it is not possible to know which of the possible other sentences (P, Q, R, S, ...)[7] will follow. When a story starts with "Once upon a time, there was... " nothing can be predicted about the content to follow. It is true that not all combination of sentences or propositions constitutes an interesting or a true text nor even a valid proof. Just as it is equally untrue that all associations of input features constitute a complete description of an object. Other operations are necessary in order to attain an accurate description. So, if a vector resembles a set of associated propositions, then it is a semiotic system in the strict classical sense, but this does not mean that its structure is regulated by some sort of grammar as one can find in a natural language. The proposition that constitutes a vector resembles sentences in a text or in a narrative structure. No grammatical rule can explain the generation of a sequence of sentences in a text - no more than the syntax of logical language can explain the structure of a demonstration.

6. Representation, cognition and semiotics

We hope to have shown that a knowledge representation, whether it be expressed in a logical language or in a vectorial or linear algebraic language, is still something grounded within a semiotic paradigm. A representation, whatever it may be about, and because "it stands for something else", can not escape this semiotic dimension. All information theories are ultimately semiotic theories.

But we also hope to have shown that there are many ways to understand a semiotic system and more importantly that not all of them are to be equated with a particular conceptual structure understood as an ideational, psychological or linguistic structure. Indeed many semiotic systems, in humans, animals and in machines, are "fined grained" informational systems but without "fined grained" conceptual structures attached to all of their constituent parts. In fact most of our cognitive behaviour operates without conceptual structures.

More significantly, the structuring of these complex semiotic systems, although they may be formed in a rule-governed manner at the level of some of their basic constituents (predicates and propositions) does not necessarily need to be so at the level of their conjunction and association.

Higher level cognitive structures seem related to much more complex organisational structures than simple compositionality. If it were otherwise, in order to survive, organisms would have either to learn the grammar of their environment or to be genetically wired with it. Life would then be very simple. But as computer science has shown, even robots need more than simple propositions to deal with the outside world. They need at least what has been called a *scenario*, *scripts* if not *stories* - that is: a set of associated, coherent sentences and propositions construed in such a way as to help them form some "idea" of their environment. No compositional theory of meaning can deliver this for these theories. It can only be applied to formulae or sentences, not to whole "stories" or whole proofs!

Notes

1. This does not mean that symbols have to be manipulated with a conscious understanding of the effect on the meaning for each step of the processing. One must not identify meaningfulness with conceptuality and consciousness.

2. For a detailed analysis of this dimension see Meunier 1991.

3. There are many semiotic systems, even in a natural language, where primitive and complex configurations of symbols or signs have idiosyncratic meaning that has to be learned individually.

4. Models vary with the representation of the activation of an input. Usually it will be represented not by 0 or 1 but by a numeric value. And for reasons of conceptual clarity, we have not included here the important aspect of the weight of each input. They indeed affect the input but, as will be seen later, it will not affect the propositional structure.

5. The choice of putting into focus some information and no other is often relative to the technical operations that can be applied. For example, one does not apply the same operation on vectors as on propositions. Vectors can be multiplied, propositions not, etc. Because of specific contexts of usage, each formalism does not necessarily need to make evident all the information another one focuses on.

6. Many things could here be said about this translation. What is important here is not to confuse, in a formal system, the problem of the set of sentences with the set of constituents of the vocabulary. What is rule-governed in a formal system is the production of the sentences, not necessarily the existence of the sentences. Two topics that are often confused. It is not because one can generate through a syntax a set of well formed sentences, that one has the rules to choose the sentences that are true in that system. There are some that are true formally, whereas others are true empirically, or in a model.

7. Compositionality does not apply to the form of a sentence. In logic, at the syntactic level if one has P & X, all that can be said is that X can be replaced by a proposition. It can never be said which one.

References

Anderson, J.R. (1983) *The Architecture of Cognition.* Cambridge, Mass; Harvard University Press.

Anderson, J.A. (1986). Psychological Concepts in a Parallel System, *Physica, D* (22), 318-326.

Augustin, (1941). *De la dialectique.* in: Oeuvres Complètes. Paris; Louis Vivès.

Brachman, R.J., Fikes, R.E., and Levesque, H.J. (1983). KRYPTON: A Functional Approach to Knowledge Representation. *IEEE Computer, 16* (10), 67-73.

Brachman, R.J. (1979) On the Epistemological Status of Semantic Networks. in: Findler, N., (Ed.) *Associative Networks: Representation and Use of Knowledge by Computers.* New York; Academic Press.

Church, A. (1951). A Formulation of the Logic of Sense and Denotation. in: P. Henle, H.M. Kallen, and S. Langer (Ed.), *Structure, Method and Meaning: Essays in Honour of H.M Sheffer.* New York; Liberal Arts.

Collins, A.M. & Quillian, M.R. (1969). Retrieval time from semantic memory, *Journal of Verbal Learning and Verbal Behaviour, 8,* 240-247.

Desclées, J.P. (1987). Réseaux sémantiques: la nature logique et linguistique des relateurs, *Languages, 87.*

Dretske F.I.(1988). *Explaining Behaviour.* Cambridge; MIT Press.

Feldman, J.A. and Ballard, D.H. (1982). Connectionist Models and Their Properties. *Cognitive Sciences* (6), 205-254.

Frege, G. (1952). *Translations from the Philosophical writings of Gottlob Frege.* Edited by P.T. Geach and M. Black. Oxford; Blackwell.

Fodor, J.A. (1976). *The Language of Thought.* New York: Crowell.

Fodor, J.A. and Pylyshyn, Z.W. (1988). Connectionism and Cognitive Architecture: A Critical Analysis, *Cognition,* 28 (1-2), 3-71.

Goldstein, I.P. Roberts R.B. (1979). Using frames in Scheduling. in: Winston, P.H. and Brown, R.H., *Artificial Intelligence, An MIT Perspective.* Vol. I. Cambridge MA; MIT Press, p. 251-284.

Goschke, Th. (1990). Wissen ohne Symbole? Das Program des Neuen Konnektionismus. *Zeitschrift für Semiotik, 12* (1-2), 25-45.

Harman, G. (1979). Semiotic and the Cinema. In M.C.G. Mast (Ed.), *Film Theory and Criticism.* London: Oxford University Press.

Haugeland, J. (1978). *Mind Design, Philosophy, Psychology, Artificial Intelligence.* Cambridge; MIT Press.

Hayes, P.J., (1979). The logic of Frames. in: Metzing, D. (Ed.) *Frame Conceptions and Text Understanding.* Berlin: Walter de Gruyter, p. 46-61.
Hendrix, G. (1977). Human Engineering for Applied Natural Language Processing. *IJCAI* (5).
Hofstadter, D.R. (1985). Waking up from the Boolean Dream or Subcognition as Computation. in: D.R. Hofstadter (Ed.) *Metamagical Themes: Questing for the Essence of Mind and Pattern.* New York; Viking, p. 631-665.
Johnson-Laird, P. N. (1988). *The Computer and the Mind.* Cambridge; Harvard University Press.
Jorna, R.J. (1990a). *Knowledge Representation and Symbols in the Mind.* Tübingen; Stauffenburg Verlag.
Jorna, R.J. (1990b). Wissenrepräsentation in künstlichen Intelligenzen, *Zeitschrift für Semiotik, 12* (1-2), 9-25.
Lehnert, W. and Y. Wilks (1979). A Critical Perspective on KRL, *Cognitive Science 3* (1), 1-28.
Lévesque, H. J. (1984) Foundations of a Functional Approach to Knowledge Representation, *Artificial Intelligence*, 23, 155-212.
Locke, John. (1690). *An Essay Concerning Human Understanding.* London.
Lycan, W. (1988). Commentaries on Smolensky Papers: On the Proper Treatment of Connectionism, *The Behavioural and Brain Sciences* 11, 1-74.
Marr, D. (1982). *Vision: A computational Investigation into the Human Representation and Processing of Visual Information.* San Francisco; W.H. Freeman.
McClelland, J.L. and Rumelhart, D.E. (1985). Distributed Memory and the Representation of General and Specific Information, *Journal of Experimental Psychology: General, 114* (2), 159-188.
Minsky, M. and Papert, S. (1973). *Artificial Intelligence.* Condon lectures, Oregon State System of Higher Education, Eugene Oregon.
Montague, R. (1973). *Formal Philosophy.* Yale; Yale University Press.
Mylopoulos, J., and Delgrande, J.P. (1986). Knowledge Representation Features of Knowledge. in: W.B.E.P. Jorrand (Ed.), *Fundamentals of Artificial Intelligence.* Berlin; Springer Verlag.
Newell A. and Simon H. (1976). Symbol Manipulation. in: *Encyclopedia of Computer Science.* New York; Petrrocelli/Charter.
Peirce, C.S. (1931-1958). *Collected Papers.* Cambridge; Harvard University Press.
Pylyshyn, Z.W. (1986). *Computation and Cognition. Towards a Foundation for Cognitive Science.* Cambridge; MIT Press.
Quillian, M.R. (1968) Semantic memory. in: Minsky, M. (Ed.), *Semantic Information Theory.* Cambridge, Mass.; MIT Press.

Rosch, E. (1973). Natural Categories, *Cognitive Psychology,* 21 (3-4), 328-350.

Rumelhart, D.E. (1975) Notes on a Schema for Stories. in: D.G. Bobrow and A. Collins. (Eds.), *Representation and Understanding* (pp. 211-236). New York; Academic Press.

Rumelhart D. and McCLelland, J.L. (1987). *Parallel Distributed Processing, Vols. I and II.* Cambridge; MIT Press.

Ryle, G. (1932). Systematically Misleading Expressions. *Proceedings of the Aristotelian Society, xxxii.*

Schank, R.C. (1972). Conceptual Dependency: A Theory of Natural Language Understanding, *Cognitive Psychology,* 3, 552-631.

Schubert L.K. (1975). Extending the Expressive Power of Semantic Networks. *Advanced Papers of the 4th International Joint Conference on Artificial Intelligence.*

Schubert, L.K., Goebels, R.G. and Cercone, N.J. (1979). The Structure and Organization of a Semantic Net for Comprehension and Inference. in: L. K. Schubert and N. Cercone (Eds.), *Representation and Use of Knowledge by Computers.* (121-175). New York; Academic Press.

Sebeok, T.A. (1976). *Contributions to the Doctrine of Signs.* Bloomington; Research Center for Language and Semiotic Studies.

Shapiro, S.C. (1979). The Snep Semantic Network Processing System. in: N. Findler (Ed.), *Associative Networks: Representation and use of knowledge by computers.* New York; Academic Press.

Smith, P. (1982). *The Philosophy of Mind.* Cambridge; Cambridge University Press.

Smolensky, P. (1988). On the Proper Treatment of Connectionism. *The Behavioural and Brain Sciences,* 11, p. 1-74.

Smythe, W.E. (1990). Wie sind Symbole zu interpretieren?, *Zeitschrift für Semiotik, 12* (1-2), 47-63.

Sowa, J.W. (1984). *Conceptual structures:Information Processing in Mind and Machine.* Reading; Addison Wesley.

Sowa, J.F. (1991). *Principles of Semantic Networks.* San Mateo; Morgan Kaufman.

Wilks, Y. (1975). *Primitives and Words.* Advance Papers of Theoretical Issues in Natural Language Processing, Workshop. pp. 34-37

Winograd, T. (1972). *Understanding Natural Language.* New York; Academic Press.

Woods, W. A. (1986). Important Issues in Knowledge Representation" *Proceedings of the IEEE,* vol 74, no. 10.

Woods, W. A. (1975). What's a Link: Foundations for Semantic networks. in: D.G. Bobrow and A. Collins (Eds.), *Representation and Understanding: Studies in Cognitive Science.* New York; Academic Press.

Semiotic aspects of neurally based representation of knowledge

M.F. PESCHL (Vienna)

1. Motivation

In traditional artificial intelligence (A.I.) and cognitive science the problem of knowledge representation is very much reduced to technical issues; computer science dominates and constrains the concepts and ideas being provided by these disciplines. As is shown in the course of this paper there are some problems in the approach of symbolic knowledge representation. I will focus on one of the most serious: the problem of meaning. In the first part (section 1.1) the assumptions, basic ideas and the problems of symbolic knowledge representation will be discussed. The second part (sections 2 and 3) shows a possible alternative way of modelling more adequately this problem. This will be done in the context of computational neuro-epistemology; this is an alternative approach to cognitive science which reduces the participating disciplines to: neuro-science, computer science (restricted to the simulation of neural networks) and epistemology (cf. Peschl 1991a; 1991b). It cannot be discussed in detail here - it represents, however, the methodological framework within which we are considering these problems.

1.1 An invitation to reflect the symbol manipulation approach: problems and assumptions

If we are talking of knowledge representation we have to take into consideration at least three aspects:

(a) the aspect of how knowledge is mapped to the representation system;

(b) the aspect of how this representation is processed;

(c) the aspect of representing the representation system;

Traditionally it is implicitly assumed that knowledge representation means linguistic representation; i.e., as our (natural) language has become the most important system of representing objects, phenomena, feelings, items, etc., it has suggested itself to make use of this well-proven system for representing knowledge in computers. The development of mathematical logic and formal languages has been combined with the advantages of modern computer technology and - at first sight - seems to meet the requirements for a general system of knowledge representation. There is also a self suggesting relation between natural language and formal languages of mathematical logic; the latter are assumed to be a "metastructure" or a valid formalization of natural language ("valid" is used in the sense that formal languages are capable of adequately containing all aspects of natural language). This leads to the assumption that computers using symbols, the concepts of mathematical logic and symbol manipulation for generating "intelligent" behaviour, represent an adequate model of cognitive processes.

If we look more closely at the concept of symbolic knowledge representation, we can find a mapping which is at least fourfold:

(i) environment to neural activities: objects, symbols, phenomena, etc., are perceived by the sensory system and transformed into unspecific neural activities.

(ii) neural activities to natural language: these neural activities are interpreted in terms of natural language; in this step of mapping we are leaving the level of semantics.

(iii) natural language to formal language: natural language words are mapped to formal structures, symbols, etc. - we are entering the domain of "pure" syntax and manipulation of meaningless patterns being called symbols.

(iv) formal language to implementation: the last step of mapping brings these formal symbols and the rules of their manipulation into the computer's structure. The programming language determines very much the possibilities of this mapping.

As can be seen knowledge representation as it is understood in the traditional approach is restricted to linguistically explicit knowledge; i.e., it is possible - in the best case - to represent knowledge which can be verbally uttered. This implies, however, the question of how such a (formal) symbol gets its meaning, because otherwise we would reduce symbolic knowledge representation to the manipulation of syntactic patterns. Unfortunately it will turn out that orthodox A.I. and traditional cognitive science (both being based more or less implicitly on Newell and Simon's Physical Symbol System Hypothesis; Newell & Simon 1976; 1980; 1981; 1989; 1990) are doing nothing but manipulating meaningless patterns. Think, for instance, of an expert system for medical diagnosis: the symbols which are manipulated in the machine are just syntactic structures which only refer in the user's cognitive domain to real world phenomena. There is no other relation to the environment but via the user.

This traditional approach is pretending that a symbol in the representation system has its meaning in itself. What is called "semantic structure" can be reduced in most cases to a network of symbolic structures embedded in the syntactic level. As can be seen in figure 1 and as will be discussed below it is the observer or the interpreter who gives the meaning to a symbol. This implies that we have to completely reformulate and rethink (and perhaps have to give up) the concept of symbolic representation. Such considerations are of relevance only if we are interested in finding an adequate model for cognitive processes or for language; commercial applications will not be affected by these reflections as long as they do not intend to construct systems which are processing commonsense or non-verbal knowledge.

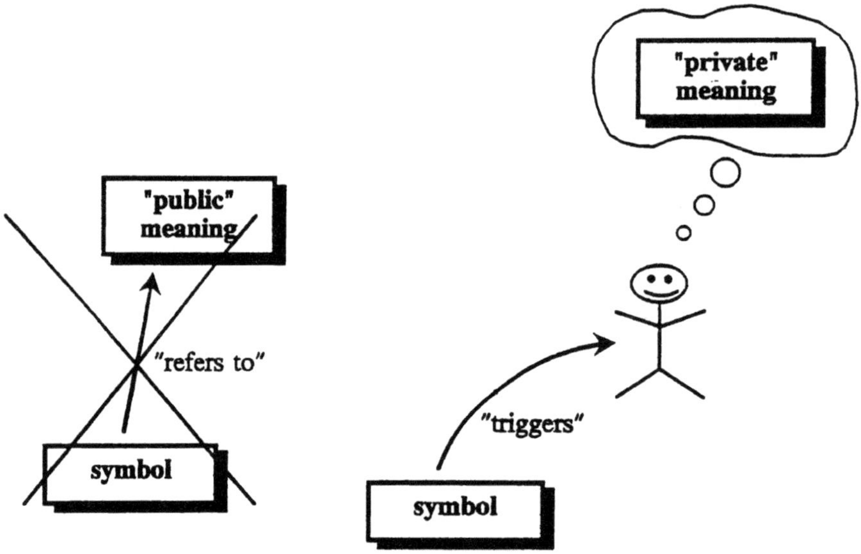

Figure 1: A computer symbol and its meaning

The approach of symbolic knowledge representation has been quite successful in the last decades. Especially in the field of commercial, technical and formal applications, such as expert systems, technical diagnosis or planning systems, this form of knowledge processing has brought about a kind of revolution in the application and possibilities of computers. From a more philosophical or epistemological point of view, however, the assumptions are implying serious problems which will be addressed in the following paragraphs; these problems become even more serious if it is our intention to achieve a better understanding of cognitive processes and/or knowledge representation in natural or artificial neural structures, such as:

Linguistic transparency

All the processes taking place in this approach to knowledge representation can be linguistically described (i.e., in natural language terms). Clark (1989) calls this phenomenon "linguistic transparency" (see figure 2) - it is an important property if we have to construct reliable technical applications; each step of processing can be followed in an explicit manner. It would be very "nice" if we could apply the same techniques for our investigations of cognitive processes. It turns out, however, that, if we are interested, for instance, in the structures and basics of (natural) language, our assumptions and concepts of language are too naive. They represent folk psychology "theories" being based on more or less commonsense assumptions (P.M. Churchland, 1986; P.S. Churchland, 1989). In the following sections I will discuss an alternative view which seems to meet the requirements of a more adequate description.

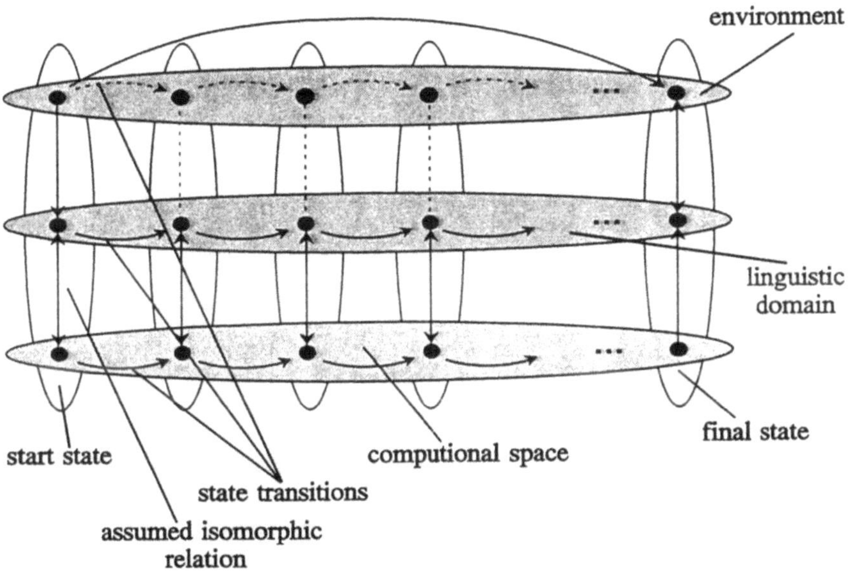

Figure 2: Linguistic transparency

Dominance of computer science concepts

One of the main reasons for linguistic transparency (besides commonsense assumptions) is the dominance of the concepts of computer science. This means that the processing structures being provided by the hardware, by the software, by the programming languages are more or less accepted as "constraints" for the models of cognition. Think, for instance, of formal languages: they represent the basis for each programming language, for most (orthodox) A.I. applications as well as for most models of cognitive processes. They are assuming that cognition takes place in natural language which can be modeled by formal languages. The ideas of von Neumann and Turing on the one hand and of Chomsky on the other hand (influencing each other, of course) are restricting the possibilities in the development of new models and concepts. They do not only determine the structures of the models but also reinforce the assumption of cognitive processes being based on the "sentence-crunching" paradigm (P.M. Churchland 1989, p. xiii).

If we are interested in finding adequate models of cognition one would expect them to be based on empirical data provided by neuroscience or cellular neuro-biology and not on ideas and concepts being constrained and determined by computer technology. From a constructivist perspective it becomes clear that these "empirical facts" are also constructs of reality (the word "fact" has its roots in the Latin word "facere" which means "to make, to create, to construct", etc.); they represent, however, a more plausible starting point than pure commonsense speculations of folk psychology, orthodox A.I. or traditional cognitive science. As will be shown there exists an alternative processing paradigm which can be also run on conventional von Neumann computers. It represents and implies, however, an untypical, non-commonsense and biologically inspired approach to modelling cognition.

Assumption of mapping

As has been mentioned above a fourfold mapping from the environment to the symbolic structures in the computer is assumed in the traditional approach of symbolic knowledge representation. This assumption implies at least three problems:

(i) loss of information;

(ii) in the process of mapping the direct relation to the environment is lost;

(iii) there is only a one-way mapping; this means that no direct feed back from the symbolic representation to the environment (and vice versa) takes place.

Reflecting on the process of mapping the assumption that there is an absolute reality which is directly accessible for everyone in the same manner becomes evident. This implies - as it is assumed in traditional symbolic representation systems - that a symbol has the same meaning in each (natural or artificial) cognitive system. This is obviously wrong, because there would not be any misunderstandings otherwise.

Sentential processing versus neural plausibility

We have seen that this traditional approach to knowledge representation and modelling cognition is based more or less on the idea that cognition is nothing but processing sentences. If we are looking more closely at these systems it turns out that symbol manipulation is understood as manipulation of the symbols' meaningless appearance (i.e., manipulation of syntactic patterns). Nothing is said about semantics. No evidence can be found for legitimizing this way of modelling cognitive processes and language in neuro-scientific investigations (cf. e.g., Churchland and Sejnowski, 1986; 1989; 1990; 1990a). Processing of syntactic structures (e.g., of formal languages, in rule applications, etc.) is seen as an adequate explanation of cognitive processes rather than a neurally based theory of cognition. There is often the excuse that "higher" cognitive processes can not be understood in terms of neural theories; neuroscience does not know enough and these "higher" processes are far too complex for being describable on the basis of neural activities. This is true only to a certain extent, because neuroscience is a dynamically developing field of research. As will be shown in section 3, the combination of neuro-scientific knowledge with newer methods from computer science even leads to a completely new understanding of neural representation and offers us unexpected possibilities in this field. As an implication we have to look out for an alternative and more adequate understanding of language and cognition in epistemology as well as in computer science (see sections 2 and 3). As has been stated above computational neuro-epistemology provides the methodological framework for our considerations: it is embedded in the constructivist paradigm (Glasersfeld, Maturana, Förster, Varela, etc.) - these constructivist considerations are the epistemological basis for the simulation and investigation of natural as well as artificial neural structures in respect to their capabilities of knowledge representation, semantic features and language.

Unsolved problem of meaning

The problem of meaning, reference, or semantics remains not only unsolved, but is not even really tackled in the approach of symbolic knowledge representation and processing. Of course, the question of semantics has been asked by traditional A.I. or cognitive science; as has been mentioned above, however, the solutions did not really leave the level of syntax. How can it be expected that language or meaning of language can be explained, described or modeled in terms of sentence processing or language itself? We would have to leave the level of language and search for a more basic, a more fundamental level in which language is embedded.

Only such a level could offer us the possibility of a deeper understanding of how a symbol gets its meaning.

As can be seen there remains a lot of unsolved and unanswered questions in the orthodox approach of symbolic knowledge representation. In the following sections I want to focus on such an alternative approach which is based on a "non-sentential" processing and representation paradigm.

2. Some considerations regarding the problem of knowledge representation and its relation to language

Before presenting a number of computer science issues, more basic and epistemological considerations have to be discussed. The problem of meaning can not be understood without considering some basic questions concerning knowledge representation. As we have seen above we have to clearly differentiate between the domain of knowledge representation and the domain of the representation of the representation system. In our case of an adequate model of cognition and language we even have to differentiate within the domain of representation: in traditional cognitive science (natural) language is understood as the ultimate representation system. This dominance of language, however, is not justified as it has neither neuro-scientific nor epistemological evidence. It is just the result of obvious and commonsense considerations. That is why I am suggesting to rethink these assumptions and to introduce the following differentiation of domains which is influenced by constructivist concepts:

* environment: we do not have direct access to this domain. We can perceive it only via the sensory system. It is the world we are living in and with;
* cognitive domain: from an internal perspective this domain is realized in (natural) cognitive systems in neural "wet-ware". Processing takes place by spreading neural activities in a highly complex and recurrent network of neurons and synapses. From an external observer's perspective the activities in the neural network are interpreted as behaviour (the motor system is responsible for the "translation" of these internal neural activities to observable behaviour);
* linguistic domain: the neurally realized cognitive domain represents the basis for this domain. It is embedded in neural activities and is understood as a very complex form of behaviour. This domain exists only in the interpreter's or observer's cognitive domain. He/she gives meaning to the behaviour patterns and interprets them as

language. The linguistic domain is not the level of processing any more; it is rather the result of the more fundamental level of neural processing which is interpreted as linguistic behaviour.

The concept being suggested here is based on constructivist ideas mainly influenced by Maturana (1970; 1975; 1978; 1978a; 1980), by von Glasersfeld (1976; 1981; 1982), Goodman and Elgin (1978; 1988), Varela (1976; 1981; 1990) and von Förster (1973; 1984). The idea common to their approaches is that the representation of the environment (i.e., the cognitive domain) is the result of a process of construction. This construction is determined by the structure and the architecture of the (natural or artificial) nervous system. The implications of this approach for traditional cognitive science and A.I. have not been realized yet. In the computational, neuro-epistemological approach to cognitive science I am consequently trying to integrate these constructivist concepts with empirical evidence from neuroscience and with simulation methods being provided by computer science, namely the Parallel Distributed Processing or connectionist approach.

Goodman (1978) discusses the problem of constructing cognitive worlds in the context of semiotics and science. One of his main claims is (very similar to the constructivists having been quoted above) that our cognitive reality is due to a process of construction implying a pluralism of representation systems in language, art and science. Our sensory systems do not perceive the world undistorted; it is rather an active process of construction taking place in the periphery and the central nervous system which determines the structure of the world as we are perceiving it. We are constructing a world, which fits into its environment. As an implication we have to give up the concept of an objective truth or of the idea that everyone has the same access to the world being out there or of the assumption that the world out there is already ready made. Of course, there is a certain structure in the world, certain regularities can be found, etc., however, it is the nervous system and its periphery being responsible for finding out or constructing exactly these structures which are useful for behaving adequately in the environment which cannot be directly perceived. This implies a multitude of cognitive worlds which have to be correlated if a kind of communication has to be established. As is pointed out by Goodman such a concept of perception, construction and truth does not imply "scientific or cognitive anarchism"; the minimal criterion of consistency and of a closed feedback loop (constructions in the brain and their test in the environment) still applies. With these ideas we are very close to Feyerabend's (1980; 1983; 1984) concepts and understanding of science and knowledge (he would not call himself, however, a constructivist).

What is the relation between the three domains having been mentioned above? We have given up the idea of a trivial or isomorphic mapping from environment to the cognitive domain in favour of the relation of construction; i.e., there is not only a one way mapping in which the cognitive domain mirrors the environment. There is rather a circular or recurrent relation between these two domains: the nervous system is understood as a complex dynamic system having its own dynamics. At each time t it has a certain state $s(t)$. It can be perturbed by external stimuli coming from the environment. This perturbation does not "instruct" (Maturana) the following state of the nervous system; it rather can bring the dynamics of activations to another trajectory. The stimuli coming from the environment are transformed into meaningless neural signals (first step of construction) which are propagated through the recurrent network. They are combined with other signals (second step of construction) and can cause a learning effect by strengthening or weakening the connections between neurons (third step of construction). These three steps of construction are forming the representation of the environment; they are determined by:

- the structure and architecture of the nervous system;
- the current state of the nervous systems;
- the history (i.e., by the previous states) of the nervous system which determine the current state;
- the perturbations from the environment.

In this constructivist concept of knowledge representation not only the flow of information from environment to the cognitive domain is of interest, but also the flow in the other direction. Of course, we cannot speak of information in the traditional sense of semantically interpreted patterns - it is rather understood as a flow of patterns which get their meaning only within the (cognitive) system perceiving these patterns; in other words, information and semantics is individually generated in the course of the process of construction by each system. The constructs of the environment (i.e., its representation, the cognitive domain) are responsible for the actions being executed by effectors in the environment. The success or failure of these actions will show whether the internal constructs fit into the environment. A circular or feedback process of perceiving, constructing and acting is established between the environment and the cognitive domain. The structures which can be found in the representation system (i.e., in the nervous system) do not have anything in common with linguistic structures - they are rather responsible for the generation of adequate behaviour ("adequate behaviour" meaning behaviour which ensures survival or continuation of life). As will be discussed in section 3 the connectionist approach (the concept of neurally based and "subsymbolic" knowledge representation (Smolensky, 1988)) can shed some light on this matter which is neither common to most epistemologists nor to computer scientists; the reason for this can be found in the problem that we have to give up the idea of "linguistic transparency" as has been discussed in section 1. This more behaviourially, neurally and bottom-up inspired approach to understanding cognitive processes represents, however, the basis for adequately modelling the problem of semantics.

As will be discussed in detail in section 2.1, the relation between the cognitive and the linguistic domain can be characterized as follows: language is embedded in behaviour and, hence, can be seen as a subset of different forms of behaviour and neural activities. Language is an emerging phenomenon (Varela 1990; Maturana 1978a; 1980) in the observer's cognitive domain.

2.1 The problem of "reference"

Generally speaking the problem of knowledge representation is how to find or to characterize the relation between a representation system and its environment; i.e., how a state in the representation system refers to the (perceived part of the) environment. As has been discussed above the computational neuro-epistemology approach does not assume the commonsense relation of isomorphically mapping or mirroring the environment in terms of natural language to the representation system (as traditional cognitive science and A.I. implicitly assume); there is rather a constructive relation between these two domains; i.e., a certain state $s(t)$ (i.e., a pattern of natural or artificial neural activations) refers to a part of the environment; see figure 3).

This part of the environment is selected by the structure, modalities and architecture of the sensory system and the nervous system. The objects, phenomena, etc., however, do not determine the state of the nervous system. This state is rather the result of the "history" (i.e., of the recurrent processes of spreading activations) plus the perturbations coming from the environment. The nervous system has to be understood as a cybernetical machine in the sense of Ashby (1964); it has its own dynamics which can be perturbed by external stimuli.

This is another reason why we have to give up the traditional assumption of a mapping from environment to the cognitive domain: we cannot find an isomorphic relation, as it is assumed in traditional A.I., between these two domains. This implies also that the same pattern of activations need not always refer to the same part of the environment and that the same part of the environment will not always cause the same pattern of activations.

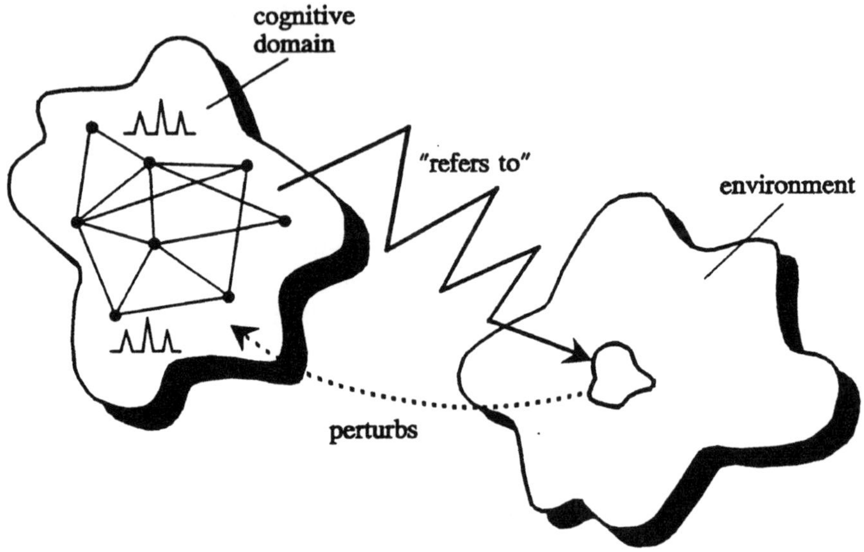

Figure 3: A certain state s(*t*) in the nervous system refers to an object, phenomenon, etc., in the environment

A threefold dynamics is involved in this approach:

(i) the dynamics of spreading activations through the recurrent architecture of the natural or artificial nervous system;

(ii) the dynamics of learning which seems to be realized in the strengthening and weakening of the connections between neurons (cf. Sejnowski and Churchland 1989; 1990);

(iii) the dynamics of the changing architecture of the nervous system, the sensors and effectors.

It must be clear that the current state of a nervous system always refers to (1) its "historical context" as well as to (2) an "external context". By "historical context" I mean the previous inner states which have a great influence on the generation of the current state. This is due tot the inner dynamics being determined by the architecture of the natural or artificial nervous system. Hence, the nervous system as representation system refers always to its inner states as well as to parts of external environment.

2.2 Language

What has been said about the nervous system is also partly valid for the representation system (natural) language. Symbols are assumed to refer to objects, phenomena or items in the environment. The central question is "how is this reference to external items realized?" (see figure 4). In the nervous system the reference is realized via sensors and effectors which "connect" the cognitive system to its environment. In artificial machines which make use of the linguistic representation system no direct reference can be found. As has been discussed above this question is not even seriously addressed - thus, the semantics, the processing of semantics and the pragmatic aspect remain unsolved problems in the traditional approach of symbolic knowledge representation and processing. Looking more closely at the epistemological aspects of the symbol manipulation approach it turns out no difference is made between semantics and syntax. Semantics is "smuggled" in by a human interpreter, user or observer who gives meaning to the meaningless patterns being called symbols on the screen by an act of interpretation. Hence the problem of reference and semantics is shifted out of the machine back to the human interpreter.

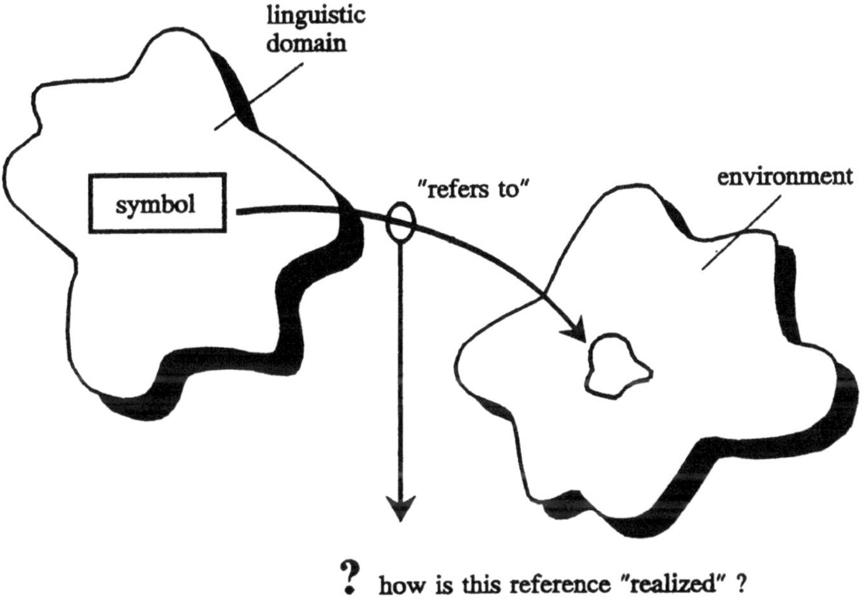

Figure 4: The symbol in the linguistic domain refers to an "external" object. How is this reference realized?

We can find a solution to this problem only if we are considering the following assumptions:

* Language itself is not an adequate and general representation system which has the same capacity as the nervous system (think of

language as a "subset" of the different forms of behaviour and their representation).

* Hence, processing language on the level of syntax (as orthodox A.I. and traditional cognitive science do) will not adequately describe cognitive processes as they are based on neural activities in the cognitive domain.
* The only solution could be to process language on a more general level of semantics. This implies that we adequately have to model the problem of reference, in other words the relation to the environment. Of course this can not be done by using other symbols - this would mean that we remain at the level of syntax.
* Embedding the representation system language in the more general representation system of the nervous system brings about a possible solution to the problem of reference: as the semiotic triangle suggests (e.g., Eco, 1972; 1973) the reference to the external object, item, etc. is realized via the meaning of a symbol.
* In terms of our constructivist concept meaning means nothing but a certain state of the nervous system (cf. Varela, 1990). As we have seen such a state is the result of the nervous system's history as well as of the input (for instance, the stimulus pattern of a symbol) triggering the dynamics.

In other words, the meaning of a symbol is the result of a process of construction. This construct is realized in physical changes of, for instance, the synaptic weights (in the natural or artificial nervous system). It is strictly "private" and is determined by the experiences having been made. We can look at this process of constructing the meaning of a symbol also as the learning of an association between two external patterns (i.e., a phenomenon in the environment and a symbol in the environment) and an internal state of the nervous system. This implies that the meaning is determined by the "private" history and of its use by the symbol's interpreter. As Maturana has worked out, consensual use can lead to communication via symbols. "Public" meaning arises by the "overlapping" use of symbols (i.e., in a commonly established consensual domain).

Another implication of this approach is that symbols are not only understood as natural language symbols but rather as patterns referring to anything else. Once again, linguistic symbols are very specialized, sophisticated and perhaps the most complex sort of symbols. Now we come full circle in our argumentation of language being embedded in behaviour and being "only" a very complex form of behaviour. It becomes also evident why "pure" symbol manipulation will never be capable of processing "meaning" or "semantics". Hence, we will have to look out for a processing paradigm offering the possibility of establishing the construction of a "private" representation of the environment (a private semantics or meaning) and of building (constructing) "semantic" references. As will be shown in section 3 the connectionist approach offers - under certain circumstances - the concepts and possibilities for building a model of cognition meeting these requirements. The meaning of a symbol is not understood as a network of other symbols any more, but rather as establishing constructed structures, a correlation between an external object, an external symbol and the internal state of the nervous system on a non linguistic, non syntactic level of neural activities.

3. Modelling cognition and language

3.1 The connectionist processing paradigm

As has been mentioned above we have to look for an alternative processing paradigm if we adequately want to model (real) semantics and understand cognitive processes and knowledge representation being based on neural structures. The "sentence-crunching" approach does not meet the requirements for the reasons having been discussed in section 1. That is why a more "neuron like approach" is suggested. It will turn out that its simulations can achieve a deeper understanding of these processes. Simulation plays an important role in the computational, neuro-epistemological approach: it is responsible for generating artificial cognitive behaviour which is based on neurally inspired processes.

I cannot go into details in this short introduction; for a detailed discussion I can recommend the "bible" of PDP: the two (three) volumes by Rumelhart and McClelland (1986; 1986a; 1988); a brief introduction and overview is given in Rumelhart (1989). The aim is to simulate neurons which are assumed to be the functional "atoms" of our brain and cognitive processes. As is well known, these (natural) neurons form a huge network of neurons being highly interconnected and all working in a parallel way. These connections are used for exchanging "information" in the form of pulses or spikes. These spikes are spreading through the whole network; they may be caused by an internal neuron or by an external stimulus being transformed into such a spike by a sensor neuron. As these neurons are all working in parallel, each of them has a certain activity $a(t)$ at a time t. This activity is - simply speaking - the result of the other neuron's (being connected to the neuron) activities. On the output side of this (highly recurrent) network these activities are transformed into action by effectors. These actions are observed and described as "behaviour".

In the PDP (Parallel Distributed Processing, connectionist) approach artificial neural networks (PDP networks) try to simulate these natural neural networks. Of course, they represent only very (mathematically) abstract and rough models of their natural originals; the relation between these artificial and natural neurons is discussed, for instance, by P.M. Churchland (1990). The connectionist approach is not so much interested in the function of a single neuron, but rather in the global behaviour of quite simple processors being called "units". One unit represents a neuron in a very abstract manner: it is connected by "weights" (they could be compared to the synaptic connections) to some other units and computes its own activation by summing up the product of the weights and the other units' activations. This activation is propagated via the weights to other units.

The possibility of learning makes PDP networks even more interesting for two reasons:

* Learning very much influences the kind of knowledge representation;
* Besides the basic architecture the knowledge being represented in such a network is determined by the process of learning which is, of course, influenced, but not governed by the stimuli coming from the environment.

We can learn a lot from these simulations for natural nervous dynamics. In the computational neuro-epistemology approach this interaction between simulated and empirical results is systematically used for the development of knowledge in this field.

As has been discussed in section 1, in the orthodox approach of symbolic representation knowledge is mapped to symbol manipulating machines in the form of symbols; they are themselves representing the result of a mapping process from the domain of natural language to the space of symbolic representation (i.e., of a formal language). Simply speaking, PDP networks are learning by associating two patterns; i.e., if we are assuming a feedforward network (meaning that activations are propagated only in one direction) a certain pattern of activations is put to the input units and represents the "input vector". These activations are propagated through the network and produce a vector of activations in the output layer. We can look at this as a process of association; i.e., the input vector is associated with the output vector. Learning means that we can change this process of mapping of input vectors to output vectors (either by an external teacher determining the input-output relation or by a process of self-organization).

This is realized by slightly changing the weights of the network - very small local changes are causing a change in global behaviour of the network. These changes in the weights are computed by a learning rule adding or subtracting a small increment to/from the weight. I cannot go into detail here - these learning rules represent a kind of self-organizing mechanism trying to minimize an error or trying to find a minimum. We can look at PDP networks being a very general information processing concept transforming any input vector of activations to any output pattern of activations by propagating patterns of activations. Hence, learning causes small changes in the weights; these weights cannot be linguistically described. This vector-to-vector (of activations) processing is the foundation for the concept of subsymbolic knowledge representation; i.e., in PDP networks it is only possible to linguistically describe knowledge representation on a global level as an emerging property of a great number of local weights. In other words: the knowledge being represented in such a network is determined by the pattern of weights being responsible for the dynamics of the network. The dynamics governs the flow of activations and, thus, the observed behaviour.

3.2 Suggesting a model of cognition

In this section I shortly want to sketch a computational model of cognition and its implications; it is based on the concepts and ideas having been discussed so far: the PDP processing paradigm represents the computational foundation for the realization of the more epistemological and semiotic ideas of constructivism presented in section 2.

This artificial organism is equipped with a recurrent PDP network. Only a recurrent architecture enables inner dynamics in the sense above. This network is connected to effectors and sensors which are acting in and perceiving the environment. The sensors perceive visual or acoustic signals; the effectors are responsible for moving around in the environment and for sending out signals. The whole simulation is realized in software; i.e., the cognitive system, its artificial neural network as well as the environment are simulated on the computer (for technical details see Peschl 1990; 1990a; 1990b). The network architecture as well as the environment can be flexibly designed. Tracing mechanisms enable the investigation of the relation between the environment and the internal representation which is built up by a Hebb-like learning algorithm.

No symbols can be found in this system: as it is connected to the environment via sensors and effectors there is no symbolic instance in between the two domains as in traditional A.I. and cognitive science. No interpreter or observer is needed in this simulation as the system directly interacts with its environment; hence, there is no need of establishing the "pragmatical" relation via a human. This is also the reason why the process of setting up symbols and their meaning can be modeled with such a model. As we have seen in section 2.2 the problem of reference is solved by the correlation (association) of two stimuli (patterns) in the environment, which are perceived via sensors, with an internal state. This concept of a model of cognition provides the possibilities for this process. The construction of an internal representation and of meaning is realized by learning; i.e., by changing synaptic weights. The architecture is responsible for primary "intentions" of the cognitive system.

We could even go further and simulate two or more artificial cognitive systems interacting with each other. For the future it is planned to design organisms which are capable of communicating on a very basic level with each other via a simple symbol system. The interesting point is, however, that each of them is capable of constructing its own representation of the environment and that language (on a very fundamental level) is embedded in this representation as one possible complex form of behaviour perturbing the other participating cognitive systems. Hence, it is possible that a symbol-like communication system is established by self-organization without ever having introduced a symbol in the traditional way.

3.3 Some semiotic issues of computational neuro-epistemology

As has been stated above no symbols are involved in the suggested model of cognition. In which sense can we understand this statement? It means that no symbols in the sense of the Physical Symbol Systems Hypothesis can be found (i.e., externally interpreted by a human observer). The objective is rather to build autonomous agents establishing their own semantics which is determined by their structure, architecture, sensory and motor system. These artificial organisms represent the basis for establishing communicative structures using simple forms of symbols. In this sense symbols are involved in this cognitive model - the difference is, however, that these symbols are not given by an external designer, but rather emerge from the interaction with the environment or with other artificial cognitive systems.

How can symbols emerge from the simulation of cognitive system which are not based on symbols? We are assuming a very general notion of a symbol: any pattern which refers to another pattern is assumed to be a symbol; by pattern any stimulus, be it visual, olfactory, acoustic, etc., is meant. The important point is, however, that it does not refer to the other pattern in the environment (perhaps it does in causal sense, but the environment in itself is, in general, not symbolic). It is only within the cognitive system's representational space that one perceived pattern refers to another. As has been discussed above neural networks are capable of learning to associate patterns. So, establishing symbols can be modeled by learning in artificial neural networks without having to use any symbols at all. An example: if such an artificial cognitive system realizes certain regularities in the stimuli coming from the environment associations are established. Think, for instance, of a certain olfactory pattern which very often is correlated with a certain visual pattern. Sooner or later it will be enough to present this olfactory pattern in order to call up the visual impression. Setting up simple forms of symbols, thus, is reduced to a kind of association or conditioning process. The meaning of these symbols is strictly private and is rather determined by the cognitive system's internal structure than by the external events; this means, of course, that these events in the environment are responsible for setting up symbols (in the sense of above), however, the meaning, which patterns are associated with each other, which patterns are associated with which internal state, etc., is determined by the cognitive system's phylogenetic and ontogenetic structure.

So far, nothing has been said about communication and the use of these simple symbols in a communicative context. Let us suppose a group of such artificial organisms described above. They all have their "private" use of symbols established by their own experiences. In such a situation communication can evolve by mutual "calibration" or, as Maturana calls it, by establishing a consensual domain. This means that the private use of each participating cognitive system is mutually adapted to the others' use of symbols in order to achieve a joint aim. Goodman and Elgin (1988) discuss these issues in the context of science: a new word (such as "quark") is not commonly used and understood at the beginning. The more participants are using it in a similar context (for instance, in physics) the better it will fit into the communicative structures of this community.

In these simulations very simple communicative structures can emerge from such interactions. Of course, one cannot expect to set up such complex linguistic structures as we humans use - however, the basic mechanisms can be studied in this bottom-up approach. What can be learned from this approach is to see more clearly how language, use of symbols and communication can be understood in terms of a neurally based concept of knowledge representation.

References

Ashby, W.R. (1964). *Einführung in die Kybernetik.* Frankfurt/M: Suhrkamp, 1984.

Churchland, P.S. (1986). *Neurophilosophy. Toward a Unified Science of the Brain.* Cambridge, MA: MIT Press.

Churchland, P.M. (1989). *A Neurocomputational Perspective - The Nature of Mind and the Structure of Science*. Cambridge, MA: MIT Press.
Churchland, P.M. (1990). Cognitive Activity in Artificial Neural Networks. In: Osherson et al. (eds.), *An Invitation to Cognitive Science*. Massachusetts: MIT Press, Vol. 3, 199-227.
Clark, A. (1989). *Microcognition. Philosophy, Cognitive Science and Parallel Distributed Processing*. Cambridge, Mass.: MIT Press.
Eco, U. (1972), *Einführung in die Semiotik*. München: Fink.
Eco, U. (1973). *Zeichen. Eine Einführung in einen Begriff und seine Geschichte*. Frankfurt/M: Suhrkamp.
Feyerabend, P. (1980). *Erkenntnis für freie Menschen*. Frankfurt/M: Suhrkamp.
Feyerabend, P. (1983). *Wider den Methodenzwang* (*Against Method*). Frankfurt/M: Suhrkamp.
Feyerabend, P. (1984). *Wissenschaft als Kunst*. Frankfurt/M: Suhrkamp.
Förster, H.v. (1973). Das Konstruieren einer Wirklichkeit. In: Watzlawick (ed.), *Die erfundene Wirklichkeit*. Piper Verlag, 39-60.
Förster, H.v. (1984). Erkenntnistheorien und Selbstorganisation. In: Schmidt (ed.), *Der Diskurs des Radikalen Konstruktivismus*, Frankfurt/M: Suhrkamp, (1987), 133-158.
Glasersfeld, E.v. (1976). Sprache als zweckorientiertes Verhalten: zur Entwicklungsgeschichte. In: E.v.Glasersfeld, *Wissen, Sprache und Wirklichkeit*, Wiesbaden: Vieweg, 1987, 63-79.
Glasersfeld, E.v. (1981). Einführung in den radikalen Konstruktivismus. In: Watzlawick, P. (ed.), *Die erfundene Wirklichkeit*. Piper Verlag, 16-38.
Glasersfeld, E.v. (1982). 'Subitizing': Die Rolle figuraler Muster in der Entwicklung von Zahlenbegriffen. In: Glasersfeld, E.v., *Wissen, Sprache und Wirklichkeit*. Wiesbaden: Vieweg, 1987, 254-274.
Goodman, N. (1978). *Ways of Worldmaking*. Indianapolis, Cambridge.
Goodman, N.& Elgin, C.Z. (1988). *Reconceptions in Philosophy and Other Arts and Sciences*. Indianapolis, Cambridge: Hackett. (German title: *Revisionen*, Frankfurt/M: Suhrkamp, 1990).
Maturana, H.R. (1970), Biology of Cognition. In: Maturana, H.R., Varela, F.J., *Autopoiesis and Cognition*, Dordrecht/Boston: Reidel, 1980, 2-60.
Maturana, H.R., Varela, F.J. (1975). Autopoiesis: The Organization of the Living. In: Maturana, H.R., Varela, F.J., *Autopoiesis and Cognition*, Dordrecht/Boston: Reidel, 1980, 63-134.
Maturana, H.R. (1978). Kognition. In: Schmidt, *Der Diskurs des Radikalen Konstruktivismus*, Frankfurt/M: Suhrkamp, 1987, 89-118.
Maturana, H.R. (1978a). Biologie der Sprache: die Epistemologie der Realität (Biology of Language: the epistemology of reality). In:

Maturana, H.R., *Erkennen: Die Organisation und Verkörperung von Wirklichkeit*. Wiesbaden: Vieweg, 1982, 236-271.

Maturana, H.R., Varela, F.J. (1980). *Autopoiesis and Cognition. The Realization of the Living*. Dordrecht/ Boston/ London: Reidel.

McClelland, J.L., Rumelhart, D.E. (1986). *Parallel Distributed Processing, Explorations in the Microstructure of Cognition*, Volume II: *Psychological and Biological Models*. Cambridge, Mass.: MIT Press.

McClelland, J.L., Rumelhart, D.E. (1988). *Explorations in Parallel Distributed Processing*. Cambridge, Mass.: MIT Press.

Newell, A., Simon, H.A. (1976). Computer Science as Empirical Inquiry: Symbols and Search, *Communications of the ACM*, 19:3, 113-26.

Newell, A. (1980). Physical Symbol Systems, *Cognitive Science*, 4, 135-183.

Newell, A., Simon, H.A. (1981). Computer Science as Empirical Inquiry: Symbols and Search. In: Haugeland, J. (ed.), *Mind Design*. Cambridge, Mass./London: MIT Press, 35-66.

Newell, A., Rosenbloom, P.S., Laird, J.E. (1989). Symbolic Architectures for Cognition. In: Posner, M.I. (ed.), *The Foundations of Cognitive Science*. Cambridge, Mass.: MIT Press, 93-131.

Newell, A. (1990). *Unified Theories of Cognition*. Cambridge, Mass.: Harvard Univ. Press.

Peschl, M.F. (1990). Cognition and Neural Computing - an Interdisciplinary Approach. In: *Proc. of International Joint Conference on Neural Networks*, Washington (IJCNN '90), Erlbaum Publ., 110-113.

Peschl, M.F. (1990a). A Cognitive Model Coming up to Epistemological Claims - Constructivist Aspects to Modelling Cognition. In: *Proc. of International Joint Conf. on Neural Networks 1990* (IJCNN '90), San Diego, IEEE, Vol. III, III-657-662.

Peschl, M.F. (1990b). *Cognitive Modelling. Ein Beitrag zur Cognitive Science aus der Perspektive des Konstruktivismus und des Konnektionismus* (*Cognitive Modelling. Constructivist and Connectionist Aspects of Cognitive Science*), Wiesbaden: Vieweg.

Peschl, M.F. (1991). From Symbol Manipulation to Understanding Cognition - A Critical Introduction to Cognitive Science from a Computational Neuroepistemology Perspective. In: Negoita, C.V. (ed.), *Handbook of Cybernetics and Systems*, New York: Dekker.

Peschl, M.F. (1991a). Knowledge, Cognition and Acting in an Environment - Computational Neuroepistemology: an Alternative Approach to Cognitive Science. In: McTear, M. et al. (eds.), *Artificial Intelligence and Cognitive Science '90*. New York: Springer.

Rumelhart, D.E., McClelland, J.L. (1986). *Parallel Distributed Processing, Explorations in the Microstructure of Cognition*, Volume I: *Foundations*. Cambridge, Mass.: MIT Press.

Rumelhart, D.E. (1989). The Architecture of Mind: A Connectionist Approach. In: Posner, M.I. (ed.), *The Foundations of Cognitive Science*, Cambridge, Mass.: MIT Press, 133-159.

Sejnowski, T.J., Churchland, P.S. (1989). Brain and Cognition. In: Posner, M.I. (ed.), *Foundations of Cognitive Science*, Cambridge, Mass.: MIT Press, 301-356.

Sejnowski, T.J., Koch C., Churchland, P.S. (1990). Computational Neuroscience. In: Hanson et al. (eds.), *Connectionist Modelling and Brain Function*, Cambridge, Mass.: MIT Press, 5-35.

Smolensky, P. (1988). On the proper treatment of connectionism, *Behavioral and Brain Sciences*, 11, 1-74.

Varela, F.J. (1976). The Architecture of Closure. In: *Proc. of III. European Meeting on Cybernetics & Systems Research*, Vienna.

Varela, F.J. (1981). Autonomie und Autopoiese. In: Schmidt, *Der Diskurs des Radikalen Konstruktivismus*, Frankfurt/M: Suhrkamp, 1987, 119-32.

Varela, F.J. (1990). *Kognitionswissenschaft - Kognitionstechnik. Eine Skizze aktueller Perspektiven* (*Cognitive Science*). Frankfurt/M: Suhrkamp.

II

Abduction and Reasoning in Expert Systems

Human-like reasoning under uncertainty in expert systems

J.C.A. van der Lubbe & E. Backer (Delft)

0. Abstract

Expert systems are thought to imitate the reasoning process of the human expert as well as possible. Considering human reasoning, it may be concluded that one of its characteristics is that it can deal with uncertain information in a very efficient way. Furthermore, with respect to human reasoning, three types of inference can be distinguished according to the semiotic and categorical framework of Ch.S. Peirce.

In this paper, these three types of inference are analyzed in the case of uncertain information, and it is studied how far these types of inferences can be implemented in expert systems in order to guarantee human-like reasoning of expert systems.
Keywords: Expert systems, Peirce's semiotic and categorical framework, certainty factor, uncertainty calculus, inference calculus, uncertainty model, deduction, induction, abduction, rule inference, classification inference, rule generation, reasoning model generation.

1. Introduction

Expert systems are computer programs that are applied in decision making about problematic cases in such a way that they operate at a level comparable to that of a human expert. Their applications are manifold. Expert systems exist, which diagnose medical diseases, which help short term weather forecasting, which advise geologists with respect to mineral exploration, etc. What all these systems have in common is that they are thought to imitate or represent human subjective reasoning as close as possible, at least with respect to the input-output performance. For this reason, one of the main problems in expert system development is how to build expert systems with a performance comparable to that of human reasoning.

With respect to reasoning or inference, usually a distinction is made between deduction and induction. However, on the basis of the semiotic and categorical framework of the American philosopher Charles Sanders Peirce (1839-1914) three types of inference can be distinguished; in addition to induction and deduction, there is also abduction. In the present paper, these three types of inference are studied and their role is discussed with respect to machine-based human-like reasoning.

Since a characteristic aspect of human reasoning is that in many cases one has to deal with uncertainty or imprecise information, it is clear that the study of uncertainty models as well as methods for the combination and propagation of uncertainties through the inference process which can be used within expert systems, is inevitable. For that very reason, spècial attention is paid to how with the three types of inference within expert systems in the case of uncertainty are dealt with.

2. Human expert versus expert system

In the foregoing section, it was mentioned that a characteristic of expert systems is that they are thought to imitate or represent human reasoning as close as possible, at least with respect to the input-output performance. The latter means that, given the application domain and given the particular problem to be solved, both the human expert and the expert system should come to the same conclusion on the basis of an identical input (see figure 1).

However, from a cognitive point of view, there are clear distinctions between human experts and currently existing expert systems (Johnson-Laird, 1989).

- First of all, there is a clear difference with respect to semantics. Human beings have knowledge about things. That means that human knowledge has a referential and denotational momentum as related to reality. The knowledge incorporated within an expert system is only denotationally interpretable by the human user, not by the expert system itself.
- Second, if a human being makes errors, this can be reason for him to revise his knowledge. However, usually expert systems are not conscious of their own errors; not to mention the fact that in general expert systems cannot update their knowledge when confronted with their own errors.

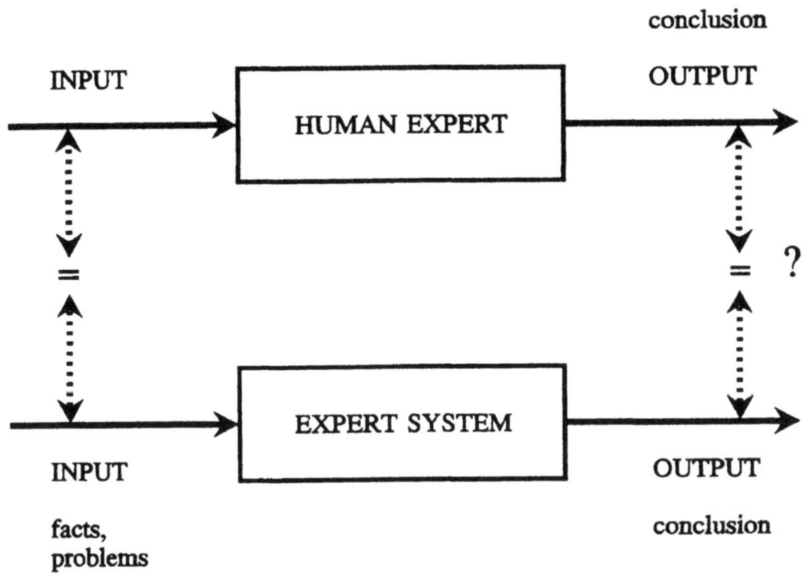

Figure 1: Human expert versus expert system

- Third, it should be noticed that expert systems are not as flexible as human beings in respect to the use of knowledge. Humans can apply their knowledge in a very flexible way to perform many different tasks and to answer a manifold of problems, this in contrast with expert systems.
- Fourth, human experts have a large amount of tacit knowledge which generally cannot be expressed in words. In addition to this, association and creativity play an important role in human reasoning processes. These aspects are those which, until now, are hardly implemented within expert systems.
- Fifth, a characteristic aspect of human reasoning is that in many cases it deals directly and very easily with uncertainty or imprecise information. In expert systems, this should be done indirectly and more digressively by using uncertainty models for the representation of uncertainty as well as inference calculi for the combination and propagation of uncertainties through the reasoning process.

The foregoing implies that an expert system should have at least the following capabilities in order to guarantee human-like reasoning: it should contain its own semantics, it should be flexible and learn from its own errors, it should include associative and creative reasoning and it should deal with uncertain information.

3. The global structure of an expert system

Before paying attention to how uncertain and imprecise information within expert systems is dealt with, the global structure of an expert system is briefly outlined.

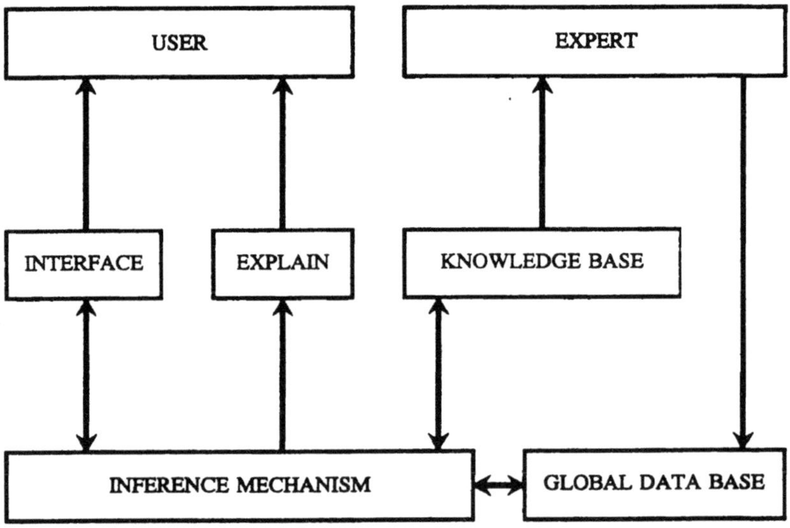

Figure 2: Global structure of an expert system

In figure 2, the global structure of an expert system is given. The key parts are:

- A global data base which contains information about the problem to be solved as well as the known facts and the intermediate results of the reasoning process;
- A knowledge base representing the application-dependent knowledge and experience of the expert;
- An inference mechanism which controls the inference process in order to solve the formulated problem.

In general, the knowledge in the knowledge base is represented in the form of if-then rules, the so-called production rules. Each production rule consists of a condition part and a conclusion part. Figure 3 gives an example of a hypothetical rule related to influenza in a medical diagnostic expert system.

IF PATIENT HAS:

□ FEVER

AND

□ SORE THROAT

AND

□ COUGH

THEN PATIENT HAS:

□ INFLUENZA

Figure 3: Example of a production rule

The inference mechanism performs inferences on the basis of the production rules in the knowledge base in order to solve a problem requested by the user, e.g., diagnosing the disease of a patient.

4. Certainty factors

As a matter of fact the contents of qualitative concepts like "having fever", etc. (see figure 3), which are used in the production rules, can be related to a numerical scale with respect to the body temperature. To what extent qualifications like "having fever" hold in concrete situations is expressed by so-called certainty factors. They express whether fever is really "fever" in a concrete situation (see figure 4).

Certainty factors can also be attached to the production rules as a whole, hence expressing the certainty of the conclusion part if the condition part of the production rule is completely certain. With respect to the example of figure 3, the certainty factor of the rule expresses the certainty that a patient has influenza, if there is complete certainty that the patient has fever, a sore throat and is coughing.

It is remarked here that certainty factors can be related to different types of certainty: e.g., statistical certainty, fuzziness, credibility, reliability, distinctness, etc. Referring to the example of figure 3, the relation between having fever and having influenza can be related to statistical certainty, but also to credibility, as such expressing to what degree the relation between having fever and having influenza is credible.

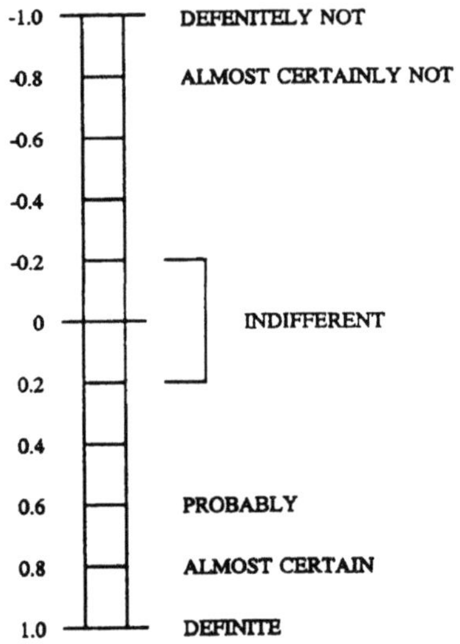

Figure 4: Scale of certainty factors

On the basis of the different types of (un)certainty, various uncertainty calculi are introduced in literature which deal with the mathematical representation of (un)certainty, finally resulting in a certainty factor. In addition to this, inference calculi are needed to deal with the combination and propagation of (un)certainties through the inference process. Both uncertainty calculus and inference calculus form the so-called uncertainty model.

5. Ch.S. Peirce and the three types of inference

With respect to inferring under uncertainty, distinction should be made between different types of inference. In general, two types of reasoning are distinguished: deductive and inductive reasoning; this corresponds to commonly accepted ideas. However, according to the American philosopher Peirce, a third type of inference should also be distinguished: abductive reasoning. It is this type of inference which plays a dominating role in human reasoning and which is inevitable for expert systems in order to have a performance compatible with that of a human expert.

Peirce's distinction between deductive, inductive and abductive reasoning is closely related to his semiotic and categorical framework, which is fundamentally triadic. This triadic categorical framework is a clear answer to a way of thinking which, until then, was mainly characterized by descriptions in terms of dyadic relations (compare Descartes' strong distinction between reality and the image we have of this reality: between object and subject, etc.). For Peirce thinking is basically a triadic relation. In Van der Lubbe and Nauta (1991), this is discussed in more detail. Here it suffices to conclude that there are three types of inference as a consequence of his triadic categorical framework.

The differences between the three types of inference can be illustrated with the help of the following examples.

Deduction:	Rule	: All the apples from the box are red
	Fact	: These apples are from the box
	Result/conclusion	: These apples are red
Induction:	Fact	: These apples are from the box
	Result/conclusion	: These apples are red
	Rule	: All the apples from the box are red
Abduction:	Rule	: All the apples from the box are red
	Result/conclusion	: These apples are red
	Fact	: These apples are from the box

Clearly, these three types of inference have different starting points. In the case of deduction, one tries to make a conclusion or to find a result on the basis of an observed fact by application of a rule. Induction is related to the generation of a general rule on the basis of a fact and a conclusion. Finally, in the case of abduction, on the basis of a rule and conclusion the fact is inferred in the form of a hypothesis.

In itself, the terms for the types of inference mentioned above are related in general to situations whereby the facts, conclusions, etc. are assumed to be either true or false. In the present context, the definitions are extended to situations in which some degree of uncertainty is present in the inference process. As such, the distinction between deduction and induction is not related to the fact that the first can lead to true outcomes and the second cannot, but to the fact that they have different starting points.

6. Deductive reasoning under uncertainty

In the case of deductive reasoning under uncertainty, a conclusion is made on the basis of a fact (premise) and by application of a general rule. Therefore, this type of inference is also called deductive rule inference. Here it is assumed that both premise and rule are coupled with uncertainty in terms of so-called certainty factors.

Let the degree of certainty of the premise be denoted by cf-premise. Analogously, cf-rule and cf-conclusion are the certainty factors of the rule and the conclusion, respectively. In practice, in human reasoning an estimation is performed of the certainty of the conclusion on the basis of the certainty factors of both the premise and the rule. In order to guarantee human-like reasoning, there should be a mechanism in the expert system which expresses the certainty of the achieved conclusion as a function of the certainty factors of the premise and the applied rule. This means that there should be a procedure such that cf-conclusion can be determined on the basis of cf-premise and cf-rule, and in such a way that the computed cf-conclusion corresponds with the degree of certainty adjudged to the conclusion by a human expert.

The so-called inference calculus is comprised of this procedure, together with other procedures for combination and propagation of certainties in the case of conjunctions and disjunctions of clauses forming part of the premise or in the case of the combination of rules.

In literature, various inference calculi have been introduced. One that is well-known was introduced by Shortliffe and Buchanan (1975). According to this model (see also figure 5) it holds that the certainty factor of the conclusion is just the product of the certainty factors with respect to premise and rule: cf-conclusion = cf-premise x cf-rule.

In figure 3, an example of a rule was given whereby the premise consists of three clauses. According to Shortliffe-Buchanan, the certainty factor, in respect to the premise, is equal to the minimum value of the separate certainty factors of the clauses. On the basis of the obtained certainty factor of the premise, the certainty factor of the conclusion can be computed according to the formula given above. This is illustrated for the rule given in figure 3.

□ PREMISE, m CLAUSES, AND-CONNECTED:

cf-premise = min (cf-clause 1,...,cf-clause m)

□ PREMISE, m CLAUSES, OR-CONNECTED:

cf-premise = max (cf-clause 1,...,cf-clause m)

□ CONCLUSION:

cf-conclusion = cf-premise x cf-rule

□ CO-CONCLUDING RULES:

cf-conclusion = a + b(1-a),

whereby a = cf-conclusion 1 and b = cf-conclusion 2

Figure 5: The inference calculus of Shortliffe-Buchanan

Let the certainty factors relating to "fever", "sore throat" and "cough" be given by 0.7, 0.3 and 0.4, respectively. According to the inference calculus of Shortliffe-Buchanan, the overall certainty factor of the premise now equals 0.3. Let the certainty factor of the rule be equal to 0.9; that means that if there is no doubt that the patient suffers fever, a sore throat and cough, then the degree of certainty that the patient has influenza is 0.9. However, because the facts of the premise are not completely clear, the certainty factor of having influenza in this particular case becomes:

cf-conclusion = cf-premise x cf-rule
= 0.3 x 0.9 = 0.27.

The minimum operation in the case of and-connected clauses guarantees that that clause which gives the least support to the conclusion determines the certainty factor of that conclusion. Analogously, if a premise consists of or-connected clauses, the overall certainty factor of the premise is the maximum of the certainty factors of the clauses.

In practice it often occurs that the same conclusion is achieved along different paths. E.g., in addition to the rule with respect to influenza as given in figure 3, there can also be another rule such as "If patient has headache then patient has influenza". Both rules lead to the same conclusion, although their certainty factors can be different. Figure 5 also demonstrates how to combine certainty factors in the case of co-concluding rules, whereby it is assumed that both certainty factors are positive. In general, the resulting overall certainty factor, as may be expected, will then have a value between the initial certainty factors of the conclusions.

7. Inductive reasoning under uncertainty

In the method mentioned above, it is assumed that the expert knowledge can be expressed in terms of general rules along with some certainty measurement. However, depending on the application domain, it can occur that the expert knowledge is available only in the form of pieces of knowledge (samples), e.g., previously analyzed patient cases in a medical diagnostic expert system with respect to influenza.

In inductive reasoning general rules are generated on the basis of samples/instances related to facts representing premises and conclusions. The underlying assumption is that the facts expressed in premises and conclusions of the samples are really related to each other. Strictly speaking, inductive reasoning is always subjected to uncertainty due to the fact that the generated general rule is not per se true, even if the premises and conclusions of the samples are true. This is caused by the fact that the number of samples is by definition limited. Moreover, the uncertainty also depends on the fact that the knowledge with respect to the samples is not per se certain.

On the basis of the uncertain and incomplete knowledge, a general rule is generated together with the corresponding certainty factor. As a matter of fact, the rules which are the result of this so-called inductive rule generation process can again be used in a deductive reasoning process as such leading to conclusions about new/other cases.

However, sometimes the generalization from samples to a general rule is not performed. Then the samples are directly used for making conclusions about new cases: the so-called classification inference. Although classification inference is not induction in the pure sense, it can be considered as a type of inductive reasoning, since the generality of the samples is assumed in the sense that the relations between premises and conclusions of the sample set of known cases (the learning set) also apply to a new case.

7.1 Classification inference

Assume n cases (e.g., patient cases), whereby the certainty factors of premise (e.g., having fever, sore throat and cough) and conclusion (e.g., having influenza) are given for each case. Let cf be the certainty factor as related to case r, r = 1,...,n. With respect to patient case r, the certainty factors of premise and conclusion can now be denoted by cf-premise and cf-conclusion, respectively. Assume a new patient case for which the degree of certainty regarding the premise (e.g., having fever etc.) is given by cf-premise and for which the certainty factor cf-conclusion that he suffers influenza should be determined. Then the problem can be formulated as follows:

Given certainty factors of n known cases:

cf-premise, cf-conclusion

. .

. .

cf-premise, cf-conclusion

Determine with respect to new case:

cf-conclusion on the basis of cf-premise.

In fact, inference is now reduced to a classification problem. For each case the certainty factor of the premise can be represented as a point on a line. The corresponding certainty factor of the conclusion can be considered as a "label" to that point (see points denoted by x in figure 6). Also the certainty factor of the premise of the patient for which a diagnosis should be made can be represented as a point (see point p in figure 6). However, for this point the label cf-conclusion should be determined.

For this, classification methods as used in statistical pattern recognition can be applied e.g., the m-nearest neighbour classifier. The m-nearest neighbour classifier searches for the m-nearest neighbours of the new case and determines the certainty factor of the conclusion with respect to this new case. This is done by taking the average of the certainty factors of the conclusions of the m nearest neighbours.

Thus, if m = 1 the certainty factor of the conclusion for the new case is uniquely determined by the certainty factor of the conclusion of the nearest point. Referring to figure 6, this implies that, for m = 1, cf-conclusion of the new case is equal to 0.5. This means that, according to classification inference the patient, for which a diagnosis should be made, has influenza with a degree of certainty equal to 0.5.

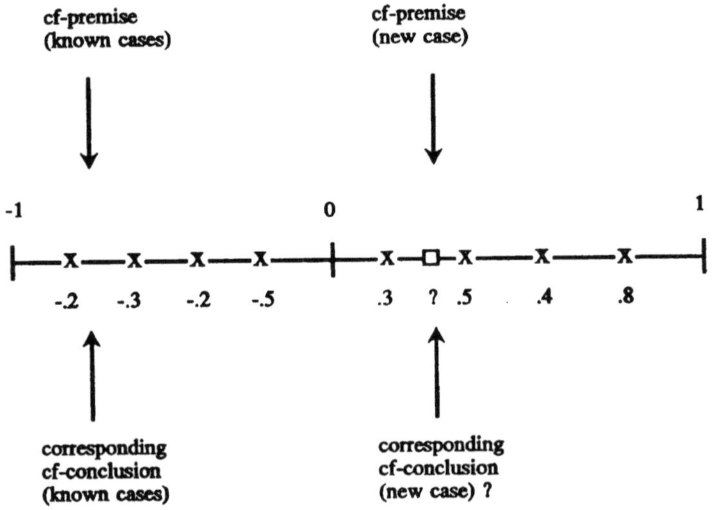

Figure 6: Classification inference

7.2 Inductive rule generation

Above, attention was paid to inference in situations whereby the knowledge is available in terms of (patient) cases. However, in addition to this, it is also possible that the knowledge concerns information about samples related to judgements of expert panels.

In the situation of cases, one expert is analyzing a specific phenomenon in various cases, e.g., a medical doctor testing patients for influenza. In the situation of an expert panel each member of the panel analyzes one specific case, e.g., a group of medical doctors individually analyzing a specific patient case resulting in various estimates of the presence of influenza for that patient.

More generally, the differences can be summarized in figure 7. It is remarked here that real inference is possible only for cases. Expert panels can give at most an assessment of the certainty factor with respect to the conclusion for one particular case on the basis of the individual judgements of the experts. Hence, expert panels tell more about the consistency of the expert knowledge than about the case itself. For that very reason, expert panels are mainly used for inductive rule generation whereby information about various cases can still play a role.

CASES	PANELS
- one expert - knowledge about various cases - main aim: knowledge about new case; classification inference	- various experts - knowledge about one case - main aim: acquisition of expert knowledge; inductive rule generation

Figure 7: Difference between knowledge on the basis of cases and expert panels

The problem of rule generation now is the formulation of general rules with their corresponding certainty factors on the basis of samples related to cases and panel judgements. Various methods can be applied.

The first way for determination of the certainty vector of the rule is direct estimation of the rule certainty factors by means of a panel of, say, m experts. On the basis of individual assessments concerning the certainty factor of the rule, cf-rule, whereby s denotes that it concerns the judgement of expert s (s = 1,...,m), the final rule certainty factor can be obtained by using all the assessments by the m experts and by computing some average certainty factor for the rule. This method is direct since information about the cases themselves is not used at all.

The other possibility for the determination of the rule certainty factor is indirect. Let cf-premise and cf-conclusion be the certainty factors with respect to premise and conclusion, respectively, related to case r as assessed by expert s. Now the problem is the determination of individual assessments of the cf-rule on the basis of all values of cf-premise and cf-conclusion. This method is appropriate if it is difficult for the expert to express his knowledge in terms of general rules directly. However, this indirect method can only be applied if one has some idea about the underlying reasoning model of the expert concerning the relation between the certainty factors of premise, conclusion and rule. E.g., if all experts are reasoning according to the Shortliffe-Buchanan model, i.e., the certainty of a conclusion is the product of the certainty factors of premise and rule (compare figure 5), then estimations of cf-rule are obtained for all s by computing cf-rule from:

cf-rule = cf-conclusion / cf-premise,

and by averaging over all cases.

It should be mentioned that if there are some cases for which the certainty factor of the premise tends to be 1, the certainty factor of the rule is identical to that of the conclusion (see also the foregoing formula). This is due to the definition of the certainty factor of a rule, which is defined as the certainty factor of the conclusion if the premise is absolutely certain. This is rather independent of the underlying reasoning model.

Finally, it is remarked here that also in the case of samples relating to both cases and panel judgements, classification inference, as introduced in section 7.2, can be performed. We now have, in fact, a classification problem in a 2-dimensional space which can be solved in a similar way as mentioned in that section. For more details, one is referred to Van der Lubbe et al. (1990a).

8. Abductive reasoning under uncertainty

In section 5, abduction was introduced as inferring hypothetical facts on the basis of a rule and a result/conclusion. As such, this corresponds to the inverse process of deduction. This type of inference is also called abduction to a fact/premise or abductive rule inference. In addition, there is also abduction to explanatory rules or abductive rule generation. Both types of abduction have in common that they are related to finding the most explanatory hypothesis of puzzling phenomena.

8.1 Abductive rule generation

Abduction is the only type of reasoning which can extend knowledge by taking together the known and unknown. Sometimes abduction to rules is confused with inductive rule generation as mentioned in section 7.2. However, whereas induction is based on a large number of instances/samples, in abduction a specific case is hypothesized on the basis of information about a single situation. Moreover, whereas in induction the relation between premise and conclusion is a priori assumed, this is hypothesized in abductive reasoning. If we see somebody caressing a cat, the conclusion can be that that person is a nice person. The underlying assumption and rule is that nice people caress their cats. The creative element in this abductive reasoning process is that kindness of people and caressing cats are related to each other. In the same way (see example in Section 5), the fact "These apples are from the box" is a possible explanation of the observed fact "These apples are red". The underlying hypothetical rule is "All apples in the box are red", as such, expressing the relation between red and coming from the box.

The problem of abductive rule generation is defining relevant relations between conditional and concluding facts. In fact, the space of possible rules is infinite. However, within an application domain often there is consensus about the concluding facts which should be explained. Therefore, the remaining problem from an expert system point of view is finding the relevant conditional facts. However, this supposes that the space of candidate conditional facts should be such that the relevant conditional facts are already included in this space. This implies that the set of candidate conditional facts for the observed result "These apples are red" should include the fact "These apples are from the box", among others a priori. It is clear that, in practice, this hinders building expert systems with a performance compatible with human-like reasoning. Whereas a human is superior with respect to the generation of new associations, the expert system should a priori include all possible relations and associations.

A problem which has already been solved, more or less, in respect to this, is the selection of the most explanatory relations between them, given the set of all possible conditional and concluding results.

Another unsolved problem is the assignment of certainty factors to rules generated by abduction. In general, they cannot be based on a large number of instances as already mentioned above. If a certainty factor is assigned, it is related more to certainty in terms of credibility, from which the legitimation can only be given by testing it via induction and deduction. At the level of abductive rule generation, only the expert judgement is leading.

8.2 Abductive rule inference

A similar problem concerning the determination of certainty factors occurs with respect to abduction to a fact. Even if the certainty factors of a result or conclusion and rule are known this does not per se give information about the certainty factors of the conditional facts.

First of all, consider again the production rule of figure 3. Since the certainty factor of influenza is equal to the product of the certainty factors of the premise and the rule according to the Shortliffe-Buchanan model, clearly the certainty factor of the premise is equal to the certainty factor of the conclusion divided by the certainty factor of the rule. However, since the certainty factor of the premise is some resultant of the certainty factors of the clauses, the separate certainty factors with respect to the various clauses cannot be found again. Due to the minimum operation with respect to conjunctions only the certainty factor which gives the weakest support to the conclusion is found, but not the related clause itself.

Also in the case of singular premises the computation of certainty factors can be problematic, e.g., in the case of co-concluding rules in the Shortliffe-Buchanan model. Since the certainty factors of the conclusion of the original rules, which are combined, cannot be derived from the certainty factor of the conclusion of the co-concluding rules, the same holds with respect to the conditional facts of the original rules.

In general, it should be concluded that only in well-defined situations abduction to a fact can be performed and the corresponding certainty factors can be computed.

9. Comparison of the three types of inference

In the foregoing, three types of inference under uncertainty were considered. Deductive and abductive rule inference and inductive classification inference differ in the type of knowledge they use as well as with respect to learning aspects. Clearly, in deductive rule inference explicit knowledge is used, whereas this knowledge is implicit for classification inference. The latter means that the relation between conditional facts and conclusion is given in terms of samples/cases without the possibility of making it explicit in terms of rules.

	Knowledge	Learning
Deductive rule inference	explicit	implicit
Inductive class. inference	implicit	explicit
Abductive rule inference	potential	potential

Figure 8: Comparison of the three types of inference

With respect to learning, the learning aspect is implicit in rule inference. In fact, here we only deal with the result of learning, i.e., the rules. Clearly, learning is inherent to classification inference where information about new cases can easily be added to the sample set. With respect to abductive rule inference, both knowledge and learning are neither explicit nor implicit, but only potential, due to their hypothetical character. Figure 8 summarizes.

In practice, in reasoning processes all the three types of inference play a role together. This is in line with Peirce's thought, according to which the three types of inference are indissoluble. Compare figure 9.

By means of abduction, it is determined what the relevant conditional and concluding facts are, as such determining the samples. Abduction is also helpful in generating hypothetical rules. These rules can be generalized by induction to general rules and tested by deduction.

Also from an implementation point of view, a combination of deductive/abductive rule inference and inductive classification inference is attractive. In general, the computational effort in the case of rule inference is lower than in the case of classification inference, whereby we are dealing with a large amount of samples. However, classification inference has the advantage of learning capability by the possibility of adding new cases to the sample set.

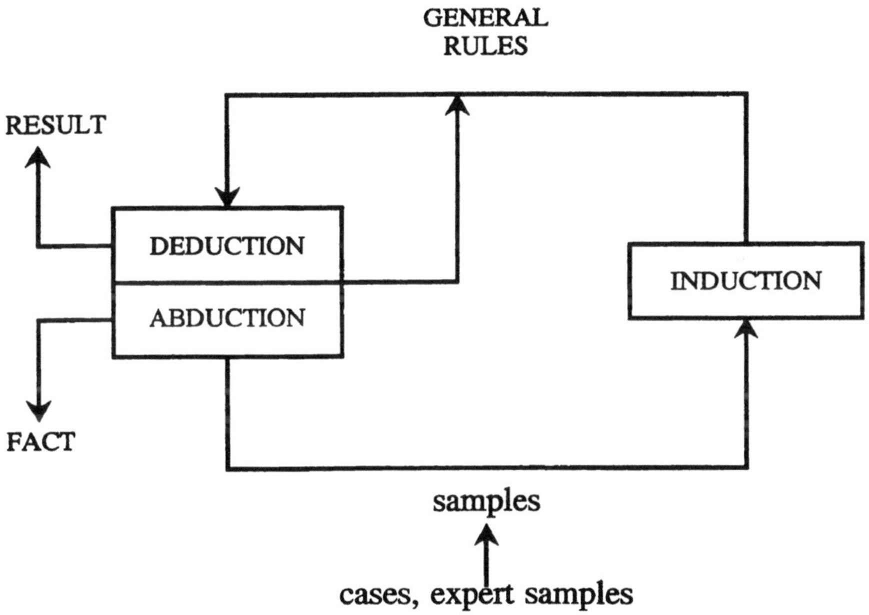

Figure 9: The cooperation between deduction, induction and abduction

In operational environments, cases can be used initially for rule generation. On the basis of the generated rules deductive rule inference can be performed for new cases. The rules are updated only periodically on the basis of new cases. New rules and new relations between conditional facts and conclusions result from abductive reasoning.

10. Reasoning model generation

In figure 10, a survey is given of all methods for rule generation and inference which were considered in this paper. What has been left out of consideration until now is the characteristic of the reasoning model, the inference calculus itself. In the foregoing, it was assumed that the human being thinks according to the Shortliffe-Buchanan model or at least it was assumed that there exists such a thing as an inference calculus, which can be considered as characteristic for all expert reasoning and which is suitable for all applications. However, from experiments in the field of medical and meteorological applications, it is known that human reasoning is highly inconsistent. This means that general reasoning models, like Shortliffe/Buchanan which is suitable within one context or application, do not hold per se in other contexts/applications. This has been underlined by experiments performed at the Delft University of Technology.

For that very reason it can be important to address the question to what extent, within the context of the general methods mentioned above, some form of reasoning model generation either is or can be incorporated in order to enhance human-like reasoning of expert systems. This also holds if one has no clear idea about the underlying reasoning model of the experts.

Consider the certainty factors with respect to premise, rule and conclusion for various cases and on the basis of expert panels. Taking e.g., the modus ponens the underlying reasoning model can now be obtained as follows. Let F be some parametrical function or formula of cf-premise and cf-rule and let F be in such a way that the outcome of F may be assumed to be an estimation of cf-conclusion. Then the optimal reasoning model for the modus ponens is that function F for which, on the average, the outcome of the function F on the basis of the certainty factors of premise and rule is more or less equal to the certainty factor of the conclusion.

As a matter of fact, the optimal function, determined in this way, can be identical to the one given by Shortliffe-Buchanan for some applications but different in the case of other applications. It is beyond the scope of this paper to deal with reasoning model generation in more detail. For further information one is referred to Van der Lubbe et al. (1990a).

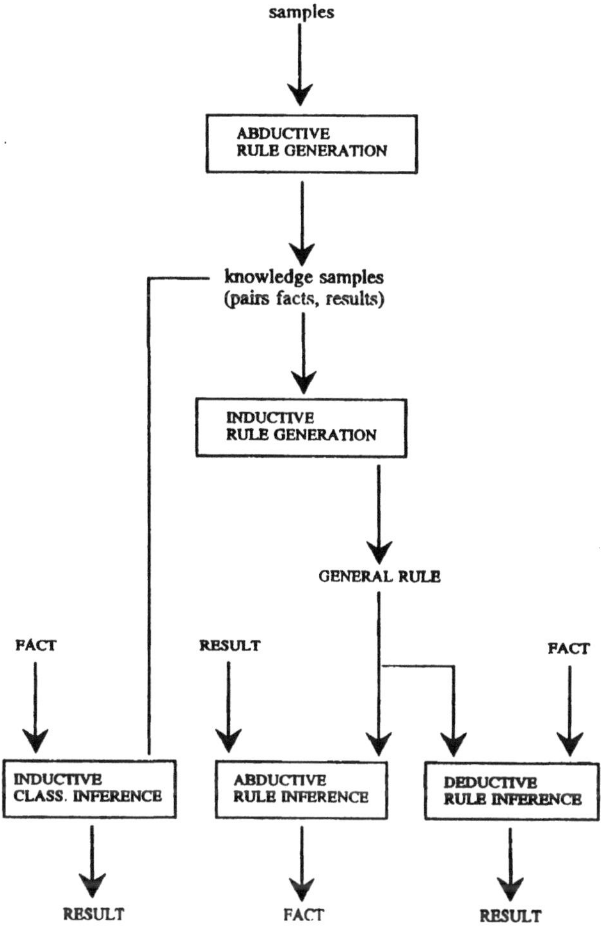

Figure 10: Survey of rule generation and inference types

11. Conclusions

In the foregoing, attention was paid to the three different types of inference under uncertainty which are important with respect to human reasoning according to Peirce's semiotics. It was studied how far these types of inference as well as methods for rule generation can be realized within present expert systems.

From this analysis it may be concluded that the three types of inference are related to each other in such a way that implementation of all of them together within expert systems seems inevitable.

Methods for inductive classification inference and deductive rule inference were discussed along with the role of cases and expert panels with respect to inference and rule generation. However, the implementation of abductive reasoning is still a hard problem in expert systems. Under strong assumptions, some form of abduction can be performed, although this is not sufficient, at this moment, in order to guarantee human-like reasoning of expert systems in every way. For this reason, abduction is one of the greatest challenges for the development of expert systems at this time.

Finally, it was concluded that, if human reasoning is highly inconsistent, then reasoning model generation within expert systems can also be necessary.

References

Backer, E., Van der Lubbe, J.C.A., Krijgsman, W. (1988). On Modelling of Uncertainty and Inexactness in Expert Systems. In: *Proceedings of the Ninth Symposium on Information Theory*. Mierlo, The Netherlands, 105-111.

Backer, E., Gerbrands, J.J., Reiber, J.H.C., Reijs, A.E.M., Krijgsman, W., Van den Herik, H.J. (1988). Modelling Uncertainty in ESATS by Classification Inference, *Pattern Recognition Letters*, 8, 103-112.

Bonissone, P.P., Tong, R.M. (1985). Reasoning with Uncertainty in Expert Systems, *Int. J. Man-Machine Studies* 22, 241-250.

Buchanan, B.G., Shortliffe, E.H. (1984). *Rule-Based Systems*. Massachusetts.

Buxton, R. (1989). Modelling Uncertainty in Expert Systems, *Int. J. Man-Machine Studies* 31, 415-476.

Dubois, D., Prade, H. (1987). A Tentative Comparison of Numerical Approximate Reasoning Methodologies, *Int. J. Man-Machine Studies* 27, 717-728.

Ho, T.B., Diday, E., Gettler-Summa, M. (1988). Generating Rules for Expert Systems from Observations, *Pattern Recognition Letters* 7, 265-271.

Johnson-Laird P.N. (1989). Human Experts and Expert Systems. In: Murray, L.A. and Richardson, J.T.E. (eds.). *Intelligent Systems in a Human Context*. Oxford, 35-46.

Peirce, Ch.S., *Collected Papers of Ch.S. Peirce*, edited by Hartshorne, C. and Weiss, P., Cambridge (Mass.). 1931-1935.

Prade, H. (1985). A Computational Approach to Approximate and Plausible Reasoning with Applications to Expert Systems. In: *IEEE Pattern Anal. Mach. Intell.*, Vol PAMI-7, 3, 284-298.

Shafer, G. (1975). *A Mathematical Theory of Evidence*. Princeton Univ. Press.

Shortliffe, E.H., Buchanan, B.G. (1975). A Model of Inexact Reasoning in Medicine, *Math. Biosciences*, Vol. 23, 351-379.

Van der Lubbe, J.C.A., Backer, E., Krijgsman, W. (1990a). Models for Reasoning with Multitype Uncertainty in Expert Systems. In: *Proc. Third Int. Conf. on Information Processing and Management of Uncertainty in Knowledge-based Systems*. Paris, July 2-6, 1990, 40-43 (to be published by Springer-Verlag, Vienna, 1991).

Van der Lubbe, J.C.A., Borger, J.B., Van den Berg, W.D. (1990b). METEODES: An Expert System for the Automatic Analysis of Cloud Types in METEOSAT-imagery. In: *Proceedings of the 8th METEOSAT Scientific User's Meeting*. Norrkoping, Sweden, August 28-31 1990, Eumetsat, Darmstadt, 1990, 395-402.

Van der Lubbe, J.C.A., Nauta, D. (1991). Expert Systems, Culture and Peirce's Semiotics. To be published in: Slikkerveer, L.J., Van Heusden, B., Jorna, R.J. & Van den Broek, G. (Eds.). *The Expert Sign - Semiotics of Culture and Expertise*. Leiden, 1992.

Abduction: The creative process

A.H. MAROSTICA (Los Angeles)

1. Introduction

Among the components of the process of reasoning, Charles S. Peirce finds three important classes: abduction, deduction and induction. This paper will not dwell on the different types of reasoning, rather, I shall concentrate on the first type, abduction, and its relationship to problem solving methods. I shall emphasize, and support with examples, that Peirce's explanation, or abduction, is able to provide a solution to a qualitative type of problems, that a problem solving system cannot solve satisfactorily.

2. Abduction

According to Peirce, abduction is the process of making an explanatory hypothesis for a surprising fact. The hypothesis is conceived as a mere conjecture, or a fair guess. Broadly speaking, abduction covers all the processes by "which theories and conceptions are engendered." (CP 5.590, 1906) For Peirce, the natural form of that inference is:

> The surprising fact, C, is observed;
> But if A were true, C would be a matter of course,
> Hence, there is reason to suspect that A is true. (CP 5.189, 1903)

In this inference, (C) is the statement expressing the surprising fact, and (A) is the statement expressing the explanatory hypothesis. According to Peirce, the general form of an abduction is:

> Any M is, for instance, P', P'', P''', etc.
> S is P', P'', P''', etc.
> Therefore, S is M. (CP 2.511-514, 1893)

In this context, (C) is "S is P', P'', P''', etc.", (A) is "S is M" and the material leading principle is the law-like statement "Any M is, for instance, P',

P'', P''', etc." The leading principle is the missing premise that connects the surprising fact, (C) with the explanatory hypothesis, (A).

Any type of argument is for Peirce, a particular type of sign. In 1902, he explained that "abduction is an iconic argument..." (M L75).

It is not my purpose here to discuss in detail the iconic property of abduction. However, I would like to stress the most relevant similarity between abduction and an icon. We can say that abduction is iconic because it shares with the icon the following properties: First, abduction and icons are the only types of signs which start new ideas. Furthermore, abduction is the type of argument closest to the function performed by an icon. The mind through abduction tries to resemble nature. Both the abductive process and the icon try to exhibit the properties of facts, or object, in some relevant respect. Sometimes abductive processes and icons resemble their objects not at all in looks; it is only in respect to the relevant relations of their parts that their likeness exists. Sometimes abduction tries to explain the surprising fact by connecting, in a creative way, fields that nobody connected before. The mind appeals to a type of instinct. That "rational instinct" is what Peirce called "*il lume naturale*." (CP 6.477, 1908). With this power, abduction is able to create models that will help to find an explanation for a given surprising fact. What Peirce called "*il lume naturale*, in modern terminology is called "*illumination*." (Gilhooly, 1982)

As an example of an abductive process, Peirce offers the abduction performed by Kepler, as it is presented in his *Astronomia nova* (1609). Peirce considered this famous example of abduction as the greatest piece of reasoning ever performed. (CP 1.71-74, c. 1896)

In a very simplified way, Kepler's natural abduction is as follows:

(I) Mars has problems with calculations of positions related to a circular orbit. (i.e., Mars has positions P_i,....P_n, and P_i,....P_n, are not positions related to a circular orbit) (C)

Therefore, Mars has an elliptical orbit.(A)

The leading principle of this argument is as follows:

All planets with elliptical orbits have problems with calculations of positions related to circular orbits.

According to Peirce, abduction, as a whole, is a type of sign. Therefore, the sign of that process is expressed in the surprising fact, (C). The object of abduction is related to its explanatory hypothesis, (A), and the interpretant is given by the leading principle: (LP).

In Kepler's case, the recognition of the iconic representation of the sign, (C), was a matter of discovery that took several years of inquiry. The surprising fact resembles its real object (i.e., the elliptical orbit) at the end of a process.

Before Kepler discovered the real orbit of Mars, nobody knew what the shape of the orbit was. Kepler was convinced that circularity was not the solution. In the terminology of Artificial Intelligence, we may say that Kepler knew the initial state, but he did not know what the goal state would be. This is because, in abduction there is not a previous model or basic search pattern. That plan or model, is the one that the inquirer may use when he is trying to find what is the explanatory hypothesis (goal state) for a given surprising fact (initial state). In order to solve the problem the inquirer has to create the model that will allow him to find what the goal state is. The creations of that basic search pattern is a problem of a qualitative nature, for it is related to the creative power of the mind. The mind through abduction creates the model.

As another illustrative example of the function performed by abduction, we may consider the case of the Bayes' Theorem. It is a surprising fact that a "boring" and simple corollary of the multiplicative law of the Calculus of Probability (due to Thomas Bayes, 1702-1761) became through the years to be an "interesting" theorem in Confirmation Theory.

In symbols the Bayes' theorem says:

$$p(h/e\&a) = P(h/a) \,.\, P(e/h\&a) \;/\; P(e/a)$$

The theorem states the resulting probability of the hypothesis *h* upon the evidence *e* and the antecedent body of knowledge *a* is equal to the product of the probability of *h* upon *a* alone times the probability of *e* upon *a*.

In Confirmation Theory this theorem is "interesting" because we can consider the application of Bayes' theorem as a method of confirming hypotheses *à la* Hempel. This is the reason that some authors considered the Hypothetico-Deductive Method as a type of application of the Bayes' theorem (Shimony, 1970).

The abductive process involved in the adoption of Bayes' theorem as an "interesting" theorem in the Confirmation Theory can be reconstructed as follows:

> Any generalization of the H-D Method is an "interesting" theorem in the Confirmation Theory. (LP)
> Bayes' theorem is an "interesting" theorem in Confirmation Theory.(C)
> Therefore, Bayes' theorem is a generalization of the H-D Method. (A)

In both, Kepler's and Bayes' cases, the recognition of the iconic representation of the sign (C) was a matter of discovery that took several years of inquiry. As far as I know, Pierre Simon De Laplace was the first scientist that used the Bayes' theorem as a method of confirmation of a hypothesis when the initial probabilities are unknown. (Laplace 1798-1814) In our century, the application of Bayes' theorem is called "Bayesian confirmation", and it is commonly used in Confirmation Theory (Salmon, 1967).

Making a creative connection between two fields, like the fields of Probability Calculus and the one of Confirmation Theory, was the reason that a "boring" theorem in one field became an "interesting" theorem in the other field. That connection is the result of the qualitative job performed by abduction. In this case, as well, the mind, through abduction, created the model, or the basic search pattern. Besides, it had to find too, which would be the goal state to pursue in the state space.

3. Problem solving

Reasoning and problem solving overlap considerably, and some researchers have attempted to combine theories of the two processes (e.g., Newell, 1980). Certain types of reasoning like deduction and induction share with problem solving some common techniques. For example, in various methods of representing a problem by a state space, and solving it by searching this state space, these may be handled in a uniform manner by deductive logic. The problem is usually represented by first-order predicate calculus, and solved by using inferences of a deductive type.

On the other hand, the rules used by expert systems, sometimes, are based on inductive procedures in which statistical types of inferences are used. For example, DENDRAL presents its results as a list of the most likely alternatives.

One of the most effective problem solving strategies is to use a plan or a basic search pattern, in which a simplified version of the problem as a whole is used as a *model* for solving the problem.

We can consider the process of problem solving as a search through a *state space* in which each point corresponds to a situation that might arise, the search starting with an *initial* situation and performing a sequence of allowable operations until a situation corresponding to a goal (the *goal state*) is reached. We can describe a variety of ways of moving through such a search space in an attempt to find a solution to a particular problem. We may say that problem solving, in general, uses a basic search pattern. That pattern allows the problem solving method to convert a given initial state into a goal state in a given state space.

We can apply this type of mechanical process, not only to the solution of the "3-Block" problem, but to the solution of some word problems in physics.

For example, the "3-block" problem could be represented as follows:

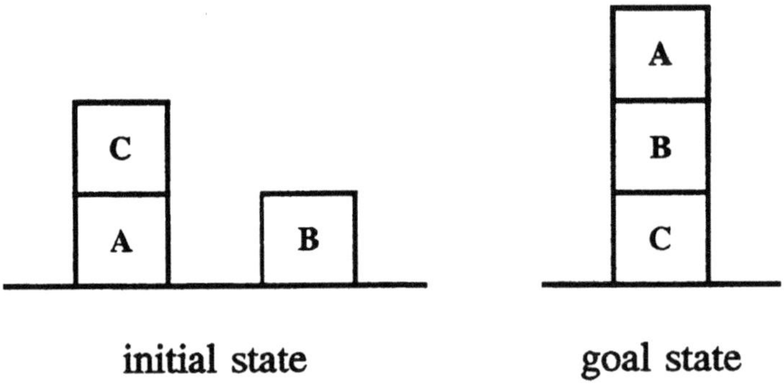

Figure 1: The 3-block problem

We can use LISP to implement a program that could solve the "3-block" problem. We can illustrate this implementation in the following way: The state space of the problem can be expressed by the database LDATA (a variable that expresses a list of facts). The initial state could be presented by the following list:

((ON C A) (ON TABLE B) (EMPTY))

The problem here is to make the LDATA contain (ON B C) and (ON A B), by moving the blocks. Some of the procedures related to the operators are, for instance, the following:

(a) (PUT ON X Y)

This procedure allows the program to take the block X and put on the top of the block Y. If X is already on the top of Y, this does nothing. If there is anything on the top of Y, it takes it off, puts it on the table, and puts X on the top of Y.

(b) (PUT AT X Y)

This is a procedure that puts block X on the top of Y. It is understood there is nothing on the top of Y. If X is already grasped, it is placed on Y, etc.

Turning now to the example of the word problem in physics, we find the same general pattern. There is a state space in which the solution can be found, an initial state, and a goal state. The person (or the program) has to follow a certain basic search pattern. For example, Larkin studied in which way a beginning physics student operates (Larkin, 1981). Larkin wrote a program ("barely ABLE") based on the same strategy. He discovered that the student operates in what he called an *algebraic problem space*. Based on Larkin's work, Stilling (1987) illustrated in which way the student works. To get the optimal solution of a word problem, which consists of variables whose values are given in the initial state of the problem, the student working backward, has to calculate the solution of the problem that is the desired goal state.

Let me consider the following word problem proposed by Stilling:

> An object dropped from a balloon descending at 4 meters per second lands on the ground 10 seconds later. What was the altitude of the balloon at the moment of the object was dropped?

The algebraic problem space, or basic search pattern, could be the following common physical formulas:

$$E1.\ v f = v_o + a t$$
$$E2.\ x = v_o t + .5 a t^2$$
$$E3.\ v_f 2 = v_o 2 + 2 a x$$
$$E4.\ v_a = (v_o + v_f) / 2$$
$$E5.\ x = v_a t \ ;\ a\text{: } 9.8 m / s_2$$

The initial state is the information in the word problem, and the goal state is the solution of the problem.

The search for the solution given by the beginning student is presented in figure 2:

Although solving a problem in physics and solving the "3-block" problem may look different at a first approach, the methods they use have the same general features. For example, both require a previous model, or a basic search pattern, and in both cases the initial and the final state are known. Besides, both use operators that reduce the difference between the initial state of the problem and the desired goal state. In this way they achieve the solution to the problem.

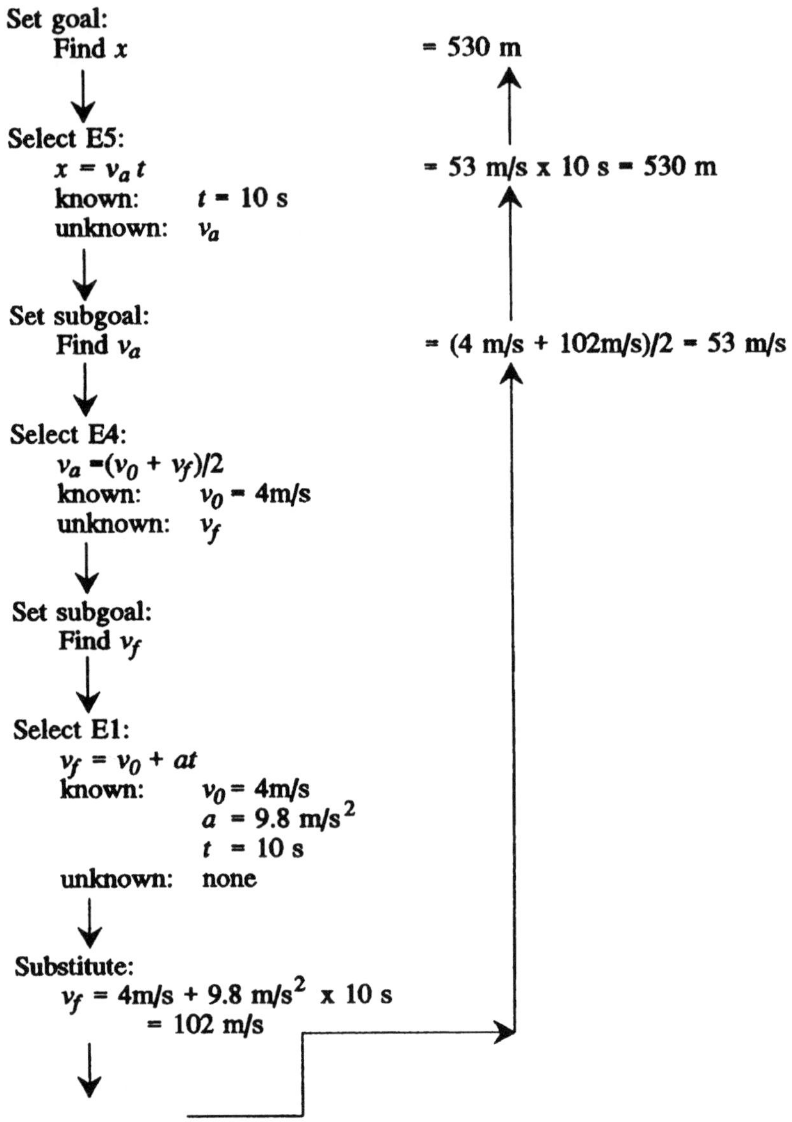

Figure 4: A problem space description of a physical problem

4. Quality *versus* quantity

In order to give a brief logical characterization of abduction, we need the grammar of a first order language and the restrictions of the relevance logic (See Anderson & Belnap, 1975; Dunn, 1986).

The dynamic aspect of the logical mechanism involved in a natural abduction can be explained by using a modified version of the model given by Belnap and Steel (1976; Marostica, 1991).

The standard form of and abductive inference in a first-order language is as follows:

$$\text{(II)} \qquad \frac{\begin{array}{ll} (x)\,(\,Fx \rightarrow_R Gx\,) & \text{(LP)} \\ Ga & \text{(C)} \end{array}}{\begin{array}{ll} Fa & \text{(A)} \end{array}}$$

In the abductive type of inference, the form is not enough to make a distinction between good and bad inferences, because all of them have the same form. In order to avoid the problem of bad abductions, the explanatory hypothesis (A) ought to fulfil several conditions to be good. For Peirce, the most important criteria for good abductions are, first, the *explanatory power* of the hypothesis, i.e., the hypothesis must explain the surprising facts, or part of them (CP 5.189, 1903). The second criterion is *simplicity*, i.e., the hypothesis must be as simple as possible (CP 5.60, 1903).

For making rigorous the explanatory power of a hypothesis, I shall appeal to the *equilibrium principle* (Peirce called this principle "Harmony") involved in Müller's graphs (1989; 1990).

With the help of the *harmony principle*, the mind through qualitative induction, (a type of qualitative checking which hypotheses obtained by abduction might work), can select the hypothesis showing the maximum local harmony (or equilibrium). The following graphs (figure 3) shows the work performed by abduction, with the supervision of qualitative induction:

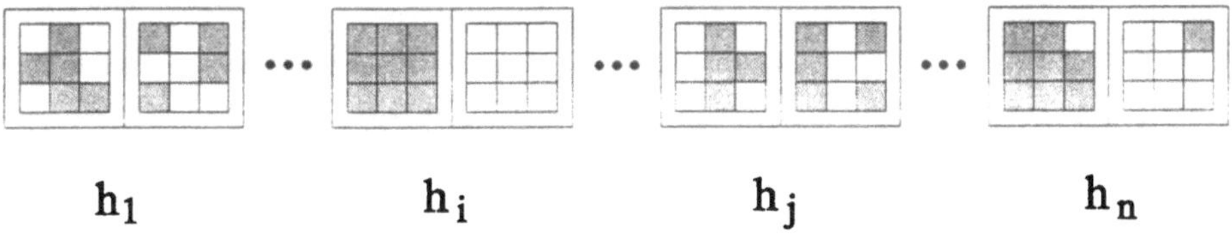

Figure 3: Qualitative induction supervising abduction

Qualitative induction supervises the work performed by the different elements of the semantic hybrid architecture of the process of the scientific inquiry. The local harmony of a hypothesis may vary in each specific situation. Qualitative induction exhibits a *heuristic* function (let us call it *E*) which selects between two possible hypotheses the one with maximum local harmony, namely, that hypothesis that explains with great precision the surprising fact. By using Müller's harmony function and graphs, we may define, informally, the explanatory power of hypotheses in the following way:

(III)
$$E\ (h_i\ ,\ h_j) = \begin{cases} h_i, & if\ H(h_i) > H(h_j) \\ h_j, & otherwise \end{cases}$$

Where "h_i" and "h_j" are sentences of a given language, "$E\ (h_i\ ,\ h_j)$" means "the explanatory power of h_i with respect to h_j", and "$H\ (h_i)$" means "the local harmony of the internal state of "h_j"

For example, if we have a series of explanatory hypotheses for a given surprising fact, in the first search, $E\ (h_i, h_j) = h_i$ because h_i is the most promising hypothesis, i.e., the most harmonious hypothesis.

In order to cope with the problem of *simplicity* as a criterion for good hypotheses, I shall use McCarthy's (1980) circumscription method of non-monotonic reasoning. McCarthy's circumscription is a *rule* of conjecture that can be used by a person (or a program) for jumping to a certain conclusion (For a more complete account, see Marostica, 1991).

McCarthy defines the circumscription formula A(P), by using the predicate parameter ϕ. The following scheme for circumscription describes from the metalanguage a set of well-formed formulas in the object language:

(IV)
$$A(P)/P = df A(\phi/P) \,\&\, (x_1)...(x_n)\ [\phi(x_1,...,x_n) \rightarrow_R P(x_1,...,x_n)] \rightarrow_R \cdot$$
$$(x_1)...(x_n)\ [P(x_1,...,x_n) \rightarrow_R \phi(x_1,...,x_n)]$$

In (IV), A is a statement of first order language containing a predicate P; ϕ is a predicate parameter for which we may substitute an arbitrary expression. The connective $\rightarrow_R$ is the relevance entailment (Dunn, 1986). The second part of the formula, the consequent, is the converse of the first entailment. This is the reason that, in (IV), P and ϕ must coincide.

Let me consider the application of the circumscription rule (IV) to the conclusion of the abductive process related to the conclusion of the abductive process related to the Bayes' theorem (For the application of (IV) to Kepler's case, see Marostica, 1990).

(V) Bayes' theorem is an "interesting" theorem in Confirmation Theory.

[A(*P*)/*P*] Bayes' theorem is a generalization of the H-D Method.

The predicate (P) means "to be a generalization of the H-D Method." In this case, the predicate "P" is related to the relevant and irrelevant elements involved in the application of the Bayes' theorem. For example, among the relevant elements in the predicate "to be a generalization of the H-D method," we have that it is a method of confirming hypothesis *à la* Hempel. Among the irrelevant elements in the application of this theorem, we have the type of probabilities involved in the application. For example, Laplace used the classical conception of probabilities. On the other hand, Salmon (1967) used the relative frequency conception of probabilities. Making a distinction between the relevant and irrelevant type of properties is the natural circumscription performed by anyone using the Bayes' theorem as a method of decision.

Now, in order to express this circumscription in relation to the argument (V), I shall use the circumscription scheme (IV). There we must circumscribe the predicate "to be a generalization of the H-D Method." In a simplified way the scheme (IV) does the job for:

(VI) $\emptyset$(Bayes' theorem) &

$$(x)\ [\emptyset(x) \rightarrow_R \text{Generalization of the H-D Method } (x)] \rightarrow_R \bullet$$

$$[\text{Generalization of the H-D Method } (x) \rightarrow_R \emptyset\ (x)]$$

(VI) means that the predicate parameter ϕ contains only those essential elements included in the predicate of being a generalization of the H-D Method. In that formula Bayes' theorem is one of those entities satisfying the restriction of ϕ. In the second part of the scheme, the essential elements are the only elements considered in the concept of being a generalization of the H-D Method.

5. Automatic abduction?

Turning to Peirce's conception of abduction, we can say that his analysis of this type of reasoning leads to the recognition that abduction is completely different from quantitative induction and occurs prior to this type of reasoning. Besides, Peirce considered abduction, deduction and quantitative induction as different type of inferences. (See Peirce's *Studies in Logic*, 1883)

A very different approach is presented by Thagard (1988). This author tried to incorporate abduction in an artificial intelligence program called PI (Processes of Induction). PI implements "in the programming language

LISP a general model of problem solving and inductive inference..." (*Op. cit.*, p. 15) According to Thagard, PI performs induction only in the context of problem solving. The following graph shows the central activity of PI:

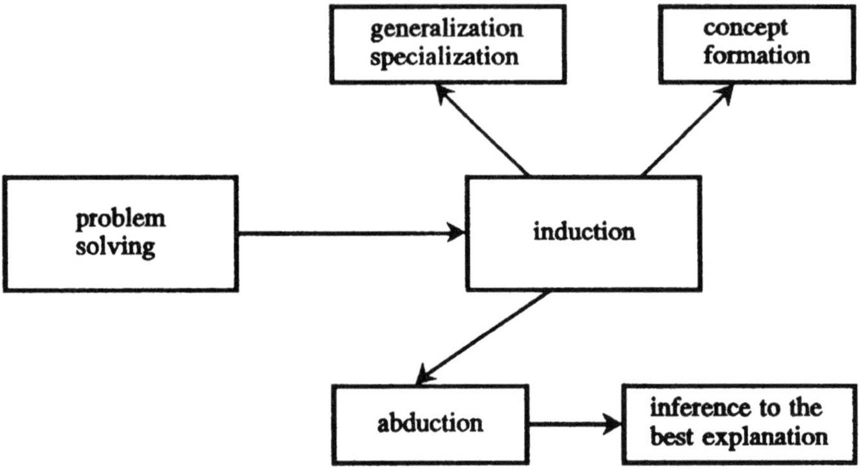

Figure 4: The central role of the process of induction

In this context, abduction depends on problem solving and quantitative induction. The role of deduction is not specified here. Thagard mentions only "novel predictions". It seems to me that predictions in this context, are inductive inferences.

It is not my purpose to discuss Thagard's approach. However, a critical comment is pertinent here. To me his approach involves a deeply anti-Peircean view. For Peirce, abduction is not a type of quantitative induction. Besides, in the process of the scientific inquiry, neither deduction nor induction are creative types of reasoning. Therefore, since predictions have to be either inductive or deductive, there is not such a thing as "novel prediction". I think that all the problems and limitations of PI mentioned by Thagard (*Op. cit.*, pp. 29-30), are due to the role that abduction wrongly has in his approach. Thagard conceives abduction as depending on problem solving and induction. They are different types of inferences.

For Peirce, the process of the scientific inquiry starts with the observation of a surprising fact. Then, the logical mechanism in our minds starts. First, we have the adoption of an explanatory hypothesis (abduction); after that we deduce observable predictions (deduction). Finally, we make an inductive verification of those predictions, and obtain a degree of probability (quantitative verification) (CP 7.202-222, 1901). The role of qualitative induction is to supervise the performance of the whole process. Qualitative induction works by using two heuristic principles, plausibility and verisimilitude. Plausibility performs an heuristic search among the explanatory hypotheses arrived at by abduction. It selects the hypothesis with maximum local harmony. When the job of plausibility is complete, qualitative induction activates deduction in order to predict observable consequences of the hypothesis with the maximum local harmony. After that qualitative induction uses verisimilitude to evaluate if the sample set has the elements required for a good generalization. Finally, qualitative induction allows quantitative induction to generalize for the population set. A graph showing the semantic architecture of the process of the scientific inquiry follows below:

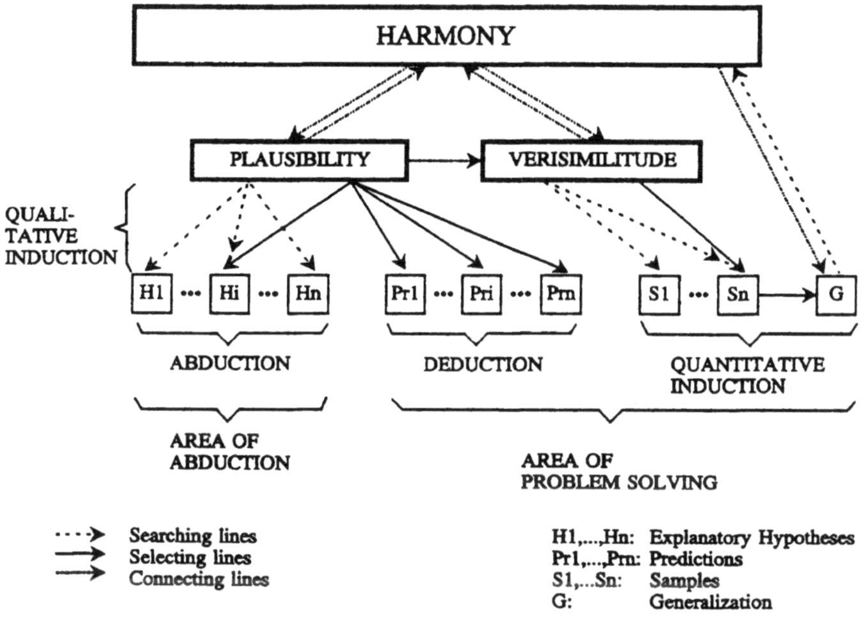

Figure 5: The semantic architecture of the process of scientific inquiry

Turning now to the possibility of implementing the abductive process on a computer, we find that the overall structure of a programming language, such as PASCAL, is the most suitable for that purpose. This is because, in PASCAL, we can implement in a very accurate way and at a given time *harmony* functions and principles, that are important elements ruling the performance of abduction.

The purpose of this paper is not to write an actual PASCAL program, but to give a pseudo code of what I consider the main features of an actual implementation of abduction in PASCAL.

The program heading may vary according to the specific abductive process we are considering. For example, in the case of Bayes' theorem, we may have:

```
PROGRAM INTERESTING (INPUT, OUTPUT, EXPERTS)
(*THIS PROGRAM EVALUATES INTERESTING THEOREMS IN CONFIR-
MATION THEORY*)
```

Some description of the data in the declaration part of the program could be, for instance, the definition of an external file (the file connected to the semantic architecture supervised by qualitative induction explained above). We can call that file EXPERTS. It provides the program with the relevant information of what is considered "interesting" (or "boring") in a specific field. The information given by the experts related to the file EXPERTS will allow, as well, the program to perform circumscription to the conclusion of abduction.

In the variable declaration part, we must introduce the objects of the system through the different types of variables. In the example of Bayes' theorem, we may have the following variables: THEOREM, METHOD, EVALUATION, etc.

In the procedure declaration we have the declaration of the criteria for good abduction. The criteria are types of procedure related to semantic rules (or EBNF rules, i.e., Extended Backus-Naur Forms).

The criterion of *explanatory power* (given in definition III) could be implemented in the following way:

PROCEDURE EXPLANATORY POWER
(VAR A,B: BOOLEAN EXPRESSION)
BEGIN
IF $(H\ (h_A) > H\ (h_B)$**THEN** WRITE (h_A)
ELSE WRITELN (h_B)
END

The second criterion of *simplicity*, or circumscription, could have the following implementation:

```
PROCEDURE SIMPLICITY
VAR    A: BOOLEAN EXPRESSION
       O: RELEVANT PREDICATE PARAMETER
       P: PREDICATE
```

```
BEGIN
IF A (SUBS (O,P))
AND R-ENTAILS (O(x_n), P(x_n))
THEN R-ENTAILS ( P(X_n), O(X_n))
END
```

Among the special heuristic algorithms in the declaration part, we could have the declaration of the relational R-ENTAILMENT and the implementation of the local harmony function. The global harmony function belongs to the semantic architecture discussed above.

The implementation of the R-ENTAILMENT function could be as follows:

```
FUNCTION R-ENTAILS (A, B: BOOLEAN EXPRESSION):
TRUTH VALUE;
BEGIN (*ENTAILS*)
IF H(h_A) > H(h_B) THEN R-ENTAILS: = TRUE
ELSE R-ENTAILS: = FALSE
END
```

The above procedure is the one that captures the logical definition of the *relevant entailment*:

(VII)
$$I(h_A \rightarrow_R h_B) = \begin{cases} T, \text{ if } H(h_A) > H(h_B), \\ F, \text{ otherwise} \end{cases}$$

Where "I" is an interpretation of a first order language, h_A and h_B are sentences, "$\rightarrow_R$" is the relevant entailment, and "$H(h_A)$" means "the local harmony of h_A". (VII) is the procedure in which a statement changes the local harmony in the direction of truth, or maximum local harmony.

The global Harmony function, known from neural network theory, is composed by many local Harmony functions. The global and Local Harmony functions were implemented on PASCAL by Müller (1990). The Harmony functions (global and local) in the simplest version says:

(VII)
$$H = \sum_i \sum_j W_{ij} X_i X_j$$

Where "X_i" and "X_j" are points, or vectors of the search state space, "W_{ij}" is a parameter linking X_i and X_j. W_{ij} accurately gives the values of the strength of the connection between X_i and X_j to the database EXPERTS, (in this way it links different domains). The Maximum of the Harmony function is obtained by forcing the system to go in a certain direction.

In order to force a system to change or move, that system needs a disturbing element that will introduce a change inside it. The local Harmony function will allow that system to remove the disturbing element and to reach equilibrium (or harmony). The values of the Harmony function will vary according to the changes of the disturbing element introduced inside the system. The values obtained by the Harmony function are only approximations because the Harmony function works in a heuristic way.

In abduction, the disturbing element is the surprising fact (C). This fact functions as a driving force that impels the system to change in the direction of an explanatory hypothesis (A) that will restore the lost equilibrium, or harmony. (CP 5.372-374, 1877)

Turning back to the implementation of the abduction in PASCAL, we may have in the statement part of the program "*harmony statements*". Those actions statements will give the group of instructions that cause the computer to carry out certain actions. These statements are the ones ruling the process. They could be compound statements having the form:

WHILE BOOLEAN EXPRESSION DO STATEMENT

To sum up: the purpose of automated abduction, (helped by Harmony functions, working in the whole system which is a hybrid architecture), is to create the model or basic search pattern that can help the program to find the best explanatory hypothesis for a given surprising fact. The surprising fact, as a disturbing element, could be provided by the environment (this environment could include human beings, even other machines).

If creativity can be considered as depending upon the development of a large, rich, organized, and accessible store of information, abductive programs can be creative, too. They can create the model by connecting fields that were disconnected before. Abduction can create the model with the help of the information given by the experts belonging to the semantical hybrid architecture. The heuristic results given by automated abduction will be correct most of the time. In the same way, human abduction yields good results most of the time, but not always. Automatic abduction will parallel systems in the real world.

6. Conclusion

The main differences between the processes of abduction and problem solving can be summarize as follows: (i) abduction is creative, because it has, what Peirce called *il lume naturale* or illumination, that is the essential ingredient of a creative process. Abduction employs qualitative procedures when it is trying to find the best explanatory hypothesis for a given surprising fact. (ii) In contrast, classical problem solving models are not creative, and employ mechanical procedures (i.e., repetitive and fixed procedures) that are efficient for solving mainly mathematical or quantitative types of problems. (iii) Even though abduction and problem solving can be considered in a broad sense as types of explanations, abduction is the process that creates the model or basic search pattern to be used in creating the goal state (the explanatory hypothesis). At the beginning of abduction, we know only the surprising fact, or initial state. In the problem solving process, however, we have already the basic search pattern. Besides, the initial and goal states are known from the beginning.

Finally, my tentative pseudo code is obviously only an outline for the implementation of abduction in a PASCAL program, using Müller's neural network theory and Harmony functions. These functions are necessary, because by using those functions at the global and local level, we can implement programs that works approximately in the same way that natural systems do.

References

Anderson, A., Belnap, N.D. Jr. (1975). *The Logic of Relevance and Necessity*. Princeton, New Jersey: Princeton University Press.

Belnap, N.D. Jr., Steel, T.B. (1976). *The Logic of Questions and Answers*. New Haven and London: Yale University Press.

Dunn, M. (1986). Relevance Logic and Entailment. In: *Handbook of Philosophical Logic* III, 117-224.

Gilhooly, K. (1982). *Thinking Directed, Undirected and Creative*. London: Academic Press.

Laplace, P.S. de (1798). *Exposition du système du monde*. Paris.

Laplace, P.S. de (1814). *Essai philosophique sur les probabilites*. Paris.

Larkin, J.H. (1981). Enriching Formal Knowledge: A Model for Learning to Solve Textbook Physics Problems. In: N.J. Anderson (ed.), *Cognitive Skills and Their Acquisition*, New Jersey: Erlbaum Associates, 122-138.

Marostica, A. (1990). Mind. A Sign Creator. In: Proceedings of the Deutsche Gesellschaft fur Semiotik (DGS) e.V. 6. Internationaler Kongress. Universität Passau.

Marostica, A. (1991). The Nonmonotonic Approach to Tychist Logic. In: N. Houser e.a. (eds.), *Studies in the Logic of Charles Sanders Peirce*, Bloomington: Indiana University Press.

Müller, A. (1989). Signal Systems as Emergent Properties of Interacting Processes - Signs and Meaning in Artificial Intelligence." In: *Proceedings of the IV Congress of the International Association for Semiotic Studies (IASS).* Barcelona-Perpignan.

Müller, A., Neumann, J. (1990). Classification with Neural Networks. In: Bock, H., Ihm, P. (eds.), *Classification, Data Analysis, and Knowledge Organization.* Berlin/New York: Springer, pp. 32-42.

Newell, A. (1980). Reasoning, Problem Solving, and Decision Procedures: The Problem Space as a Fundamental Category. In: R.S. Nickerson (ed.), *Attention and Performance* VIII, Hillsdale, N.J.: Erlbaum Associates.

Peirce, Ch.S. (1960). *Collected Papers of Charles S. Peirce.* Vol. I-VIII. ed. Hartshorne Ch., Weiss P., and Burks A.W. Cambridge, Mass.: The Belknap Press of Harvard University Press.

Peirce, Ch.S. (1967). *Manuscripts and Letters. As Arranged in Annotate Catalog of the Papers of Charles S. Peirce.* ed. R.S. Robin Cambridge, Mass.: University of Massachusetts Press.

Salmon, W.C. (1967). *The Foundations of Scientific Inferences.* Pittsburgh: University of Pittsburgh Press.

Shimony, A. (1970). Scientific Inference. In: R. Colodny (ed.), *The Nature and Function of Scientific Theories,* Pittsburgh: University of Pittsburgh Press, 79-172.

Stilling, N.A. (1987). *Cognitive Science: An Introduction.* Cambridge, Mass.: The MIT Press.

Thagard, P. (1988). *Computational Philosophy of Science.* Cambridge, Mass.: The MIT Press.

Expert systems and the abductive circle

G. LUGER & C. STERN (Albuquerque)

0. Abstract

The current generation of expert systems is becoming more and more successful at functioning in a collaborative role with human users in abductive problem solving. We first show how these systems implement a symbol processing architecture which allows for a cyclical pattern of description, explanation, and action. We next analyze the structure of abductive problem solving and evaluate the ability of current expert systems to engage in a semiotic interpretation of evidence. We show where epistemological understanding has not kept pace with expert system problem solving practice. Finally, we argue that a new epistemology, based on a clearer understanding of abductive problem solving, could provide a basis for integrating many of the tools now emerging from areas of A.I. research.

1. Introduction

Expert systems problem solving was one of the first A.I. technologies to migrate on a large scale from the research environment to a commercial setting. An important part of the widespread use and success of expert systems has been their adaptability to many problem solving contexts. This adaptability has involved the integration of a variety of knowledge representation and reasoning techniques.

In the section 1.1 we trace the roots of A.I. programming techniques in structuralist models of problem solving. We examine exploratory programming, proof trees and rules stacks, and show how these tools have been used to describe and explain the problem solving process. We then show how much of the versatility of expert systems derives from the robustness of these original techniques. In section 1.2 we point out many of the current limitations of expert systems, including brittleness, and lack of meta-level integration, and the inability to model common sense.

In section 2 we analyze abductive problem solving, describing an architecture which includes interwoven elements of description, explanation and intervention. We give an example from our own expert system development work of abductive problem solving in the area of discrete semiconductor failure analysis.

Finally, in section 3, we propose an epistemological foundation for current expert systems practice that offers a possibility of extending their semiotic sophistication.

1.1 Expert systems: a "use driven" technology

Seymour Papert in the mid-1960s described for the computing and education communities what has come to be referred to as "exploratory programming". Papert exemplified this approach with his LOGO language coupled with the use of "turtle graphics" and an interactive programming environment. Papert first proposed this methodology as part of a theory of education where a program actively represented a student's reasoning process in a particular situation and the computer's interpretation of the student's code allowed the student to comprehend problems, called "bugs," in his or her thought process (Papert, 1980). Figure 1 shows a student's code/thought of a tree with the computer's interpretation demonstrating "bugs" in the thought process. Progressive refinement of the tree code, first adding a recursive termination condition, and then creating a "procedure invariance" so that the turtle ends each recursive call having the same orientation with which it started, finally produces the intended result.

Papert's ideas are built on the Piagetian (structuralist) paradigm in psychology, where humans learn new relationships in their world through a process of accommodation to discrepancies in the structures of their current understanding. In this "genetic epistemology" new invariances constantly update and replace current limited (buggy) understandings of situations. Papert translated these ideas into a computational environment and they subsequently became an important aspect of the artificial intelligence and expert systems programming methodology.

Expert systems designers use exploratory programming under several guises, but most importantly in exploring the problem space and in developing the early prototype. We explore the problem space of an application to determine the salient features for a program design. These features might include the choice of data or goal driven inferencing, of breadth, depth of best first search strategies, or representation through decision trees, rule systems, objects or some hybrid combination. Throughout this process we seek to align the computer's interpretive process with that of the human expert interpreting the phenomena of the problem situation.

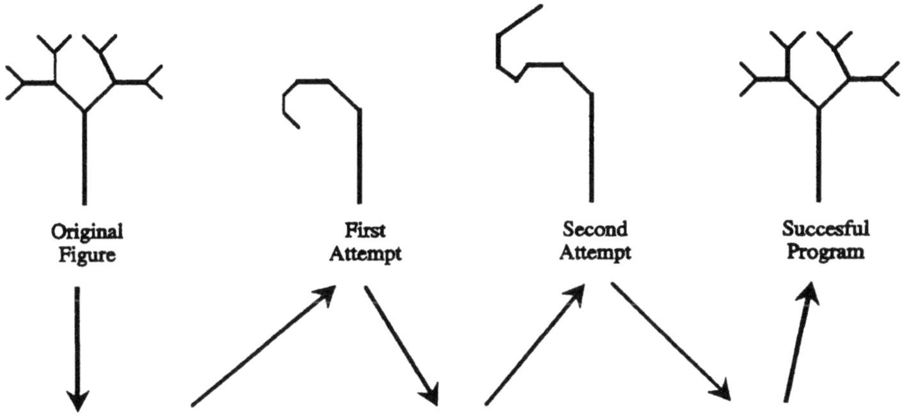


```
TO TREE :SIZE
FD :SIZE
LT 20
TREE :SIZE/2
RT 40
TREE :SIZE/2
END
```

```
TO TREE :SIZE
IF :SIZE<2 [STOP]
FD :SIZE
LT 20
TREE :SIZE/2
RT 40
TREE :SIZE/2
END
```

```
TO TREE :SIZE
IF :SIZE<2 [STOP]
FD :SIZE
LT 20
TREE :SIZE/2
LT 20
BK :SIZE
END
```

Figure 1: The progressive refinement method used to develop the computer code for drawing a tree

Once the base representation and search strategies are selected the expert system designer begins to fashion the rules or knowledge structures of the particular application. In developing the early prototype the A.I. programmer attempts to fashion a knowledge base reflective of the expert's interpretation of the application. In this situation it is perfectly acceptable to say, "Even though I don't know the full details of what I am doing, let me explore with a few ideas..." Through this progressive refinement model, the computer's interpretation, directly reflecting the programmer's evolving understanding of the domain, gradually comes to capture the understanding and interpretative skills of the human expert working in that application area.

Exploratory programming has come to be one of the designer's most important tools. John McDermott, in reflecting on his preliminary work and successes in building the computer configuration program, XCON, at Digital (McDermott 1981; McDermott & Bachant, 1984) insists that the exploratory programming methodology made his program possible, whereas two previous attempts by Digital, not using a very high level language and the exploratory methodology, had failed at the task.

We include as Figure 2 a flow chart describing the exploratory programming model. There are two important features: first, try an idea and see if it works, in particular "watch where it fails", and revise (the code representing) your idea accordingly.

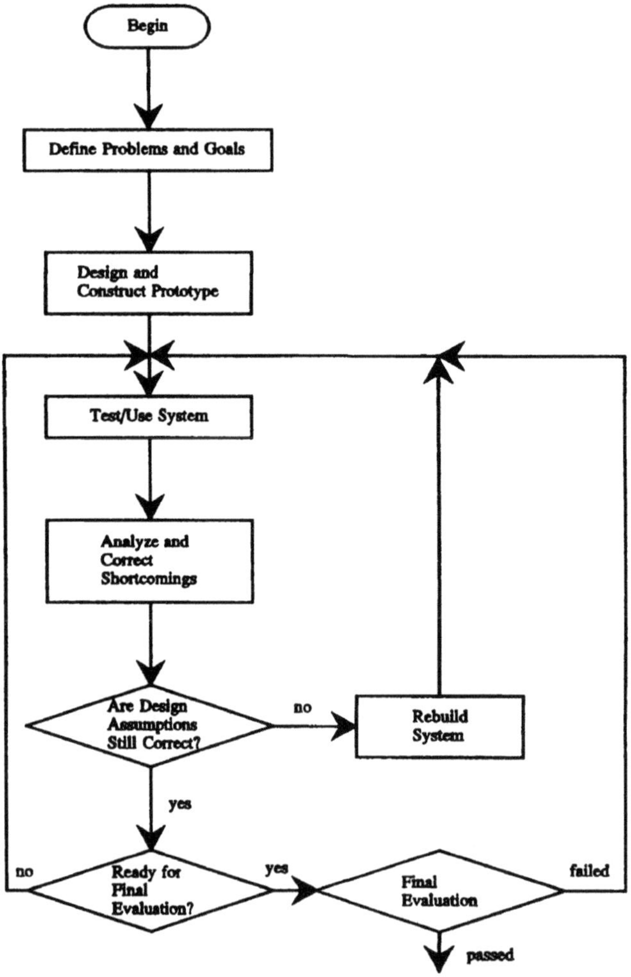

Figure 2: The explanatory development cycle for rule based expert systems

The second feature is, once the designer has worked through the thought process until the application is understood, be ready to scrap the rule or object design that resulted from the exploratory mode, and rewrite it from the beginning to reflect directly the new understanding of the problem situation. When McDermott did this with an early version of the XCON program he found that he could build a program of identical competencies with one third fewer rules, from 750 down to 500 (McDermott, 1981).

An important A.I. tool to assist in the exploratory approach is a powerful user interface design. With the object-oriented interface first seen in Interlisp and the Smalltalk world at Xerox PARC, and later reflected in the Flavors environment at MIT, active tracing and debugging tools have became a part of the expert system designer's tool kit. Besides offering an important assist in removing syntactical miscues, the interface allows the designer to oversee the computer's interpretive process. With the assistance of a sophisticated interface, the program designer is able to view failure within the context of the interpretive process.

The exploratory programming methodology, combined with the rule or object centered data structure, makes it possible for the program designer to view an appropriately grained analysis of miscues. This allows the programmer to see misconceptions in the context where they occur. A proof tree or rule stack gives the exact location in the computer's interpretative process of the programmer's misconception. This means, of course, that the program designer is dealing not just with some abstract mistake (array variable out of bounds, stack underflow) but a conceptual mistake in the context of an interpretation (this disk drive requires two controllers and there are no such devices available).

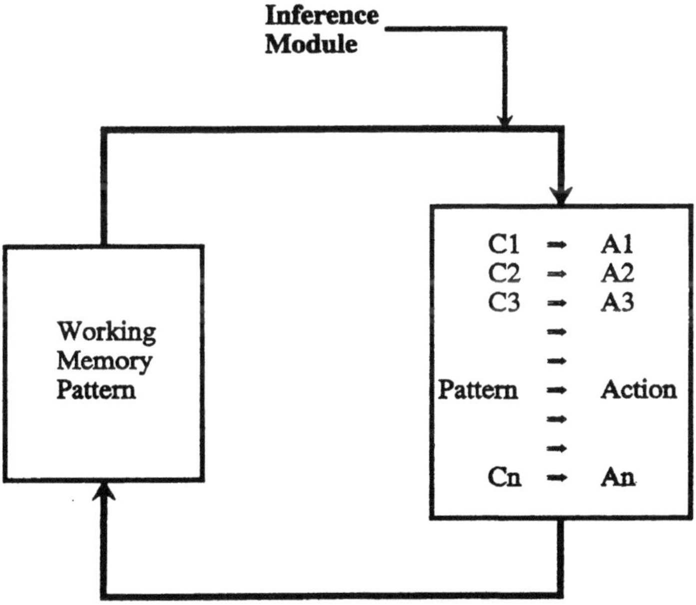

Figure 3: The production system architecture. The inference module takes patterns from working memory to the rule set and returns revised patterns

To make this notion of "interpretive context" for rule debugging clear, we offer a simple example. Using a expert system controller such as the traditional production system, rule based inferencing exactly reflects progress through an and/or graph, and that graph gives the context for each rule as it is interpreted. Figure 3 presents a diagram of the production system model of computing with its traditional division of logic (the encoded rules of expertise) from inference engine. The inference module goes to the rule base with the context of the information in working memory to match a production rule and generate another step in the search process.

The rule stack, as part of working memory, reflects the progress through the graph of possible solutions. With each successful rule invocation, that rule is placed on the stack. Thus, if the user is asked a question (does the probe light register positive?) the program can present the rule as the justification as to why the question was asked (because if the probe light registers positive and ... then the fault is in ...). If and when a rule later fails to be part of a successful solution path, it is popped off the rule stack. Thus the stack reflects both the chaining of rules together and the context of any particular interpretation. A reflection of the rule stack as progress through a graph is given as figure 4.

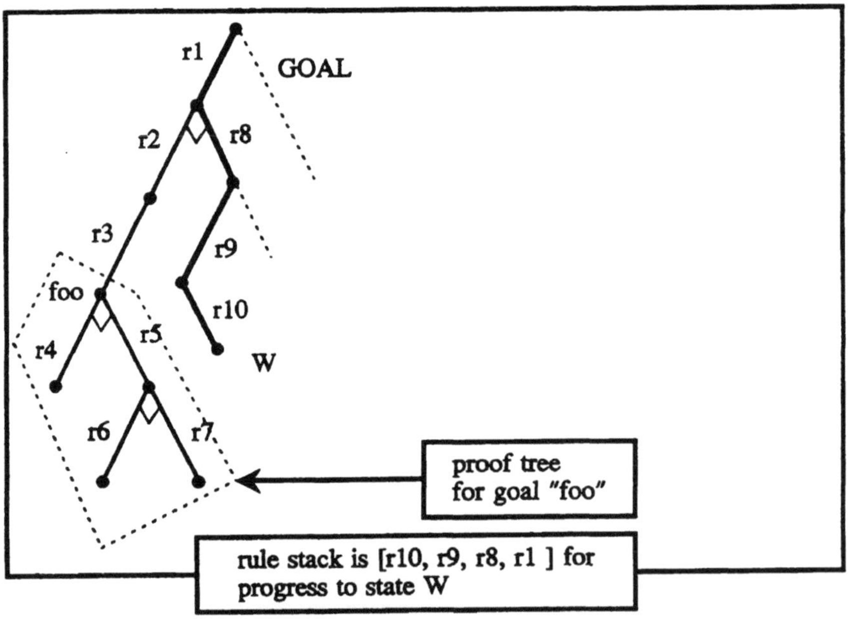

Figure 4: Proof tree that reflects reasoning

The result of any solution, or even partial solution in the problem is reflected in a proof tree. A proof tree is that portion of the graph, along with the path through its states, that captures the completed reasoning process in the problem or subproblem. When the program designer and later the user asks the system "How did you come up with this particular result?," the program responds with the proof tree that reflects its reasoning in that situation. This situation is captured in Figure 4, where the user has asked the program how it knows "foo" is true. The encircled portion of the graph is the system's response.

Two important points can be made from the analysis of the proof tree and rule stack concepts: First, in exploratory programming mode, the designer or programmer has an interpretive context for understanding her misconceptions or bugs. Her mistakes are made in a context, and interpreting and correcting them is a conceptual accommodation (in the full genetic epistemological sense) to the world as it is. The second point is that the eventual expert system user is also always problem solving in a context. Accompanied by a rule stack with solutions reflected in proof trees, inference rules and explanations are fundamentally linked to a focus or context, that is, they are interpretations.

The explanation/justification powers of the expert system methodology are a hallmark of this genre of programs: if the justification of decisions in the search process is not available, the program is not an expert system. As we see in subsequent sections explanations are also an essential part of human communication, and even more mature justifications will be part of our description of the abductive circle: requirements for a symbol system to achieve semiosis.

Current research in expert systems is attempting to address difficult problems, such as the design of intelligent editors to help, by automation of the process, the human domain expert interact with the expert system program in debugging the knowledge base. The Teiresias work at Stanford (Davis, 1982; Davis & Lenat, 1982) shows us an example. A "metatheory" of the MYCIN rule base was built for the domain expert to reason about the objects (rules and facts) in the MYCIN knowledge base. Using "schemas" the Stanford researchers built explicit models of classes of rules. These schemas contained information on how to create new instances of a class of objects, how information about a set of rules is to be obtained, how certain infections can enter the system, and so on. In the dialogue below, when the doctor attempts to enter a new rule in the knowledge base, Teiresias is able to "understand" it, attempt to enter it into a class of already existing rules, and to determine why the rule is not appropriate.

T: Is there a rule missing?
D: Yes

T: Would you like to give me such a rule now?
D: Yes.

If	1. The patient's infection is primary-bacteremia
	2. The site is one of the sterile sights
Then	There is suggestive evidence (.8) that the category is enterobacteriacae.

(Teiresias parses this rule into its internal representation and then presents it again so the expert can check it. After the expert agrees, Teiresias attempts to integrate this new rule into the knowledge base....)

T: I hate to criticize, Dr Davis, but did you know that most rules about what the category of an organism might be that mention the site of a culture, and the infection also mention the portal of entry of the organism? Shall I try to write a clause to account for this?
D: Yes
T: How about:
The portal of entry is gastrointestinal. OK?
D: Yes

The proof tree and rule stack are also used by Teiresias, as one would expect, in the debugging process. Teiresias asks the user if a particular rule stack or proof tree justification are appropriate in a situation. Teiresias is in effect asking the human doctors if their interpretation is the same as MYCIN's interpretation of a particular medical situation! Teiresias also provides a "meta-meta" level where new schemas, for new classes of rules can be created.

In spite of this growth and widespread adoption of the expert systems methodology, there has been no unifying computational epistemology that has kept pace with these evolutionary developments. The theoretical understanding of expert system problem solving has remained rooted in the denotational semantics of Tarski and the deductive model of human problem solving.

Even the so called "uncertain" reasoning systems, using techniques such as the Stanford Certainty Factor Algebra (Buchanan & Shortliffe, 1984) and Zadeh's fuzzy set theory (Zadeh, 1983; Luger & Stubblefield, 1989), are seen as weak deductive methods rather than as genuine instances of an inference process. Many expert systems technologists, with their rationalist origins, seem comfortable only with deductive inference. Sound inference schemes may make good mathematical theorem provers but they make little psychological sense. We believe that these and other problem solving processes which expert systems use are by and large abductive in nature. Furthermore, we feel that the epistemological foundations of expert problem solving requires a more sophisticated account of the functioning of symbol systems and the role of interpretation.

In this context we will define the abductive circle. Roughly, this term refers to the linkage of description, explanation, and action within the context of abductive problem solving. We believe that the need for expert systems to capture this dimension of problem solving in humans has motivated the incorporation of features that support abductive problem solving. We will propose a theoretical account of abduction which we believe will provide direction for the future evolution of expert system technology. Before we do this we will briefly mention several of the current limitations of the expert or knowledge based technology.

1.2 Current limitations of the expert systems technology

Despite their successes, expert systems are still subject to a number of fundamental limitations. We see these limitations as a reflection of the semiotic poverty of our current knowledge representation and reasoning techniques. We enumerate several of these limitations before continuing with our definition of abductive circularity.

Brittleness: This correlates with simplistic sharp-edged concept modeling. Brittleness comes from two aspects of the current technology. First, a Tarskian semantics that maps elements of a symbol system onto items "in the world." We feel this simplistic mathematical approach to a semantic model is fundamentally flawed, as we discuss in subsequent sections. Second, the matching algorithms in expert systems, so crucial for chaining rules as well as matching rules to descriptions of the world, are performed by simplistic, context independent techniques such as unification (Luger & Stubblefield, 1989). Matching is never within a context that could support near (syntactic) misses, alternative (equivalent) descriptions, or any guidance based on deeper (semantic) understanding.

Shallow versus deep reasoning: The "shallowness" of a problem specification is sometimes related to surface or descriptive, rather than deep, explanatory, or semantic representations. In MYCIN, for example, medical situations are often described by temperature levels and presence of nausea and headaches, rather than explained through a theory of bacterial infecting agents. The failure to produce a solution with the shallow model is sometimes responded to by model-based reasoning (Iwasaki, 1989). Transfer between different levels of reasoning remains an unsolved problem due to the lack of semantic cohesion between the representational levels (Skinner & Luger, 1991).

Weak explanation facilities: This is related to the previous point. The best expert systems currently produce explanations which are built from literal statements of rules from the rule stack or rebuilt into proof trees. Explanation in humans is a much richer process, often including deeper clues to the "intervention process" and the eventual problem solution. For example, human explanations often include contexts for switching between shallow and deep reasoning models (Skinner & Luger, 1991).

Lack of (semantic) metalevel integration: Rule based expert systems, or even rule sets attached to object based specifications are little more than a loosely coupled collection of information. We refer to this as the "woodpile" model of skill representation: when you want to encode a new skill just write it in an if.. then.. format and throw it into the pile of other rules. Rules can be modular and "additive" to the point of absurdity. What is desired is (at the minimum) more metalevel coherence. The exception to this approach, and important data points in meta level modeling are the Metadendral and Teiresias research (Lindsay et al., 1980; Buchanan, 1984).

Common sense: Common sense in human problem solvers functions in background to support flexibility of expertise. We don't know how to model this background knowledge very well. This skill is related to our embodiment in the world and our repository of basic motor and coping skills (Winograd & Flores, 1986). We discuss these ideas further in subsequent sections.

Difficulty in paradigm selection for expert reasoning systems: At the present time there does not exist a mechanism under which we can decide which problems or classes of problems will be amenable to the expert systems approach. In many cases the way to deal with this decision is to engage in exploratory programming, a semiotic exploration of the problem solving space.

Lack of learning potential: The present generation of knowledge based systems lacks even rudimentary potential to automatically integrate new information, even that from successful runs, into its knowledge base. Current research in model and case based reasoning offer hope in this regard.

The account of abduction offered in this paper we believe will show both the sources of these limitations and a means for addressing and overcoming them.

2. Expert problem solving and abduction

2.1 Introduction

Expert systems manipulate symbolic representations. Their computations are symbolic in two senses. First, they manipulate non-numeric symbols representing qualitative properties and relationships. Second, it is intended that these symbols have the same internal or computational semantics as that attributed to them by the human user.

In order to encode the knowledge of an expert, the expert system designer must have a clear view of the semantics of the symbols which the expert uses. In this section we shall argue that such a view requires an understanding of the functioning of symbol systems within a fundamentally abductive problem solving process.

Symbol systems serve as instruments for the effective interaction of experts and their problem-solving domain. They organize and codify the domain phenomena as well as the expert's understanding and response to those phenomena. The semantic structure of the expert's symbol system cannot be divorced from the problem solving knowledge to which it gives form. The three phases of problem solving, description, explanation, and intervention, are inextricably linked together as three aspects of a single problem solving practice. What weaves them together is an abductive structure embodied in the semantic linkages of the expert's symbol system.

We now flesh out these observations by showing that the semantics of the expert's language is defined by its relationship to description, explanation, and action, and that this semantics carries the linkages between these three phases of the problem solving process (see figure 5). We also observe the abductive character of this problem solving in the dynamic alternation of these phases.

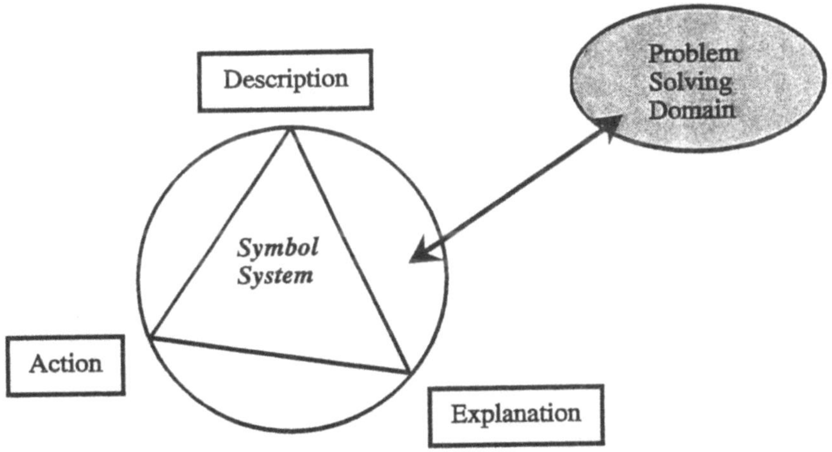

Figure 5: The abductive circle

Description:

Problem solving begins with a description of the problematic situation. This description is more than a list of facts innocently gathered and assembled from the problem solving environment. The effective selection of facts and the ordering of these facts into a coherent description presupposes 1) an ability to recognize in the situation features and constellations of potential significance and 2) fluency in a set of domain specific descriptive forms. Novices can rarely recognize and isolate the salient features of a situation, and their descriptions are often full of omissions and irrelevancies. This is of course why doctors and auto mechanics refuse to make diagnoses on the basis of a layman's description. Domain experts stand indeed further above their less skilful colleagues in their ability to construct descriptions which are at the same time both more concise and more revealing.

Problem solving generally begins with an initial description of the problem solving situation. This description is then developed and elaborated in conjunction with a process of inquiry. New information is acquired through measurement, testing, interviewing, etc., information which is then reintegrated into the situation description.

The acquisition and integration of new information has associated costs in time and resources. This process thus requires focus and direction from a goal or set of goals in order for the effort to efficiently converge. These goals are formed by the expert's response to the current state of the description, its completeness or incompleteness, its coherent or anomalous character, the categorizations and explanations which it suggests. At various stages of the inquiry, the expert will adopt an hypothesis or set of hypotheses. These then direct the course of inquiry until they are refuted or replaced by more probable hypotheses. This means that the elaboration of the description is an ongoing, abductive process organized and informed by the expert's domain knowledge.

Description and explanation do not represent distinct and separate processes but rather locations in a continuum. Description evolves, in the process of inquiry and elaboration, in the direction of explanation. At each stage in the process the description projects, through its structure and content, a certain presence or absence of intelligible form. The description may initially be sketchy and incomplete, too inchoate to allow for any explanation. Later it may contain aspects which are coherent and which suggest a spectrum of possible explanations, and others which are anomalous and which drive inquiry further. Finally, if the inquiry is successful and the problem situation matches closely one of prototypical or well understood cases, then the description may be so lucid and self-explanatory as to require only the most perfunctory explanation. The progress of the problem solving process thus involves an adaptive interaction between descriptive and explanatory forms, an interaction mediated in part by the semantic relations implicit in the expert's symbol system.

Explanation:

Explanation of a situation is relative to description of the situation: how we specify *what* is to be explained partly determines *how* it is to be explained. The relationship is, however, bidirectional. Explanation may locate key features of the situation which determine others; this may in turn lead us to change the organization and structure of our description.

Classical theories of explanation have tended to focus on law and causality. Hempel (1965), for example, elaborates a view of scientific explanation as a process of connecting the particular situation to the operation of general or universal laws of nature. The general form of explanation is thus that of subsuming the particular under the universal. (There is a rough correspondence between this and the proof tree model of explanation in current expert systems: The rules involved in the proof correspond to the "universal laws".)

Currently work is underway in A.I. to develop a formal model of abductive explanation. One account is that of Levesque (1989) who proposes a definition of abductive explanation in terms of a (mathematical) relation called EXPLAIN. The sense of this relation is given by the axiom:

$$\text{EXPLAIN}_e((P \rightarrow Q), Q, P)$$

which is interpreted as follows: If, in a given epistemic state *e*, P together with the background beliefs of that state entails Q, then P is one explanation for Q relative to *e*. We have shown (Stern and Luger, 1991) that entailment-based accounts of explanation fail to capture the semantic characteristics of *good* explanations, e.g., edification (non-triviality), clarity and coherence.

To this we add that the characterization of explanation must be domain- and context-specific. Expert explanations take many different forms (not merely subsumption of the particular under a universal rule). The defining feature that all these differing forms have in common is that they serve a purpose in the expert's problem solving process, providing direction for further inquiry or problem solving intervention.

Abduction, hypothesis, and intervention:

Problem solving under limitations of time and/or resources requires a special form of reasoning and decision making. The expert must navigate in conditions of uncertainty, using a method of informed hypothesis to find an expeditious path to a solution. While uncertainty is an unavoidable concomitant of the journey, it must be minimized by the time the destination is reached.

The formulation of an hypothesis serves either as a means to focus the course of inquiry or as a prelude to action. In both cases, the hypothesis stands between the problem description, on the one hand, and a decision or commitment on the other. The hypothesis functions as an explanation of currently known facts and at the same time as the ground of a commitment either i) to the verifiability of certain new facts or ii) to the success of a certain form of intervention. In both cases, the hypothesis represents the abductive gathering of known and unknown, of past and future.

Hypothesis formation relies both on a body of theory and a body of experience. While the theory provides the descriptive terms and linkages which comprise the fabric of the explanation, experience provides a set of successfully handled or well-explained cases which schematize the application of the theory. Often the formulation will begin with the postulation of a relationship between the current instance and some previous instance(s), a set of correspondences and differences which locate the current instance in a space of paradigmatic cases.

The case-based hypothesis is then elaborated through a mapping process, where the domain theory together with these correspondences are used to extract testable consequences or a tentative course of action. It is generally here that the expert's skill is most sharply distinguished from that of the newly schooled novice. While the novice may possess the same abstract level of theoretical understanding, the expert's richer background of interpreted experience allows her to identify suggestive patterns in the domain phenomena and to formulate hypotheses which focus problem solving more quickly and effectively.

The expert's problem solving is organized to serve two purposes: to provide effective problem resolution and also to provide significant feedback about the problem solving situation. If the intervention is unsuccessful, the results of the intervention should provide as much information as possible about what didn't work and why. The interpreted results should be able to inform the direction of continued efforts.

Even if the intervention is successful, the results of the intervention must still be evaluated. The expert must *know* that it is successful and have a clear understanding of why it worked. The expert must have confidence in the solution and a well defined set of expectations about when it will work again in the future. The reason for this is that the expert's problem solving is not, in general a "single shot" process; it is part of an ongoing evolving practice. To achieve the capacity for adaptability and growth, the expert's interaction with the environment must be organized from the outset dialogically. This involves a semiotic structure in which the outcome of the interaction is itself a message, a carrier of useful information which can be folded back into the expert's problem solving representations.

2.2 Abductive problem solving: an example

In this section we present an example of expert problem solving derived from one of our current projects. We are designing a "discrete semiconductor failure analysis expert system" for Sandia National Laboratories. "Discrete semiconductor" here refers to transistors and diodes as opposed to integrated circuits.

Failure analysis, in this case, is generally performed on a device with which the expert is already familiar. Either he or someone in his work team was involved in drafting a procurement specification for the device and in evaluating original manufacturer's samples. Based on this initial understanding of the device, the expert is responsible for monitoring the device through its life cycle. This means assisting in the handling of problems in the manufacturing process, in incoming-receiving inspection, circuit assembly, and finally, in the field.

Detecting the source of failures requires demanding detective work. There are several different potential problem sources. These include:

i) Problems in the manufacturing process, such as volatile or particle contamination, improper bonding or welding, improper or inconsistent silicon doping, or a cracked silicon chip.
ii) Device level design problems, such as adjacent materials which are chemically reactive or bonded materials with different coefficients of expansion.
iii) Screening problems[1], such as a screen that is not tight enough or does not cover the right characteristics.
iv) Handling problems, such as damage due to faulty test equipment, rough handling during installation, or electrostatic damage.
v) Circuit problems, such as the circuit damages the device through over-exercise or improper temperature control.
vi) Circuit level design problems: the device is the wrong part for the job.

A typical problem solving process proceeds through the following series of stages:

i) Evaluation of failure background, including circumstances of the failure and past history of the device.
ii) Failure verification by establishing that the device indeed failed in the way that was reported.
iii) External physical analysis: a precise description of the device's external physical and electrical characteristics.
vi) Internal physical analysis. This usually involves opening up the package and examining the device with optical and electron microscopes or performing chemical analyses; it is generally a destructive process.
v) Causal analysis that determines the source of defects or damage at the physical level.
vi) Developing a fix or cure for the problem.

The first phase in the expert's problem solving is to assemble and assess background information. Where did the device fail? After what period of testing or use? How many devices failed? Are the circumstances of failure similar to some previous event for the same device? For a similar device? Do the circumstances of failure suggest a pattern, e.g., the manufacturer has a history of contamination problems, or many low power devices have been failing after testing on a certain piece of test equipment?

By the time failure analysis reaches the stage of electrical testing, it has already become, to a great extent, data-driven. Because this testing is time consuming, and more importantly, because it can cause further damage to the device, thus destroying the evidence, the selection and ordering of electrical tests requires a good deal of skill. The choice of test parameters as well as voltage and current levels is determined, for each test, by the results of previous tests and the expert's reading of their contextual significance. The device's electrical characteristics are interpreted as indicators of damage or defect at the level of physical structure. The tests are orchestrated so as to narrow or constrain the range of hypothesis about physical structure while at the same time preserving the possibility of pursuing alternative hypotheses should the current ones fail.

Not until progress has been made in identifying a strongly suggestive pattern of evidence at the external electrical and behavioural level is physical analysis undertaken. This is because i) physical analysis is irreversibly destructive, and ii) because the required physical evidence is commonly located at the microscopic level and hence cannot be found without first knowing where to look.

The final step in failure analysis is the identification of the cause and offering a cure. These often proceed hand-in-hand. Conceptually, of course, the identification of cause should determine the selection of cure, but in actual practice it is often the case that a tentative form of problem intervention is undertaken partly to verify the correctness of the causal analysis.

For example, if a small number of failures of a certain component begin to appear after some period of time, it might be hypothesized that a few marginal devices which barely passed an original screen eventually degraded through the rigors of use. The cure, on this analysis, would be to tighten the requirements of the screening procedure so that marginal devices are screened out. This "cure" has the virtue of simplicity and relative low cost. Were this kind of "cure" to fail, moreover, the failure itself would be revealing. It would indicate that the failures are "latent", meaning that apparently good devices experience significant degradation over time. Since "latent failures" have a restricted range of possible causes, this information would be quite useful.

2.3 Reflections and analysis

One of the striking features of the analytical process described above is the progression of stages (figure 6).

In the initial failure report what is described are gross physical or electrical behaviours. Extensive testing then gives a more and more detailed and precise account of the device's external physical and electrical characteristics. This characterization not only illuminates the earlier failure event but also serves as a road map to the hidden landscape of physical structure. Internal physical analysis then encounters that landscape firsthand, discovering the structural causes of these physical and electrical characteristics.

Levels of Description	
Initial failure report	Rough description of failure event, e.g. intermittent base emitter open, degraded BV
External physical and electrical analysis	Precise characterization of electrical charateristics, package intergrity, residual gas analysis
Internal physical analysis	Delid package and examine under electron microscope; perform chemical analysis
Causal failure analysis	Use physical indications to decipher environmental causation

Figure 6: Progression of stages as a feature of the analytical process

Finally, causal analysis uses indications from the level of physical morphology to track down the sources of these physical defects, whether these factors be traceable to design flaws, manufacturing problems, mishandling, or other environmental influence.

The structure of inquiry organizing this progression is thus a semiotic spiral (Figure 7) in which each level of description illuminates its predecessor while at the same time anticipating and pointing to its own explanation at the next higher level.

The implicit reference of level to level is registered in many of the descriptive terms which are used. A term like "overstress", for example, refers both to an excessive voltage or current applied to a device and also to the pattern of distress that such an excessive voltage or current can produce.

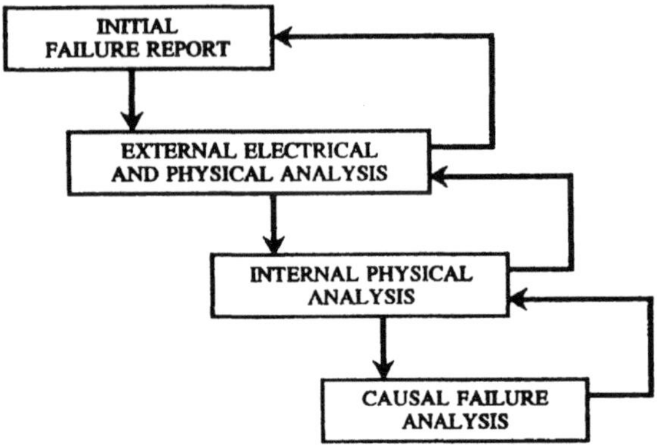

Figure 7: The abductive spiral

This pattern can be a recognizable physical indicator of a past event. Thus the expert talks about a "signs of overstress" or "overstress damage" visible under a microscope. "Volatile leakage" is another example of a physical indicator. "Volatile leakage" refers to a leakage characteristic of reverse breakdown voltage which improves with elevated temperature.

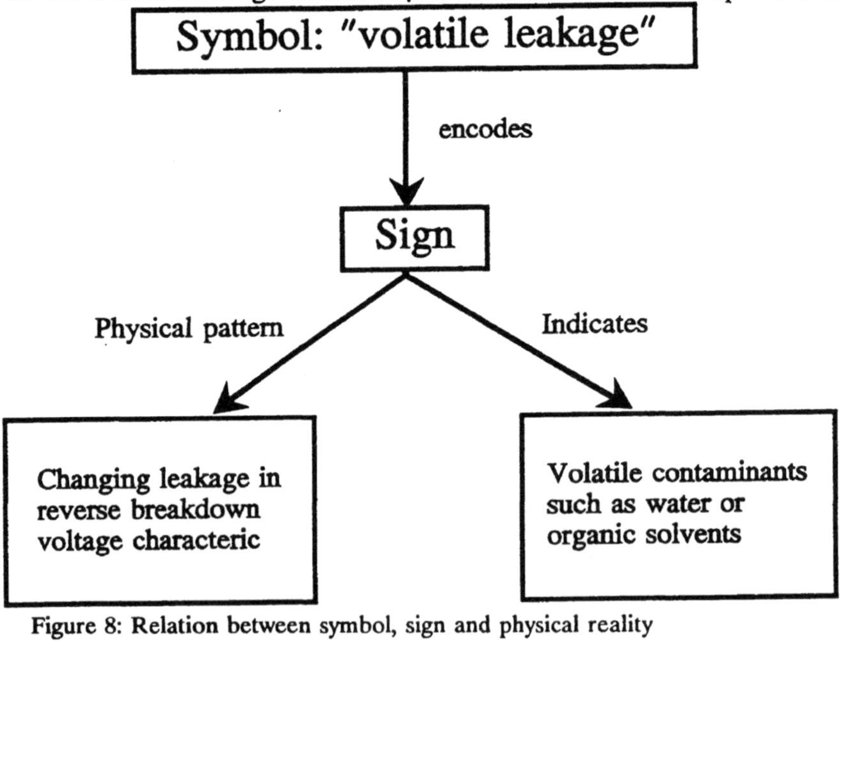

Figure 8: Relation between symbol, sign and physical reality

"Volatile leakage" provides clear indication of the presence of volatile contaminants such as water or organic solvents (Figure 8).

Terms such "soft knee", "intermittent open", "walking breakdown", etc., also encode the semiotic relationship between a physical pattern (generally on a laboratory instrument) and the causal factors to which that pattern points. It is in this sense that the expert's symbol system embeds his problem solving knowledge. Although we do not have the time to expand the observation here, we further note that the expert's instrumentation has been designed to perspicuously display those patterns deemed indicative or significant. In this sense, the expert's explicit linguistic representations are themselves comprised within a larger system of signs which organizes the expert's problem solving environment.

3. Areas of research and growth

As a result of the entry of expert system technology into the commercial marketplace, it has undergone an evolution that has moved it well beyond the goals of its original designers. Its epistemology has also outgrown its rationalist foundations (Luger and Stern, 1990)

In spite of its successes, there remain some fundamental flaws and limitations in expert system technology. We see this in its brittleness and its lack of ability to provide deeper justification than that of proof trees and rule stacks. We also note the absence of a rule/model symbiosis that would allow the system to employ either technology when appropriate. Finally, it is still well beyond the ability of current expert systems to improve performance through accumulated experience. We would like to see some limited learning ability in the next generation of expert systems, at the very least the integration of successful cases into its knowledge and practice.

Early efforts in A.I. were biased towards deductive inference. Limitations of deduction in areas such as diagnosis and theory formation have led to increased interest in abductive inference. Our description of the "abductive circle" provides the basis for a more realistic understanding of abductive problem-solving and the symbol systems which support it. In our ongoing work (Stern and Luger, 1991) we are developing a sign-based account of abductive explanation which offers significant advantages over the current entailment-based account.

The research challenges ahead necessitate a re-evaluation of the epistemological foundations of expert system problem solving. The epistemologies prevalent in A.I., based on formal logic and Tarskian semantics, are characterized by a self-imposed poverty which limits their ability to grasp the implications of current practice. Our analysis of abductive problem solving comes closer to a structure for understanding current expert system tools and practices. Our analysis, coupled with some of the techniques now emerging from A.I. research (Luger and Stubblefield, 1992), offer the promise for understanding and creating more semiotically mature computational systems.

Note

1. It is not cost effective to eliminate variability in the semiconductor manufacturing process; it is more cost effective to screen out the small percentage of a manufacturing lot which is lower quality.

References

Buchanan, B., Shortliffe, E. (eds.) (1984). *Rule Based Expert Systems: The MYCIN Experiments of The Stanford Heuristic Programming Project*. Reading, MA: Addison Wesley.

Davis, R. (1982). Applications of meta level knowledge to the construction, maintenance and use of large knowledge bases. In: Davis & Lenat 1982.

Davis, R., Lenat, D. (1982). *Knowledge Based Systems in Artificial Intelligence*. New York: McGraw Hill.

Eco, U. (1976). *A Theory of Semiotics*. Bloomington: Indiana University Press.

Hempel, C.G. (1965). *Aspects of Scientific Exploration and Other Essays in the Philosophy of Science*. N.Y.: Free Press.

Iwasaki, Y. (1989). Qualitative physics. In: A. Barr, P. Cohen. and E. Feigenbaum (eds.), *Handbook of Artificial Intelligence*, vol IV, Palo Alto: Addison Wesley.

Levesque, H. (1989). A knowledge level account of abduction. In: *Proceedings of the Eleventh International Joint Conference on Artificial Intelligence*, San Mateo, Calif.: Morgan Kaufmann.

Lindsay, R.K., Buchanan, B. G., Feigenbaum, E. A., and Lederberg, J. (1980). *Applications of Artificial Intelligence for Organic Chemistry: The DENDRAL Project*. New York: McGraw-Hill.

Luger, G.F., Stern, C. (1990). *The Role of Interpretation in the Representational Methodology* (Tech Report, Computer Science Department, University of New Mexico, Albuquerque New Mexico).

Luger, G.F., Stubblefield, W.A. (1989; 1992 sec. ed.). *Artificial Intelligence and the Design of Expert Systems*. Palo Alto: Benjamin Cummings.

McDermott, J. (1981). R1: The formative years, *AI Magazine*.

McDermott, J., Bechant, J. (1984). R1 revisited, four years in the trenches, *AI Magazine,* 5:3.

Papert, S. (1980). *Mindstorms*. New York: Basic Books.

Peirce, C.S. (1955). *The Philosophical Writings of Peirce*. New York: Dover Publications.

Skinner, J., Luger, G. (1991). A synergistic approach to reasoning for autonomous satellites. Presented at The Conference of Machine Intelligency for Aerospace Electronic Systems, Lisbon, 1991.

Stern, C., Luger, G. (1991). Towards a Sign-based Theory of Abduction. (submitted to the 1991 Conference on Robot Epistemology, copies available from authors).

Tarski, A. (1944). The Semantic Conception of Truth, *Philosophy and Phenomenological Research*, Nr. 4, 341-375.

Winograd, T., Flores, F. (1986). *Understanding Computers and Cognition.* Norwood NJ: Ablex.

Zadeh, L. (1983). Commonsense knowledge representation based of fuzzy logic, *Computer*, Nr. 16, 61-65.

Can machines compensate for biased human reasoning? Case studies in medical decision making

B.G. SILVERMAN (Washington, D.C.)

"Tis with our judgments as our watches, none go just alike, yet each believes his own."
- Alexander Pope; Essay on Criticism, 1711, Part I, Line 9

0. Abstract

This talk introduces the reader to criticism based problem solving, a theory that is useful when it is necessary to doubt, trap, and repair expert judgment. With the use of this theory, the machine's criticism achieves a semiotic property. The human recognizes the criticism as a sign of his own fallibility and he takes corrective action also suggested by the machine. A number of extensions to traditional knowledge engineering technique are seen to be useful in the methodology suggested here. Traditional knowledge engineering often answers the questions delineated in Generic Task (GT) theory. In general, however, GT theory must be extended to provide four additional sets of questions that must be answered in order to engineer a knowledge base when the expert is prone to bias. This extended theory is called here 'critic engineering' and it accounts for the cue, bias, remediation strategy, and semiotic factor levels of criticism based problem solving.

This talk concludes with a discussion of attempts to empirically investigate whether knowledge based systems can achieve the desired semiotic property and thereby enhance human collaborator performance. In keeping with this goal several machine collaborator case studies are also described. The talk closes with a discussion of the lessons learned and research questions answered and raised.

1. Introduction

As use of knowledge based systems spreads, the likelihood also grows that the machine will support domain personnel who are competent but not fully unbiased experts. Even acknowledged experts have judgment blind spots and bias tendencies. In such cases, human professionals exhibit improved performance during problem solving tasks when the machine is not simply a student. That is, they improve when the machine can signal occurrences of bias and help identify and repair inappropriate judgment heuristics. Criticism based problem solving provides a deep knowledge that helps the machine fill this semiotic role.

Criticism based problem solving has been introduced in Silverman (1990, 1991a-b, 1992a-b). The purpose of the present article is threefold. (1) It better defines an implementable version of the theory. This includes first principles, generic question sets, and a library of bias triggers and collaboration strategies. (2) It hypothesizes, tests, and evaluates such improvements for specific tasks in specific domains. Of particular importance is a more precise theory of question asking for problem solving tasks. This more precise theory takes the form of a general model of a knowledge engineer's process for acquiring and assessing knowledge (section 2). The case studies (section 3) examine whether that model, when captured within a criticism based problem solving system, serves as a successful semiotic device or not (sections 4 and 5).

1.1 Judgment theory as an epistemological basis for knowledge based systems

Two great, but contradictory traditions exist in the study of human expertise as illustrated in figure 1. The judgment/decisionmaking (J/DM) literature is older, more mature, and theory-rich. That literature's principal strength lies in the vast number of tasks or situations it has catalogued in terms of normative cues, biases likely to arise, and theoretically sound solution techniques: e.g., see Kahneman, Slovic, & Tversky (1982) or Arkes & Hammond (1986). For example, any management science, operations research, or decision science textbook is filled with chapters enumerating how to solve specific classes of problems. Just locate the relevant chapter for a new problem and find out how to solve that problem. This is not to say that all of operations research, management science, or decision analysis was created to solve problems arising in human expert bias or error. However, it has often proved useful in that regard and the distinction is not germane to this discussion.

The other great tradition, that of artificial intelligence/expert systems (A.I./E.S.), offers no similar resource. On the contrary, for each new problem, the solutions that experts would consider normative can only be discovered through laborious knowledge engineering effort. The knowledge engineering field has reduced some of this bottleneck by developing models of the problem solving process. But, the process of documenting these models is just beginning: e.g., see Bylander and Chandrasekaran, 1987; McDermott, 1988).

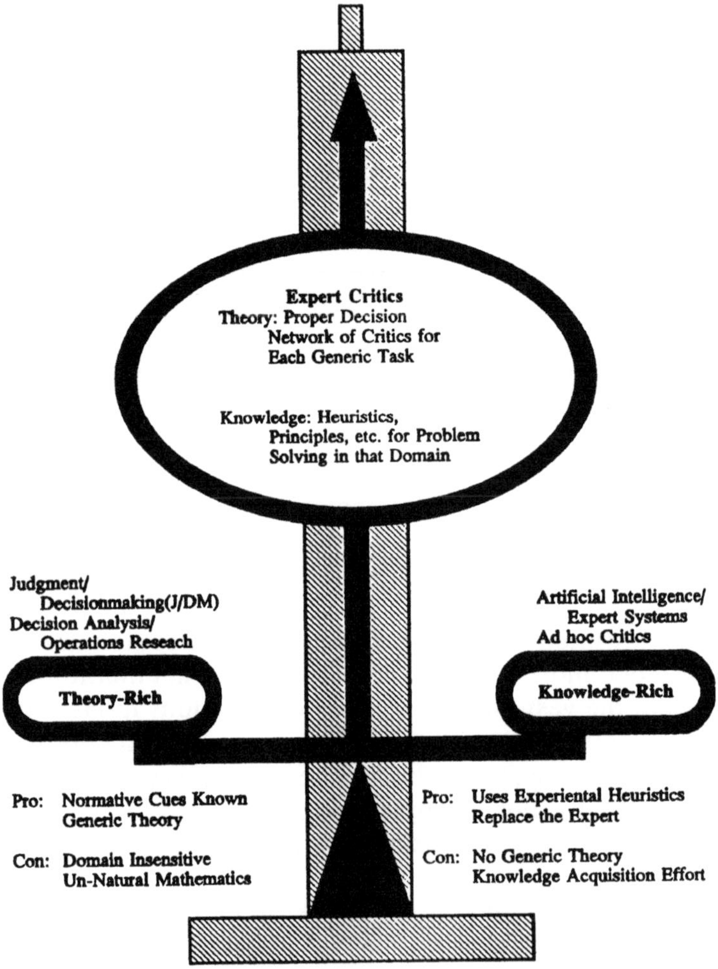

Figure 1: Unifying theory and knowledge with expert critics

Documenting knowledge models of different tasks has been, to date, restricted primarily to the expert systems subfield of A.I./E.S. That is, the attention is upon the replace-the-expert paradigm rather than upon the support-the-expert one. To put it another way, the knowledge modelling effort, by design, ignores the biases and errors that experts typically make when applying their intuition to planning, decisionmaking, and problem solving situations.

This is doubly unfortunate, since, many of the successful A.I./E.S. applications to date involve programs that support, rather than replace, human experts. While this raises a series of interesting questions concerning what should be the central paradigm of the artificial intelligence field, that debate is not the focus of this discussion. The focus here is upon the knowledge vs. theory polarity of existing approaches to expertise.

At the other end of the scales (see right hand side of figure 1), the advantage of the knowledge-rich A.I./E.S. approaches is the very commodity which makes them difficult to develop - i.e., knowledge. The use of expert heuristics in problem solving systems is attractive because it is sensitive to the particulars of the situation. After all, it has resulted from years of experience with every subtlety and nuance that can arise in that specific task-environment. No generic theory can hope to match the breadth of the expert. Further, the strict mathematical nature of the theory-rich approaches often renders them inappropriate for situations that demand heuristic methodology.

One paradigm that bridges this gap is that of critiquing and argumentation. If "semiotic machines" are to better support the human expert, the best role often might be for them to critique human generated solutions from the perspective of missing knowledge viewpoints as well as for recurring judgment errors. Expert systems, and expert advisory systems, produce their own independent solution to a problem. In contrast, critiquing requires the machine to examine the user's solution and to attempt to signal him to improve his own performance. Traditional decision support and analysis systems automate mundane computing chores (e.g., helping with repeated trials to generate a tradeoff diagram) but leave the highest levels of decision forming to the user. In contrast, again, critics are able to react on their own and to provide intelligent feedback and argumentation about the higher level thinking and intuition processes. In this paradigm the machine need not know how to solve the entire domain problem but must excel at helping the human to do so.

More importantly as shown in the centre of figure 1, critics can unify theory and knowledge to provide intelligent support for enhancing user performance. On the theory side, critics can exploit what is known about expert bias and error from the J/DM literature plus the prescriptive suggestions of the decision analytic approaches. This is called a theory of bugs and repairs for expert intuition. By using this theory, the problem solving of biased experts is improved. On the knowledge side, critics can exploit the advantages of domain sensitive knowledge, heuristics, and rules plus other strengths of A.I./E.S. technology. They need not rely solely upon un-natural, mathematical techniques. They can converse with humans via whatever heuristic, knowledge-rich strategies are appropriate to the task - such as, but not limited to, arguing, analogizing, cuing, tutoring, persuading, or directing.

Expert critics have existed as an A.I./E.S. technique for almost a decade but they have never had the benefit of a general theory of human error and bias, a theory of "bugs", or a theory of repair strategies. That is what J/DM offers. For example, Miller (1983, 1986), the founder of the critiquing approach, gave critics a domain-specific knowledge base of errors or "bugs." This knowledge base is guided exclusively by knowledge specific to the domain of interest. Thus most critics are listed on the right side of figure 1 as "ad hoc" since they are knowledge-rich but theory-impoverished. This paper is an extension to the critiquing approach and it is the first time that a general theory of reasoning error and remediation has been applied to assist the critic design process. There is no comparable synthesis elsewhere in the literature.

Similarly, J/DM has existed for over four decades as a theoretical discipline but it has never been fully operationalized. This is particularly true for the cognitive bias side of the J/DM literature. Expert critics, via their heuristic form of knowledge communication, pose a vital pathway toward implementing what has heretofore been primarily an area of scientific study. As a contribution in this direction, the general model of cognition and the bias identification rules of Section 2 plus figure 3 are a first step toward operationalizing this literature. Since operationalization must happen on a generic task by generic task basis, the case study at the end of this paper takes a second step by illustrating how to operationalize the J/DM literature for selected aspects of a generic task.

1.2 What is a critic/How does it mitigate the problem?

Expert critiquing systems are a class of program that receive as input the statement of the problem and the user-proposed solution. They produce as output a critique of the user's judgment and knowledge in terms of what the program thinks is wrong with the user-proposed solution. Some critic programs also produce corrective repairs while others attempt to prevent the user from committing some more common judgment errors in the first place. Critic programs may be user invoked (passive critic) or active critics. They may work in batch mode (process the entire solution after the user has finished it) or in incremental mode (interrupt the user during his problem solving task).

Simple, yet widely used, examples of critics are spell and grammar checkers. These are passive critics the user may invoke in a batch mode. They make use of table lookup functionality to check the user's task result for a variety of syntactic errors. Yet, more sophisticated critics are appearing at an ever increasing rate in medical clinician support systems (e.g., Miller 1983, 1986 or Langlotz and Shortliffe, 1983), in computer aided design environments (e.g., Spickelmeier and Newton, 1988, Zhou et.al., 1989), in high function environments (e.g., Fischer, 1988), and in judgment debiasing during automated knowledge base acquisition (Silverman, 1990, 1991a-b, 1992a). In these applications, users can attempt their task solutions the (active) critic interrupts them if it finds a serious error of judgment or knowledge.

Also these applications use a more sophisticated algorithm that takes advantage of artificial intelligence techniques. While these critics contain an expert system capability (it produces the critic's solution to selected aspects of the problem statement), that is only a portion of their algorithm.

They also, contain two further modules shown in figure 2. (1) The differential analyzer compares the user- and machine-generated solutions. It isolates any differences, decides if the difference is worth bothering the user about, and infers a way to explain the difference in terms least disruptive to the user-proposed solution. (2) The dialogue generator that attempts to put the criticism and feedback into a form of 'natural language' using canned text strings. We postpone discussion of the other components of figure 2 until later on.

At this point, it is worth mentioning that expert critics are different from either expert systems or expert advisory systems. Both of the latter only accept the problem statement as input and provide their machine-generated solution as output. Unlike the expert critic, expert systems and expert advisory systems do not evaluate the user-proposed solution. This difference means that expert critics are for a different class of applications.

Expert critiquing systems are ideal when the user can generate his solution to a recurring problem. Critics help when users commit the types of errors that machines are good at eliminating. Specifically, critics can cause the user to notice and use more cues. In engineering design applications this means they fill in missing knowledge.

Unlike an expert system, expert critics are usually unable to solve a task problem entirely on their own. They exist solely to cue the domain expert and to act as an intelligent prosthesis device that makes expert system technology palatable to the human expert. Thus as the spell/grammar checkers are unable to author a memo so are the more sophisticated engineering design critics unable to draw a design. Yet, both types of critics are useful adjuvants to help the expert improve his performance on a minimal interference basis.

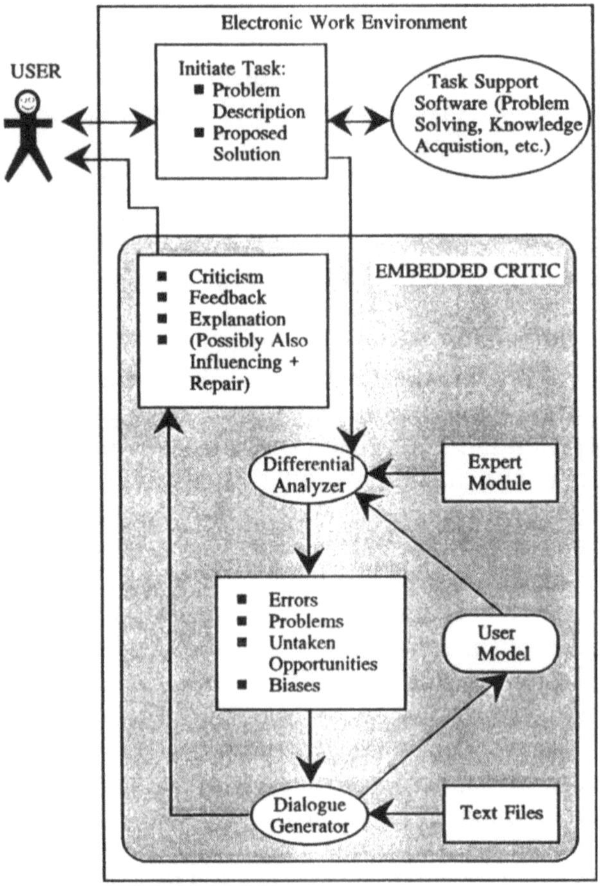

Figure 2: Overview of the critiquing process

Interestingly, a critic can be deployed in an application with unknown answers. For example, one may use spelling or grammar checkers to help in word processing tasks where these critics don't know the final document focus. Yet, critics cannot be deployed where they don't know the proper cues of the sub-tasks of interest. Thus, there could be no spell checker in the absence of a formalized language. Likewise, there can be no design critic in the absence of engineering discipline knowledge and heuristics.

While the niche just described may be a necessary set of conditions for the expert critiquing class of programs, it is insufficient for assuring the critic is as effective as possible. Additional conditions exist that dictate how a given critic should interact with its users. Discovering what those additional conditions are is the purpose of the lessons learned here.

2. Theoretical elements of a generic, semiotic critic

Criticism based problem solving concerns the use of normative cues or heuristics during tasks, the biases that arise, and the strategies and factors involved in mitigating those biases. This theory is summarized as a multi-level question driven approach in figure 3 and as further described in what follows. Figure 3 is a guide to the theory and to the types of questions a good collaborator should know how to ask.

At the top, one picks a domain (e.g., purchasing clothing, running a power plant, or software programming) that one decomposes into generic tasks (e.g., monitoring and detection, heuristic classification, planning). It is useful in the Task Level of figure 3 to quote a set of Generic Task questions from Bylander and Chandrasekaran (1987). In their approach tasks are understood via a series of questions such as listed in the top Level of figure 3. There is an interaction between representation and inference technique within each task that they recommend be exploited in designing a knowledge acquisition system.

For a given domain there will be:

Task Level - Domain Task-Structural Questions

Generic Tasks: For a given domain, what are the type of tasks that occur? What is the function (input and output) of the generic task? What is the Generic Task good for?

Representation an Inference Interaction: For a given Generic Task, how do the representations and inference strategies interact with each other and with the task? How should knowledge be organized and structured to accomplish the function of the generic task? What inference strategy can be applied to the knowledge to accomplish the function of the generic task?

Concepts: What concepts are the input and output about? How is knowledge organized in terms of concepts? How does the inference strategy operate on the concepts?

Exploitation: How can the generic task-structure model (functions, interactions, concepts) be exploited by the knowledge acquisition methodology to extract and select the appropriate knowledge? Have all the specific categories of knowledge been collected and are all their interactions functional, and/or conceptual roles understood? What structural errors (e.g., inconsistency, circularity, dead-endedness, etc., have occurred? How can these be removed?

Cue Level - Normative Cue Utilization Questions

What normative cues must be utilized to finish this subtask properly? What cues are the experts focusing on? Which of those are normative? inappropriate? What normative cues are usable by the expert that aren't now being used and why aren't they used? Which normative cues are beyond the expert's states of knowledge? How are cues judged, weighted and scaled by the expert and is that done properly?

Bias Level - Epistemological assessment (Bias Identification) Questions:

External: What theory(s) of the world does the user appear to subscribe to? Does the user remember why the Knowledge is being transferred and who will ultimately benefit from it? How did the user come to know that fact? How can I strain the validity and robustness of the user's input? What errors of commission and omission is the user succumbing to?

Internal: What do the user's external answers tell us about his cognitive model/biases? What would I have to have had in memory to reach the user's input? What kind of heuristics (e.g., availability, representativeness, etc.) might he have used to have reached that kind of answer? How are they biased? misused? What formal reasoning steps has he omitted or relaxed?

Strategy Level - Credibility Refinement And Critiquing (Influence, Debias) Questions:

Positive Influence Strategies: How should I better cue the user to dampen his biases? errors? What principles, examples, references should I refer him to that would alter the way he solved the problem? What successful analogs and lessons learned can be shown to him that have similar characteristics as the current one? What directors (formal reasoning) might he benefit from?

Negative Debiaser Strategies: How should I repair/modify his answers so they appear more credible yet will still be acceptable to him? What alternative views of what he's authored will cause him to think about its clarity, workability, and correspondence with reality? What instance of the FMECA paradigm will help him overcome his biases/errors? What directors should the user be required to follow?

Dimension/Collaboration Factor Level - Fine Tuning Questions:

How should bias and strategy information be modulated and presented so as to enhance the collaborative relationship? How should each of the critic dimensions (e.g., process, timing, mode) and collaboration factors (deep knowledge, cognitive orientation, intention sharing, control plasticity, mutual learning, dynamic memory) be set for a given user type to improve critic success and user productivity? (Silverman, 1992a)

Figure 3: Cognitive task analysis requires the critic engineer to get the machine critic to ask five levels of questions

The Task Level questions define an intelligent actor's cognitive model. This is a structural model of the domain. It includes the inputs, outputs, representations, vocabulary, concepts, sub-tasks, work packages, interactions, and acquisition system features for each generic task. For example, consider a domain of purchasing clothing. A GT might include obtaining the likely price information. One defines the structural model of that task by answering each of the questions of the Task Level of figure 3.

GT analysis leads to a normative view of the domain. All the Task Level questions of figure 3 lead to the kind of insight one gleans from retrospective analyses of successfully completed tasks. That is, the resulting cognitive or structural model lacks an account for errant expert behaviour. To obtain accounts of the errors, one needs descriptive analyses. One must collect these while watching individuals work (and think aloud). The goal is to uncover the reparative processes that experts use to recover from errors. Section 2.2 addresses this too.

For critic engineering purposes, the outcome of the task level analysis leads to the identification of the normative cues one must use to finish a task properly (see Cue Level of figure 3). For example, cues might exist on where to look for price information, on how to structure that information to complete the task and solve the problem, etc. This is the first step in introducing the theory into what has been a domain knowledge engineering activity up to now.

Expert task performance is more than simply a matter of adhering to normative cues. Experts often follow only high level cues. They rely on holistic, analogical reasoning from experience. This implies that ignoring normative cues need not correlate with poor performance. Still, normative cues are a measurable entity and a useful point of departure for critic design. For example, no one would argue that a Pulitzer is won just by following cues of outstanding spelling, grammar, penmanship, and topic selection. Also, no one would argue that a Pulitzer winner won't redefine some normative cues. Still, in 99 out of 100 cases, overlooking some significant fraction of the normative cues accounts for failure to win the Pulitzer.

Let us make this idea a little more explicit. A critic design for a generic task requires the study of "buggy" behaviour and likely remediation strategies in addition to study of the normative task outcome. The elements of the critic are as follows.

Critic (Task i) = F{ Cue(j), Error Type(j,k), Decision Network(j,l), Design Dimension Settings(m) }

where,

Critic (Task i)	=	the critic design for the ith generic task,
F{.}	=	reusable expert critic design for that generic task,
Cue(j)	=	vector of j=i, J cues for the ith task,
Error Type(k)	=	vector of k=1, K biases and errors in using the jth cue,
Decision Network(l)	=	lth combination of strategies (i.e., influencers, debiasers, and directors) that is optimal for reducing the K biases and errors for the jth cue,
Design Dimension Settings(m)	=	recommended setting of the mth design dimension and collaboration factor.

In figure 3 the Bias Level questions the epistemological status of the individual who is providing the answers to Task Level questions. Like a dialectical or devil's advocate, Bias Level questions attempt to poke holes in the answers of level 1. At this level, criticism based problem solving taps the deep knowledge of human judgment processes that has been gleaned from judgment/decisionmaking (J/DM) theory. Most of the common biases (availability, representativeness, co-variation, etc.) committed in generic tasks arise in the second level of figure 3. Consider an example in the clothing procurement domain. An availability bias occurs if a consumer thinks all shoes are expensive based on examining the only (readily available) catalog he finds lying around the house. Availability is the internal cause of the bias. The external manifestation is in mistakenly thinking all shoes are expensive. The expert omitted the cues "find and compare alternatives."

The Strategy Level, in turn, exists to prevent bias from occurring. It also attempts repairs after a biased judgment occurs. The Strategy Level includes the common strategies (hint, tutor, explain, repair, etc.) defined in criticism based problem solving (see below). This level holds prescriptive knowledge as opposed to the normative (presumed always correct) knowledge of the Task Level. Strategies for helping the example consumer find a potentially better estimate of the cost of shoes might overcome his availability bias by preventively suggesting he looks at several catalogues. Or, corrective strategies might show him the information and point out a better price for the same pair of shoes.

Critic design dimensions, the lowest Level of figure 3 provide the questions that one must answer to fine tune the strategies and make them work in a semiotic sense. For example, this asks how to point out the user's error without upsetting him, information overloading him, or otherwise overly adversely affecting his abilities to react to signs. Dimensions and factors are an important part of criticism based problem solving. They play a vital role in the success of the collaboration. They are treated further in Silverman (1991a,1992a).

Finding specific instantiations to the questions of the Cue, Bias, Strategy, and Dimension Levels for real applications is the methodological aspect of building semiotic properties into critics. Further discussion appears in the ensuing sections.

2.1 Categorize the types of cues relevant to each task

For each (generic) task identified in the domain, it's necessary to categorize the task cues as figure 4 shows and as this section elaborates. Specifically, Figure 4 shows that for any task there is a universe of cues, F. This universe contains those cues, E, the expert can use to complete the task. There are also other cues in F that are unusable. For example, the E cues a medical doctor can use to diagnose a patient's disease are limited to those he can observe, query, or test for. Other cues may be useful from F, yet, medical science doesn't know the correlation to the disease. Or, it lacks a way to test for and measure them. Also included in the unusable cue portion of F are the cues labelled D that the particular expert perceives as unusable but could use. "Not D" occurring in a problem is a missing knowledge error. It may be due to insufficient training or, more likely, to failing to keep up as new knowledge gets added to the field.

The region labelled A + B in figure 4 is the cues the expert initially focuses on. Due to cognitive biases and missing knowledge errors, A + B differs from the normative set of cues, B + C + D. Yet, the correct solution to the problem requires that one uses the B + C + D set. Those normative cues that are within the purview of the expert's selective attention are B. The normative cues within the expert's usable cue set, E, but outside his current focus are called C.

The cues labelled C are the external manifestations of cognitive bias by the expert. For whatever internal reason - e.g, selective perception, availability, recency effects, and so on - the expert selectively focuses his attention on A + B. He neglects to factor C into his task completion effort. In a similar vein, the cues labelled D are the external manifestation of the expert's missing knowledge errors.

Knowing these different categories of cues is central to understanding where the expert is repeatedly going astray. Even more importantly, it is the only way to design strategies to drive his attention back from A + B to the full set of normative cues, B + C + D. For example, it is useful to know whether a given normative cue falls into C vs. D. The critic uses this to determine whether to use critiquing vs. "situated" (or on the spot) tutoring. That is, critiquing helps to mitigate bias of type "not C." Missing knowledge errors, "not D," require on the spot tutoring to inform the expert of the knowledge he needs to assimilate.

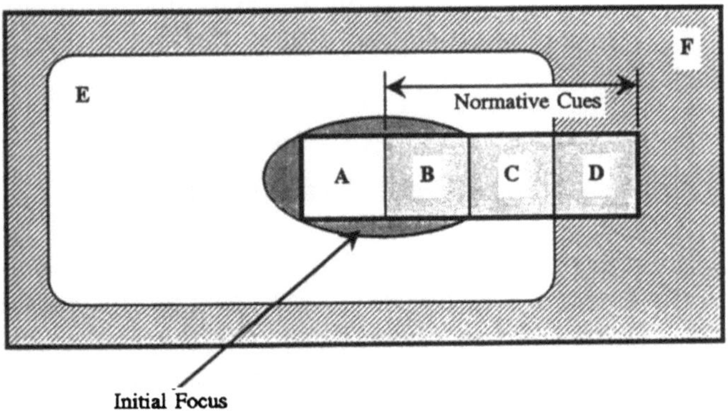

F - the universe of cues in cue space
E - the cues that are usable by an expert in the task-domain
A + B - cues in the focus of attention of the expert
B + C + D - set of normative cues needed to complete the task properly

B - normative cues already being focussed upon by the expert
C - normative, usable cues that the expert is not focussing (bias)
D - normative, non-usable cues that the expert isn't focussing on (missing knowledge)

Figure 4: Central to the cognitive task analysis is a categorization of the various types of cues in a given task

As a second example, knowing precisely what cues the expert has biases for helps the designer decide what cognitive process they fall under. For example, biases can fall under the categories of knowledge acquisition, knowledge processing, intended output, and so on. With the aid of Silverman (1991a-b, 1992a-b), this helps the designer and the critic pinpoint the type of cognitive bias, the strategy to deploy, and the design to assume. As a third example, knowing the cues that appear in A gives a clue to what the expert is focusing upon and why. Knowing what is distracting the expert can help one find strategies that change his focus.

2.2 Bias identification and repair strategy based on principles of criticism

The idea captured by the Bias and Strategy Levels of figure 3 is as follows.

PRINCIPLE: The machine should have a library of functions that serve as bias identification triggers, influencer strategies, and debiaser strategies.

To implement critics, it is useful to have a library of "functions" or specifications for identifying when flawed answers, biases, and general cue usage failure modes arise. It includes general triggers that one can specialize for a specific domain or application. These trigger functions ease the job of the designer of the machine critic. They help the untrained (in the field of human judgment/decisionmaking theory) designer find important internal manifestations of bias.

In the same vein the function library offers multiple corrective strategies. One can deploy these in a partially redundant fashion. This will "blanket" the set of likely causes of unwanted cue use and normative cue non-use. The alternative strategies include the ones that follow.

Influencer strategies that help prevent a bias:

- o Hinting, cueing, and attention focusing to minimize potential biases,
- o Showing defaults and analogs to provide good starting anchors,
- o Explaining principles, examples, and references to assist anchoring and adjusting processes,
- o Repetition, often in different form, to be sure points get through,
- o Visualization of the big picture to avoid selective focusing,

Debiaser strategies that help correct a bias:

- o Identifying Failure Modes (FM),
- o Explaining Effect (E) and Cause (C) to try and elevate the subject's awareness,
- o Attempting Repair Actions (A) such as but not limited to specializing, generalizing, analogizing, substituting, adjusting, and attention re-focusing to try and move the subject to a more productive pathway,
- o Visual feedback in the form of colorization, highlighting, etc. of imperfections in the task artifact.

These are many strategies. Few users will need this much criticism. One must design triggers so redundant strategies only interrupt the user if earlier strategies fail to remove the error. This serves to preserve the semiotic nature of the relationship. This leads to a useful and conservative approach.

Redundancy and repetition have a chance to operate on potentially stubborn strategies without loss of semiotic properties.

2.3 Create decision networks that define the criticism sequences

The idea of libraries of redundant critics, multi-step critics, critics combined with situated tutors, etc. suggest potentially complicated sequences of critics will be useful in numerous applications. To see the alternative paths through this network of critics, it is useful to prepare a network flow diagram as one of the design products. This is called a decision network of critics.

The implications of the Levels of figure 3 are for a question-driven human-machine intelligence where neither entity is "in charge." Instead, the machine's semiotic model and question sets prompt the human to use normative cues to reach more valid and robust knowledge bases. The generic model of task performance/cue usage/bias identification/strategy/collaborator factor setting is the central focus of criticism based problem solving. It relates tasks, cues, biases, and strategies in a generic way. Although it is far from exhaustive, the general network model is implementable. For many, though not all, decision networks the computer's basic cycle would be something like the following.

(1) Influence While Asking Level 1 and 2 Task/Cue Oriented Question Sets (Influence, Direct)
(2) Notice Potentially Flawed Answers
(3) Ask Epistemological Assessment Question Sets (Influence Further, Identify Bias)
(4) Isolate Cue Usage Failure Modes and Biases
(5) Ask Credibility Refinement Question Sets (Influence Still Further, Debias)
(6) Offer Repair Ideas and Modifications (Debias, Direct)

This typical cycle implements the question-driven model of figure 3. It's useful for designing a bias identification and corrective strategy system. To facilitate this process, there is a criticism based problem solving system language called, COPE. COPE sits atop the C language and is available on DOS and UNIX platforms (see Staff, 1989; 1990). In this paper the six step algorithm has been applied to a medical decision problem structuring task.

3. Case study to illustrate the unified knowledge- and theory-rich approach

In this section, a simple non-computerized example shows how the human judgment theory can serve as a deep model that guides the epistemological analysis of expert reasoning. This will serve both to illustrate the theory as well as to introduce a number of concepts and strategy details that will be useful to readers attempting to understand the full significance of criticism based problem solving.

In particular, two major uses of critics are described in this case study. (1) In the realm of *Knowledge*, critics inform the user with knowledge and constraints, or criticize the knowledge the user has offered. (2) In the realm of *Judgement*, they critique the user's reasoning, judgment, and decision processes. These two categories correspond to the distinction between "knowledge base" and "inference engine" used in the expert systems field. The knowledge base holds the domain insight. The inference engine performs domain-independent reasoning that manipulates the knowledge to solve problems.

3.1 An example of the role for knowledge critics

It is probably best at this point to proceed right to the example which will facilitated if the reader also consults figure 5 while reading the following Scene.

Scene

> Upon moving to a new city, I found an MD with a well-regarded, general practice not too far from my home. I visited him to obtain a diagnosis of why I was having trouble swallowing at meal time. Dr. Ready examined me but could find nothing wrong. Since the problem occurred only once a month he sent me home saying "chew more carefully and lets see what develops." When the problem progressed to twice a month, I revisited Dr. Ready. He sent me to a Lab for a procedure (esophagus x-rays while swallowing barium). This revealed nothing out of the ordinary. Dr. Ready again sent me home with the same advice as before. The problem reached a weekly level. A third trip to Dr. Ready lead him to proclaim "It's probably in your mind. There's nothing more the medical profession can do." Being an engineer, but probably just following common sense, I reasoned that the esophagus is just a pipe. If there is nothing wrong in the pipe one must examine the outlet area (i.e., the stomach). So I scheduled a visit with a gastro-intestinal specialist. Dr. Willing immediately recognized it as one of about three possible conditions associated with an o-ring that exists between the esophagus and the intestine. This ring is parallel to the plane of view of the earlier xray machine tests. A brief exam with the

proper equipment (this time I only had to swallow a camera and a light source!) confirmed the hypothesis. It identified a tightening of the muscle ring. Dr. Willing prescribed a commonplace medicinal prescription. This drug promptly cleared up the by now over one year old problem.

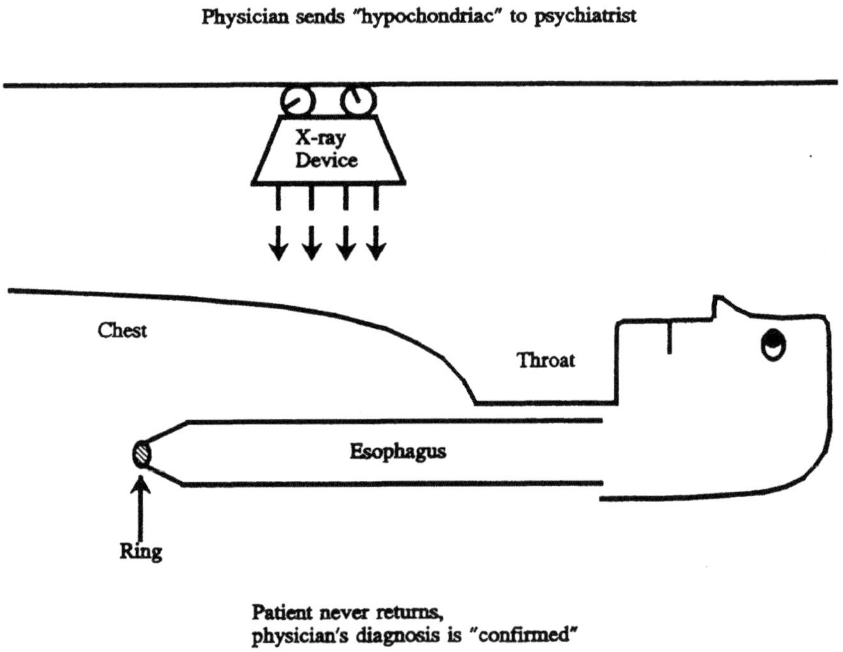

Figure 5: Physiscian with missing knowledge can't find problem which is parallel to the plane of the X-ray device

This scene illustrates two general points about the critiquing approach. For one thing, one must make a distinction between judgment and knowledge. For another, one also must distinguish between judgment and formal reasoning methods. Let us begin with a discussion of the first of these distinctions. Dr. Ready has category B knowledge about certain swallowing disorders (esophagus-related ones viewable from old-fashioned xrayography). He lacks category D knowledge about others (intestine-connection ones viewable by the more modern fiber optic technology). His knowledge also covers the idea of sending the patient to a specialist for a test procedure in an area unfamiliar to him. Yet, it apparently doesn't include sending a patient to other specialists (or contacting them) when the situation stumps him. Apparently, Dr. Ready does not recognize that his knowledge about the problem is out of date. So, he introduces category A knowledge into his final diagnosis. This leads him to incorrectly conclude the patient is a hypochondriac who should visit the "mind-doctor."

It is all right to have incomplete knowledge. Yet, this person is the primary clinical decisionmaker. In such a role, it is important to know what to do at the edges of one's knowledge base. We call this case management. It relies upon either reasoning or judgment processes. Judgment is a person's ability to come to an understanding, opinion, and sense of things. It is separate from domain knowledge and it includes the values, preferences, and intuitions that set the stage for the decisions one ultimately makes. For example, when confronted by a decision, it is one's judgment that leads one to conclude: (1) when one looks at enough alternative diagnoses, (2) whether the one has the correct set of dimensions along which to evaluate the alternatives, or (3) what is the most appropriate way to reason about the results.

Just as judgment is distinct from knowledge, it is also different from formal reasoning methods. When situations for formal reasoning or decision-making are not present, or perceived to be absent, humans allow judgment to guide their behaviour and reach conclusions. Judgment heuristics require less effort than formal reasoning ones do. So, judgements may be made for reasons of time, habit, stress, or perceived efficiency. This is acceptable if no significant errors occur. When errors of judgment do arise, we call them *biases*. As the ensuing section explains, many biases arise in human cognition.

To clarify, this discussion makes two points. (1) Although judgment often serves us well, it often is a relaxation of more formal reasoning methods (e.g., logic or rationality). (2) Biases are recurring errors arising from systematic repetitions of these relaxations.

Most professionally trained personnel take many courses and receive on-the-job training in their subject matter of expertise. Many even receive training in decision theory, decision making, and reasoning processes. At the same time, very few give serious thought to or receive education concerning judgment, introspection, and people skills. In particular, there is no training in the judgment processes that they use to manipulate substantive knowledge. Dr. Ready has a deficit in his knowledge base. He also has one in the judgment processes he uses to reason through his knowledge deficit. So, Dr. Ready is unaware of how deficient his diagnosis is. When he offers it, he feels no loss of face.

By the way, if a knowledge engineer interviewed Dr. Ready for a knowledge base of rules about swallowing disorders, that knowledge base would replicate the performance that Dr. Ready himself gave. The knowledge engineer would test this knowledge base on real patients to see if it is valid. Since most patients, like myself, receiving this poor of a diagnosis would never return for future help, the knowledge engineer would conclude that the diagnosis is correct and that the patient has got the cure from the psychiatrist. The knowledge engineer would be using the same biased feedback as does Dr. Ready.

Alternatively, to design a criticism based problem solving system for Dr. Ready is a fairly straightforward process given that his error categories are now clarified and given that one is aware of human judgment theory for epistemological analysis purposes. In particular, the goal will be to design a support system rather than a replacement system. As Dr. Ready has trouble visualizing what knowledge he is missing, it seems prudent to equip him with a visual diagram on his personal computer screen of the digestive system. The critic would receive his initial diagnosis that the esophagus should be checked. Since the critic would concur, it would have no output. After the results came back, however, the critic would disagree with Dr. Ready. It would use a simple model of the digestive track to conclude that the patient should be sent to the Gastro-Intestinal Specialist.

The critic would also know by this point that Dr. Ready is either biased or missing knowledge. It would invoke human judgment theory to better pinpoint the source of his error and to isolate the proper strategy to repair his error. A decision network could easily be configured to first cue him (e.g., by flashing the intestine in the drawing on the PC screen) as if he were biased and forgetful. If that failed to precipitate the desired behaviour, the machine could then assume he had a missing knowledge error and, the decision network could proceed with a set of increasingly aggressive, on the spot tutoring and repair strategies. Dr. Ready would be shown principles, examples, analogies, and references that all would attempt to sway him in a corrective fashion.

3.2 An example of the role for judgment critics

Up to this point, Dr. Ready has been receiving a lot of criticism. So that readers will not view the "Scene" above as a lionization of Dr. Willing, a postscript is in order that will make use of figure 6.

Postscript

> After switching my family to Dr. Willing's general practice, he later misdiagnosed a symptom in my wife. The problem called for a highly likely explanation and a routine solution. (Three independent MDs later confirmed this. This advice lead to successful results). Instead, Dr. Willing concluded he should test for a rare disease. This was apparently because

of a recent case in his practice that had a small overlap in symptoms with those of my wife's. Dr. Willing clung to the rare, low probability diagnosis though it required expensive and potentially dangerous procedures to disconfirm it.

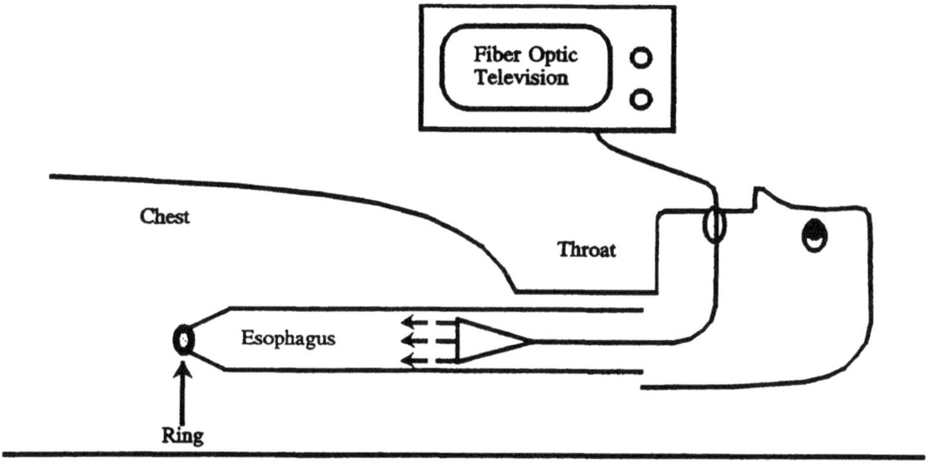

Same physician uses biased heuristics in diagnosing a rare disease due to recency effects in his practice

P(disease) = F(recency of malpractice event)

Ignore: cost/danger of required tests
P(disease) = F(# of relevant symptoms)

Figure 6: Physician with correct knowledge immediately finds problems and solution

Dr. Willing has judgement biases that are different, but just as problematic as Dr. Ready's. Dr. Ready has difficulty dealing with the edges of his knowledge. Dr. Willing, in turn, has trouble discerning biases resulting from "recency effects" and "low-probability events." The recency effect points out how category A knowledge of the previous case affects Dr. Willing's judgement. Also, the rare disease diagnosis is a low-probability event due to ignoring category C knowledge. That is, Dr. Willing ignores most symptoms (category C). Instead, he overly focuses on a few symptoms (category B). His concern is to avoid a repetition of an earlier mistake (category A). Dr. Willing lacks training in (or forgot) the proper methods for reasoning under uncertainty in a case like this. He jumps into a judgment heuristic that leads him astray. The same thing might happen to a new homeowner who recently had a burst water pipe. The homeowner jumps to conclusions when he next sees water on the floor.

In retrospect, one other problem with Dr. Willing's judgement is evident. That is, he is not so willing to discuss his decisions. The reason this is a problem points out a difficulty of working with expert knowledge. That is, when one is learning a subject, the student easily retrieves knowledge about that subject. When one masters a domain, the knowledge of what to do (and why) is frequently no longer available to conscious reflection. Instead, situations trigger this knowledge. It's almost as if the knowledge chunks and heuristics are instinctive. We call this "chunking." Due to chunking, one can't state precisely why this or that decision is good. Again, this is a hallmark of one who mastered his or her domain. Chunking is desirable if the situation triggers correct responses. It is potentially dangerous if the "expert" has bad habits or incorrect information. It is also dangerous if the field of knowledge changes or if the expert has incomplete training about matters of judgment.

One cannot always rely on reasoning to verify important decisions. So, keeping judgment processes to oneself does a disservice to all involved. Exposing these processes to criticism leads to better results. Still, the two cognitive behaviours - chunking and communicating one's judgment processes - are at odds with each other. Chunking is a characteristic of expert skill, but inhibits communication. However, the communication of judgment processes is vital for improving the veracity and validity of results.

In the J/DM literature there is an often cited caution that it is easier to prevent bias from forming then it is to eliminate an already formed bias. In terms of Dr. Willing's critic, this implies the decision network should attempt before-task influencers, although it might also need to include after-task debiasers and directors. In particular, the influencers would be triggered upon noticing the patient's symptoms even before Dr. Willing input his own diagnosis. These influencers would compare this case to others where he had committed recency bias. They would attempt to prevent his faulty heuristic from being used by showing him hints, proper default reasoning pathways, and examples/analogs from the similar cases. If he still persists in his recency bias, the after-task directors might try to walk him through the normative reasoning steps. In this fashion, the critic network integrates formal reasoning theory based on rational principles of probability and statistics with a knowledge-rich approach. The latter allows the critic to notice the tendency of Dr. Willing to succumb to recency heuristics in the history of the cases in his practice.

3.3 Not even the story teller can be trusted

It seems that nobody escapes this story without criticism. In fact, my own judgment biases and knowledge absences are also partially to blame in the medical cases delineated above. First I was overconfident, and I had an illusion that I could simply select an M.D. for myself and my family based on the doctor's certification, lack of malpractice suits, size of practice, and location (Dr. Ready was near to my house) as illustrated in the top half of figure 7. The last item on this list is category A knowledge while the others are category B. Later, I was equally biased in switching my family to Dr. Willing. The original reference to him and his successful treatment of me was only a small sample of his overall abilities.

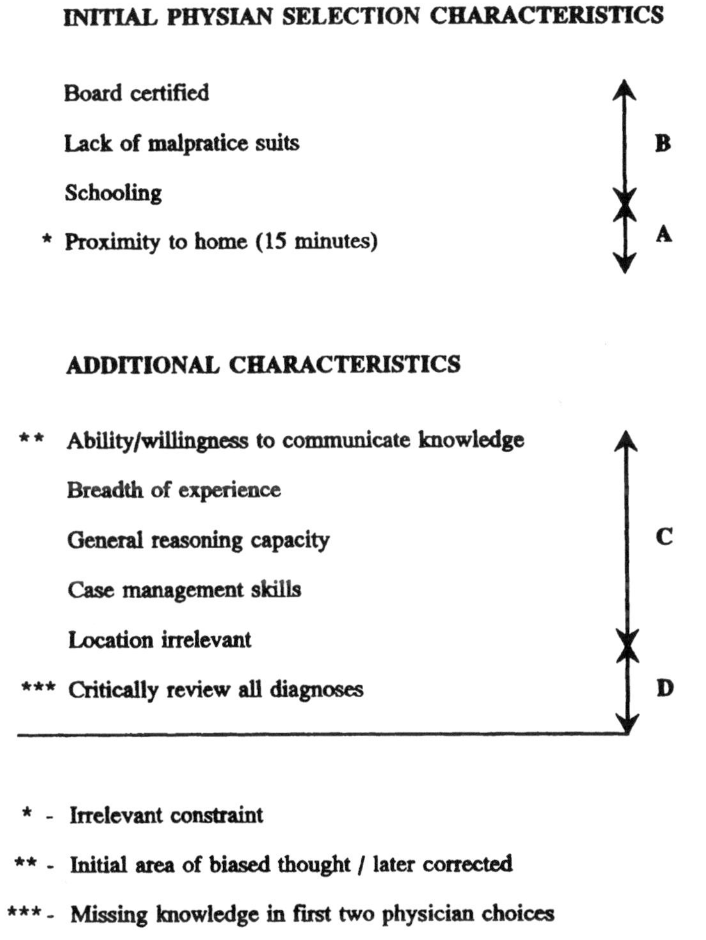

Figure 7: The story teller's decision criteria

Furthermore, since my swallowing problem fell directly into his specialty, this small sample of his abilities unduly favoured him. Not only did I ignore these "sampling" problems, but I also selectively filtered out several other unsettling category C facts such as Dr. Willing's general reticence to discuss his decisions, and his relative youth and inexperience in general practice. After my experiences with Drs. Ready and Willing, I have critiqued my own judgment processes and I have extended my knowledge base to include additional (category C and D) criteria for selecting a GP. These are shown in the bottom half of figure 7 to be whether he or she is (a) a good case manager, (b) a good general diagnostician, and (c) a user of robust judgment heuristics - all of which he or she is (d) willing to discuss. Applying these criteria I have successfully located "Dr. Able" and have been happily (though critically) following his medical advice ever since.

The points raised here are not peculiar to the practices of Drs. Ready and Willing, nor is the intent to suggest that medicine is an isolated profession where critiquing is appropriate. A survey of the Medline on-line catalog of journals in the medical field reveals over 350 citations annually under the keyword "diagnostic error" with each citation documenting between one and several thousand cases of judgment or knowledge error. Similar studies in other domains would probably reveal at least as large a sample of evidence of cognitive bias and missing knowledge error by "experts" in those professions and trades. As a further confirmation of pervasiveness of expert bias, one of the principal examples used in my research, that of a U.S. Army application, is rife with information on the nature and extent of bias in professionals as well as on the role that knowledge-based critics can play in mitigating that bias.

The opportunity facing professions and organizations is that tasks and decisions can be accomplished better with the assistance of expert critics. These critics are applied by recognizing where formal reasoning processes have been replaced by weak judgment heuristics, without loss of confidence on the decision maker's part - or - where knowledge is deficient. That is, the first step toward utilizing the framework of figures 3 and 4 is to identify what categories of knowledge are involved in a given expert's behaviour, and to pinpoint which judgment processes he is using. The second step in applying critics is to isolate the proper strategy and design that will mitigate the categories of knowledge and judgment errors that arise. Putting these two steps together is the subject of criticism based problem solving.

4. Experiments to test/validate the unified theory- and knowledge-rich approach

The value of criticism based problem solving up to this point has been illustrated by "thought experiments". To verify that it is more than just conjecture we initiated several experiments in both the laboratory and in real world applications. These experiments will be very briefly summarized below. For more details, the reader is referred to the citations provided there.

COPE has been developed over the past several years during the construction of critics for five distinct task areas and in running a couple of dozen formal experiments to test out aspects of those critics. The five task areas are heuristic classification knowledge base acquisition, forecasting, design, planning, and probabilistic reasoning. The first two of these task areas, along with other sub-tasks, have been encompassed by a large scale critic (over fifteen hundred rules, fifteen hundred objects, and two thousand rules). That critic assists in a document authoring task that is the principal case study cited in Silverman (1991b). It addresses a generic task known in the J/DM literature as "decision problem structuring" or in the A.I./E.S. literature as heuristic classification knowledge base acquisition. The latter three task of the five task areas are documented, respectively, in Zhou et.al. (1989), Silverman (1990a), and Silverman (1992a).

By researching and developing a shell for multiple task areas, much has been learned about what is and isn't yet known in the field of critics. An effort has been made to ensure: (1) that the resulting insights are reusable across domains and (2) that lessons learned are fed back to improve the theory. A poorly designed network of critics will interrupt the expert at the wrong time (too early or too late) or with the wrong level of information and thereby fail in its semiotic objective. Improving the predictive ability of the theory is important.

At the outset of this research it was initially believed that *decision networks should include all three types of critics*: influencers, debiasers and directors. In the more cognitively difficult task areas such as forecasting or probabilistic reasoning, however, the users seemed to be too absorbed in the task or, alternatively, their biases were too deeply embedded for them to effectively notice and respond to the influencers. In the case of the forecasting task area, the influencers were simply removed from the network with the result that error reduction is unaffected. This is a task area for which *100% bias reduction* was achieved by debiasers and directors.

Contrary to these results, *influencers proved so highly valuable* in the knowledge base acquisition and planning domains that subsequent debiasers and directors were rarely triggered. Further, in the design domain where only debiasers were initially tried, users uniformly indicated a dissatisfaction with the negativity of being criticized after the task. They objected to the debiasers only telling them why they couldn't do a certain design action (what is referred to as the "why not" characteristic) and wished the *critics could also be suggestive*.

Trying to understand what does influence and debias users leads to the question of how well do the various criticism strategies work? The *decision network of critics is somewhat of a "safety in numbers"* approach. That is if an early criticism strategy such as hinting fails to sway the user, there are a number of backup strategies left for the decision network to try (the ultimate strategy is to place a non-removable task failure notice in the user's final work product). In one experiment in the knowledge base acquisition task area, the decision network was replaced by a single strategy. This involved using successful past analogs to show the user where his error lay and to give him a better anchor from which to make target problem adjustments. The results of that experiment showed that many users, while benefiting from the corrective advice of the analog, copied the past solution so closely that they re-introduced other errors they earlier eliminated. That is, while analogs help improve performance on one of the cues, since backup strategies aren't available to warn them, *users tend to lower their performance on the cues not directly relevant to the analog they see*.

This and other evidence (e.g., the low user satisfaction with the single debiasing strategy in the design domain) suggest that *attempts to reduce the numbers of strategies of criticism in a given decision network are unlikely to be successful* until more is known about how users' performance is affected by individual strategies. Clearly, one or two strategy criticism should be achievable for simpler domains. For example, the spell/grammar/style critics only use two strategies: video inversion and repair suggestion. However, if one is working in more complex domains where higher level, inherently uncertain (judgment would be unnecessary if formal reasoning applied), and multiple judgments are involved, then decision *networks* of critics seem desirable to cover the many ways in which user performance needs to be improved. In the same fashion, more road signs are needed in more difficult driving conditions.

5. Discussion of results and conclusions

This article presents an extension to criticism based problem solving including a more specific theory of question asking. There is also a principle to guide application of the algorithm to specific types of bias situations. Thought experiments or cases illustrate several implementational details in the medical decisionmaking domain. A summary of results of real experiments shows the validity of the theory and principle. Details of the methodology for creating collaborators, called cognitive task analysis, were sacrificed in order to be able to devote more attention to questions of significance to the theory and its verification. In the remainder of this article, some final points about the items that were covered here will be highlighted.

5.1 Examination of lessons learned

This article has covered several items that are crucial to the process of designing decision networks of critics and which will now be summarized and clarified. In some cases these lessons learned lead to the extension of traditional, long held beliefs in the knowledge engineering for knowledge based systems community.

1. Judgment Heuristics and Substantive Knowledge Should Be Treated Equally: The traditional knowledge based systems approach does not discriminate between the substantive knowledge of a domain that an expert accumulates through years of experience and the intuitional heuristics such as availability and recency, among others, that the expert uses to manipulate his substantive knowledge. In traditional knowledge based systems all heuristics are treated equally. The points made in this paper and the lessons of J/DM theory shed serious doubt on the validity of this practice and raise the prospect of knowledge engineers having to treat (at least) two types of knowledge.

2. Judgment Theory Offers a "Deep Knowledge" for the Design of Knowledge Based Systems: Most expert systems to date have succeeded with shallow heuristics. The idea of "deep knowledge" in expert systems, where it is beginning to be used, is often meant to refer to first principles about the substantive knowledge of a domain (e.g., laws of physics or of nature). This definition ignores the heuristics that experts use to manipulate substantive knowledge. The mis-use of these can lead to errors remaining in the knowledge base for years to come. Human judgment theory refocuses this definition and raises the prospect that one should closely examine the epistemology of a given expert's intuition. Such examinations have been shown in this research to confirm widespread occurrences of bias even among professionals.

3. J/DM Theory is Relevant to More Than Lay-Persons: Many of the J/DM experiments on human cognition have illustrated that lay persons are biased in their processing of probability and statistics notions. While that was not necessarily the goal of J/DM research, it has become a widespread belief in other fields. There J/DM theory is often dismissed by stating that experts do not commit such biased judgments. There is substantial evidence in the literature as well as in the studies presented throughout this article that most of the biases of lay persons can also be observed in experts as well. For example, the biases of medical diagnosticians were illustrated in this article. The point is that J/DM is a fertile field that can be ploughed for theoretical guidance useful to the design of either critics or other types of knowledge based systems.

4. Critic Engineering Successfully Extends Knowledge Engineering: Knowledge engineering leads to a qualitative, structural model of the domain. The structural model via the help of GT theory is a vital element of knowledge acquisition. It is the critical breakthrough that permitted the field to reach the level of performance it has attained.

Developing a structural model is equivalent to answering the Level One questions of figure 3. But, critic theory suggests designers (of knowledge acquisition systems or of any knowledge based system) go even further. They should go further, not just on their own initiative as often happens, but in a systematic, theoretically supported fashion. That is the purpose of Levels Two through Five of figure 3.

Thus, while traditional knowledge structure modelling or GT description of the domain (Level One of figure 3) helps define a knowledge base, the critic theoretic approach forces the designer to confront the root cause of the errors and biases. By applying the full five levels of figure 3, preparatory subtasks are discovered, biases in doing those subtasks are analyzed, and criticism based problem solving is deployed for a new domain.

The point of this discussion is to introduce the designer to a formal procedure he can follow for any domain. This extends GT rooted structural modelling into criticism based knowledge acquisition system engineering. This is referred to here as critic engineering.

5.2 Judgment theory is a source of deep knowledge models of expert error and repair

The current generation of knowledge based systems has pursued the definition and use of models of specific task types. The same holds true for the design of critics. A library of bias identification triggers and standard critiquing strategies appropriate to specific task types is needed. Developing that library, however, involves a "critic engineering" process that is markedly different from traditional knowledge engineering. The steps of critic engineering illustrated in this article is the author's attempt to extend knowledge engineering in the directions needed to model the error commission and repair processes of domain experts. Extensions to generic task theory have been offered for the case where critic, rather than expert, systems are the design goal. These results should enhance the semiotic properties of any joint man-machine cognitive system as well as of human-computer collaboration in general. I believe this is relevant to a principal focus of the field of semiotics that is concerned with the meaning and understandability of symbols and knowledge.

References

Arkes, H.R., Hammond, K.R. (1986). *Judgment and Decision Making: An Interdisciplinary Reader*. Cambridge: Cambridge Univ. Press.

Bylander, T. Chandrasekaran, B. (1987). Generic Tasks for Knowledge Based Reasoning: The Right Level of Abstraction for Knowledge Acquisition, *International Journal of Man-Machine Studies*, vol. 26, 231-243.

Fischer, G. (1989). Communication Requirements For Cooperative Problem Solving Systems, *International Journal of Information Systems* (to appear in a special issue on Knowledge Engineering).

Kahneman, D., Slovic, P. Tversky, A. (1982). *Judgment Under Uncertainty: Heuristics and Biases*. Cambridge: Cambridge Univ. Press.

Langlotz, C.P., Shortliffe, E.H. (1983). Adapting A Consultation System To Critique User Plans, *Int. J. Man-Machine Studies*, vol. 19, 479-496.

McDermott, J. (1988). Exploiting Task Structure to Automate Knowledge Acquisition. Invited AAAI-88 talk (tape recording and flip charts) available from M. Kaufman, Palo Alto, 1988.

Miller, P.L. (1986). *Expert Critiquing Systems: Practice-Based Medical Consultation By Computer*. New York: Springer-Verlag.

Miller, P.L. (1983). ATTENDING: Critiquing A Physician's Management Plan, IEEE Trans. On PAMI, *PAMI-5*, n. 5, 449-461.

Silverman, B.G. (1990). Critiquing Judgment Bias Via Knowledge Acquisition Systems, *AI Magazine*, vol. 11:3, 60-79.

Silverman, B.G. (1991a). Expert Critics: Operationalizing the Judgment/Decisionmaking Literature as a Theory of "Bugs" and Repair Strategies, *International Journal of Knowledge Acquisition*, vol. 3, 175-214.

Silverman, B.G. (1991b). Criticism Based Knowledge Acquisition in Document Generation. In: *Innovative Applications of Artificial Intelligence*, Menlo Park: AAAI Press, 291-319.

Silverman, B.G. (1992a). *Critiquing Human Error: A Knowledge Based Human-Computer Collaboration Approach*. London: Academic Press (book manuscript in process).

Silverman, B.G. (1992b). Evaluating and Refining Expert Critiquing Systems, *Decision Sciences Journal*, accepted for Jan.Feb.'92.

Spickelmier, R.L., Newton, A.R. (1988). Critic: A Knowledge-Based Program for Critiquing Circuit Designs. In: *Proc. of the 1988 IEEE International Conf. on Computer Design: VLSI in Computers and Processors*, IEEE Computer Soc. Press, 324-327.

Staff (1989). *Knowledge Engineers Guide to COPE*, Potomac: IntelliTek.

Staff (1990). *COPE Users Guide*, Potomac: IntelliTek.

Zhou, H., Simkol, J., Silverman,B.G. (1989). Configuration Assessment Logics for Electromagnetic Effects Reduction (CLEER) of Equipment on Naval Ships, *Naval Engineers Journal*, vol. 101:3, 127-137.

Procrustes, or the future of flexibility

H. VISSER (Tilburg)

1. Introduction

In the early days of automatic information processing, sceptics expressed their doubts about the possibilities for computers to perform other than elementary information processes and combinations of such processes. They believed that it would be impossible to construct machines that could perform "higher" processes such as processes for means-end analysis and planning. However, the success, notably of computer-chess programs, has contributed a lot to the disappearance of this kind of criticism. The sceptics had to look for other weaknesses of computers and this time they produced another trump-card: computers might be programmed for performing "deep" information processing tasks, but not for carrying out ordinary, every-day knowledge and information processing activities. Nevertheless, A.I.-scientists tried to demonstrate that the task of programming computers with "common sense" would not be insurmountable.

In this paper, the controversy between the optimists, who believe that "common sense" can be programmed, and their critics is reduced to what is seen as the hard core of common sense: the availability of a flexible instrument with which common sense activities can be carried out. Successively, the following subjects are dealt with: an overview of some attempts to address the problem of programming common sense, starting with McCarthy's early contribution to the 1958 Symposium on Mechanisation of Thought Processes (§ 2); an analysis of the shortcomings of these attempts (§ 3); the presentation of alternatives (§ 4); and, finally, an outline of possible prospects of programs *without* common sense in human society, in short, the future of flexibility (§ 5).

2. Programs with common sense

John McCarthy's early paper "Programs with common sense" is notable for at least three reasons; (1) it contained a characterization of the notion of common sense, in connection with computer programs; (2) it gave translations of statements in the English language into a kind of formalized language, in which it was possible to draw "automatic conclusions"; (3) it assumed that there is a straightforward connection between (a) wanting something, together with (b) believing that it is possible to achieve, by a sequence of actions, what is wanted, and (c) initiating the first of these actions. McCarthy's (1959) characterization was as follows:

> We shall (...) say that a program has common sense if it automatically deduces for itself a sufficiently wide class of immediate consequences of anything it is told and what it already knows.

This means that McCarthy assumed that a program with common sense might be "told" (1) atomic formulas of the form: $A^{(n)}a_1a_2 \dots a_n$, in which $A^{(n)}$ is a n-place predicate symbol, and (2) general formulas of the form: For all x_1, x, ..., x_n, if ... and ... and ..., then ..., made up from atomic formulas, variables and constants. However, in the course of the article, McCarthy imposed the requirement that his purported program, called "the advice taker", should also have present *in his memory* some specified atomic formulas, containing the information about where specific "objects" such as a desk, a car, a home and an airport, are at a given time; moreover, he stipulated that his program should also contain general formulas, describing what can be done with these objects. He said that "we must impose this requirement if we are to be able to say that the advice taker exhibits common sense".

One cannot but conclude that the distinction between "common sense" and "real world knowledge" was not drawn at that time. But knowing that one's car is at home, is quite different from knowing, for example, that if one can achieve, in a situation in which p_1 is the case, by doing a_1 that p_2 is the case, and in a situation that p_2 is the case, by doing a_2 that p_3 is the case, then one can achieve, in a situation that p_1 is the case, by doing first a_1 and then a_2 that p_3 is the case. (This is a translation of one of McCarthy's general formulas.)

In a later elaboration of this original paper, McCarthy assumed that an artificial system with common sense would have in its memory not only representations of general properties of action, but also representations of general properties of causality and time. But in order to "solve" problems derived from experiments by Wolfgang Köhler with chimps - actually caricatures of these experiments - McCarthy (1968) attributed to the system an "axiom" which says that each person who can perform a certain action a_1 and an action a_2, can also perform the action (a_1 and a_2). This shows that the problem of integrating action theory into first order logic was not yet solved. Though McCarthy did not notice the inadequacy of his theory of action, he admitted that "there is at present no formal theory in which one can express the kind of means-end analysis used in ordinary life".

Similarly, McCarthy and Hayes (1969), in their well-known paper "Some philosophical problems from the standpoint of artificial intelligence", still saw that the task "to define a naive, common sense view of the world precise enough to program a computer to act accordingly" was far from solved. But they maintained the view that a kind of first-order logical formalism was the obvious means for "epistemologically adequate" representations of the world, in the sense that the solution of problems, requiring intelligence in humans, would follow from the facts expressed in these representations. As a matter of fact, they began to lean on results in the field of philosophical logic (modal logics, tense logics, epistemic logics). Simultaneously, their attention shifted from problem solving to representing real world properties without reference to possible problems.

This also holds for Hayes' (1979) well-known "naive physics" papers, in which a subfield of common sense knowledge, called naive physics, is distinguished. Hayes' aim was explicitly "to construct a formalisation of a large part of ordinary everyday knowledge of the physical world". He made the proposal to look for so-called clusters of concepts, supposing that there are sets of related concepts, all of which have to do with a certain general domain, such as "liquids" and "places and positions of physical objects". For each cluster, a formalization of the constituent concepts has to be given, together with an axiomatization of properties of the corresponding domain. (Hayes' own work on the "ontology of liquids" serves as a paradigm.) The goal of each axiomatization is that all (and only) the immediate, plausible properties of the domain under consideration follow from the axioms of the formalization. In due times, the theories for different clusters have to be combined in order to cover "the whole range of everyday physical phenomena".

With this approach, Hayes departed from earlier attempts to give a general theory for, say, causality. Causality, to put it simply, is not considered a cluster: "there is no useful, more-or-less self-contained theory of causality"; what happens when other things happen, depends on circumstances, and is different for different clusters. Similarly, Hayes regarded the traditional approach of first trying to develop a general theory for change and action as an obstacle to the development of formalizations of the physical world.

3. Shortcomings of programs for "programs with common sense"

The contributions to Artificial Intelligence mentioned in section 2, show several defects. Three of them will be dealt with: the first has to do with the explicit neglect of questions of implementation or even the lack of any indication which problems should be solved and in what way; the second has to do with the underlying notions of common sense knowledge and naive physics; the third has to do with the question of the piecemeal formalizations of separate theories.

The *first* point, the explicit neglect of questions of implementation is obvious from Hayes' (1985) second manifesto: "It is *not* proposed to make a computer program which can 'use' the formalism in some sense". Thus, McCarthy and Hayes (1969) suggested that it is possible to separate questions of "epistemologically adequate" representations from "heuristically adequate representations". One wonders why these writers keep calling their work "Artificial Intelligence". Who has ever heard of "intelligence" apart from "acting intelligently"? How great the temptation is to distinguish two questions instead of seeing one, can be seen from Israel's (1985) statement "What must an intelligent, though artificial, creature know, and what must it be able to do with what it knows?". The effect is that a so-called "knowledge base" is separated from an ability to do something. Strange: do these authors realize that the separation is *not* made in research on *natural* intelligence; where does the separation between knowing and doing come from? From philosophy? But not all philosophers are that one-sided - as can be seen from the opening sentences of C.I. Lewis' (1946) *An analysis of knowledge and valuation*: "Knowledge, action, and evaluation are essentially connected. The primary and pervasive significance of knowledge lies in its guidance of action: knowing is for the sake of doing. And action, obviously, is rooted in evaluation."

That A.I. people take logicians and linguists as their examples rather than psychologists, becomes unbearable in the naive physics stream: there is no mention at all of the classic work by Lipmann at the Institute for Applied Psychology at Berlin in the twenties. In their book *Naive Physik* of 1923, Lipmann and Bogen described several experimental situations in which children are tested for their ability to solve practical problems such as getting a piece of chocolate out of a cage with the help of some object, say a stick, which is on a table in front of them. I shall return to these experiments.

The *second* point addresses the so-called formal theories of the common sense world more directly. It is concerned with the alleged theoretical background and with the content of these theories. What do these authors mean by "common sense knowledge"? McCarthy's original proposal, quoted at the beginning of section 2, sounds as if McCarthy joined the so-called Frege-Davidson program for a theory of logical form, which, according the Harman (1974), "must account for all implications that speakers take to be obvious by means of a finite set of axioms or obvious rules". Apart from the obvious inadequacy of this proposal, it is interesting to see that McCarthy also believed that "the intelligence, if any", of his advice taker, "would not be embodied in the immediate deduction routine", but "in the procedures which choose the lists of premisses to which the immediate deduction routine is to be applied". For, as McCarthy (1959) assures us, "of course, the program should never attempt to apply the immediate deduction routine simultaneously to the list of everything it knows. This would make the deduction routine too long".

Apparently, an important part of common sense knowledge is concerned with the selection of the "right" data with which a given problem can be solved, including search procedures. However, a given problem usually leaves room for more than one solution and solution method. This may mean either that the advice taker should *evaluate* different solutions or methods, or that special "common sense solutions" are within his reach. It looks as if the distinction of epistemological and heuristic adequacy was emphasized in order to avoid such questions.

Hayes' (1985) "Second Naive Physics Manifesto" bears witness to this: it is presented as a proposal for "the construction of a formalisation of a sizable portion of common sense knowledge about the every day physical world of objects, space, movements, substances (solids and liquids), time, etc.," which "should cover the whole range of everyday physical phenomena". Nowhere is the insight shown that our common sense knowledge of the external world manifests itself in our actions and our ways of acting. As a matter of fact, intelligence has always been connected with the ability to solve certain problems - sometimes in thought, but often by manipulating things. Why should we not also bring the ability to solve problems under the concept of common sense?

The *third* point of criticism is the question of the piecemeal formalisation of separate theories; this might be interesting, from a mathematical point of view, as an exercise in axiomatization, but it is a fact that the instrument human beings use successfully in their descriptions of the so-called common sense world, a natural language, does not have this neat division. Words as 'at' and 'between', to mention a few, are used in connection with places as well as with time, and also with regard to pitch and other phenomenal qualities. Constructing partial theories gives rise to a cumulation of instruments fitted for special tasks, but lacking any kind of flexibility.

Admittedly, Hayes occasionally shows some insight into the flexibility or openness of ordinary concepts: "if a concept makes intuitive sense in a wide variety of circumstances, but its candidate theory somehow presupposes a more limited framework, then something is wrong". He also draws the attention to mathematical concepts, but as soon as he thinks of formalization, he falls back upon his "cluster" approach.

4. Alternatives

4.1 Proposals

It is time to make a new start by giving more operational proposals for the way in which we are going to use terms like 'common sense knowledge' and 'naive physics'. Since this subject is extensively dealt with in another paper (Visser, 1991), only an outline of the main ideas is given. One of the starting-points is a problem, given by Duncker (1935) in his classical treatise on productive thinking: "On the occasion of a mountain-trip, in which the descent occurred on the same road as the ascent of the preceding day, I wondered whether there would be a place on the road, at which I was at the same time in the descent as well in the ascent, presupposing that they took place at the same time of day (say from 5 a.m. to 12 a.m.)?" Duncker used it as an illustration of "the original function" of a proof of presenting direct "readableness". As a matter of fact, the problem has one solution that is immediately understandable: "Divide ascent and descent between two persons on the same day; then they must meet each other". There is indeed a world of difference between this "common sense solution" and an appeal to the intermediate value theorem for continuous functions; within the context of the problem, a mathematical solution is even far-fetched.

From this and other problems, it seems plausible to explicate the notion of a common sense solution of a problem as a solution of that problem that can be described in ordinary language in such a way that it is immediately understood and recognized as a solution by anyone who understands the problem formulation.

Common sense knowledge then can be defined as that which is needed to produce common sense solutions of problems. The well-known eight-puzzle may serve as another illustration. The problem of transforming the position

7	8	1		1	2	3
6		2	into	8		4
5	4	3		7	6	5

admits a common sense solution, as the reader can easily verify. The same holds for the problem of transforming

5	6	7		1	2	3
4		8	into	8		4
3	2	1		7	6	5

even if its solution takes thirty so-called elementary moves.

It is possible that a computer program also gives the same elementary moves which constitute a common sense solution. Indeed a program, based on Nilsson's evaluation function, solves to a depth of four moves, the second problem by moving successively the pieces 6, 5, 4, 3, 2, 1, 8, 7, 5, 4, 3, 2, 1, 8, 7, 5, 4, 3, 2, 1, 8, 7, 5, 4, 3, 2, 1, 8, 7, and 6. However, this program is clearly inadequate, since to a depth of eight moves, it does not solve this problem at all, for by successively moving the tiles 6, 5, 4, 6, 5, 4, 6, 5, 4, 6, 5, 4, it gets into a loop. Another computer program, based on a Manhattan distance function, does solve the problem of transforming

4	5	6		1	2	3
2		7	into	8		4
3	1	8		7	6	5

by successively moving the pieces 2, 3, 1, 8, 7, 6, 5, 4, 3, 1, 8, 7, 6, 5, 4, 3, 1, 8, 7, 6, 5, 4, 3, and 2, so that it looks as if the computers gives the common sense solution! However, the same program solves the problem of transforming

5	6	7		1	2	3
4		2	into	8		4
3	1	8		7	6	5

by successively moving the tiles 6, 5, 4, 6, 1, 3, 6, 1, 5, 7, 2, 5, 3, 8, 5, 3, 7, 4, 1, 7, 8, 6, 7, 8, 4, 2, 3, 4, in stead of first bringing piece 2 into the middle, then "turning" all other pieces clockwise "round" till they have reached their proper place, and finally moving tile 2 into its proper place.

By analogy, I characterize the notion of a *naive physics solution* of a problem as a solution of that problem which can be demonstrated in such a way that it is immediately understood by each person who understands the problem. From experiments carried out by Lipmann and Bogen (1923) it can be seen that natural language indications help test-subjects to find the solution; for example: 'take a stick and push the piece of chocolate'. But it is not clear whether mere showing how to do it is enough to make them understand. Experiments with imbecile children who cannot even understand the instruction and only repeat part of the solution shown - such as taking the stick - suggest that here too natural language activities play more than an accompanying role. Perhaps a naive physics solution has to be *described* somehow by the test-person - in inner speech - before she understands the way of solution shown ("I see, you have to push the piece of chocolate!").

4.2 Natural languages

That natural languages are so adequate for describing some solutions to some problems asks for an explanation. As a first approach to such an explanation, I point again to the enormous flexibility or multi-functionality of words or expressions of a natural language. The same expression, say "to turn around", is used in many occasions, in several "language games", for several "clusters", though its different meanings are not wholly unrelated. Psychologically speaking, users of a natural language might find their common sense solutions of problems thanks to similarities and analogies with problems for which they already have encountered common sense solutions. The idea is that the descriptions of these common sense solutions make use of the same natural language expression as the newly discovered ones. This suggests that starting with isolated clusters is not an adequate way of describing common sense knowledge. Instead, we should start with general concepts and specify their fundamental properties. The part-whole relation is a good example. John McCarthy (1959) might have had something like this in mind, when he introduced a general relation between a place and a sub-place in his "program with common sense". But of course, the part-whole relation is not restricted to places.

There is a special category of words of an ordinary language which have striking properties: verbs. Verbs have the property that they bring several actions together - as Mauthner (1913) already emphasized. I restrict myself to one "story" by De Haan (1916): "A patient came to a doctor and complained that he had pain, when he stretched his right arm slantwise backwards, and then did the same with his left arm, then stretched both arms widely sidewards, and then moved them fast to each other. Asked the doctor impatiently, why it was necessary to make such strange movements. Answered the patient that without these strange movements he could not put on his jacket. In other words: when the speaker split the action 'put on a jacket' into only four or five actions, he was not understood anymore". This property of verbs is, in some sense, recognized by A.I. scientists, who seem to have invented substitutes for them. The question is whether such substitutes have similar virtues as natural language expressions.

4.3 Substitutes for natural languages?

The computer analogon of verbs is presented by the concept of a macro-operator; it brings several "elementary" operators together, for example in the eight-puzzle, where each series of elementary moves between two moves of one and the same tile first bringing it into the middle, and second into a place on the edge - can be regarded as a macro-operator. But of course, its use is not restricted to mathematical games such as the eight-puzzle. Yet the effectiveness of "an architecture for general intelligence" called SOAR, was demonstrated by Laird, Newell, and Rosenbloom (1987) with the help of this puzzle. SOAR was presented as a means to enable an artificial system "to perform the full range of cognitive tasks, employ the full range of problem solving methods and representations appropriate for the tasks, and learn about all aspects of the tasks and its performance on them". However, it may be expected that SOAR will undergo the same fate as its precursors, as long as no attention is paid to that other aspect of natural languages, flexibility. Macro-operator without flexibility are not much better than the traditional GPS-approaches to means-end analysis. Let us assume that it is possible for a program based on SOAR to create the macro-operator of twenty-eight (!) moves that can be seen to occur in the common sense solution of the second of the above eight-puzzle problems. Would it then be possible for this program to use the defined concept in other environments? This would require that the intended operator is brought under a concept that is not restricted to the eight-puzzle. Since the program cannot be expected to have a natural language at its disposal, we have to look for a substitute. Fortunately, mathematical concepts, such as orderings and transformations, are not domain-specific; they are applicable to quite different "clusters", as soon as these can be seen to share certain mathematical structures.

This means that programs, based on SOAR, should also contain procedures for pattern recognition, not in the sense that certain configurations are regarded as symbols or as pictures of certain objects, but as means for discovering mathematically describable patterns. Without evidence that this will be the case, Newell has no justification for his claim that his architecture can serve as a basis for an adequate psychological theory.

Computer chess theorists and programmers do not have the pretension of presenting psychological theories. Yet it would be very helpful if computer chess programs also had a substitute for natural language at their disposal. Consider the problem of winning a King-Bishop-Knight/King endgame; we know that White should drive the Black King into a corner with a square of the same colour as the White Bishop. With such descriptions, human chess players understand endgame strategies. From this psychological fact, a negative judgment of the advancements in computer chess can be given, which has some similarity with the criticism of SOAR: what is the practical and theoretical relevance of Thompson's (1986) solution of the problem of winning a King-Queen/King-Knight-Knight endgame, as long as it is not somehow brought under concepts of a natural language or suitable substitutes?

5. The future of flexibility

In traditional, good old fashioned communication processes, the use of natural language plays a crucial role: it can give clues for "immediate insight" - which might have pleased McCarthy when he stipulated that a program with common sense must be able to draw immediate consequences of anything it is told and what it already knows. Moreover, if, by accident, direct insight is not achieved immediately, one of the participants of the "language game" can indicate why he does not understand. It is not clear how man-machine interactions could have the same virtues as human interactions, without the means of a natural language or suitable substitutes.

An interesting example is the use of computers in schools. It is well-known that the projects on programmed instruction of the sixties were stopped. They could not compete with traditional teaching, and they were found too boring to work with. The latter problem seems absent in computer-aided instruction, but the former still remains, as long as the programs work with menus only. This requires from human users that they adapt themselves to such programs: teaching is replaced by instructing. In general, computers without common sense are as rigid as the concepts which they use. Though human beings are so "flexible" that they can adapt themselves to rigid programs, it can be questioned whether such a development should be welcomed. If the only "flexibility" of a computer program is that it offers different menus to users with different abilities and attitudes, it still remains the case that the chosen menu regulates the actions of human beings.

Suppose that there is a growing number of computer programs which *must* be used, for the simple reason that no human beings are available any more to do the job. Then one of the dangers is that people who get used to doing things with the help of computers, may *unlearn* to do this without them. It is also possible that certain activities which were formerly done in human interaction, are not taught and learned anymore. Is this harmless or not? There are critics of A.I., such as Winograd and Flores (1986), who point out that computers are dangerous because they cannot "fall back on common sense" in case of a so-called "break-down". The reply, that in such a case human beings can take over, may be beside the point, for the simple reason that the break-down might not be discovered. However, in the situation sketched above it is thinkable that the breakdown *is* discovered, but that nobody is able any more to take over, because the ability to do the task with human means has disappeared. Procrustean progress has robbed people of their flexibility. This sounds as if the computer revolution has already changed fundamentally what it is to be human, as Arbib (1985) assumed. *But the future of flexibility is still up to us*: let us leave "deep" information processing tasks to the computer, but continue to carry out ordinary, everyday knowledge processing activities ourselves.

References

Arbib, M.A. (1985). "On being human in the computer age." In: Trappl, R. (ed.) (1985). *Impacts of artificial intelligence*. Amsterdam: North-Holland, pp. 52-63.

De Haan, J.I. (1916). Rechtskundige significa en hare toepassing op de begrippen: "aansprakelijk, verantwoordelijk, toerekeningsvatbaar". Amsterdam: W. Versluys.

Duncker, K. (1935). *Zur Psychologie des produktiven Denkens*. Berlin: Springer.

Harman, G. (1973). *Thought*. Princeton: Princeton University Press.

Hayes, P.J. (1979). "The naive physics manifesto". In: D. Michie (ed.) (1979). *Expert systems in the micro-electronic age*. Edinburgh: Edinburgh University Press, pp. 242-270.

Hayes, P.J. (1985). "The second naive physics manifesto". In: J.R. Hobbs and R.C. Moore (eds.) (1985). *Formal theories of the common sense world*. Norwoord, N.U., Ablex Publishing Corporation, pp. 1-36.

Israël, D. (1985). "A short companion to the naive physics manifesto". In: J.R. Hobbs and R.C. Moore (eds.) (1985). *Formal theories of the common sense world*. Norwood, N.J.: Ablex Publishing Corporation, pp. 427-447.

Laird, J.E., Newell, A., and Rosenbloom, P.S. (1987). "SOAR: An architecture for general intelligence". *Artifical Intelligence 33*, pp. 1-64.

Lewis, C.I. (1946). *An analysis of knowledge and valuation*. La Salle, Ill.: Open Court.

Lipmann, O. und Bogen, H. (1923). *Naive Physik*. Leipzig: Johann Ambrosius Barth.

Mauthner, F. (1913). *Beiträge zu einer Kritik der Sprache*, III. Leipzig: Felix Meiner.

McCarthy, J. (1959). "Programs with common sense". In: *Mechanisation of thought processes*. National Physical Laboratory, Symposium No. 10. London: Her Majesty's Stationary Office, 1959, pp. 85-91.

McCarthy, J. (1968). "Programs with common sense". In: Minsky, M.L. (ed.) (1968). *Semantic information processing*. Cambridge, Mass.: MIT Press, pp. 403-418.

Thompson, K. (1986). "Retrograde analysis of certain endgames". *ICCA Journal* 9, pp. 131-139.

Visser, H. (1991). "Common sense, naive physics, and artificial intelligence". *Methodology and Science*. (in print).

Winograd, T., and Flores, F. (1986). *Understanding computers and cognition*. Norwood, N.J.: Ablex Publishing Corporation.

III

Communication with Expert Systems

Believing, causing, intending: The basis for a hierarchy of sign concepts in the reconstruction of communication

R. Posner (Berlin)

1. Introduction

1.1 Cybernetic ancestors of communicating machines

When cybernetics was experiencing its heyday in the 1960's, there was a team of researchers in Berlin which worked towards the development of teaching machines (cf. Cube, 1985). Felix von Cube, Helmar Frank, Herbert Stachowiak and other professors at the West Berlin Teachers' Training College prepared a scenario that became facetiously described as

> a computer sitting in the professor's armchair and talking via loudspeakers to a class of students who eagerly copied what the machine had to say on pieces of paper lying in front of them.

Docile as they were, the students involved in the project ironically proposed a seemingly even more efficient solution to the teaching and learning task:

> If we can replace the professor by a machine that teaches through loudspeakers why not replace the students by cassette recorders!

With this modification, the scenario of a fully automatized classroom was to become a proverbial nightmare of German educational planning authorities in the seventies and eighties.

What was it that made this scenario so horrifying?

It was the attempt to automatize a set of activities often considered essentially human, namely

- learning and teaching,
- gaining experiences and passing them on to others,
- forming one's personality by self-determined exposure to the circumstances of life as well as to reports about the life of others.

What intensified the horror was the blatant inadequacy of the machines designed for that purpose in the sixties. The students therefore made a good point when they ridiculed a teaching machine which consisted of little more than

- a *memory* filled with pedagogically structured data and
- a device for the *transmission* of these data through auditory or visual display

by confronting it with a learning machine which consisted of not much more than

- a device for the auditory or visual *registration* of these data and
- a *memory* in the form of a cassette tape.

If classroom communication consists in the unmodified transmission of ready-made data from one memory to another, it seems superfluous. Humans can do without it because they have more efficient ways of information intake, such as solitary reading; machines do not need it because there are devices for more direct information transfer available, such as machine-internal duplication of data from one data-carrier onto another.

1.2 Communication and Artificial Intelligence

You may ask what this story from our cybernetic ancestors can tell us today in the age of Artificial Intelligence (A.I.), where expert systems with inference machines and internal and external testing devices for incoming information have replaced the crude devices of the old days.

The irony of the story is that the shortcomings that led to the rejection of the computer in the classroom (and to the rejection of much of the cybernetic approach with it) have also turned out to be responsible for the present conceptual crisis in the development of intelligent systems (cf. Andersen, 1990 and Jorna, 1990). It is no use filling a system's memory with millions of pieces of encyclopedic data if we cannot provide it with powerful devices for organizing and reorganizing these data with respect to changing purposes. Artificial information processing systems must become capable of

- *responding to questions* by quickly restructuring their memorized data, so that they make the relevant stored information accessible within the short time typical for human interaction;
- *sustaining a dialogue*, i.e., jointly constructing relevant homogeneous pieces of complex information by putting together data that have been stored in separate systems;

jointly setting goals for their dialogue, and modifying them in mutual agreement in the course of the dialogue, so that each system can treat the encoded information made available by its dialogue partner as a contribution towards the common goal.

In other words, in order to function as intelligent systems, computers must become capable of goal-oriented information search, joint composition of information from separate sources and co-operative information processing. Possessing information and being able to encode it in some external expression does not suffice for a system to be called intelligent, it must also be able to design this expression as a contribution to a specific mutually determined dialogue goal and to process the dialogue partner's output as a contribution to such a dialogue goal. In short, for an information processing system to be intelligent, it must not only have the capacities of 'knowing' and 'saying' something but also of 'meaning' something when 'saying' it and of 'understanding' something 'said' by a co-operating system: what makes a machine an intelligent system also enables it to communicate.

One of the greatest obstacles to the design of communicating computers has until now been the application of the *code* concept in information theory. Software engineers have taken the code to be a mechanism that maps one symbol structure onto another, and have thus hypothesized understanding to consist in nothing but the activation of such a mapping device. They have not been sufficiently aware of the fact that communication involves a complex interplay of sign processes, occurring on various levels of reflection and leading to continuously modified hypotheses about the communication partner's dialogue goals, his available knowledge and knowledge deficits, the depth of knowledge sought at each stage of the communication, etc. (cf. Dennett, 1987). They have not been aware of these processes because these mostly occur beneath the surface of verbal behaviour in human communication and are rarely made the topic of an explicit exchange of information. Communication is not just encoding and decoding given information (cf. Posner, 1992), it involves

- beliefs,
- intentions to make others believe,
- intentions to modify one's own beliefs and
- intentions to make the partners act in specific ways straight away or later on.

This approach is to be discussed and elaborated upon in what follows.

1.3 The relation between semiotics and intensional logic

Before beginning this discussion, however, it is necessary to point out a further obstacle to an adequate reconstruction of the processes of communication in A.I. research - an obstacle created by cultural traditions that are entrenched in our various natural languages.

Since the days of Plato and Aristotle, two separate terminologies have been used to describe what happens in communication between organisms. On the one hand there seem to be *extraorganismic* objects: sign vehicles, signals, symbols, words, pictures, sounds etc. They appear to be endowed with magic powers that somehow make them carry messages, contain content, have sense. What can someone do who wants to study such extraorganismic objects? He must find criteria for classifying them: according to the medium in which they occur, the channel through which they are transmitted, the relation that exists between the sign vehicle and the message carried by it, etc.

In this paradigm, semioticians (cf. Eco, 1976 and Nöth, 1990) and linguists (cf. Lyons, 1977) have set up taxonomies opposing

- human versus animal signs,
- visual versus auditory, tactile, olfactory and gustatory signs,
- natural versus nonnatural signs,
- indexes versus icons versus symbols,
- nouns versus verbs, adjectives, adverbs and sentences.

Summarizing the results, we can say that this *object-oriented* approach has given access to an enormously rich realm of sign types but is now approaching stagnation due to the taxonomic methodology and the algebraic apparatus used in its description. Moreover, what happens when an intelligent system uses signs of the various types in communication has not been grasped.

On the other hand all European languages offer a rich terminology for the description of *intraorganismic* attitudes and processes such as thinking and knowing; believing, assuming and hypothesizing; wanting, wishing and intending; inferring, concluding and proving. These appear to happen internally without a material basis. Someone who wants to study them seems bound to investigate the so-called "inner life" of a person or animal. Psychological introspection and logical analysis of rules of inference are the methodological procedures usually applied in this *subject-oriented* approach (cf. Finocchiaro, 1989, who develops an alternative empirical methodology).

As a result, elaborate theories were developed, e.g., about cognitive dissonance or about proof procedures in 2-, 3- and n-valued logics. However, what happens when an intelligent system thinks, believes, intends and infers during a communication process has not really been grasped.

And a psychology and a logic that cut themselves off from analyzing actual communication are bound to stagnate and become marginal, too.

In the subject-oriented paradigm it is often said that one thinks, believes, assumes, hypothesizes, infers, concludes and proves on the basis of "evidence". But what the status of that evidence is, remains generally unasked (however, cf. Chisholm, 1966: ch. 4). Logicians and psychologists have to realize that what they call evidence is exactly what is analyzed as sign, index, icon and symbol in semiotics. And semioticians and linguists have to realize that what they call a message does not exist without

- someone conceiving of it,
- someone wanting someone else to receive, believe, infer it and
- someone making someone else do something by producing it.

It so happens that English has a word which bridges the gap between objectified external signs and messages on the one hand and subjectified internal beliefs, intentions and inferences on the other. It is the word "meaning", which can occur in both contexts (cf. Grice, 1957 and 1982; as well as Schiffer, 1972 and 1987). We use it to denote the mysterious semantic force of an external object, this being either a symbol or symbol complex as in "word meaning" and in "the meaning of this text, picture, symphony"; or an artifact as in "the meaning of the Berlin wall" and "the meaning of the tunnel under the Channel"; or a natural phenomenon as in "the meaning of the dark cloud in the sky" and "the meaning of the high waves on this lake". And we use it to denote the mysterious pragmatic force of a personal act as in "Peter means Mary", "the hooligan meant to hit you" and "John meant that you are mistaken".

It is my contention that the two correlative mysteries will disappear once we start seeing the meanings of external objects and the internal acts of meaning as two sides of the same coin.

In what follows I will therefore engage you in the actual analysis of sign processes occurring in various types of human interaction, including what can be called communication. My aim will be to present a semiotic framework for the analysis of all possible sign processes. I will introduce semiotic concepts for each sign type and will define these semiotic concepts on the basis of three central concepts of intensional logic, namely 'believe', 'cause' and 'intend'. For the purpose of this presentation I will take it for granted that 'believe', 'cause' and 'intend' can be characterized in a sound way within intensional logic (cf. Kutschera, 1976; for the logic of 'believe' cf. Lenzen, 1978 and 1980, Stalnaker, 1984, Mudersbach, 1984 and Gärdenfors, 1988; for the logic of 'cause' cf. Beckermann, 1979, Kutschera, 1980, Meixner, 1987 and Aqvist & Mullock, 1989; for the logic of 'intend' cf. Wright, 1963, 1968: ch. 2 and 1977, Meggle, 1981, Bealer, 1982: ch. 10 and Cohen, Morgan and Pollack, 1990).

My conceptual apparatus provides a set of definitions for infinitely many types of sign processes, covering all possibilities of semiosis. It is offered as a first step towards both the reconstruction of what happens in human communication and the construction of communication behaviour in artificial intelligent systems.

2. A hierarchy of sign types

2.1 Basic sign types: signal, indicator, expression, gesture

(I) Let me proceed from the assumption that sign processes are special types of causal processes. A causal process can be characterized as a process connecting the occurrence of an event *f* with the occurrence of an event *e*, where (the occurrence of) *f* is called a cause and (the occurrence of) *e* is called its effect. Think of yourself sitting in a room where a sudden loud noise makes the window rattle: we say that the occurrence of the noise *f* is a *cause* for the occurrence of the rattling *e* in the windowpanes, the latter being its *effect*. Think of a mountain slope covered with snow where an increase in the weight of the snow load sets off an avalanche: we say that the occurring increase of the snow's weight is a *cause* for the avalanche *e*, which is its *effect*. Think of a lake where the water temperature falling below 0 degrees centigrade makes the water freeze: we say that the occurring decrease of the water temperature is a *cause* for the freezing of the water, which is its *effect*.

In these processes no organs of perception are needed; there is no representation necessary for the event *e* and no memory required that can store this representation; there is no program involved (e.g., a 'rattling program') that produces the effect *e* in these circumstances; nor do we have to assume any intention (e.g., by the noise to make the window rattle). Instead we have a direct causal relationship → which connects the occurrence of the event *f* with the occurrence of the effect *e* without a third system intervening.

Causal processes can be described by the formula $E(f) \rightarrow E(e)$, where "*f*" and "*e*" are terms denoting events, "→" is a two-place sentence operator denoting the cause- and-effect relation and "*E*" is a one-place predicator denoting the property that the event denoted by its argument term occurs (at a certain time and place). "$E(f) \rightarrow E(e)$" is to be read: "the fact that *f* occurs causes the fact that *e* occurs"; or shorter: "the occurrence of *f* causes the occurrence of *e*".

(II) The scenario becomes different, when we have a bird (*a*) sitting on a tree and a loud noise (*f*) makes this bird fly off (*r*). Here the occurrence

of the noise *f* is a cause for the flying off *r* of the bird, and we say that this cause functions as a *signal* for the bird *a* to fly off *r*. The signal process is only possible because the bird has organs of perception which register the noise, and a program of reaction which makes it respond with flight behaviour. The bird *a* is a behavioural system intervening between the occurrence of the cause $E(f)$ and the occurrence of the effect $E(e)$. The effect consists in *a* performing the flight behaviour *r*: $T(a,r)$.
If the bird's response is a simple physiological reflex, we do not require the bird's memory coming into action by storing an internal representation of the noise: the bird need not believe anything when flying off. Nor do we, of course, assume any intention on the part of the noise to make the bird fly off.
Signal processes can be described by the formula $E(f) \rightarrow T(a,r)$, where "*a*" is a term denoting a behavioural system, "*r*" is a term denoting its behaviour and "*T*" is a two-place predicator denoting the relation of performance that holds between the behavioural system (denoted by its first argument term) and the behaviour (denoted by its second argument term). In this constellation, *a* is called a reacting system, $T(a,r)$ is called its response or interpretant, and *f* is called a signal for *a* to do *r*.

(III) Now think of a scenario with a skier (*a*) standing on a snowy mountain slope when a sudden grumbling noise (*f*) comes from below that makes him believe that the snow under him might start sliding downhill (*p*). Here the occurrence of the noise *f* is a cause for the occurrence of a belief by *a* in a proposition *p*, and we say that this cause functions as an *indicator* of *p* for the skier *a*.
The indicator process can occur because the skier has not only organs of perception, which register the noise, and a program of reaction, which makes him perform a response, but also an internal representation system that enables him to have an internal response such as a belief. However, we still do not have to assume the involvement of intentions (e.g., on the part of the rocks wanting to warn the skier of the coming avalanche).
Indicator processes can be described by the formula $E(f) \rightarrow G(a,p)$, where "*p*" is a sentence denoting a proposition and "*G*" is a two-place operator having a behavioural system as its first argument and a proposition as its second, and denoting the relation of belief that holds between the behavioural system and the proposition. In this constellation, *a* is again called a reacting system, $G(a,p)$ is called its response or interpretant, *p* is called the message of *f* for *a*, and *f* is called an indicator of *p*.

(IV) The next scenario we take as an example is the apartment next door where a door is banged (*f*), which makes the neighbour (*a*) believe that the tenant (*b*) is angry (*Z*). Here the occurrence of the noise *f* is a cause for the occurrence of a special type of belief in *a*, namely the assumption that there is someone *b* who caused the bang and that this person *b* is in a certain state *Z*. In this case we say that the noise functions as an *expression*, for the neighbour *a*, of the state of anger *Z* in its producer *b*. The expression process can occur because the reacting system *a* not only perceives the noise but also assumes the existence of an acting system *b* and infers that it is in a certain state.

Note that we do not have to presuppose that the acting system assumed by *a* exists in reality nor if it exists, that it really is in the state in question. For the noise to function as an expression, it suffices that the reacting system assumes it to have been produced by someone in a certain state. Expressions thus are indicators of special types of propositions. Being indicators, expressions do not require the involvement of intentions on the part of the reacting system, nor on the part of the acting system: the alleged tenant might have banged the door without wanting to and without intending to make someone aware of the fact that he was angry.

Expression processes can be described by the formula $E(f) \rightarrow G(a, Z(b))$, where everything is as in the formula for indicator processes except that p is replaced by $Z(b)$; "*b*" is a term denoting a behavioural system and "*Z*" is a one-place predicator denoting the property of its argument being in a certain state. In this constellation, *b* is called an acting system, *a* is called a reacting system, $G(a, Z(b))$ is called *a*'s response or interpretant, $Z(b)$ is called the message, and *f* is called an expression of *b*'s state for *a*.

(V) The last scenario to be considered on this level of our exposition is that of a person (*a*) walking through a parking lot and suddenly hearing the noise (*f*) of a car engine being started nearby. When the occurrence of the noise *f* is a cause for *a* to believe that the person (*b*) who started the engine intends (*I*) to drive away (*g*), then we say that *f* functions as a *gesture*, for *a*, of the intention *I* of *b* to drive away *g*. A gesture is an expression where the expressed state of the sign producer is an intention to produce another event.

Again, the assumption of a sign producer and of his intention may be mistaken, so that a noise can be taken by someone as a gesture without having in fact been produced by anyone. This is why the acting system involved is called a virtual system. The difference between simple expressions and gestures is rather important. Imagine yourself walking through a construction site when a giant bulldozer approaches you: what horror, when the machine continues to follow you wherever you turn to get out of its way! Taking the course of the machine as an expression of its general work task constitutes no problem for you. But the situation becomes alarming if you find yourself forced to attribute a more abstract intention to the machine, particularly the intention of running over you.

Gesture processes can be described by the formula $E(f) \rightarrow G(a, I(b, T(b,g)))$, where everything is as in the formula for indicator processes except that p is replaced by $I(b, T(b,g))$. Here "I" is a two-place operator having a behavioural system as its first argument and a proposition as its second, and denoting the property of the behavioural system having the intention to realize the proposition. "$T(b,g)$" is to be interpreted in a way analogous to "$T(a,r)$", with "T" as a two-place predicator, and "g" as a term denoting the behaviour of the first argument of T. In this constellation, b is called an acting system, a is called a reacting system, $G(a, I(b, T(b,g)))$ is called a's response or interpretant, $I(b, T(b,g))$ is called the message, $T(b,g)$ is called the gestured behaviour, and f is called a gesture of b's intention for a.

Figure 1 shows a synopsis of the concepts introduced so far. It should have become clear that they constitute a series, such that each following concept is a specialization of the preceding one; the specific differences can be seen by comparing the structure of the effects given in the response formulas of figure 1:

(I) If there are no behavioural systems involved, we have to do with a simple causal process; f is a cause and the occurrence of f causes the occurrence of e: $E(e)$.

(II) If there is a reacting system a intervening between cause f and effect e, f functions as a signal for a to do r; this is because the occurrence of f causes a to do r: $T(a,r)$.

(III) If the response of a to the occurrence of f is not just any event, but consists in a believing that p, then f functions as an indicator of p for a; the occurrence of f causes a to believe p: $G(a,p)$.

(IV) If what a believes upon registering f is that there is a b that produced f and that is in state Z, then f is an expression of Z for a; the occurrence of f causes a to believe in state Z of b: $G(a, Z(b))$.

(V) If the state Z of the acting system b assumed by the reacting system a is an intention to produce a further event g, then f is a gesture of b to do g for a; the occurrence of f causes a to believe in the intention I of b to do g: $G(a, I(b, T(b,g)))$.

Thus we can summarize: every gesture is an expression (of its producer's intention), every expression is an indicator (of its producer's state), every indicator is a signal (for the recipient to believe something), and every signal is a cause (of some response in a behavioural system). But of course, the reverse is not true: only certain causes are signals, only certain signals are indicators, only certain indicators are expressions, and only certain expressions are gestures.

Now the question arises, which of these types of events should be regarded as signs. The answer is straightforward: everything that causes a response in a behavioural system can be called a sign. This criterion

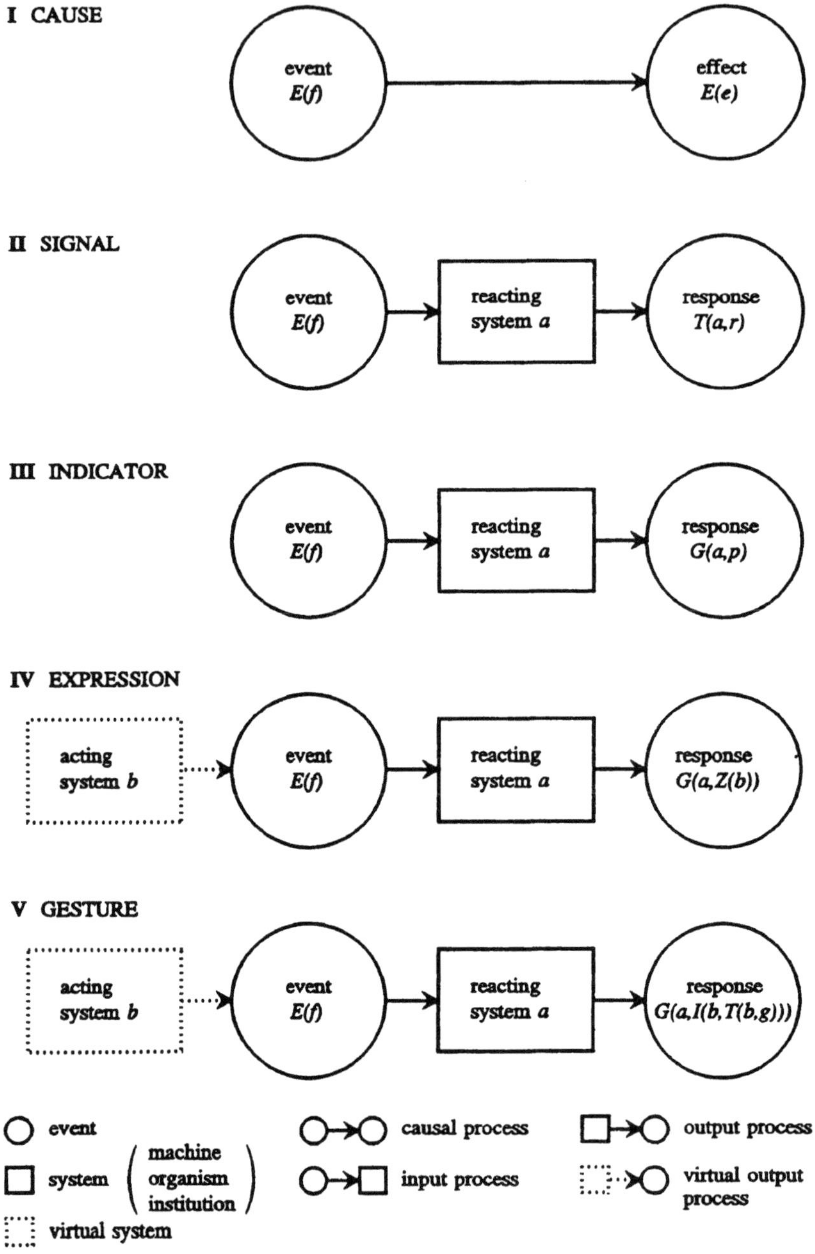

Figure 1: Basic sign types: signal, indicator, expression, gesture

enables us to treat gestures (**V**), expressions (**IV**), indicators (**III**), and signals (**II**) as types of signs and to exclude simple causes (**I**) from the realm of signs. Another consequence of this criterion is that *f*, which is a simple cause in the case of I, becomes a sign (a sign vehicle) in the cases of **II** through **V**.

When we speak of a behavioural system in this context, we have in mind any organism, such as a plant, an animal, or a human individual. A behavioural system is characterized by a program which determines its response to an event registered by it. In terms of computer science, we can also say that a behavioural system is any system that accepts an input and responds with an output according to its program. Taken in this general sense, behavioural systems can also be social institutions such as a national state, a city council, a corporation, a university or a publishing house. And, of course, we also consider artificially constructed systems such as computational information processing systems as behavioural systems since they take events of a certain type as input and respond with an appropriate output. If an information processing system is designed for tasks that experts are understood to carry out, we refer to it as an expert system. Our task is to study the conditions under which the behaviour of any such system can be called "intelligent behaviour" and "communicative behaviour".

Neither the question whether an event is a sign nor the question which type of sign it is can be answered by studying the event in isolation: simple causes, signals, indicators, expressions and gestures all have the same simple structure *E(f)*. An event becomes a sign event only through the fact that it is taken as input by some behavioural system, which then responds to it with some internal or external interpretant. A sign event can be said to function as a signal, indicator, expression or gesture only on the basis of the effect it has on the reacting system: a signal causes any type of response; an indicator causes a belief; an expression causes the assumption of the existence of an acting system and a belief as to its state; a gesture causes the assumption of the existence of an acting system and a belief in that system having a certain intention. This is why signals are said to be signs of the simplest type.

Taking the response to a given event into consideration may help to decide the question whether it is a sign event of one of the four basic types, but on the level of analysis given so far, there is no way of distinguishing a natural event (that becomes a sign only by way of causing a certain behaviour in a reacting system) from an intentionally produced sign. Even expressions and gestures are defined only on the basis of the reacting system believing in the existence of some acting system whose state or intention is indicated; the question whether they are really produced by such an acting system or not is left open. Therefore also the distinction between an attempt at signaling, indicating, expressing or gesturing something and the successful achievement of such an attempt is beyond the conceptual apparatus introduced so far (but cf. § 3.1).

A related point concerns the widely used distinction between sign events and sign types. On the present level of analysis, we are only dealing with concrete events that either function as signs or that are not signs at all. An *f* which does not cause some behavioural system to react in one of the four ways specified is not a sign, even if it is of a type which characterizes events that function as signs in other contexts. We are therefore not yet in a position to distinguish between instances of coded signs (which might or might not function as signs in concrete circumstances) and uncoded signs. However, the present approach is open for the introduction of such a distinction on a higher level of analysis (cf. § 5).

A question often raised by semioticians pertains to the relationship in indicators between the sign vehicle *f* and the message *p*. In indexical signs, the occurrence of *f* is said to either cause or be caused by the message *p*: $E(f) \rightarrow p$ or $p \rightarrow E(f)$. Thus, the occurrence of a shadow $E(f)$ under a tree may be said to cause coolness and thus become an indexical sign, for some reacting system, of it being cool under the tree (*p*). Indexical signs in this sense, however, must not be confused with indicators: while indexical signs require a causal relationship to hold between the occurrence of the sign vehicle and the message, indicators require a causal relationship to hold between the occurrence of the sign vehicle and the interpretant (which consists in a belief, in this case): $E(f) \rightarrow G(a,p)$. How exactly the reacting system *a* arrives at this belief is left open. Thus, our concept of an "indicator" is wider than the notion of an "indexical sign" in Peirce (cf. Peirce, 1931-1966: II, § 283-291). It more resembles the notion of an "Anzeichen" in Husserl (1901: II 1, § I2) and of "indication" in Prieto (1966: ch. I2). This is why one can find indexical as well as iconic and symbolic indicators, depending on the relationship between *f* and *p* being either a cause-and-effect relation, a resemblance or neither of these. While the relationship between *f* and *p* need not be causal, the relationship between *f* and $G(a,p)$ always is.

These special questions should not, however, turn the reader's attention away from the central idea of the series of basic sign concepts introduced so far. Apart from the predicators $E(...)$ and $T(...,---)$, which play a primarily technical role, only three concepts of intensional logic are necessary to define these sign concepts: causing $... \rightarrow ---$, believing $G(...,---)$ and intending $I(...,---)$. What counts is the configuration of these attitudes and processes. This is what determines the differences between the sign types. Signs of the basic types discussed turn out to be extraorganismic correlates of attitudes and processes. In what follows, we will demonstrate that signs of all types

	I	II	
2b com	declaration *(f,b,a,e)* =df T(b,f) ∧ I(b, E(f) → G(a, T(b,f) ∧ I(b, E(f) → E(e)))) ∧ G(b, (E(f) → G(a, T(b,f) ∧ I(b, E(f) → E(e)))) → (E(f) → E(e)))	directive *(f,b,a,r)* =df T(b,f) ∧ I(b, E(f) → G(a, T(b,f) ∧ I(b, E(f) → T(a,r)))) ∧ G(b, (E(f) → G(a, T(b,f) ∧ I(b, E(f) → T(a,r)))) → (E(f) → T(a,r)))	assertive *(f,b,a* T(b,f) ∧ I(b, E(f) → G(a, T(I(b ∧ G(b, (E(f) → G(a, T I(
2b	indicating an action *(f,b,a,e)* =df T(b,f) ∧ I(b, E(f) → G(a, T(b,f) ∧ I(b, E(f) → E(e))))	indicating a signaling *(f,b,a,r)* =df T(b,f) ∧ I(b, E(f) → G(a, T(b,f) ∧ I(b, E(f) →T(a,r))))	indicating an T(b,f) ∧ I(b, E(f) → G(a, T(I(b
2a	indicator of action *(f,b,a,e)* =df E(f) → G(a, T(b,f) ∧ I(b, E(f) → E(e)))	indicator of signaling *(f,b,a,r)* =df E(f) → G(a, T(b,f) ∧ I(b, E(f) → T(a,r)))	indicator of in E(f) → G(a, T(b,f) ∧ I(b, E(
1b	action *(f,b,e)* =df T(b,f) ∧ I(b, E(f) → E(e))	signaling *(f,b,a,r)* =df T(b,f) ∧ I(b, E(f) → T(a,r))	indicating *(f,b,* T(b,f) ∧ I(b, E(f) → G
1a	cause *(f,e)* =df E(f) → E(e)	signal *(f,a,r)* =df E(f) → T(a,r)	indicator *(f,a,* E(f) → G(a,p)

Figure 2: Levels of reflection up to communicating

f)) → G(a,p))))) → G(a,p)))) → G(a,p)))	expressive *(f,b,a,Z)* =df T(b,f) ∧ I(b, E(f) → G(a, T(b,f) ∧ I(b, E(f) → G(a,Z(b))))) ∧ G(b, (E(f) → G(a, T(b,f) ∧ I(b, E(f) → G(a,Z(b))))) → (E(f) → G(a,Z(b))))	commissive *(f,b,a,g)* =df T(b,f) ∧ I(b, E(f) → G(a, T(b,f) ∧ I(b, E(f) → G(a,I(b,T(b,g)))))) ∧ G(b, E(f) → G(a, T(b,f) ∧ I(b, E(f) → G(a,I(b,T(b,g)))))) → (E(f) → G(a,I(b,T(b,g)))))
ng *(f,b,a,p)* =df)) → G(a,p)))	indicating an expressing *(f,b,a,Z)* =df T(b,f) ∧ I(b, E(f) → G(a, T(b,f) ∧ I(b, E(f) → G(a,Z(b)))))	indicating a gesturing *(f,b,a,g)* =df T(b,f) ∧ I(b, E(f) → G(a, T(b,f) ∧ I(b, E(f) → G(a,I(b,T(b,g))))))
g *(f,b,a,p)* =df) a,p)))	indicator of expressing *(f,b,a,Z)* =df E(f) → G(a, T(b,f) ∧ I(b, E(f) → G(a,Z(b))))	indicator of gesturing *(f,b,a,g)* =df E(f) → G(a, T(b,f) ∧ I(b, E(f) → G(a,I(b,T(b,g)))))
df	expressing *(f,b,a,Z)* =df T(b,f) ∧ I(b, E(f) → G(a,Z(b)))	gesturing *(f,b,a,g)* =df T(b,f) ∧ I(b, E(f) → G(a,I(b,T(b,g))))
	expression *(f,b,a,Z)* =df E(f) → G(a,Z(b))	gesture *(f,b,a,g)* =df E(f) → G(a,I(b,T(b,g)))
	IV	**V**

have that property. The correlation between the terminologies of semiotics and intensional logic will therefore continue to be of concern to us.

2.2 Levels of reflection: iteration of intention and belief

The distinction of sign types so far was entirely dependent on the behaviour of a reacting system *a*. This lowest level in the hierarchy of sign types to be set out is therefore named "**1a**". In the present section, we will not only have to do with a virtual acting system assumed by *a*, but include a real acting system *b*, and analyze various simple interactions which are possible between the two systems *a* and *b*.

When an acting system *b* comes into play, *b* can produce an event *f* because *b* intends this event to cause *a* to do or believe something. *a* can then believe that a certain event *f* was produced by *b* because *b* intended *f* to cause *a* to do or believe something. *b* can even intend this, i.e., intend *a* to believe that a certain event *f* was produced by *b* because *b* intended it to cause *a* to do or believe something. And *a* can in turn have reason to believe in that complex intention of *b*, etc.

This describes a series of intentions with embedded beliefs of increasingly complex structure on the part of the acting system *b* and a series of beliefs with embedded intentions of increasingly complex structure on the part of the reacting system *a*. The resulting ordered set of increasingly complex beliefs and intentions will be called *levels of reflection*:

level **1a**	$G(a,p)$
level **1b**	$I(b, G(a,p))$
level **2a**	$G(a, I(b, G(a,p)))$
level **2b**	$I(b, G(a, I(b, G(a,p))))$
.	.
.	.
.	.

On level **1**, *a* believes something, and *b* intends something. On level **2**, *a* believes that *b* intends *a* to believe something, and *b* intends *a* to believe that *b* intends something. The iterated beliefs and intentions could also be attributed to one and the same individual, or to more than two individuals; but for reasons of exposition, we base our description on two different individuals *a* and *b* that play complementary roles in the sign processes studied. This enables us to refer to the levels as **1a**, **1b**, **2a**, **2b**, ... respectively.

Proceeding from the basic sign processes introduced in § 2.1, we will now use the series of levels of reflection to build up more complex sign processes that will eventually lead to what is generally called communication (in the strong sense of the word). Compare the table in figure 2, where the defining characteristics of the five basic concepts **I** through **V** are given on the bottom line, which presents level **1a**: a cause is defined by the formula in area **I1a**, a signal is defined by the formula in area **II1a**, etc. The following chapter (§ 3) presents illustrations and discussions of various formulas on the higher lines of figure 2, such as **I1b, I2a**, and **II1b, II2a.**

3. The reconstruction of communication

3.1 Acting and indicating an action

Consider the following set of culinary examples.

(I1a) In the kitchen, a cup of yogurt accidentally falls into the deep freezer: $E(f)$. The yogurt gets frozen: $E(e)$. The latter event is caused, under the given circumstances, by the former one: $E(f) \rightarrow E(e)$. What we have here is a simple *causal process* in the sense of § 2.1. Now imagine that Bernie, the son of the family, discovers the frozen yogurt in the deep freezer, tries it and likes the taste. In consequence:

(I1b) Bernie deliberately takes another cup of yogurt out of the refrigerator and puts it in the deep freezer: $T(b,f)$. He intends that the fact that the yogurt got into the deep freezer will again lead to the yogurt freezing: $I(b,\ E(f) \rightarrow E(e))$. Doing something with the intention that it will cause something else to happen is an action. Actions are described with reference to their intended effects. This is why we say that Bernie freezes the yogurt when he does nothing more than put the yogurt in the deep freezer. If the intended effect does not occur, then the action is unsuccessful. But let us assume that the deep freezer is working, and putting the yogurt in it really makes it freeze: $E(f) \rightarrow E(e)$. Under these circumstances Bernie can regard his action as successful.

Generalizing the example, we can say: if *b* produces an event *f* and intends that the occurrence of *f* will cause the occurrence of a further event *e*, then *f* is an *action*. Every action can be described by the formula: $T(b,f) \wedge I(b,\ E(f) \rightarrow E(e))$. The action *f* is successful if the occurrence of *f* causes the occurrence of *e*, as intended by the acting system *b*. Thus $E(f) \rightarrow E(e)$ is called the *condition of success* of the action *f*.

(I2a) Imagine now that, some days later, Bernie puts a cup of yogurt in the deep freezer again. But this time, he is not alone. His sister Astrid happens to see what he does, without being noticed by him. She wonders why on earth he should do so. Then she remembers that Bernie has been praising the culinary delights of frozen yogurt lately, and she reaches the conclusion that Bernie does so because he intends the fact of the yogurt getting into the deep freezer to lead to the yogurt freezing: $G(a, T(b,f) \wedge I(b, E(f) \rightarrow E(e)))$.

In semiotic terms, for Astrid the event of the yogurt getting into the deep freezer is an *indicator* of Bernie's action directed at having the yogurt frozen: $E(f) \rightarrow G(a, T(b,f) \wedge I(b, E(f) \rightarrow E(e)))$. The event of the yogurt getting into the deep freezer is the sign vehicle; the proposition that Bernie puts it there to have it frozen is the message; Astrid is a recipient of the message; Astrid's belief in the message is the interpretant.

If we compare the present example of an indicator process with that given in § 2.1 (**III**), we see that the only difference lies in the complex structure of the message *p*. An indicator *f*, where *p* has the structure $T(b,f) \wedge I(b, E(f) \rightarrow E(e))$ is called an *indicator of an action*. Note that an event can be an indicator of an action even if the system producing this event does not intend it to function as an indicator.

Indicators of actions can occur without intervening codes. An event becomes an indicator of an action simply if it causes some behavioural system to conclude that its producer intended it to cause some other event.

(**I2b**) Now, the case where an event is unknowingly taken to be an indicator of something can be compared with another case where such an event is intentionally produced to serve as an indicator of something for another person. Imagine: Bernie and Astrid both are in the kitchen, Bernie makes sure that Astrid notices what he does and then ceremoniously opens the deep freezer and puts a cup of yogurt in it. Here Bernie produces an event *f* and intends the occurrence of this event to cause Astrid to believe that Bernie produces this event with the intention for it to lead to another event *e*: $T(b,f) \wedge I(b, E(f) \rightarrow G(a, T(b,f) \wedge I(b, E(f) \rightarrow E(e))))$. In other words, Bernie acts with the intention that what he does be an indicator for Astrid that he attempts to bring about a certain effect.

In semiotic terms, if *b* produces an event *f* with the intention that *f* serve as an indicator of *p* for *a*, then *b* indicates *p* to *a*. Thus what Bernie does here is indicating to Astrid his action of making the yogurt freeze. We are dealing with someone *indicating an action*. This becomes especially clear when we compare the present example with the formula that defines indicating in area **III1b** of figure 2: $T(b,f) \wedge I(b, E(f) \rightarrow G(a,p))$. It differs from the complex formula above only in having *p* instead of: $T(b,f) \wedge I(b, E(f) \rightarrow E(e))$, which is the formula for action (cf. figure 2, **I1b**).

When someone *b* produces an event *f* with the intention that *f* serve as an indicator of some *p* for some other person *a*, then *b* cannot count on being successful: *f* may or may not be received as indicator of *p* by *a*; i.e., *f* may or may not cause *a* to believe *p* (as intended by *b*). This raises the question whether an *f*, occurring under these circumstances, may be called a sign in the sense of § 2.1: when the indicating is successful, f functions as an indicator of p for a and therefore is a sign; however, when the indicating is unsuccessful, no indicator process takes place, and f cannot therefore be regarded as a sign in the sense of § 2.1. The best way to circumvent this awkward situation is to extend our criteria for the sign concept: we now call an event not only a sign

(1) when it causes a behavioural system to respond by doing or believing something, but also

(2) when there is a behavioural system which produces this event with the intention for it to be a sign in the first sense.

A sign in the first sense we call a *recipient sign*, a sign in the second sense a *sender sign*. On the basis of this stipulation, an event produced in order to indicate, whether or not the indicating is successful, is a sign.

If an indicating of an action takes place: $T(b,f) \wedge I(b, E(f) \rightarrow G(a, T(b,f) \wedge I(b, E(f) \rightarrow E(e))))$, the acting system b is called a sender; the event f is called an indicating sign; a is its intended recipient or addressee; $G(a, T(b,f) \wedge I(b, E(f) \rightarrow E(e))$ is the intended interpretant; $T(b,f) \wedge I(b, E(f) \rightarrow E(e))$ is the intended message.

Returning to the example, let us assume that Bernie's behaviour really leads Astrid to believe that Bernie is making the yogurt freeze. In this case Bernie's indicating of this action is said to be successful. It would even be called successful if there were an electric energy breakdown and the yogurt did not in fact get frozen. It would also be so if Bernie did not really want the yogurt to freeze this time and took it out of the deep freezer immediately after Astrid left the kitchen. These eventualities should make it clear beyond doubt that the *condition of success* in indicating lies in the occurrence of f making the reacting system a believe a certain proposition p: $E(f) \rightarrow G(a,p)$, and not in the proposition p itself or one of its components being true. If we replace p in the above formula by the formula for an action, we obtain the fully explicit condition of success for the indicating of an action: $E(f) \rightarrow G(a, T(b,f) \wedge I(b, E(f) \rightarrow E(e)))$.

This case concludes a series of examples for four different but related processes having to do with simple cause-and-effect sequences (cf. column I of figure 2). On level **1a** we have a simple cause-and-effect sequence without any intervening systems. On level **1b** we have an acting system's attempt to bring about such a cause-and-effect sequence, i.e., we have to do with an action. On level **2a** the initial cause of the cause-and-effect sequence leads to a belief about this attempt to bring about the cause-and-effect sequence, i.e., the actor causes a belief about this action. This is a constellation which makes the causing event a sign: it becomes an indicator of the action. On level **2b** we have an acting system's deliberate attempt to make the initial cause produce this belief about the attempt to bring about a cause-and-effect sequence. This is a constellation which makes the action coincide with an attempt to indicate the action. Only the last two processes are sign processes. And there is no communication in the strong sense yet.

In order to reach the stage of complexity at which one can adequately talk of communication, let us now follow another series of example cases on levels **1a** through **2b**, this time in column **II** of figure 2: signals, signalings, indicators of signaling and indicatings of signaling.

3.2 Signaling and indicating a signaling

(II1a) Imagine we are in a noisy kindergarten, where the teacher Britta (*b*) has to look after a number of small children (*a*) of age 3 to 5. All of a sudden there occurs a loud bang: $E(f)$, which causes the children to interrupt their play and look up at the origin of the noise: $T(a,r)$. This is a causal process with an intervening behavioural system *a*: $E(f) \rightarrow T(a,r)$. It is a response called orientation reflex by biologists, and it can happen without any beliefs intervening.

In semiotic terms, an event that causes a behavioural system to react in a certain way is defined as a *signal* (cf. § 2.1); the reaction of the behavioural system is called its interpretant. This is why we say that the sudden noise is a signal for the children to look up in the direction of its origin. Signals such as these are signs of the simplest type.

(II1b) Now think of Britta and what she did when the bang occurred in her noisy kindergarten. She was amazed at the moment of silence, which was its effect. Next time she wants to produce a moment of silent attention in her kindergarten, she produces a sudden noise herself by loudly clapping her hands. Experienced parents know how well this method works, when the children are young enough and the clapping is loud enough. How should we analyze Britta's behaviour? Well, it is an action because Britta produces an event and intends the event to cause another event: $T(b,f) \wedge I(b, E(f) \rightarrow E(e)))$. But it is a special type of action since the event produced by Britta is intended to bring about the other event by way of being a signal: *f* is intended by Britta to cause the children to look up, be silent and pay attention: $E(f) \rightarrow T(a,r)$. Thus, Britta's handclapping is the action of producing a signal: $T(b,f) \wedge I(b, E(f) \rightarrow T(a,r))$.

In semiotic terms, a behavioural system *b* that produces an event *f* with the intention of it functioning as a signal for *a* to do *r* is said to perform a *signaling*. The event *f* is the signaling, *a* is the intended recipient or addressee of *f* and *a* doing *r* is its intended interpretant. Signaling is often nothing more than pure manipulation: the youngest children have no choice; in their case, the teacher's action is nearly always *successful*: $E(f) \rightarrow T(a,r)$. However, signaling can be as unsuccessful as any other type of action: what is necessary for behaviour to be an action is only that a certain effect is intended to happen, not that it really happens.

(II2a:c) Now let us introduce a third party into the scenario. There is a visitor - her name is Cynthia - who observes what goes on in the kindergarten without interfering herself. Cynthia hears Britta clap, and this handclapping is an indicator for her of Britta intending the children to look up, be silent and pay attention. Formulated more explicitly, the handclapping *f* causes *c* to believe that *b* does *f* because *b* intends the children *a* to do *r*: $E(f) \rightarrow G(c, T(b,f) \wedge I(b, E(f) \rightarrow T(a,r)))$; in short, *c* believes because of *f* that *b* does *f* so that *a* will do *r* because of *f*. This formulation shows that, on this level of reflection, the handclapping *f* has two different sign functions:

1. *f* causes the visitor *c* to believe something (i.e., *f* becomes an indicator for *c*).
2. *f* causes the children *a* to look up (i.e., *f* is a signal for *a* to do *r*).

For the visitor *c*, the handclapping is an *indicator of signaling*; for the children involved, it is a signal. Under these circumstances we can say that the visitor *c* *understands* the action of the teacher *b* *as* signaling.

(II2a:a) Back to the kindergarten without a visitor. Even young children are capable of making hypotheses about what happens around them. The more often the handclapping occurs, the less easily they let it interrupt their activities. They become aware of what Britta wants to bring about by her handclapping: they now believe each time when she claps her hands that she wants to make them look up, be silent and pay attention at that moment. Even if they do not react by really looking up, being silent, paying attention, they have a direct reaction; it does not consist in an external response but in an internal process: the children's interpretant of Britta's handclapping is their believing, at that moment, that Britta intends them to look up, be silent and pay attention. Just like the visitor Cynthia in the preceding example, they take the handclapping as an *indicator of signaling*. This case differs from the preceding one only in that there is personal identity between the recipient of the signal and the recipient of the indicator of signaling. The children *a* are recipients of an indicator of signaling since *f* causes *a* to believe that *b* does *f* because *b* intends the occurrence of *f* to lead to *a* doing *r*: $E(f) \rightarrow G(a, T(b,f) \wedge I(b, E(f) \rightarrow T(a,r)))$. And the children *a* are also recipients of a signal if the occurrence of *f* causes *a* to do *r*: $E(f) \rightarrow T(a,r)$. We can say that the children *understand* the teacher's action *as* signaling, even if they do not *follow* it.

(II2b:c) In order to reach the next higher level **2b**, let us return to the example with Cynthia, the visitor. Imagine that Britta knows Cynthia is observing what she is doing, and she wants to make Cynthia aware that she will signal to the children that, say, the play time is over and they must look up, be silent and pay attention. She can achieve this by modifying her signal *f*: instead of clapping her hands loudly, she might give Cynthia a meaningful look and move them only in such a way as to visually simulate handclapping for Cynthia. In such a case, *b* produces a silent handclapping f_1 because *b* intends the occurrence of f_1 to make *c* believe that *b* will soon produce a loud handclapping f_2 since *b* intends the occurrence of f_2 to make ***a*** do *r*: $T(b, f_1) \wedge I(b, E(f_1) \rightarrow G(c, T(b,f_2) \wedge I(b, E(f_2) \rightarrow T(a,r))))$; in short, *b* does f_1, with the intention that *c* believe that *b* will soon do f_2 with the intention that ***a*** do *r*.

In semiotic terms, we can say, using previous definitions: *b* produces for *c* an indicator of *b* producing a signal for ***a*** to do *r*. As in § 2.1, the production of an indicator is called indicating (cf. Fig. 2, **III1b**) and the production of a signal is called signaling (cf. Fig. 2, **II1b**). Thus what the teacher does here is *indicating a signaling*. She intends the visitor to understand that she is going to signal something to the children.

(II2b:b) The next case to be discussed is still on level **2b**, but dispenses with Cynthia, the visitor: Britta, the teacher, has in the meantime become aware that some children no longer follow her handclapping automatically, although there is no doubt that they hear it perfectly well. Being an experienced pedagogue, she also changes her own behaviour and stops trying to manipulate the children. She no longer intends her handclapping to cause an immediate external reaction; she only wants the children to notice - like the visitor - that she intends them to be silent and pay attention. This she can achieve without suddenly clapping her hands loudly. Instead, she waits for a sufficient number of children to glance at her, gives them a meaningful look and simulates handclapping. What she produces is an allusion to signaling. This again is what is called *indicating a signaling*; however, the strength of real signaling connected with it has become variable: to the extent that Britta diminishes the loudness of her handclapping, its signal effect decreases, but to the same extent the indicator effect increases.

The difference between this example and the preceding one involving Cynthia as a third party is again that there is personal identity between the addressee of the indicating of a signaling and the addressee of the signaling. In addition, the sign vehicle produced to be an indicator of a signaling is identical with the sign vehicle produced to be a signal.

In terms of intensional logic, *indicating a signaling* involves the following: *b* produces *f* because *b* intends the occurrence of *f* to make ***a*** believe that *b* produces *f* because *b* intends the occurrence of *f* to make ***a*** do *r*: $T(b,f) \wedge I(b, E(f) \rightarrow G(a, T(b,f) \wedge I(b, E(f) \rightarrow T(a,r))))$; in short, *b* does *f* with the intention for a to believe (because of f) that b intends a to do r (because of f). That is, b does f with the intention for a to *understand* that b intends a to do r.

Indicating a signaling has *conditions of success* that are very different from those of genuine signaling. This can be seen when we compare area **II1b** with areas **III1b** and **II2b** in figure 2: successful signaling requires that the occurrence of f causes a to do something: $E(f) \rightarrow T(a,r)$; successful indicating only requires that the occurrence of f causes a to believe something: $E(f) \rightarrow G(a,p)$; and successful indicating of a signaling requires that the occurrence of f causes a to believe in the intention of b for a to do something: $E(f) \rightarrow G(a, T(b,f) \wedge I(b, E(f) \rightarrow T(a,r)))$. Successful indicating of signaling is possible without successful signaling.

3.3 Communicating

Now imagine that the pure-signal aspect of the handclapping f in the last example becomes zero. The result is that f turns into a genuine higher level indicator. By producing f, Britta now indicates a signaling, but no longer performs the signaling itself. She informs the children of a wish, but no longer utters it. She indicates to the children that she wants them to do something, and if she is successful, the children will understand that she wants them to do something, but they will not necessarily feel moved to do it.

How can Britta nevertheless reach her goal of making the children who glance at her be silent and pay attention? Strictly speaking, she has no behavioural resources of her own that she could utilize for that purpose. She depends entirely on the insight and good will of the children. She can only wait for the children to become 'understanding' and 'sensible', as she likes to say.

What happens when the children become 'understanding' and 'sensible'? Well, they understand that Britta intends them to do r and this understanding suffices to make them actually do r. Semiotically speaking, they respond to the indicator of a signal produced by Britta, as if it were the signal itself. The indicator that b intends them to do r is taken by them as a signal to do r. This is what happens in a successful request. A successful request consists in a signal process (**II1a**) achieved through an indicator of signaling (**II2a**). A successful request is thus composed of two sign processes, a signal process and an indicator process, where the one causes the other to occur. The indicator process $E(f) \rightarrow G(a, T(b,f) \wedge I(b, E(f) \rightarrow T(a,r)))$ causes the signal process $E(f) \rightarrow T(a,r)$. Thus the condition of success in requesting is the following: $(E(f) \rightarrow G(a, T(b,f) \wedge I(b, E(f) \rightarrow T(a,r)))) \rightarrow (E(f) \rightarrow T(a,r))$.

This formula shows that requesting is successful if it makes the addressee do something on the basis of his belief in the sender's intention for him to do it. If we compare the indicator formula with the signal formula, it differs from it precisely in having a belief and intention component: $\ldots G(a, T(b,f) \wedge I(b, E(f) \rightarrow ---))$. When we delete this component, the indicator formula merges with the signal formula.

Now, if the teacher is still of good cheer and has not given up all hope that the children will become serious communication partners, then she will try to reinforce the positive behaviour just described, by repeating interaction of this type as often as possible. Put in semiotic terms, she will produce a signal by producing an indicator of herself producing a signal; i.e., she will signal by indicating a signaling. Formulated in terms of intensional logic: *b* produces *f*, intending the occurrence of *f* to make *a* believe that *b* produces *f* with the intention for the occurrence of *f* to make *a* do *r*, and *b* believes that if the occurrence of *f* will lead to *a*'s belief that *b* produced *f* with the intention for the occurrence of *f* to make *a* do *r*, then the occurrence of *f* really will make *a* do *r*:

$$T(b,f) \wedge I(b, E(f) \rightarrow G(a, T(b,f) \wedge I(b, E(f) \rightarrow T(a,r)))) \wedge G(b, (E(f) \rightarrow G(a, T(b,f) \wedge I(b, E(f) \rightarrow T(a,r)))) \rightarrow (E(f) \rightarrow T(a,r))).$$

This is the definition of a directive act of communicating. In it, *f* is called a directive sign event or simply a directive; *b* is the sender and *a* the addressee; $G(a, T(b,f) \wedge I(b, E(f) \rightarrow T(a,r)))$ is the intended secondary interpretant, and $T(a,r)$ is the intended primary interpretant; $T(b,f) \wedge I(b, E(f) \rightarrow T(a,r))$ is the secondary message. There is no primary message, because the intended primary interpretant does not consist in a belief.

If the occurrence of *f* makes *a* (perform the secondary interpretant, i.e.) believe that *b* wants *a* to do *r*, then *a* has *understood f as* a request and the act of communicating is *felicitous*. Thus the felicity condition of a directive is identical with the condition of success of its indicating component: $E(f) \rightarrow G(a, T(b,f) \wedge I(b, E(f) \rightarrow T(a,r)))$.

If in addition to making *a* believe that *b* wants *a* to do *r*, the occurrence of *f* makes *a* do *r* because of this belief, then *a* has *followed* the request, and the communication attempt is *successful*. Thus the condition of success of a directive includes its felicity: $(E(f) \rightarrow G(a, T(b,f) \wedge I(b, E(f) \rightarrow T(a,r)))) \rightarrow (E(f) \rightarrow T(a,r))$.

What turns indicating a signaling into directive communicating is the sender's belief that this condition of success is going to be realized by the addressee: $G(b, (E(f) \rightarrow G(a, T(b,f) \wedge I(b, E(f) \rightarrow T(a,r)))) \rightarrow (E(f) \rightarrow T(a,r)))$.

The defining formula of directive communicating can be read in the top area of column **II** in figure 2. On the same line, the reader finds analogous formulas for

- declarational communicating, which consists in acting by indicating that action,
- assertive communicating, which consists in indicating by indicating that indicating,
- expressive communicating, which consists in expressing by indicating that expressing, and
- commissive communicating, which consists in gesturing by indicating that gesturing.

These formulas claim that non-directive acts of communicating have the same structure as directive ones; the only difference between them is supposed to lie in the effect of the basic process on which they rely: it is a simple event in the case of declarations, a behaviour of *a* in the case of directives, a belief of *a* in a message *p* in the case of assertives, a belief of *a* in a state of *b* in the case of expressives, and a belief of *a* in an intention of *b* to do *g* in the case of commissives.

In order to test the validity of this generalization from the structure of directive communicating to the structure of other types of communicating, let us examine a case of declarational communicating (cf. column **I** in figure 2). When somewhere in the world, a shaman *b* declares a man and a woman husband and wife by quietly laying his hands on their joined right hands under the appropriate circumstances, he performs laying on of hands *f* because he intends the occurrence of *f* to turn his followers *a* into a married couple: $E(f) \rightarrow E(e)$. In other words, he produces *f* with the intention for the occurrence of *f* to make the required status change come about. But how does he think this status change will be achieved? Well, in laying on his hands, he also has the intention that the occurrence of *f* will make his followers *a* believe that he intends the occurrence of *f* to turn them into a married couple: $E(f) \rightarrow G(a, T(b,f) \wedge I(b, E(f) \rightarrow E(e)))$. In other words, he produces *f* with the intention for the occurrence of *f* to be an indicator of the action of making the required status change come about. And he believes that when the occurrence of *f* makes his followers *a* believe that he intends the occurrence of *f* to turn them into a married couple, then the occurrence of *f* will in fact turn them into a married couple: $(E(f) \rightarrow G(a, T(b,f) \wedge I(b, E(f) \rightarrow E(e)))) \rightarrow (E(f) \rightarrow E(e))$. In other words, he believes that the indicator process itself will be what causes the occurrence of *f* to bring about the status change in his addressees under the given circumstances.

This is what is described by the formula in the top area of column **I** in figure 2 (area **I2bcom**). As in the other formulas of figure 2, its structure is indicated by boxes enclosing the relevant constituents. The two large boxes contain occurrences of the same formula, which describe an indicator of an action (cf. the identical formula appearing in area **I2a**). The occurrence of this formula in the upper box is embedded as second argument in the intention operator *I(b, ...)*. The occurrence of this formula in the lower box is the antecedent of a formula which represents a complex causal proposition and has as its consequent $E(f) \rightarrow E(e)$, the latter describing the process intended to happen in the action indicated. The complex causal proposition is embedded as second argument in the belief operator *G(b,...)*. The belief of *b* thus described authorizes us to replace the occurrence of the indicator formula in the large box above by $E(f) \rightarrow E(e)$. As a result, the formula in **I2bcom** is transformed into $T(b,f) \wedge I(b, E(f) \rightarrow E(e))$, which describes precisely the basic action that *b* is trying to perform (cf. the formula in area **I1b**).

This formula-based reasoning demonstrates how the sender succeeds in performing an action in declarational communicating. He produces an indicator of himself performing this action, and he believes that the indicator process will cause the process which is intended to happen in the action: $E(f) \rightarrow E(e)$. This was shown to be equivalent with the sender performing the action indicated. Herein lies the justification for our statement that declarational communicating is acting by indicating that action.

Again it must be emphasized that the indicating of an action has conditions of success different from those of the action indicated. The indicating is successful if the addressees believe that the action is performed (condition of success of the indicating component or felicity condition). The action itself is successful if its intended effect comes about (condition of success of the action component). And the declarational act as a whole is successful only if the fulfilment of the condition of success of its indicating component (its felicity condition) brings about the fulfilment of the condition of success of its action component. As in directive acts of communicating, what turns indicating an action into declarational communicating is the belief of the sender that its complex condition of success will be realized by the addressees.

The formula-based reasoning above led us to the conclusion that every declarational act of communicating is an action performed by indicating that action. On this basis, it can be argued that also every other act of communicating (as defined on line **2bcom** in figure 2) is an action performed by indicating that action. Let us again proceed from levels **1a** and **1b** in figure 2 in order to show this. As demonstrated in § 2.1, every gesture is an expression, every expression is an indicator, every indicator is a signal, and every signal is a cause; thus all basic sign processes defined on level **1a** are causal processes. Now it also holds that every gesturing is an expressing, every expressing is an indicating, every indicating is a signaling, and every signaling is an action; thus all sign processes defined on level **1b** are actions. The same is true of all indicating processes described on level **2b**: they are all indicatings of an action (of one of the types defined on level **1b**). Since signaling, indicating, expressing and gesturing are all actions, and the indicating of a signaling, of an indicating, of an expressing and of a gesturing is always the indicating of an action, the formula in **I2bcom**, which claims that a declarational act of communicating is an action performed by indicating that action, carries over to each of the other types of communicating.

In conclusion, we are justified in claiming that

(1) all commissives, expressives, assertives and directives are declarations and

(2) all communicating consists in an action performed by indicating that action.

For this reason we need only think in terms of declarational communicating when we discuss general properties of communicating in what follows.

The two results of this section are highly relevant for two central tenets of traditional speech act theory. Declarational, directive, assertive, expressive and commissive acts of communicating are counterparts of the five types of speech acts postulated in Searle (1979). As Searle claims, all human speech acts belong to one of these types, but he cannot prove this claim because he does not lay open its analytical basis. If one accepts our definitions of declarations, directives, assertives, expressives and commissives as explications of Searle's speech act types, one can use our conceptual system to deduce the universality and completenes of Searle's typology. The fact that our conceptual system, which is based on an independently motivated system of simple sign processes and a general set of levels of reflection, includes Searle's typology as a special case, can be considered as a confirmation both of Searle's philosophical account and of our semiotic approach.

As with the basic sign processes, the acts of communicating defined above constitute a series of increasingly specialized sign processes. This makes it possible to consider all of them as special cases of declarations, thus confirming a position which John Austin reached late in his life (cf. 1958 and 1962), i.e., that the distinction of performative versus constative utterances is misguided when used as a general typology of verbal communicating, since all communicating is performing an action.

In addition, our approach has the advantage that it provides systematic access to kinds of sign processes other than speech acts and thus bridges the gap between speech acts and all sorts of non-communicative sign behaviour, be it verbal or non-verbal.

3.4 Felicity, openness and success in communicating

As pointed out in § 3.3, a communicating is performed in order for the addressee

- to understand what the sender wants to happen (felicity condition of communicating) and
- to accomplish that on the basis of this understanding (condition of success of communicating).

This leads to the following two questions:

1. Under what circumstances does the addressee understand what the sender wants to happen?
2. Under what circumstances does the addressee accomplish what the sender wants to happen?

In order to see how these two questions are to be answered, let us review the series of kindergarten examples once more.

Ad 1: On level **1a**, the sign event *f* was a signal to do something, which was automatically followed. On level **2a**, it became an indicator of a signaling, which was only believed.

What made the addressees believe, on level **2b**, that the teacher wanted the children to look up, be silent and pay attention? In the visitor Cynthia's case, the real handclapping served as an indicator of Britta's intention, and Cynthia could have reasoned: handclapping normally has such an effect; Britta must know that and she would not do something if she did not also approve of its anticipated main effect; this effect must therefore have been intended. In the case of the older children, we can assume the capability of a similar reasoning.

But what made Cynthia also believe, on level **2b**, that Britta intended her to believe she would soon clap her hands loudly? Well, Britta produced an *iconic indicator* of the handclapping signal and at the same time divested it of its signal force by going from the acoustic to the optic channel. Cynthia could have reasoned: Britta performs handclapping in a way that prevents it from having the effect it usually has on the children; at the same time Britta gives me a meaningful look, from which I conclude that she intends to indicate something to me; what can it be? The most probable guess is that by clapping her hands silently she intends to make me believe that she will soon perform a similar act for the children which is to have its usual effect on them, i.e., she will soon clap her hands loudly.

The children's understanding of Britta's indicating of a signaling can be explained on similar lines. The children could have reasoned: Britta performs handclapping in a way that prevents it from having the compulsive effect it used to have on us; at the same time Britta gives us a meaningful look, from which we conclude that she intends to indicate something to us;

what can it be? The most probable guess is that by clapping her hands silently she intends to make us believe that she wants us to react in the way we used to, by being silent and paying attention.

This explanation relies on the *history of sender-recipient contacts* in each case. When two people have successfully solved a coordination problem in a certain way, they tend to solve it in a similar way when it occurs again. Thus, a convention develops, which is based on the memory that the interaction partners have of previous problem solutions (cf. Lewis 1969: ch. I3 and II1). This convention of letting a certain sign type correspond to a certain type of intended interpretant can often be based on assumed causal relations (indexes) or relations of resemblance (icons), but that it is so based is not a necessary condition for its development.

Linguistic conventions are a case in point. Even if they were once based on iconic and indexical sign relations, these relations became less and less binding in the history of language. Learning from his own communication history, each communication partner lets his memory take over and help where there is no sufficient iconic or indexical sign relation. In this way, eventually the impression has arisen in some semioticians (cf. Saussure 1916: part I, ch. I2) that such signs are not iconically or indexically motivated at all. However that may be, recourse to the history of sender-recipient contacts is necessary for an explanation of the development from non-linguistic signaling by way of indicating a signaling to full-grown linguistic utterances such as "Regardez!", "Aufgepasst!", "Look here!" The latter are produced as genuine requests, i.e., as signaling by means of indicating a signaling. An intermediate step in the development from non-linguistic to linguistic requests of that kind may be seen in handclapping accompanied by verbal utterances which then gradually turns into verbal utterances accompanied by handclapping until the handclapping is entirely omitted in the end.

Ad 2: If we can assume that this is how the children learn to understand signaling acts of the various kinds, why should they follow them and do what the sign producer wants them to do? Here again, the history of sender-recipient contacts plays an important role. Being used to having many of their own wishes fulfilled by Britta, the children also tend to fulfil what they think are her wishes. And they generally do so without Britta actively trying to influence them. When Britta now performs her silent handclapping for the first time, she can profit from these habits. If the handclapping is felicitous, the children understand that she wants them to do *r*; and since this is a wish of hers, they tend in fact to do *r*: their understanding of her wish makes them fulfil the wish. In this way, Britta's silent handclapping, which is only an indicator of her signaling, becomes a signal for them to do *r*.

What happens, when Britta tries to reinforce this behaviour by performing other requests? The children start understanding not only that she wants them to do *r* but also that she believes they will do *r* when they understand that she wants them to do *r*. Her silent handclapping now causes them not only to believe that she is signaling but also that she is communicating. It turns into an indicator of a directive act of communicating. The sender's directive act of communicating as a whole becomes the content of the addressee's belief and thus occurs on a higher level of reflection. The indicator process leading to this belief has to be located on level **3a** in the hierarchy of sign types. The higher level of understanding reached in this way is not counterproductive; on the contrary, it may enhance the motivation of the children to do *r*: the children's belief that *b* wants them to do *r* (level **2a**) and their belief that *b* wants them to know that *b* wants them to do *r* (and that *b* wants them to do *r* because of this knowledge; level **3a**) work together in making them really do *r*.

Being a good teacher, Britta is, of course, bound to notice the children's increasing ability to understand; and she reacts by making her intentions and beliefs in communicating as transparent as possible. This can lead to even higher levels of understanding and indicating: Britta may now perform a directive (i.e., she may signal by indicating this signaling) simply by means of indicating the performance of this directive (i.e., she may signal by indicating this signaling and do that through indicating that she is signaling by indicating this signaling). It is left to the reader to try and reformulate this configuration of sign processes on level **3b** in the terminology of intensional logic as a configuration of attitudes and internal processes in the persons involved.

What is required of Britta in the course of mutual adaptation with the children is an increasing openness to higher levels of reflection and the will to use these levels more and more for the accomplishment of her intentions in communicating. Unrestricted reflective openness in communicating would consist in the sender *b* being able not only

(2b) to intend that *a* believes
that *b* does *f* because *b* intends the occurrence of *f* to bring about some effect;

but also

(3b) to intend that *a* believes
that *b* intends that *a* believes
that *b* does *f* because *b* intends the occurrence of *f* to bring about some effect;

and

(4b) to intend that *a* believes
that *b* intends that *a* believes
that *b* intends that *a* believes
that *b* does *f* because *b* intends the occurrence of *f* to bring about some effect;

etc.

Put in formulas, unrestricted reflective openness of the sender *b* in an act of communicating is the ability of *b* such that

(2b) $\qquad\qquad\qquad I(b,\ G(a,\ T(b,f) \wedge I(b,\ E(f) \rightarrow E(e)))),$
(3b) $\qquad\qquad I(b,\ G(a,\quad '' \quad\quad '' \qquad\qquad\qquad)),$
(4b) $\quad I(b,\ G(a,\quad '' \quad\quad '' \quad\quad '' \qquad\qquad\qquad)),$
. . . . . .
. . . . . .
. . . . . .

The corresponding openness on the side of the addressees *a* in an act of communicating can be defined in a parallel way:

(2a) $\qquad\qquad\qquad G(a,\ T(b,f) \wedge I(b,\ E(f) \rightarrow E(e))),$
(3a) $\qquad\qquad G(a,\ I(b,\quad '' \quad\quad '' \qquad\qquad)),$
(4a) $\quad G(a,\ I(b,\quad '' \quad\quad '' \quad\quad '' \qquad\qquad)),$
. . . . . .
. . . . . .
. . . . . .

Of course, in real-time communication, reflective openness is never realized in an unrestricted way. Due to the finite character of human and artificial brains, an infinite number of intentions (on the part of the sender) and beliefs (on the part of the addressee) can never be activated. However, even if this were possible, it is unnecessary. Felicitous communicating requires intentions and beliefs to occur on levels **1** and **2**. Reflective openness thus consists simply in being prepared to additionally activate levels **3** and **4**, etc. according to the levels anticipated to be activated by the communication partner. This account has the advantage of sparing us the unrealistic assumption implicitly or explicitly made by many another theorist that communicating requires the occurrence of infinitely many propositional attitudes (cf. Schiffer, 1972; Meggle, 1981; Sperber & Wilson, 1986; and Barwise, 1989).

In addition to mutually-adapted reflective openness, there are further circumstances that contribute to the success of an act of communicating. They have already been comprehensively discussed in the relevant literature (cf. Searle, 1969, 1979 and 1983; Bennett, 1976; Kasher, 1976, 1979 and 1988; Bach & Harnish, 1979; Recanati, 1981; Savigny, 1983; Searle & Vanderveken, 1985; Sperber & Wilson, 1986; Grandy & Warner, 1986; Burkhardt, 1990; Hall et al., 1990; as well as Searle et al., 1992) and it may therefore suffice to summarize them in our own terms here:

a. If the addressee is to do what he understands the sender intends him to do, he must assume that the sender is *serious*. In the kindergarten case, this implies that the teacher really wants the children to be silent and pay attention when she produces a directive to that effect. In the shaman case, this implies that the shaman really wants the man and woman to become husband and wife when he performs the declarational laying on of hands: $I(b, E(f) \rightarrow E(e))$. This formula describes the primary communicative intention of the sender and can be called the *seriousness condition* of communicating.

b. The addressee must assume that doing what the sender intends him to do *is not a mistake*. This implies in the case of directives that it lies in the addressee's (short or long term) interest (cf. Posner, 1980: ch. 5). In the case of assertives, expressives and commissives, what the sender wants the addressee to do is to believe something, and this is not a mistake if what is supposed to be believed is true. This condition can be called the *unmistakenness condition* of assertive communicating.

c. In the case of assertives, expressives and commissives, the sender's own psychological state is a relevant circumstance in the addressee's decision whether he can believe what the sender wants him to believe. In an assertive, the sender himself must appear to believe the proposition he intends the addressee to believe: *G(b,p)*. In an expressive, this proposition specifies a certain state of the sender, and so the sender must appear to be in that state: *Z(b)*. In a commissive, that state consists in the sender's intention to do something, and so the sender must appear to have that intention: *I(b, T(b,g))*. This condition is sometimes called the *sincerity condition* of communicating.

These circumstances are important enough to justify our considering them in relation to the constituents of the complex formula that defines the act of communicating.

4. The anatomy of communication

In § 2 and § 3 we introduced a hierarchy of sign types based on complex configurations of believing, causing and intending. We started on level **1a** with signals, indicators, expressions and gestures and showed that they are all causes with effects of increasing complexity. We then introduced signaling, indicating, expressing and gesturing on level **1b** and showed that they are all actions with intended effects of corresponding complexity. We then demonstrated how signs of higher levels are constructed by combining the concepts of levels **1a** and **1b**. This led us to the definition of five types of communicating. Communicating occurs in the form of a declaration, a directive, an assertive, an expressive or a commissive, and it consists in acting by indicating that action, signaling by indicating that signaling, indicating by indicating that indicating, expressing by indicating that expressing and gesturing by indicating that gesturing. All communicating thus has the same structure: it is an action performed by means of indicating that action. Since communicating is a sign process of high complexity, there are many conditions determining its performance, and the time has now come to give a systematic account of them.

4.1 Conditions of communicating

As a result of the analysis in the preceding paragraphs we know that when someone *b* performs an act of communicating, *b* produces a certain event *f* and intends (primary intention) the occurrence of *f* to cause a certain effect *e* (primary effect); *b* also intends (secondary intention) the occurrence of *f* to cause (secondary effect) someone else *a* to understand his primary intention; and *b* believes that this understanding will bring about a process leading to the primary effect. We also know what is required of the addressee *a* to make *b*'s act of communicating a success on the various levels: *a* must accomplish the primary effect (condition of primary success); *a* must accomplish the secondary effect (condition of secondary success or felicity condition); and the accomplishment of the secondary effect must cause the accomplishment of the primary effect (communication condition). And we know that this complex response is enhanced if *a* has the reflective openness to become aware of intentions of *b* on still higher levels and if *a* believes in the sender's seriousness and unmistakenness and assumes his sincerity.

Let us now look at the various conditions in detail (cf. figure 3).

1. *The sincerity condition*. If someone asserts some proposition *p* which he does not believe in himself, or expresses some state which he is not in, or promises to do something without intending to do it, he is called insincere. The sincerity condition of an assertive is therefore *G(b,p)*, that of an expressive is *Z(b)*, and that of a commissive is *I(b, T(b,g))*. These formulas are written on the bottom line of the list of conditions of communicating given in figure 3. They all describe psychological states of the sender with respect to the proposition which is the primary message of the act of communicating. The latter consists in *p* for assertives, *Z(b)* for expressives and *I(b, T(b,g))* for commissives. If the sender wants to convince the addressee of the primary message, he must give him the impression that it is true or at least that he is convinced of it himself. In the case of declarations and directives there is nothing the sender wants to convince the addressee of on this level of reflection; instead he wants the addressee to bring about some external effect (possibly in cooperation with himself, as in many declarations). Therefore declarations and directives have no sincerity conditions (Searle, 1979: 19, acknowledges that there is no sincerity condition for declarations, but for directives he postulates a sincerity condition of the type: *b* wants *a* to do *r*; cf. also 1979: 14 and 44. As our systematic account shows, this requirement lies on a level that is different from the sincerity conditions for assertives, expressives and commissives: it is one of the seriousness conditions treated in point 6; cf. also Falkenberg, 1990).
2. *The minimal propositional content*. When someone performs an act of communicating, he wants to achieve a certain primary effect by indicating that he wants to achieve that effect. A natural way of verbal communicating therefore is the utterance of a verbal expression which refers to the intended primary effect by means of its coded content. The propositional content of a verbal declaration can be expected to be simply *E(e)*, of a verbal directive *T(a,r)*, of

	Declaration	Directive	Assertive	Expressive	Commissive
12. Communication condition	$(E(f) \rightarrow G(a, T(b,f) \wedge I(b,E(f) \rightarrow E(e)))) \rightarrow (E(f) \rightarrow E(e))$	$(E(f) \rightarrow (G(a,T(b,f) \wedge I(b,E(f) \rightarrow T(a,r)))) \rightarrow (E(f) \rightarrow T(b,r))$	$(E(f) \rightarrow G(a,T(b,f) \wedge I(b,E(f) \rightarrow G(a,p)))) \rightarrow (E(f) \rightarrow G(a,p))$	$(E(f) \rightarrow G(a,T(b,f) \wedge I(b,E(f) \rightarrow G(a,Z(b))))) \rightarrow (E(f) \rightarrow G(a,Z(b)))$	$(E(f) \rightarrow G(a,T(b,f) \wedge I(b,E(f) \rightarrow G(a,I(b,T(b,g)))))) \rightarrow (E(f) \rightarrow G(a,I(b,T(b,g))))$
11. Secondary action	$T(b,f) \wedge I(b,E(f) \rightarrow G(a,T(b,f) \wedge I(b,E(f) \rightarrow E(e))))$	$T(b,f) \wedge I(b,E(f) \rightarrow G(a,T(b,f) \wedge I(b,E(f) \rightarrow T(a,r))))$	$T(b,f) \wedge I(b,E(f) \rightarrow G(a,T(b,f) \wedge I(b,E(f) \rightarrow G(a,p))))$	$T(b,f) \wedge I(b,E(f) \rightarrow G(a,T(b,f) \wedge I(b,E(f) \rightarrow G(a,Z(b)))))$	$T(b,f) \wedge I(b,E(f) \rightarrow G(a,T(b,f) \wedge I(b,E(f) \rightarrow G(a,I(b,T(b,g))))))$
10. Secondary intention	$I(b,E(f) \rightarrow G(a,T(b,f) \wedge I(b,E(f) \rightarrow E(e))))$	$I(b,E(f) \rightarrow G(a,T(b,f) \wedge I(b,E(f) \rightarrow T(a,r))))$	$I(b,E(f) \rightarrow G(a,T(b,f) \wedge I(b,E(f) \rightarrow G(a,p))))$	$I(b,E(f) \rightarrow G(a,T(b,f) \wedge I(b,E(f) \rightarrow G(a,Z(b)))))$	$I(b,E(f) \rightarrow G(a,T(b,f) \wedge I(b,E(f) \rightarrow G(a,I(b,T(b,g))))))$
9. Secondary process (felicity condition, condition of secondary success)	$E(f) \rightarrow G(a,T(b,f) \wedge I(b,E(f) \rightarrow E(e)))$	$E(f) \rightarrow G(a,T(b,f) \wedge I(b,E(f) \rightarrow T(a,r)))$	$E(f) \rightarrow G(a,T(b,f) \wedge I(b,E(f) \rightarrow G(a,p)))$	$E(f) \rightarrow G(a,T(b,f) \wedge I(b,E(f) \rightarrow G(a,Z(b))))$	$E(f) \rightarrow G(a,T(b,f) \wedge I(b,E(f) \rightarrow G(a,I(b,T(b,g)))))$
8. Secondary interpretant (intended secondary effect)	$G(a,T(b,f) \wedge I(b,E(f) \rightarrow E(e)))$	$G(a,T(b,f) \wedge I(b,E(f) \rightarrow T(a,r)))$	$G(a,T(b,f) \wedge I(b,E(f) \rightarrow G(a,p)))$	$G(a,T(b,f) \wedge I(b,E(f) \rightarrow G(a,Z(b))))$	$G(a,T(b,f) \wedge I(b,E(f) \rightarrow G(a,I(b,T(b,g)))))$
7. Secondary message (primary action)	$T(b,f) \wedge I(b,E(f) \rightarrow E(e))$	$T(b,f) \wedge I(b,E(f) \rightarrow T(a,r))$	$T(b,f) \wedge I(b,E(f) \rightarrow G(a,p))$	$T(b,f) \wedge I(b,E(f) \rightarrow G(a,Z(b)))$	$T(b,f) \wedge I(b,E(f) \rightarrow G(a,I(b,T(b,g))))$
6. Primary intention (seriousness condition)	$I(b,E(f) \rightarrow E(e))$	$I(b,E(f) \rightarrow T(a,r))$	$I(b,E(f) \rightarrow G(a,p))$	$I(b,E(f) \rightarrow G(a,Z(b)))$	$I(b,E(f) \rightarrow G(a,I(b,T(b,g))))$
5. Primary process (condition of primary success)	$E(f) \rightarrow E(e)$	$E(f) \rightarrow T(a,r)$	$E(f) \rightarrow G(a,p)$	$E(f) \rightarrow G(a,Z(b))$	$E(f) \rightarrow G(a,I(b,T(b,g)))$
4. Primary interpretant (intended primary effect)	$E(e)$	$T(a,r)$	$G(a,p)$	$G(a,Z(b))$	$G(a,I(b,T(b,g)))$
3. Primary message (unmistakenness condition)	$\varnothing$	$\varnothing$	p	$Z(b)$	$I(b,T(b,g))$
2. Minimal propositional content	$E(e)$	$T(a,r)$	p	$Z(b)$	$T(b,g)$
1. Sincerity condition	$\varnothing$	$\varnothing$	$G(b,p)$	$Z(b)$	$I(b,T(b,g))$
	I	II	III	IV	V

Figure 3: Conditions of communicating

a verbal assertive *G(a,p)*, of a verbal expressive *G(a, Z(b))* and of a verbal commissive *G(a, I(b, T(b,g)))*. So the shaman might simply say to his marriage couple "You are now husband and wife"; and the teacher might say "Keep silent and pay attention" ("Silence and attention, please!"). However, in the case of assertives, expressives and commissives, where the intended primary effect involves a propositional attitude of the addressee (his belief), it is also possible to omit the verbalization of that attitude and just to specify its intended content. Thus in an assertive act of communicating one simply says "The door is closed" instead of "Believe that the door is closed". In an expressive one says "How happy I am!" instead of "Believe how happy I am". And a commissive may be reduced even further so that one says "I will bring you the book" instead of "Believe that I intend to bring you the book!". This simplification is made possible by the fact that communicating is acting by indicating the action concerned. It is often enough to utter a minimal proposition in order to bring about the intended indicator process in the addressee (cf. line 2 in figure 3).

3. *The primary message (unmistakenness condition).* In an assertive, expressive and commissive, the sender tries to make the addressee believe a certain proposition *p*, *Z(b)*, and *I(b, T(b,g))* respectively. This proposition is called the primary message of the act of communicating. A message is something the sender intends the addressee to believe. In declarations, however, the sender intends some change to come about on the social level, and in directives, the sender intends the addressee to respond with some behaviour other than belief. Therefore, declarations and directives have no primary messages. When the addressee really believes what the sender intends him to believe, he is not mistaken if the respective proposition holds. The unmistakenness condition for the response to an act of communicating is therefore identical with its primary message. One could construct a similar argument for directives (cf. circumstance b in § 3.4), requiring that the behaviour the sender tries to make the addressee perform is in the addressee's interest. However, the formula describing this behaviour, *T(a,r)*, is not embedded in a belief operator and therefore specifies no message in the sense given above. This is why an unmistakenness condition is specified only for assertives, expressives and commissives on line 3 in figure 3.

4. *The primary interpretant (intended primary effect).* The primary interpretant of an act of communicating is what the addressee must do, if the act of communicating is to be successful. The primary

interpretant is thus identical with the intended primary effect of the act of communicating. It consists in *E(e)* for declarations, *T(a,r)* for directives, *G(a,p)* for assertives, *G(a, Z(b))* for expressives and *G(a, I(b, T(b,g)))* for commissives. The primary interpretant of an act of communicating is constituted by something happening (on the social level) in declarations, the addressee doing something in directives, and the addressee believing something in assertives, expressives and commissives. What the addressee is to believe can itself be a complex attitude of the sender as in the case of *I(b, T(b,g))* for commissives.

5. *The primary process (condition of primary success).* The occurrence of the intended effect alone is not sufficient for an act of communicating to be successful. Closing a door before being requested to do so cannot be regarded as fulfilment of that request. Communicating by producing a sign event *f* is successful only if the occurrence of the intended effect is caused by the occurrence of *f*. Causal processes of this kind were described as basic sign processes in § 2.1 above. They are what we call the primary processes of acts of communicating, and their occurrence is the condition of primary success for these acts of communicating. As pointed out in § 3.3, it is important to note that an act of communicating can be performed without the corresponding primary process occurring. In this case we say that it is unsuccessful with respect to its condition of primary success. It can still be felicitous (cf. point 9).

6. *The primary intention (seriousness condition).* When someone produces a sign event *f* in an act of communicating, he intends the respective primary process (which is the condition of primary success of this act of communicating) to occur. This intention is called the primary intention of the sender. It is *I(b, E(f) → E(e))* in the case of declarations, *I(b, E(f) → T(a,r))* in the case of directives, *I(b, E(f) → G(a,p))* in the case of assertives, *I(b, E(f) → G(a, Z(b)))* in the case of expressives, and *I(b, E(f) → G(a, I(b, T(b,g))))* in the case of commissives. If the sign producer does not have one of these intentions, his production of *f* is not a serious act of communicating. Our definitions of the five types of communicating do not directly require the primary intention to occur, but they do specify that the sign producer intends the addressee to believe in it and that the sign producer assumes that this belief will cause the content of the primary belief to be realized.

7. *The secondary message (primary action).* As was established in point 3 above, a message is what the sender tries to make the addressee believe in an act of communicating. The definitions of all types of

communicating require that the sender tries to achieve the intended primary effect by making his addressee believe that he is trying to achieve it. Thus all communicating involves a message on this secondary level. The secondary message is what the addressee must be made to understand (by means of the occurrence of *f*), if the act of communicating is to be felicitous. What the addressee understands in a felicitous declaration is that the sender performs an action, in a felicitous directive it is that the sender performs a signaling, in a felicitous assertive it is that the sender performs an indicating, in a felicitous expressive it is that the sender performs an expressing, and in a felicitous commissive it is that the sender performs a gesturing. The formulas for the secondary messages on line 7 of figure 3 are identical with the formulas specifying the respective actions on level **1b** in figure 2. These actions can be called primary actions.

8. *The secondary interpretant (intended secondary effect)*. When someone produces a sign event *f* in order to communicate something, he performs a primary action by indicating that action. The intended effect of the primary action is the primary interpretant of the act of communicating, the intended effect of the indicating is the secondary interpretant. It consists in the addressee believing that the sender is performing the primary action. The formulas for the secondary interpretants in line 8 of figure 3 therefore all start with *G(a, ...)*, where the second argument consists in the primary action performed. The secondary interpretant of an act of communicating is a belief on the part of the addressee in the sender's intention to bring about the occurrence of the primary interpretant by producing the sign event *f*. The secondary interpretant includes the belief of the addressee that the sender's production of *f* is a serious act of communicating (cf. point 6).

9. *The secondary process (felicity condition, condition of secondary success)*. When the occurrence of the sign event *f* in an act of communicating leads to the addressee understanding that the sender is performing a certain primary action, then the act of communicating is felicitous. The felicity condition thus requires the occurrence of *f* to be an indicator of the primary action performed. This indicator process (cf. level **2a** in figure 2) is called the secondary process of the act of communicating concerned. It is directly intended by the sender, as can be seen in the formulas defining communicating of the various types (upper box on level **2bcom** in figure 2). Therefore the felicity condition of an act of communicating can be said to be its condition of secondary success. The

conditions of primary (cf. point 5) and secondary success must both be fulfilled if an act of communicating is to be successful.

10. *The secondary intention.* When producing an event *f* in order to communicate, the sign producer has the intention that the occurrence of *f* will make the addressee understand that he is performing a certain primary action. This intention is called the sender's secondary intention in communicating. It is characterized by the formulas on line 10 in figure 3. They show that the sender's secondary intention can be understood as his intention to have the felicity condition fulfilled by the addressee. The secondary intention is the intention involved in indicating the performance of the primary action to the addressee (cf. level **2b** in figure 2).

11. *The secondary action.* Producing an event *f* with the intention to make the addressee understand that one is performing a certain primary action is the secondary action involved in communicating. The secondary action thus consists in the production of *f* connected with the secondary intention. It aims at bringing about the secondary process (fulfilment of the felicity condition), and its intended effect is the secondary interpretant. The secondary action in an act of communicating is the action of indicating the primary action. The formulas for the secondary action on line 11 of figure 3 are therefore identical with the formulas specifying the indicating of an action on level **2b** in figure 2.

12. *The communication condition.* The essential feature of communicating lies in the sender producing a secondary sign process (of level **2a**) (i.e., performing a secondary action of level **2b**) with the belief that it will bring about a primary process (of level **1a**): he uses an indicator of himself producing a causal process in order to bring about that causal process (in declarations); he uses an indicator of himself producing a signal process in order to bring about that signal process (in directives); he uses an indicator of himself producing an indicator process in order to bring about that indicator process (in assertives); he uses an indicator of himself producing an expression process in order to bring about that expression process (in expressives); and he uses an indicator of a gesturing process in order to bring about that gesturing process (in commissives). This is described by the formulas for the communication condition on line 12 in figure 3. They have a peculiar structure, which becomes evident when one compares the effect of the secondary process with the effect of the primary process caused by it: while the effect of the secondary process is $G(a, T(b,f) \wedge I(b, E(f) \rightarrow E(e)))$, the effect of the primary process is simply $E(e)$. The difference between the

formulas of these two effects consists in *G(a, ... I(b, ---))*, which characterizes one step down in the hierarchy of levels of reflection. Thus one is justified in claiming that the whole point of communicating lies in reducing a higher level process to a corresponding process on the next lower level of reflection. The sender of an act of communicating believes that this reduction will be carried out by the addressee, and whenever this is the case, the act of communicating is successful in the full sense (including the fulfilment of the conditions of both secondary and primary success). The condition of communication implies that behavioural systems not reaching at least the second level of reflection are incapable of performing acts of communicating or of appropriately responding to them: communication is impossible without a certain degree of intelligence.

Let us now compare the various formulas that specify attitudes and processes connected with communicating. The following conclusions emerge.

(i) With the exception of the formulas for the sincerity condition, the minimal propositional content and the communication condition, the formulas in each column of figure 3 constitute a sequence where each formula contains an occurrence of the preceding one as its constituent.

(ii) The formulas for the primary process (the condition of primary success) are identical with those of level **1a** in figure 2; the formulas for the primary action (secondary message) are identical with those of level **1b**; the formulas for the secondary process (the felicity condition, condition of secondary success) are identical with those of level **2a**; and the formulas for the secondary action are identical with the formulas of level **2b**.

(iii) Even the circumstances which enhance primary and secondary success in communicating find a place in this system of formulas: when the primary message is true, the addressee is *unmistaken* in believing it (as intended by the sender). When the sender himself believes the primary message or is in the corresponding state, he is *sincere*. When the sender has the primary intention necessary for the act of communicating, he is communicating *seriously*.

Since the formulas in each column from line 3 to 11 in figure 3 are embedded in one another and the formula on line 11 is a constituent of the formula defining the respective act of communicating, all these formulas can be said to describe aspects of communicating. However, this does not imply that they are all true when an act of communicating of the respective type takes place: when an act of communicating is unsuccessful on the primary level, the primary message (3) is not believed and the primary interpretant (4) does not occur, nor does the primary process (5). When an act of communicating is not serious, the primary intention (6) does not occur. When an act of communicating is not felicitous, the secondary message (7) is not believed and the secondary interpretant (8) does not occur, nor does the secondary process (9). Of all the attitudes and processes noted in figure 3, only the secondary intention (10) and the secondary action (11) are necessary components of an act of communicating; this follows from the upper section of the definitions on line **2bcom** in figure 2. The second necessary feature of communicating is the sender's belief in the validity of the communication condition (12) under the given circumstances, which follows from the lower section of the definitions on line **2bcom** in figure 2.

The conclusions (i) and (ii) above confirm our claim that communicating is a complex sign process that requires at least the level of reflection **2**, and is constructed on the basis of sign processes of level **1a** and **2a**.

4.2 Action, understanding and communicating

In § 4.1 we studied the conditions of communicating in relation to the components of the belief-and-intention configuration involved in communicating. Let us now analyze the components of the belief-and-intention configurations involved in other kinds of sign processes. Above, communicating was repeatedly characterized as a primary action performed by means of a secondary action aimed at making the addressee understand the sender's intention to perform the primary action. Felicitous communicating thus involves two kinds of action on the part of the sender and (at least) one kind of understanding on the part of the addressee. What role do action and understanding play in the other kinds of sign processes of the hierarchy given in figure 2?

On level **1a** there is no action defined yet, nor does any understanding occur in simple causal processes and in signal processes. However, when a sign event *f* is an indicator, its occurrence causes a belief in a reacting system: $E(f) \rightarrow G(a,p)$, and this in itself justifies speaking of understanding, if only in a very rudimentary sense. Indicator processes turn out to be central building blocks of communicating: they not only occur in expression and gesture processes, which are both special cases of indicator processes; they also reoccur on level **2a**, as can be seen from the structure of the respective formulas: $E(f) \rightarrow G(a,...)$.

The simplest type of action specified in our hierarchy occurs on level **1b** in column **I**. Someone is said to perform an action by doing *f* if he intends the occurrence of *f* to cause a certain effect. Performing an action is thus characterized as doing something with a certain intention: $T(b,f) \wedge I(b,...)$. All other processes on level **1b** are special cases of actions, and action processes also reoccur on a higher level in **2b**, as can be seen from the structure of the respective formulas: $T(b,f) \wedge I(b,...)$.

From these observations it follows that, with the exception of simple causal and signal processes, all processes specified in our hierarchy up to level **2b** are configurations of indicator processes and actions. In principle, the construction of complex sign processes by combining indicator processes and actions can be continued beyond the second level of reflection. The discussion of interactive openness in § 3.4 made it clear that such higher-level sign processes exist. But the higher one gets the more they tend to lose their point, since they are not systematically connected with responses on the lower levels of reflection. This is, however, what communicating is supposed to achieve through the communication condition.

If we stay with the apparatus of intensional logic in constructing higher-level sign processes, the resulting formulas soon become too complicated to be handled easily. Let us therefore make use of the semiotic terminology, which was introduced in § 2 and § 3, and synoptically presented in figure 2, in order to abbreviate the higher-level formulas. This is possible if we allow the area codes of figure 2 to be substituted for the formulas occurring in these areas:

- the formula for an action in area **I1b**, which contains the formula for a causal process $E(f) \rightarrow E(e)$ as specified in area **I1a**, can thus be replaced by $T(b,f) \wedge I(b,\mathbf{I1a})$;
- the formula for an indicator of an action in area **I2a** can be replaced by $E(f) \rightarrow G(a,\mathbf{I1b})$, as well as by $E(f) \rightarrow G(a, T(b,f) \wedge I(b,\mathbf{I1a}))$;
- the formula for an indicating of an action in area **I2b** can be replaced by $T(b,f) \wedge I(b,\mathbf{I2a})$ and by $T(b,f) \wedge I(b, E(f) \rightarrow G(a,\mathbf{I1b}))$ as well as by $T(b,f) \wedge I(b, E(f) \rightarrow G(a, T(b,f) \wedge I(b,\mathbf{I1a})))$;
- the formula for a declarational act of communicating in area **I2bcom** can be replaced by $T(b,f) \wedge I(b,\mathbf{I2a}) \wedge G(b,\mathbf{I2a} \rightarrow \mathbf{I1a})$ as well as by what can be obtained by spelling out ***I2a*** and ***I1a*** as in the other example cases.

The abbreviated formulas are a convenient instrument for showing that:

- *f* is an action if it is produced with the intention of bringing about a certain effect,
- *f* is an indicator of an action if its occurrence causes a recipient to believe that it is an action,
- *f* is an indicating of an action if it is produced with the intention for it to be an indicator of an action, and

- *f* is a declaration if it is produced with the intention for it to be an indicator of an action and with the belief that this indicator of an action will cause the primary process intended in the action.

Abbreviated formulas of this kind can be used not only to describe the relations among the levels in column **I**, but also in the other columns of figure 2. If one omits the column signs, the formulas characterize the general relations among the sign processes on the various levels of reflection in all columns, that is for all types of sign processes. This procedure has been used in the presentation of sign structures in figure 4.

Figure 4 shows the general principles of construction of the hierarchy of sign processes. In the horizontal dimension, it is based on a series of causal processes with increasingly complex effects. These processes are characterized on level **1a** in the same way as in figure 2.

In the vertical dimension, we also have a series of increasingly complex processes, but the principles of construction here are different from those in the horizontal dimension:

- on level **1a**, we have a formula for a simple causal process $E(f) \rightarrow E(e)$;
- on level **1b**, this formula reoccurs as a constituent of the formula $T(b,f) \wedge I(a,...)$; the latter characterizes *b*'s intention to bring about ... by producing *f*, i.e., it characterizes an action;
- on level **2a** the formula ***1b*** reoccurs as a constituent of the formula $E(f) \rightarrow G(a,...)$; the latter characterizes an indicator process, i.e., it characterizes ***a***'s understanding of ***1b***;

The construction procedures for formula ***1b*** out of ***1a*** and for formula ***2a*** out of ***1b*** are then repeated on the higher levels:

- level **2b** is reached from level **2a** in the same way as level **1b** is reached from level **1a** by embedding the respective formula into $T(b,f) \wedge I(b,...)$; i.e., on level **2b** we are dealing with an action;
- level **3a** is reached from level **2b** in the same way as level **2a** is reached from level **1b** by embedding the respective formula into $E(f) \rightarrow G(a,...)$; i.e., on level **3a** we are dealing with an indicator process, that is, an understanding.

This dual progression of action and understanding can be continued without end. However, there is a complication on level **2b**, which lies in the special way communicating is constructed on the basis of action and understanding: communicating is performing a first-level action by making the addressee understand that one is performing that action. Communicating is the indicating of an action, combined with the sender's belief that the level-reducing communication condition holds. Thus the first part of the formula for communicating is identical with the formula **2b** for indicating an action: $T(b,f) \wedge I(b,2a)$; its second part represents the level-reduction:

G(b,2a → 1a). As the configuration of belief and intention operators shows, the level-reducing formula belongs to the same level of reflection as the formula for indicating an action. This is why the reflection level of communicating is characterized as **2bcom**.

In figure 4, the formulas on level **3a** etc. take the formula for communicating, ***2bcom***, as constituent. As pointed out above, an alternative progression could simply take the formula for indicating an action, ***2b***, as constituent.

The addition of the sender's belief in the communication condition, which constituted an act of communicating on level **2bcom**, is also constitutive of communicating on higher levels of reflection. One must, however, add to this as many level-reducing beliefs as are necessary to reach the basic level of reflection. On level **3bcom**, the formula ***3b***, which represents the indicating of a declaration, has to be conjoined not only with the formula *G(b,3a → 2a)*, which reduces the indicator of a declaration to the indicator of an action, but also with the formula *G(b,2a → 1a)*, which reduces the indicator of an action to the primary process intended in the action. The higher the level of reflection of an act of communicating, the more level-reducing operations must be assumed by the sender to be performed by the addressee.

It is not difficult to find examples for higher-level communicating on level 3: take a chairperson trying to reopen a formal session when the intermission is over. Instead of formally reopening the session by saying "I hereby reopen the meeting", which would be a standard declaration, he can indicate this declaration by producing a noticeable cough *f*, and believe that the occurrence of *f* will be accepted as a declaration to the same effect as the standard reopening declaration. Another example of higher-level communicating was outlined in our discussion of communicative openness in the kindergarten (cf. § 3.4). When the teacher *b* tries to have the children be silent and pay attention without uttering an explicit verbal request to that effect, she can just hint at herself uttering an explicit verbal request by producing a noticeable cough *f*. In both cases, *f* can take over the function of indicating since it is indexically connected with the verbal utterance indicated (coughing is a preparatory step to a verbal utterance). The acts of communicating indicated, however, are different in the two cases; their type and content have to be inferred from the circumstances.

These examples may suffice to provide evidence for the wealth of complex higher-level sign processes that result from combinations of the three procedures described. Taking into account reflective openness in the sender and the addressee, they can be recapitulated as

(1) action: producing an event *f* with the intention that the occurrence of *f* be a cause for a certain lower-level process: $T(b,f) \wedge I(b,...)$,

(2) understanding: being made to believe something by the occurrence of *f*: $E(f) \rightarrow G(a,...)$, and
(3) communicating: producing an indicator of an action with the belief that it will cause the process intended in the action: $T(b,f) \wedge I(b,\mathbf{na}) \wedge G(b,\mathbf{na} \rightarrow \mathbf{n\text{-}1a})$, where $\mathbf{n}$ is any natural number above 1.

When higher-level communicating is performed to achieve the effect of one of the five types of communicating defined on level **2bcom**, it has the form:

$$
\begin{aligned}
T(b,f) \wedge I(b,\mathbf{na}) & \\
\wedge\, G(b,\mathbf{na} \rightarrow \mathbf{n\text{-}1a}) & \\
\wedge\, G(b,\mathbf{n\text{-}1a} \rightarrow \mathbf{n\text{-}2a}) & \\
\vdots \qquad \vdots & \\
\wedge\, G(b,\mathbf{n\text{-}(n\text{-}2)a} \rightarrow \mathbf{n\text{-}(n\text{-}1)a}), & \text{ where } \mathbf{n} \text{ is any natural number above } 1.
\end{aligned}
$$

4.3 Sign use and type-switching

If a sender *b* produces an event *f* with the intention that *f* serve as a sign, we can say that *b uses f as* a sign, as already pointed out in point 12 of § 4.1. Thus *b* uses *f* as a signal when *b* performs the action of signaling: $T(b,f) \wedge I(b, \mathbf{II1a})$; *b* uses *f* as an indicator when *b* performs the action of indicating: $T(b,f) \wedge I(b, \mathbf{III1a})$; etc. And *b* uses *f* as an indicator of signaling, when *b* performs an indicating of signaling: $T(b,f) \wedge I(b, \mathbf{II2a})$; etc.

In the case of communicating, *b* produces an indicator of an action and believes it to cause the process intended in that action. Here again we can formulate that *b* uses an indicator of an action as a cause for the process intended in that action. In directives, for instance, we can say that *b* uses an indicator of signaling as a signal: $T(b,f) \wedge I(b,\mathbf{II2a}) \wedge G(b,\mathbf{II2a} \rightarrow \mathbf{II1a})$.

The concept of sign use enables us to analyze the composition of more complex sign processes obtained by combining selected sign processes from our hierarchy. Let us study them on the basis of a final series of examples connected with expressions, expressings and expressive acts of communicating (cf. column **IV** in figure 2 and figure 4). In area **IV1b**, *b* expresses some state *Z*: $T(b,f) \wedge I(b, E(f) \rightarrow G(a, Z(b)))$; i.e., *b* uses *f* as an expression of that state: $T(b,f) \wedge I(b,\mathbf{IV1a})$. In area **IV2b**, *b* indicates expressing; i.e., *b* uses *f* as an indicator of expressing: $T(b,f) \wedge I(b,\mathbf{IV2a})$. In area **IV2bcom**, *b* performs an expressive act of communicating, i.e., *b* uses an indicator of himself expressing some state as an expression of that state: $T(b,f) \wedge I(b,\mathbf{IV2a}) \wedge G(b,\mathbf{IV2a} \rightarrow \mathbf{IV1a})$.

Imagine an apartment where Brenda (*b*) is in the kitchen, preparing supper, while Amanda (*a*), who shares the apartment with Brenda, is sitting at her writing desk in the room next to the kitchen. The kitchen door is open and the radio is not on, since Amanda wishes not to be disturbed while working.

(IV1a) One evening, while Amanda is concentrating on her work, she suddenly hears a cry of pain from the kitchen: $E(f)$, which makes her believe that Brenda has hurt herself (Z) while preparing the supper: $E(f) \rightarrow G(a, Z(b))$. Let us assume that Brenda has in fact hurt herself and in the process did not think of any other person present. She cried out involuntarily. Amanda hears the cry, believes that Brenda is in pain and, as a consequence, jumps up from her writing desk and runs into the kitchen to see if she can help. This is to have more consequences.

(IV1b) One evening, Brenda is preparing supper again and she has another mishap, which is slightly less serious than the first one. There is no involuntary cry. But after a short reaction time, Brenda intentionally produces a cry of pain that resembles the one she would have produced involuntarily if the pain had been severe enough. She produces a cry with the intention that its occurrence cause Amanda to believe she is in pain: $T(b,f) \wedge I(b, E(f) \rightarrow G(a, Z(b)))$. This is what we call expressing pain. The difference between an expression of pain and an expressing of pain is that the latter, but not necessarily the former, is an action: $T(b,f) \wedge I(b,\mathbf{IV1a})$; cf. § 3.1 and area **IV1b** in figures 2 and 4.

(IV1b → II1b) Now it may well be that Amanda cannot tell the difference and takes Brenda's cry as an expression of pain in the same way as in the first case. In consequence, she may run to help Brenda, bandage her finger etc. And this may be what Brenda wanted to achieve. If so, Brenda manipulated Amanda: she produced an event with the intention that it be taken as an expression of a bodily state (independent of what her bodily state actually was) and she believed that this expression would serve as a signal for Amanda to come to help; in other words, Brenda used an expression as a signal: $T(b,f) \wedge I(b,\mathbf{IV1a}) \wedge G(b,\mathbf{IV1a} \rightarrow \mathbf{II1a})$. Manipulation always takes place when one tries to make someone else do or believe something without indicating that intention to him. The difference between manipulation and communication lies in the communication condition. When the latter is fulfilled, the addressee is intended to understand what the sender wants him to do or believe, and this understanding is even supposed to cause the addressee to do or believe that.

(IV2a) Back to the kitchen: if Brenda repeats her manipulation too often, Amanda may become aware of it. In this case, Brenda's cry makes Amanda believe that Brenda produced it with the intention for the cry to make Amanda believe that Brenda is in pain: $E(f) \rightarrow G(a, T(b,f) \wedge I(b, E(f) \rightarrow$

$G(a, Z(b))))$. Semiotically speaking, Amanda takes Brenda's cry as an indicator of Brenda expressing pain: $E(f) \rightarrow G(a, IV1b)$. The discovery that Brenda sometimes voluntarily cries in order to make Amanda believe she is in pain when in fact she is not may make Amanda less eager to run to help. Amanda may even accuse Brenda of misleading her and simulating pain by producing fake pain behaviour.

(II2a) However, if Amanda is very fond of Brenda, she might eventually accept Brenda's simulated cry *f* as a direct signal for her to come into the kitchen and help. In this case, *f* serves as an indicator of signaling for Amanda, and it is no longer relevant whether she has any specific belief about Brenda's bodily state: $E(f) \rightarrow G(a, T(b,f) \wedge I(b, E(f) \rightarrow T(a,r)))$; in semiotic terms: $E(f) \rightarrow G(a, II1a)$.

(IV2b) Amanda's way of responding might influence Brenda's habits of interaction in such a way that she now tries to avoid giving any reasons for being accused of simulating. So the next time Brenda hurts herself, she does not dare to produce her pseudo-natural pain cry but simply utters the word "ouch", in a tone that indicates that she has not lost control of herself. In this case, Brenda produces a conventional sound, intending its occurrence to make Amanda believe that she produces this sound with the intention of making Amanda assume she is in pain: $T(b,f) \wedge I(b, E(f) \rightarrow G(a, T(b,f) \wedge I(b, E(f) \rightarrow G(a, Z(b))))))$. Semiotically speaking, Brenda indicates to Amanda that she is expressing pain: $T(b,f) \wedge I(b, IV2a)$.

(IV2b → II1b) Of course, Brenda indicates expressing pain only in order to make Amanda come into the kitchen again. Thus Brenda produces an indicator of expressing pain with the belief that it will serve as a signal for Amanda to come; in other words, Brenda uses an indicator of expressing as a signal: $T(b,f) \wedge I(b, IV2a) \wedge G(b, IV2a \rightarrow II1a)$. However, when using an indicator of expressing as a signal, Brenda manipulates Amanda in a way similar to herself using an expression as a signal. In either case, Amanda may or may not be aware of the manipulation.

(IV2bcom) When Brenda uses *f* as an indicator of expressing her state, Amanda is relieved that Brenda is no longer simulating. She therefore takes Brenda's indicating of expressing pain more seriously than the previous pseudo-natural pain behaviour. However, indicating that one expresses something is not the same as expressing something, and so Brenda cannot count on Amanda automatically believing that she is really in pain. She rather counts on an intermediate process taking place in Amanda. She believes that when her utterance of "ouch" makes Amanda understand that she wants her to believe she is in pain, then it will also make Amanda believe that she really is in pain. This corresponds to the communication condition. By applying it, Brenda makes Amanda's belief in Brenda's pain dependent on her understanding of Brenda's utterance; i.e., Brenda performs an expressive act of communicating: $T(b,f) \wedge I(b,\mathbf{IV2a}) \wedge G(b, \mathbf{IV2a} \rightarrow \mathbf{IV1a})$.

(IV2bcom → II1b) Of course, Brenda has not given up her hope that Amanda will come to her when she believes that Brenda is in pain. She performs the expressive act of communicating in the belief that it will serve as a signal for Amanda to come; in other words, she uses the expressive as a signal: $T(b,f) \wedge I(b,\mathbf{IV2a}) \wedge G(b,\mathbf{IV2a} \rightarrow \mathbf{IV1a}) \wedge G(b,\mathbf{IV1a} \rightarrow \mathbf{II1a})$. What Brenda achieves in this way is signaling by expressively communicating. Her primary expressive intention is conveyed communicatively, but her primary directive intention is still supposed to be satisfiable by manipulation. In Austin's terminology (cf. 1962: 121ff), she uses an act of communicating to perform a perlocutionary act. She uses an expressive as a signal without intending her addressee to be aware of that; she does not indicate to Amanda that she believes a successful act of expressive communicating will serve as a cause for her to come into the kitchen. If this is her aim, she cannot achieve it by simply using a communicatively produced expression as a signal.

(IV2com → II2b) When Brenda performs an expressive act of communicating with the additional belief that communication success will make Amanda come into the kitchen, she manipulates Amanda into *doing* something. Alternatively, Brenda can perform an expressive act of communicating and believe that communication success will make Amanda *understand* that she wants her to come into the kitchen. In this case she indicates signaling by expressively communicating; she uses an expressive as an indicator of signaling: $T(b,f) \wedge I(b,\mathbf{IV2a}) \wedge G(b,\mathbf{IV2a} \rightarrow \mathbf{IV1a}) \wedge G(b,\mathbf{IV1a} \rightarrow \mathbf{II2a})$; in short: $\mathbf{IV2bcom} \wedge G(b,\mathbf{IV1a} \rightarrow \mathbf{II2a})$. However, even if Brenda is successful, Amanda will only believe that Brenda is in pain and that she wants her to come. Amanda will not feel she is being asked to come into the kitchen because of Brenda's pain. Amanda can again accuse Brenda of manipulating her, since Brenda does not openly request her to come. In order to circumvent this objection, let us try the following version.

(IV2bcom → II2bcom) Brenda produces an expressive *f* in the belief that communication success will make Amanda receive *f* as a directive. In this case, Brenda uses an expressive sign *f* as a directive sign. Spelled out in a little more detail, Brenda signals to Amanda to come (by indicating this signaling) through expressing her pain (by indicating this expressing):

$T(b,f) \wedge I(b,\mathbf{IV2a}) \wedge G(b,\mathbf{IV2a} \rightarrow \mathbf{IV1a}) \wedge G(b,\mathbf{IV1a} \rightarrow \mathbf{II2bcom})$;

put more explicitly:

$T(b,f) \wedge I(b,\mathbf{IV2a}) \wedge G(b,\mathbf{IV2a} \rightarrow \mathbf{IV1a}) \wedge G(b,\mathbf{IV1a} \rightarrow \mathbf{II2a}) \wedge G(b,\mathbf{II2a} \rightarrow \mathbf{II1a})$;

and in the shortest version:

$\mathbf{IV2bcom} \rightarrow \mathbf{II2bcom}$.

However, even this complicated configuration of beliefs and intentions is not appropriate as a communicative attitude geared to making Amanda aware of Brenda's dual intention. Although Brenda tries to perform two acts of communicating (based on the same sign event *f*), the connection between the two acts is manipulative. Amanda can still accuse her of using communication for the purpose of manipulation. Brenda is still involved in what we can call manipulative indirectness. In order to achieve *communicative indirectness*, Brenda must *indicate* to Amanda that she produces the *f* with the intention to use it as a signal. A possible way of doing this is the following.

(com (IV2bcom → II1a)) *b* produces *f* with the intention that the occurrence of *f* make *a* understand that *b* intends *a* to believe in *b*'s state; and *b* believes that when this understanding occurs, the belief in *b*'s state will occur (expressive). In addition, *b* intends that the occurrence of *f* make *a* understand *b*'s intention that when the occurrence of *f* leads to *a*'s belief in *b*'s state then the occurrence of *f* will also lead to *a* doing *r*; and *b* believes: when the occurrence of *f* makes *a* understand *b*'s intention (that when the occurrence of *f* will lead to *a*'s belief in *b*'s state, the occurrence of *f* will also lead to *a* doing *r*), then the occurrence of *f* will really lead to *a* doing *r* (communicative indirectness). Spelled out in a formula, this amounts to:

$$T(b,f) \wedge I(b, E(f) \rightarrow G(a, T(b,f) \wedge I(b, E(f) \rightarrow G(a, Z(b)))))$$
$$\wedge\ G(b, (E(f) \rightarrow G(a, T(b,f) \wedge I(b, E(f) \rightarrow G(a, Z(b)))))$$
$$\rightarrow (E(f) \rightarrow G(a, Z(b)))) \qquad \text{(expressive)}$$
$$\wedge\ I(b, E(f) \rightarrow G(a, T(b,f) \wedge I(b, (E(f) \rightarrow G(a, Z(b))) \rightarrow (E(f) \rightarrow T(a,r)))))$$
$$\wedge\ G(b, (E(f) \rightarrow G(a, T(b,f) \wedge I(b, (E(f) \rightarrow G(a, Z(b))) \rightarrow (E(f) \rightarrow T(a,r)))))$$
$$\rightarrow (E(f) \rightarrow T(a,r))) \qquad \text{(communicative indirectness)}$$

In semiotic terms, *b* produces an indicator of herself producing an expression of her state, and *b* beliefs that this indicator will serve as an expression of her state:

$$T(b,f) \wedge I(b,\mathbf{IV2a})$$
$$\wedge\ G(b,\mathbf{IV2a} \rightarrow \mathbf{IV1a}) \qquad \text{(expressive)}$$

In addition, *b* produces an indicator of herself intending the expression of her state to serve as a signal for *a* to do *r*, and *b* believes that this indicator will in fact serve as that signal:

$$T(b,f) \wedge I(b, E(f) \rightarrow G(a, T(b,f) \wedge I(b,\mathbf{IV1a} \rightarrow \mathbf{II1a}) \qquad \text{(communicative}$$
$$\wedge\ G(b, (E(f) \rightarrow G(a, T(b,f) \wedge I(b,\mathbf{IV1a} \rightarrow \mathbf{II1a}))) \rightarrow \mathbf{II1a}) \quad \text{indirectness)}$$

In other words, *b* produces *f* as an indicator of expressing and uses that indicator as an expression; in addition, *b* produces *f* as an indicator of *b*'s intention for this expression to serve as a signal and uses that indicator as a signal. In short, *b* uses an expressive as an indirect directive.

A complex sign process thus structured satisfies the communication condition in two different ways. On the one hand, *b* performs an expressive

⋮	⋮	⋮	
3bcom	f is a declaration through an indicating of this declaration $T(b,f) \wedge I(b,\mathbf{3a})$ $\wedge G(b,\mathbf{3a} \rightarrow \mathbf{2a})$ $\wedge G(b,\mathbf{2a} \rightarrow \mathbf{1a})$	f is a directive through an indicating of this directive	f is a throu of th
3b	f is an indicating of a declaration $T(b,f) \wedge I(b,\mathbf{3a})$	f is an indicating of a directive	f is a asser
3a	f is an indicator of a declaration $E(f) \rightarrow G(a,\mathbf{2bcom})$	f is an indicator of a directive	f is a asser
2bcom	f is a declaration, i.e., f is an action through an indicating of this action $T(b,f) \wedge I(b,\mathbf{2a})$ $\wedge G(b,\mathbf{2a} \rightarrow \mathbf{1a})$	f is a directive, i.e., f is a signaling through an indicating of this signaling	f is a f is a throu of th
2b	f is an indicating of an action $T(b,f) \wedge I(b,\mathbf{2a})$	f is an indicating of a signaling	f is a indic
2a	f is an indicator of an action $E(f) \rightarrow G(a,\mathbf{1b})$	f is an indicator of a signaling	f is a indic
1b	f is an action $T(b,f) \wedge I(b,\mathbf{1a})$	f is a signaling	f is a
1a	f is a cause $E(f) \rightarrow E(e)$	f is a signal $E(f) \rightarrow T(a,r)$	f is a E(f)-
	I	II	

Figure 4: The hierarchy of sign types and its principles of construction

	. . .	. . .
rtive indicating rtive	f is an expressive through an indicating of this expressive	f is a commissive through an indicating of this commissive
ating of an	f is an indicating of an expressive	f is an indicating of a commissive
ator of an	f is an indicator of an expressive	f is an indicator of a commissive
tive, i.e., ating indicating ating	f is an expressive, i.e., f is an expressing through an indicating of this expressing	f is a commissive, i.e., f is a gesturing through an indicating of this gesturing
ating of an	f is an indicating of an expressing	f is an indicating of a gesturing
ator of an	f is an indicator of an expressing	f is an indicator of a gesturing
ating	f is an expressing	f is a gesturing
ator	f is an expression $E(f) \rightarrow G(a,Z(b))$	f is a gesture $E(f) \rightarrow G(a,I(b,T(b,g)))$
	IV	V

act of communicating; on the other hand, *b* utilizes this expressive act of communicating in a communicative way for the purpose of signaling. *b* no longer manipulates *a* to do *r* by means of the expressive, but indicates to *a* *b*'s wish for the expressive to serve as a signal for *a* to do *r* and believes that this indicating will bring about the signaling. In other words, by communicatively expressing her bodily state, *b* indirectly requests *a* to do *r*. If *a* really does *r*, then this no longer constitutes the intended effect of a covert perlocutionary act of *b*, but the satisfaction of an indirectly communicated wish of *b*.

The examples we are considering in this section differ from the ones discussed earlier in that they combine basic processes of two different types: an expression (column **IV** in figure 2) serves as a signal (column **II** in figure 2) for the addressee to do something. As was pointed out, there are various ways in which this can be achieved. In the example **IV1b → II1b** there is double manipulation: *b* manipulates *a* into doing something by manipulating *a* into believing something. The example **IV2b → II1b** is not essentially different: here *b* manipulates *a* into doing something by indicating that *b* wants to manipulate *a* into believing something. In **IV2bcom → II1b**, there is only simple manipulation: *b* manipulates *a* into doing something by communicating *b*'s state to *a*. Here we are dealing with manipulation by means of communication. This is also the case in **IV2bcom → II2bcom**, where we have two acts of communicating of different type linked through the same sign event *f*. This link itself is produced uncommunicatively. Thus *b* produces *f* as an expressive act of communicating and manipulates *a* into taking it as a directive act of communicating.

Only in the last example is the change from one type of basic process to the other performed communicatively. In **com (IV2bcom → II1a)** *b* not only performs an expressive act of communicating but also communicates the intention for this act of communicating to serve as a signal for *a* to do *r*. This is typical of what is called an indirect speech act in Searle, 1979 (cf. also Morgan, 1978). Indirect acts of communicating satisfy the communication condition in at least two ways: they are based on an act of communicating of type *x* and they communicate its utilization to achieve the result of an act of communicating of type *y*. Such type-switching can take an act of communicating of any type as basis and lead to an act of communicating of any other type.

This may be illustrated by a final example. When, in concluding this chapter, I say to you "I am sorry about the complexity of my formulas", I communicatively intend you to take that as an apology for the complexity of my formulas: I perform a declaration by means of an expressive. This indirect declaration is a felicitous act of communicating only if you understand my intention for you to take my expressive as a declaration.

And it is successful if you do take the expressive as a declaration because you understand my intention for you to do so.

5. Consequences for Artificial Intelligence research

With the analysis of type-switching sign processes, our trip through the realm of semiosis has come to a provisional end. This gives us an opportunity to assess the advantages and disadvantages which our approach to communication has in A.I. research.

The leading concern of this article was the question what happens in communication between humans. It was asked with the aim of giving an answer to the question what should happen in communication between information processing systems in A.I. The reconstruction of basic processes in human communication was carried out with a view to the construction of such processes in human-machine communication and in machine-machine communication. It was done on the basis of the claim that machines lacking the capacity to communicate cannot be called intelligent in any adequate sense of the word.

In reconstructing communication, we proceeded from the claims (made in § 1) that communicating is a sign process and that in sign processes external objects or events are registered or produced in connection with attitudes and processes internal to recipients and senders. We then introduced (in § 2) five elementary concepts of intensional logic that can be used to describe occurrences of external events and internal attitudes and processes. We used two event-predicators, one of them denoting the occurrence of an event: *E(...)*, and the other denoting the production of an event by a behavioural system: *T(...,---)*; and we applied three sentence operators, one of them denoting the cause-and-effect relation: ...→ ---, the second denoting the belief by a behavioral system in a proposition: *G(...,---)*, and the third denoting the intention of a behavioural system to realize a proposition: *I(...,---)*. These few concepts were all we needed to define (in § 2 and § 3) a hierarchically structured set of infinitely many sign concepts. As was pointed out in § 3, the sign concepts defined on this basis are characterized by the fact that the type of a sign event is always dependent on the type of sign process in which it occurs, the latter being determined by the belief-and-intention configuration of the recipient or the sender. In § 4 the sign concepts on the various levels of the hierarchy were shown to be reached in a dual way by alternatively applying an action and an indicator concept to lower-level sign concepts and by using a device for level-reduction, which we called the communication condition. The sign hierarchy includes, as a sub-hierarchy, a set of (infinitely many) concepts of communicating on the various levels of reflection. Among them are five types of communicating which correspond to the five types of speech acts defined in Searle, 1979. To round off the conceptual apparatus, a type-switching device was introduced in § 4.3, which makes it possible to combine a sign process of a given type with a sign process of another type, thereby creating indirect sign processes and, particularly, indirect communicating.

The concepts of an action and an indicator, together with the communication condition and the type-switching device, constitute a powerful set of tools for providing the structure of all kinds of sign processes that occur in human life. At the same time, the fact that all these devices are, by definition, based on the five elementary concepts of intensional logic mentioned above, gives this formal apparatus an explicitness and a transparency that allows its application in computer programming.

The present reconstruction of human communication processes as a sub-hierarchy within the hierarchy of sign processes can therefore function as a basis for the construction of intelligent systems that develop the capacity to communicate. At the same time the implementation of the present hierarchy of sign processes in a computer can serve as a test procedure for the consistency of our approach. In addition, this implementation can be the first step towards further elaboration of special communication tasks to be carried out by expert systems of various kinds.

Presupposing that these applications of our hierarchy of sign processes will prove successful, what consequences do we foresee concerning the role which sign processes of the various types and, in particular, communication can play in A.I.?

1. What type of sign is realized by a given event depends largely on the internal belief-and-intention configurations of the sign producer and the recipient. Thus the key to constructing communication in artificial information processing systems lies not so much in the syntactic and semantic structures of the external sign events, but in the capacity of the systems to activate appropriate internal states, i.e., belief-and-intention configurations.
2. When a system capable of decoding its sign input also has the capacity to form hypotheses about the beliefs and intentions of the sign producer,
   - it can increase the number of inferences from the sign input and thus intensify its information processing,
   - it can check the decoded information against the hypothetical communication intentions of the sign producer, and thus detect errors (and correct them according to its hypotheses or change its hypotheses),

- it can understand signs of one type as indirectly conveying messages normally carried by signs of other types, i.e., it can understand acts of indirect communicating,
- it can decide to respond in a way not directly determined by the sign input but based on the results of its own intensified information processing, error correcting and indirect understanding.

3. Analogous points can be made about the sign producer: when a system capable of producing signs by encoding information selected from its data base also has the capacity to form hypotheses about the beliefs and intentions of the addressee,
   - it can more adequately chose the appropriate information to be encoded,
   - it can decide about the possibility of abbreviations or the necessity of redundancies,
   - it can make use of coded meanings to convey other messages by way of indirect communicating,
   - it can leave to the addressee the decision of how to respond in the light of a shared goal, thus relying on the addressee's capacity for rational behaviour.

   These modes of behaviour in the sign producer and the addressee offer enormous advantages over systems whose capacities are restricted to decoding and encoding information. Information processing systems endowed with belief-and-intention configurations will approximate the efficiency and flexibility of human information exchange. The possible increase in misunderstanding can be counteracted in the same way as in human communication, i.e., by allowing the interacting systems to thematize any puzzling behaviour of their communication partners straight away.
4. Previous approaches to the interaction between information processing systems only had available either the simple code model or the highly refined speech act analysis of Searlian provenance. The code model is too rigid to be of use in the flexible interaction required in the application of expert systems. Speech act theory provides five highly specialized types of sign processes. But when one looks at human interaction, it seldom consists merely of simple decoding or encoding activities, nor does it always involve acts of communicating that correspond to Searlian speech acts. There is a vast field of interaction lying between these two extremes which has never been sufficiently studied and systematically analyzed up to now. Our conceptual approach can be of help in filling this gap. We started with a set of basic sign processes and increased their

complexity step by step until we reached ones corresponding to speech acts. However, we did not stop there, but provided means for the (re)construction of sign processes that are slightly more complex and slightly less complex than speech acts. This makes our approach comprehensive enough to grasp what goes on in actual human interaction: the majority of sign processes occurring between humans are below the threshold of communication, and when there is communication it never occurs without accompanying lower-level sign processes (involving contextual indicators) and higher-level sign processes (involving the reflectional integration of the communicated messages with the messages of previous communication and of contextual indicators). Only a comprehensive semiotic approach such as ours can do justice to human interaction, and it follows that only this kind of approach can lead to a successful modeling of human interaction in A.I.

5. The structure of codes in general, and of natural and machine languages in particular, was given little attention in the present essay. This was deliberately done in order to use the available space for an analysis of the complex mutual relations between sender and addressee in human interaction. However, it is clear that communication would not be very efficient without conventional codes that provide a potentially infinite set of types of sign events and assign them fixed meanings. Nevertheless, the possibility of solving the complicated tasks of advanced expert systems simply on the basis of the generative power of such codes has been highly overestimated in the history of A.I. It seems that humans use linguistic expressions with conventional meanings largely as instruments to convey messages that differ from those meanings, as in metaphors, ellipses and indirect speech acts. Indirect communicating is a way of constructing new messages on the basis of given meanings. The more complex the meanings given by our conventional codes, the more elaborate the messages can be that we construct by relying on mutual belief-and-intention configurations. This argument confirms the traditional assumption that language and thinking must have developed in close relation to each other. The point made in the present article is that this would have been impossible without communicating. From this it is merely a small step to the claim that artificial information processing systems will develop intelligence only if they are programmed so that they can communicate.

6. One of the important consequences of our approach is the claim that communicative competence in the strict sense discussed here cannot be programmed as such into an information processing

system. It must rather be trained. The history of sender-recipient contacts between two information processing systems must be arranged in such a way that system *a* starts expecting the complex belief-and-intention configurations in system *b* that are required for *b*'s sign to function as a communicative sign. Only when systematically confronted with increasingly complex sign processes and when guided by reinforcing responses, can an information processing system develop the habit of presupposing communicative belief-and-intention configurations in the sign producer. And only under such circumstances can it develop the habit of presupposing such internal configurations in the addressee of a self-generated sign process. This implies that communication-oriented behaviour cannot be acquired by the addressee independently of the sender and vice versa; i.e., role change between systems is a necessary component in the training of communicative competence.

7. The training approach to the introduction of communicative competence in information processing systems has a further consequence concerning the roles a system should take in communicative interaction. Full communicative competence cannot be reached by training the pairwise exchange of information within simple dialogue constellations. Communicative competence includes the ability to distinguish ratified communication partners from non-ratified participants, addressed ratified communication partners from non-addressed ones, eavesdropping non-ratified participants from bystanders, etc., and this ability can only be trained by putting the information processing system into each of these roles vis-a-vis a given sender (and vice versa). Similar differentiations must be learned concerning the roles of author, principal and animator in the function of a sender. An information processing system that cannot make adequate hypotheses about these various roles and cannot switch quickly from one to the other will not have the flexibility necessary for appropriate behaviour as an advanced expert system. In learning to assess its momentary role in an ongoing communication, the system must rely on the ability to respond to the contextual signals, indicators, expressions and gestures that accompany the acts of communicating performed by the sender.

8. Of course, the necessary training programs for computers cannot be developed on the basis of armchair analyses of the processes to be trained. The appropriate belief-and-intention configurations of the participants in communication have to be known in principle on the basis of empirical research. Two fields of study are promising in this respect. One of them includes the complex communication

constellations presented on the stage in theatrical plays, where the plot (a special version of the history of sender-recipient contacts) determines the hypotheses of the actors and actresses and of the audience about their mutual belief-and-intention configurations. Another promising object for empirical research is the pathology of human interaction, where the belief-and-intention configurations mutually projected onto one another are again results of the history of sender-recipient contacts within the group of humans concerned. This is not the place to go into the methods to be used in such research. Its results, however, must make it possible

- to predict the level of reflection necessary and sufficient for a given task of interaction,
- to diagnose situations where interaction partners take either too high levels of reflection (as in certain types of paranoia) or too low ones (as in certain types of bureaucracy),
- to find ways for therapeutic treatment that is level-reducing in one case and level-raising in the other.

From a semiotic point of view, communication training for computers will eventually differ very little from therapeutic training for paranoic persons and management reorganization in bureaucratic institutions, thus confirming our approach that the sign users we are studying can be (human) organisms as well as information processing machines and social organizations.

Acknowledgment

I am grateful to Arnold Günther, René Jorna, Sabine Kowal, John Orman and Klaus Robering for extensive comments on earlier drafts of this paper.

References

Andersen, P.B. (1990), *A Theory of Computer Semiotics: Semiotic Approaches to Construction and Assessment of Computer Systems*. Cambridge, England: Cambridge University Press.

Aqvist, L. and P. Mullock (1989), *Causing Harm: A Logical-Legal Study*. Berlin and New York: de Gruyter.

Austin, J.L. (1958), "Performatif - constatif". *Cahiers de Royaumont, Philosophie IV: La philosophie analytique*. Paris. English translation in J.R. Searle (ed.), *Philosophy of Language*. Oxford, England: Oxford University Press 1971: 13-22.

Austin, J.L. (1962), *How to Do Things with Words*, ed. by J.O. Urmson, Oxford, England: Clarendon Press.
Bach, K. and R.B. Harnish (1979), *Linguistic Communication and Speech Acts*. Cambridge, Massachusetts: The M.I.T. Press.
Barwise, J. (1989), "On the Model Theory of Common Knowledge". In: J. Barwise, *The Situation in Logic*. Stanford: Center for the Study of Logic and Information Lecture Notes Nr. 17: 201-220.
Bealer, G. (1982), *Quality and Concept*. Oxford, England: Oxford University Press.
Beckermann, P. (1979), Intentionale vs. kausale Handlungserklärungen". In: H. Lenk (ed.), *Handlungstheorien interdisziplinär*. Vol. 2,2. Munich: Fink: 445-490.
Bennett, J. (1976), *Linguistic Behaviour*. Cambridge, England: Cambridge University Press.
Burkhardt, A. (ed.) (1990), *Speech Acts, Meaning and Intentions: Critical Approaches to the Philosophy of John R. Searle*. Berlin and New York: de Gruyter.
Chisholm, R.M. (1966), *Theory of Knowledge*. Englewood Cliffs, N.J.: Prentice-Hall.
Cohen, P.R., J. Morgan and M.E. Pollack (eds.) (1990), *Intentions in Communication*. Cambridge, Massachusetts: The M.I.T. Press.
Cube, F. von (1985), "Fünfundzwanzig Jahre kybernetische Pädagogik". *Semiosis 9-10*: 34-45.
Dennett, D.C. (1987), *The Intentional Stance*. Cambridge, Massachusetts: The M.I.T. Press.
Eco, U. (1976), *A Theory of Semiotics*. London: Indiana University Press.
Falkenberg, G. (1990), "Searle on Sincerity". In: Burkhardt 1990: 129-148.
Finocchiaro, M.A. (1989), "Methodological Problems in Empirical Logic". *Communication and Cognition 22*: 313-335.
Gärdenfors, P. (1988), *Knowledge in Flux: Modeling the Dynamics of Epistemic States*. Cambridge, Massachusetts: The M.I.T. Press.
Grandy, R.E. and R. Warner (eds.) (1986), *Philosophical Grounds of Rationality: Intentions, Categories, Ends*. Oxford, England: Clarendon Press.
Grice, H.P. (1957), "Meaning". *Philosophical Review 66*: 377-388.
Grice, H.P. (1982), "Meaning Revisited". In: N.V. Smith (ed.), *Mutual Knowledge*. New York: Academic Press: 223-264.
Hall, K. et al. (eds.) (1990), *Proceedings of the Sixteenth Annual Meeting of the Berkeley Linguistics Society: General Session and Parasession on the Legacy of Grice*. Berkeley, California: Berkeley Linguistics Society.
Husserl, E. (1901), *Logische Untersuchungen*. 3 vols. Jena: Niemeyer.

Jorna, R.J. (1990), *Knowledge Representation and Symbols in the Mind: An Analysis of the Notion of Representation and Symbol in Cognitive Psychology*. Tübingen: Stauffenburg.

Kasher, A. (1976), "Conversational Maxims and Rationality". In: A. Kasher (ed.), *Language in Focus: Foundations, Methods and Systems*. Dordrecht: Reidel: 197-216.

Kasher, A. (1979), "What is a Theory of Use?" In: A. Margalith (ed.), *Meaning and Use*. Dordrecht: Reidel: 37-55.

Kasher, A. (ed.) (1988), *Cognitive Aspects of Language Use (= Journal of Pragmatics, 12)*. Amsterdam: North-Holland.

Kutschera, F. von (1976), *Einführung in die intensionale Semantik*. Berlin and New York: de Gruyter.

Kutschera, F. von (1980), "Grundbegriffe der Handlungslogik". In: H. Lenk (ed.), *Handlungstheorie interdisziplinär*. Vol. 1. Munich: Fink: 67-106.

Lenzen, W. (1978), *Recent Work in Epistemic Logic*. Amsterdam: North-Holland.

Lenzen, W. (1980), *Glauben, Wissen und Wahrscheinlichkeit: Systeme der epistemischen Logik*. Vienna: Springer.

Lewis, D. (1969), *Convention: A Philosophical Study*. Cambridge, Massachusetts: Harvard University Press.

Lyons, J. (1977), *Semantics*. 2 vols. Cambridge, England: Cambridge University Press.

Meggle, G. (1981), *Grundbegriffe der Kommunikation*. Berlin and New York: de Gruyter.

Meixner, U. (1987), *Handlung, Zeit, Notwendigkeit: Eine ontologisch-semantische Untersuchung*. Berlin and New York: de Gruyter.

Morgan, J.L. (1978), "Two Types of Convention in Indirect Speech Acts". In: P. Cole (ed.), *Syntax and Semantics*, Vol. 9: *Pragmatics*. New York: Academic Press: 261-280.

Mudersbach, K. (1984), *Kommunikation über Glaubensinhalte: Grundlagen einer epistemischen Logik*. Berlin and New York: de Gruyter.

Nöth, W. (1990), *Handbook of Semiotics*. Bloomington, Indiana: Indiana University Press.

Peirce, C.S. (1931-66), *Collected Papers*, ed. by Ch. Hartshorne, P. Weiss and A.W. Burks. 8 vols. Cambridge, Massachusetts: Harvard University Press.

Posner, R. (1980), "Semantics and Pragmatics of Sentence Connectives in Natural Language". In: J.R. Searle, F. Kiefer and M. Bierwisch (eds.), *Speech Act Theory and Pragmatics*. Dordrecht: Reidel: 169-204.

Posner, R. (1992), "Research in Pragmatics after Morris". In: M. Balat and J. Deledalle-Rhodes (eds.), *L'homme et ses signes*. Berlin and New York: Mouton de Gruyter.

Prieto, L.J. (1966), *Messages et signaux*. Paris: Presses universitaires de France.

Recanati, F. (1981), *Les énoncés performatifs: Contribution à la pragmatique*. Paris: Minuit.

Saussure, F. de (1916), *Cours de linguistique générale*, publié par C. Bally, A. Sechehaye et A. Riedlinger. Paris: Payot.

Savigny, E. von (1983), *Zum Begriff der Sprache: Konvention, Bedeutung, Zeichen*. Stuttgart: Reclam.

Schiffer, S.R. (1972), *Meaning*. Oxford, England: Clarendon Press.

Schiffer, S.R. (1987), *Remnants of Meaning*. Cambridge, Massachusetts: The MIT Press.

Searle, J.R. (1969), *Speech Acts: An Essay in the Philosophy of Language*. Cambridge, England: Cambridge University Press.

Searle, J.R. (1979), *Expression and Meaning: Studies in the Theory of Speech Acts*. Cambridge, England: Cambridge University Press.

Searle, J.R. (1983), *Intentionality: An Essay in the Philosophy of Mind*. Cambridge, England: Cambridge University Press.

Searle, J.R. and D. Vanderveken (1985), *Foundations of Illocutionary Logic*. Cambridge, England: Cambridge University Press.

Searle, J.R. et al. (1992), *(On) Searle on Conversation*. Amsterdam: Benjamins.

Sperber, D. and D. Wilson (1986), *Relevance: Communication and Cognition*. Oxford, England: Blackwell.

Stalnaker, R.C. (1984), *Inquiry*. Cambridge, Massachusetts: The MIT Press.

Wright, G.H. von (1963), *Norm and Action: A Logical Inquiry*. London: Routledge and Paul.

Wright, G.H. von (1968), *An Essay in Deontic Logic and the General Theory of Action*. Amsterdam: North-Holland.

Wright, G.H. von (1977), *Handlung, Norm und Intention: Untersuchungen zur deontischen Logik*. Berlin and New York: de Gruyter.

On knowledge representing interacting systems

A. MÜLLER (Göttingen)

1. Introduction

In this paper I will try to show, that two recent developments in the field of cognitive science are linked with interesting semiotic questions:

(a) The problem of adaptation or on-line learning: It is well known, that the question how humans are able to adapt rapidly and spontaneously to noisy and complex environments whose structures may change unexpectedly, is a key issue in cognitive science (e.g., Machlup & Manfred, 1983). In William James' engaging phrase: How do we cope with the 'blooming buzzing confusion' of every day life?

(b) The concept of coordination (distributed reasoning): N agents (processes) operate independently and in parallel on a problem space. In order to reach a common solution these agents have to communicate their partial solutions. This 'interactive turn' implies answers to (at least) three important questions:

    (1) The channel problem (communication topology): How to connect numerous processes?

    (2) The semiotic problem: How can one guarantee, that these processes understand each other, i.e., that the interpretation functions for the symbol 'x', for instance, are identical?

    (3) The problem of conflict resolution: Given the solution of (1) and (2), how to handle situations in which inconsistencies appear, e.g., if for process 1 'x is true' holds and for process 2 'x is false'?

In order to illustrate (2) and (3), let us consider two persons A and B, who want to exchange some information stored in their data bases. Person A has called a field *neural networks*, B *connectionist models*. Although both persons may mean exactly the same thing, an automatic exchange of information in their decentralized data bases will fail, since the labels are different (de dicto misunderstanding, case (2)). Moreover, person A has, for instance, judged the contributions of an author as "low", B classified the same author's contributions as "high" (de re dissence, case (3)). It is well known, that even in natural communication this conflict is not easily settled (if ever).

What is the semiotic relevance of these issues? In this paper mainly (2) will be considered. This problem can be formulated in vaious ways. According to Meunier (1991) one may first ask how a physical object (e.g., a pattern of electric energy in a computer system) gets its semiotic status.

> For a physical object, to acquire the status of symbol implies a promotion where the physicality does not count for much. Indeed, to become a symbol in a representational system is not firstly to have a physical substratum but to occupy a function. It is something like becoming a minister in a government. To be a 'minister' is defined more by the function than by person's physicality...More precisely, becoming semiotic depends on the function it occupies in regard to the interpreting system to which it is related. (p. 15)

In addition, since in distributed reasoning at least two interpreting systems are involved, one has to demand that the semiotic function of a physical object is present for all systems that are using this object.

> I use the word 'sign' in the widest sense for any medium for the communication or extension of a form (or feature)...In order that a form may be extended or communicated, it is necessary that it should have been really embodied in a subject independently of the communication; and it is necessary that there should be another in which the same form is embodied only in consequence of the communication. (C.S. Peirce, Letter to Lady Welby (Draft), dated '1906 March 9'; cited after Marty, 1990, p. 12)

However, how is the semiotic function assigned to a physical object, is a sign embodied in a system such that the communicative aim is fulfilled, such that both systems have 'teridentity'?[1]

It is not intended to give a complete overview on the various answers to this problem, given, for instance, in the context of discussions on the origin of languages (e.g., Hewes, 1977).

However, one may roughly separate three different positions:

- The agents are synchronized a priori by biological mechanisms on a phylogenetic time scale:

> Any two cultures are seen as superficially different representations of one abstract structure, namely of human culture, and it is this isomorphism which accounts for the feasibility of communication across cultures. (Sebeok, 1968, p. 4).

- The agents are synchronized a priori by adaptive mechanisms on an ontogenetic time scale:

> This dialectical approach [the Institutional Analysis (Lourau, 1970)] to social phenomena allows us to consider the sign-object relation as a social datum which exists before the particular use of the sign and that social individuals realize on each occasion. They are the micro-institutions which governs, more or less successfully, the relations between individuals and the exterior world. They are essentially interfaces which possess some plasticity accordingly to a society's development, because they are compelled to govern new facts. (Marty, 1990, p. 11f)

- The agents have to solve the problem of understanding in a self-organized way on an actual genetic time scale. This view challenges the importance of social rules and conventions a priori prepared for speaker and listener.

> I conclude, that there is no such thing as a language, not if language is anything like what many philosophers and linguists have supposed. There is therefore no such thing to be learned, mastered, or born with. We must give up the idea of a clearly defined shared structure which language-users acquire and then apply to cases. And we should try again to say how conventions in any important sense is involved in language; or, as I think, we should give up the attempt to illuminate how we can communicate by appeal to conventions. (Davidson, 1989, p. 446) [2]

According to this view, understanding in conversations is a local process depending on "passing theories", rules of thumb, wit, luck, wisdom, rough maxims, private vocabularies and grammars. Nevertheless, it is not denied that there is convergence in speech behaviour among those who exchange words, which is supported by empirical evidences (cf. Müller & Strack, 1992). However, no prepared rules in the strict sense are involved. The position that the "generation of meaning" is due to a local and decentralized process on a short (actual genetic) time scale is also held by ethnomethodologists and symbolic interactionists. Moreover, in the social theory of mind (Mead, 1910b; 1913; 1934) this process is considered as conditio sine qua non for the emergence of consciousness.

Let us come back to the relation of semiotics and cognitive science. The central question can now be posed as follows: Can the sign-object relation be formed dynamically by interacting artificial systems? Is it possible, that these "interfaces" are generated in a self-organized way on a small time scale such that they possess plasticity, i.e., that they are adaptive?

This necessity is very important, since if several systems are confronted with new facts (non-stationary environments), they have to adapt not only their individual representations, but their communication structure as well.

This point can be stated more rigorously by a radical scenario given by Müller (1989). Let us consider the worst case, which probably marks the upper bound of such kind of plasticity: Two strangers meet each other in a strange world - there is neither a familiar environment nor a common communication structure. Obviously, no physical object of this world has a semiotic function. If, for instance, two astronauts from two different galaxies are stranded on a third one, can they manage to communicate? One may question the possibility of this enterprise in general:

> Critics have wondered how, in the absence of an existing language, the participants in such a conference have carried on their deliberations as they determined which sounds to assign to different meanings. (Hewes, 1977, p. 44)

However, the question to ask is rather: Under what conditions is a 'bootstrap semiogenesis', the self-organized generation of a common code, possible? Which assumptions and internal mechanisms of these strangers are necessary in order to reach a "common ground"?

These questions are, obviously, very complex and only a brief consideration is possible here. However, the discussion of this problem may illustrate some interesting recent topics both in the fields of cognitive science and semiotics. The general line of the argumentation goes as follows: In the next section the concept of distributed reasoning is explained in a knowledge based (now usually called "symbolic") framework. There will be a discussion, whether these models can contribute to the central question. In section 3, possibilities and limitations of classical neural networks in relation to the problem of "bootstrap semiogenesis" are considered. The following section introduces some recent developments in neural network theory: so called structured or modular networks. In section 5 a model of a "classification couple" is introduced. This system contains two automata, which perform interactive concept and sign generation. The self-organized process is governed by genetic algorithms, a very powerful class of adaptive methods. These are employed in machine learning and in hybrid architectures, which try to combine the benefits both of the symbolic and subsymbolic approach. Some related philosophical considerations concerning the emergence of meaning will be given in section 6.

2. Knowledge based protocols in symbolic distributed systems

2.1 Foundations

It is commonly accepted (Lamport, 1984) that a network of N distributed processes can be expressed in a form similar to flowcharts or Petri-nets. The run of a single process can be viewed as a sequence of states, which are transformed by actions

$$x_1^0 \rightarrow^{\alpha_0} x_1^1 \rightarrow^{\alpha_1} x_1^2 \rightarrow^{\alpha_2} \dots x_1^t \rightarrow^{\alpha_t} \dots \qquad (1)$$

with x_1^t state of process 1 and α_t action at iteration t.

For a network of N processes there is a corresponding global state transformer T

$$x^{t+1} = T(a_u, a_1, \dots a_j, \dots a_N)(x^t) \qquad (2)$$

with $A = (a_u, a_1, \dots a_j, \dots a_N)$: common action of the N processes j and of the environment (a_u), $x = (x_u, x_1, x_2, \dots x_N)$ is a global state.

Typical action sets A include local computations and the sending and receiving of messages. The actions are governed by an action-protocol H (algorithm or strategy), H: X → A. *Standard-action-protocols* may simply be viewed as function from states to *if ... then ... else ....-statements*. The local states of each process are altered by the messages from the other processes or from the environment.

A more technical matter is the concurrency problem in distributed systems (e.g., deadlock in a CRCW PRAM concurrent read concurrent write parallel random access machine, cf. Goldschlager, 1982; Vishkin, 1983). A program is a set of equations which relates the output arcs of a node (process) to a function or operator applied to the input of other nodes. One example is the programming language LUCID, which is suitable for the implementation of operator nets, which are non-knowledge based systems solving cooperatively tasks like the Hamming problem. A detailed discussion of these systems, which generate a continuous algebra on the elementary data objects and the corresponding fix-point theory is given by Ashcroft & Jagannathan (1985).

More interesting is the notion of knowledge in distributed processing. Unfortunately, there are only a few conceptualizations available in this recent field of research. It is helpful, to think of a knowledge-based protocol as a function from states to *if...then...else...-statements* with prior tests for knowledge. Halpern & Fagin (1988) have given an interpretation of

knowledge in distributed systems, which satisfies the axioms of modal logic S5.
Let Φ be a set of basic facts $p \in \Phi$, ψ, φ, $\varphi \wedge \psi$, $\neg\psi$ and $K_i\psi$ (read: 'process i knows ψ') formulas.

- $K_i\varphi \rightarrow \varphi$
- $(K_i\varphi \wedge K_i(\varphi \rightarrow \psi)) \rightarrow K_i\psi$
- $K_i\varphi \rightarrow K_iK_i\varphi$
- $\neg K_i\varphi \rightarrow K_i\neg K_i\varphi$

together with the rule of inference

- from φ infer $K_i\varphi$

In particular, it implies:
- a process knows only true facts
- a process' knowledge is closed under logical implications
- in combination with the rule of inference (a process knows all valid formulas): processes are 'perfect reasoners'
- a process knows what it knows (knows what it does not know), axioms of introspection

Of further interest is the notion of common knowledge. A group G of processes has *common knowledge* of a fact φ, if everyone in G knows φ and knows, that everyone in G knows φ, etc. E_G ('every process in G knows φ') and C_G ('φ is common knowledge in group G'). It can be shown (Halperin & Moses, 1985) that a complete axiomatization for this extended language (which may also include temporal operators like 'always', 'until', etc.) can be given by adding the axioms:

- $E_G\varphi \equiv \bigwedge_{i \in G} K_i\varphi$
- $(C_G\varphi \wedge C_G(\varphi \rightarrow \psi)) \rightarrow C_G\psi$
- $C_G\varphi \equiv E_G(\varphi \wedge C_G\varphi)$

together with the rule of inference

- from $\varphi \rightarrow E_G\varphi$ infer $\varphi \rightarrow C_G\varphi$

2.2 Illustration and limitations

Let me illustrate this framework and its limitations by a famous puzzle, which is given here in the version of the "cheating husbands" puzzle (Moses et al., 1986). It is isomorphic to the "muddy children" puzzle of Halpern & Moses (1984).

> It has always been common knowledge among the women of Mamajorca (all of them are perfect reasoners), that their queens are truthful, and that the women are obedient to the queens. It was also common knowledge that all women heard every shot fired in Mamajorca. Queen Henrietta I awoke one morning with a firm resolution to do away with the male infidelity problem in Mamajorca. She summoned all of the women heads of households to the town square, and read them the following statement:
>
>> There are (one or more) unfaithful husbands in our community. Although none of you knew before this gathering whether your own husband was unfaithful, each of you knows which of the other husbands are unfaithful. I forbid you to discuss the matter of your own husband's fidelity with anyone. However, should you discover that your husband is unfaithful, you must shoot him on the midnight of the day you find out about it.
>
> Thirty-nine silent nights went by, and on the fortieth night, shots were heard.

Obviously, the question is to explain, how many cheating husbands there were and why they are shot just on the 40th night. In fact, it can be proven by induction, that if there were exactly k unfaithful husbands, they would have been shot on the kth night. Is $k = 1$ the only unfaithful husband is shot on the first night, since his wife, not knowing about other unfaithful husbands, concludes at the very time, she receives the message from the queen that only her husband is unfaithful and will shoot him at the first night. If there are $k + 1$ unfaithful husbands, their wives know about k cases (every husband besides their own). If in the kth night no shots are heard, they conclude that there could not have been exactly k unfaithful husbands. Since if there were, they would have been shot on that night. Thus each wife of an unfaithful husband can deduce in the $(k + 1)^{st}$ night that her husband is unfaithful and so will shoot him on that night. She could not have acted earlier, since the situation is dependent on the actions and states of the other women.

Now the women are regarded as the processes, which receive a message from the environment (the queen) at $k=0$ and follow the simple protocol "if you discover, that your husband is unfaithful, shoot him on this night and send this event as message to the other processes".

The deeper sense of this puzzle is to show, under which conditions this proof by induction breaks. These conditions exhibit the problems of communication and distributed reasoning in parallel symbolic (knowledge based) architectures:

- The processes need mutual knowledge about the knowledge of the other processes. As it is shown in Halpern & Moses (1984), none of the women would have been able to conclude anything about their own husband's faithfulness without the apparently useless statement of the queen, that there are unfaithful husbands (since all women were already aware of it). This statement, however, insures that every process knows what every other knows.

- The processes have to be perfect reasoners. Moreover, they have to know, that each knows, that this is in fact the case. Although there are a lot of interesting efforts to surmount this restriction for a single system (using heuristics, non-monotonic approaches etc.; Levesque, 1984; Fagin & Halpern, 1988a; Marostika, 1992; this volume; van der Lubbe & Backer, this volume), it is an open question how to handle this problem if a whole group of non-perfect reasoners is involved. Moses (1988) gives a detailed discussion of this topic in the context of distributed reasoning and tries to find a semantic for it.
- If there are minimal errors in the message-system (delays or noise, for instance), the incorporation of error handling procedures is Np-hard in the general case.
- In the framework given above the knowledge is externally ascribed to the system. If the processes have to generate knowledge about the basic facts themselves it is possible, that inconsistencies appear both within and between the processes. There are yet no isolation strategies available if N systems are involved.

2.3 Semiotic implications

Let us first discuss, how the three central problems of distributed reasoning mentioned in the introduction are solved within this architecture:

(1) The communication topology is given by an all-relation: All processes can communicate directly with each other (in contrast to blackboard models).

(2) There is no problem of understanding: The "internal language of thought" is identical to the "external" one used in formulating messages.

(3) Since this language, the basic facts and the corresponding basic constituents, are defined and ascribed to all processes by the system designer, no dissense can appear. The agents are externally and a priori synchronized.

Jorna (1990) and Meunier (this volume) have given detailed semiotic analyses of the notion of symbol and representation within this logico-linguistic framework for a single, "monadic" agent. Hence it may be sufficient to discuss some consequences for the central question.

Roughly, within this architecture not only "mind is modeled in the spirit of proof theory" (Smolensky, 1988) but also communication. This kind of modelling, however, hides exactly those phenomena, which should be explained.

It has been pointed out by Meunier (1991) that the existence of symbols or semiotic primitives used in knowledge based systems

> ..comes from a baptismal act that consists in choosing a physical mark of some sort and giving it a name. [...] It is an act like one read about in the Book one of Genesis. One could read, in the bible of the logician, the following passage: 'In the first day, Russell took his pencil and said: Let there be the following symbols: a,b,c,d', and these symbols were! A few years later Carnap, seeing that these symbols were alone, created by more complex rules and called these rules the syntax of the language! (p. 9).

However, "there is no voice in the burning bush". This means, that in real situations there is no voice telling us the proper description and labelling of the objects of the world, there are no external ascriptions which guarantee such logical coherence and a mutual understanding.

Perception may roughly be defined as the discrimination of an object or event and its separation from the background or from other objects. One fundamental task of an intelligent system is to carry on adaptive perceptual classification in an "unlabelled" world. However, no closed lists of singly necessary and jointly sufficient conditions for the classification of objects exist. This does, obviously, not mean, that the world is without structure, rather that categorization depends upon cues, context, salience and the momentary state of the system. In Müller & Strack (1992) some of these issues are discussed in the context of empirical studies on concept formation.

On the other hand, the "baptismal act" of the definition, nomination and even interpretation of the constituents (in Meunier's words: semiotic primitives) guaranties both consistency and mutual understanding in distributed systems.

Unfortunately, this act leaves exactly those operations unexplained, which

> become fundamental for sustaining any cognitive science enterprise that wishes to understand or simulate the learning, manipulation, recognition and production of symbols by some agent, be it human or mechanical. The simple presentation of symbols under the form of a list or a definition does not suffice any more. (Meunier, 1991, p. 10)

To summarize: Concepts like communication and common knowledge are important ingredients of these models. However, since the semiotic functions are defined a priori by the system designer, these models cannot contribute very much to the problems raised in the introduction. Since they are restricted to an invariant "symbolic world" (no sensory interface to the environment) it is not hard to imagine, that these agents would fail immediately in the "two stranger in a strange world"- situation.

3. Cybernetics: neural networks

3.1 Foundations

Neural networks seem to be more promising candidates since they are able to generalize, extract prototypes and recognize even distorted and noisy input-patterns - like the identification of the beauty (figure 1) even if she is noisy or present in an incomplete form.

Figure 1: Pattern recognition, examples (Müller & Neumann, 1990)

These networks consist of numerous simple threshold automata (the neurons) interacting by low-level signal flows. By these local interactions emergent or global properties, i.e., such pattern recognition or CAM-qualities (Content Addressable Memory) are generated. Moreover, since the number of such simple threshold automata is usually very large, there is a high degree of redundancy in these systems yielding default tolerance, i.e., the acceptance or handling of errors both in local computations and in the message exchange.

3.1.1 Autoassociative neural networks

An autoassociative neural network Ξ may be described as a quintuple

$$\Xi = \{X, W, U, T, \Lambda\}$$

with

- **X:** representation space (short-term memory)
- **W:** a matrix space, the connections between the threshold automata (synaptic weights or long-term memory, LTM)
- **U:** set of input patterns, which may be given by a distribution function $\mathbf{P}_U$.
- **T:** a non-linear state transition operator, T: X → X, governing the short-term memory dynamics

$$x^{t+1} = Tx^t \quad Tx = S(W \cdot x) \quad x = (x_1 \cdots x_N): \ \textit{state vector} \quad W = (w_{ij}) \quad W \cdot x: \ \textit{inner product} \tag{3}$$

  with $\mathbf{x} \in \mathbf{X}$, S threshold function (e.g., signum, heavyside, deterministic and stochastic sigmoid).
- **Λ:** a learning function **Λ**: U → **W**. As learning function **Λ** often the Hebbian rule is borrowed from neurophysiology. Two neurons x_i and x_j strengthen their connection w_{ij} if their activities (their inputs) are correlated. Two versions of this rule are given by either a passive decay

$$\frac{dw_{ij}}{dt} = -F_{ij} + G_{ij} f_i(x_i) h_j(x_j) \tag{4}$$

  or a gated decay

$$\frac{dw_{ij}}{dt} = h_j(x_j)\left[-F_{ij} + G_{ij} f_i(x_i)\right] \tag{5}$$

  of the synaptic weights where F and G are constants and the activation x are due to inputs u.

Generalization of CAM-networks: It can be shown (Carpenter & Grossberg, 1987) that every network the dynamics of which can be stated as in equation (6), can have such abilities. Among these systems are the Hopfield model, Brain-State in the Box, Boltzmann machine and various PDP-models:

$$\frac{dx_i}{dt} = c_i(x_i)\left(\sum_{j \neq i}^{N} w_{ij} d_j(x_j) - b_i(x_i)\right) \tag{6}$$

where c_i : amplification function, d_j : other-signal function and b_i : self-signal function.

Note, that in this formula the non-linear functions of a sum are written as a sum of non-linear functions. Interestingly, a lot of physical or biological systems can be rewritten in this form: the Eigen-Schuster model of macromolecular evolution (the hypercycle) and the famous Lotker-Volterra model of population biology, for instance.

Fix-point theory: From a mathematical point of view the crucial question is how to construct a system with prototypes as stable states (attractors), such that Ξ realizes a classification function ϕ: U → X. Fortunately there exists a functional over the representation space, which can be formed such that exemplars fall in the basins of attractors (minima of this functional).

$$V = -\sum_{i=1}^{n} \int^{x_i} b_i(\xi_i) d_i'(\xi_i) d\xi_i + \frac{1}{2}\sum_{j,k=1}^{n} w_{jk} d_j(x_j) d_k(x_k) \tag{7}$$

Using an analogy from physics the functional (7) is often called energy function. Another expression is 'harmony function' since the system settles to a state of maximum harmony, i.e., maximum a posteriori probability for a correct classification, which is equivalent to a state of minimal energy.

3.1.2 Backpropagation (multi-layer perceptrons)

Backpropagation is a mapping neural network, which learns to classify arbitrary input-patterns if we present the system a set of examples. The structure of the network is multi-layered with feed-forward signal flow. Units between the input and output layer are usually called hidden units.

The learning procedure employs a generalization of the Widrow-Hoff rule, which is basically a steepest (gradient) descent minimizing the means square error defined by error signals as deviations of the actual output from the desired output. This is a relatively simple though widely used method in function minimization. Note, that a "desired output" is defined by an external teacher (supervised learning). Some applications of these systems are: The backpropagation network SNOOPE, which is employed in baggage control at airports and recognizes plastic explosives by neutron radiation;

the (backpropagation) classification of highly non-linear spectral data (Müller & Neumann, 1990). Another example is the popular NETtalk model (Sejnowski & Rosenberg, 1986), which uses a phoneme-by-phoneme matching scheme and classifies auditory patterns of phonemes to visual (written) phoneme codes.

3.1.3 Semiotic implications

There are detailed semiotic analyses of these "subsymbolic" systems (Goschke, 1990; Müller & Strack, 1990; Meunier, this volume; Peschl, this volume). Hence again, only the question how these architectures give some answers to the problems raised in the introduction may be discussed here.

The notion of knowledge and representation is, obviously, weak in these cybernetical models (cf. Fodor & Pylyshyn, 1988) and just related to perceptual classification.

Comparable to the brain, which maps about 10^9 bits/sec sensory information to 10^2 bits/sec contents of consciousness, these artificial neural networks may roughly be regarded as statistical machines. They extract certain statistical properties of the environment and map the input information to the corresponding classes. A class (prototype) is represented as a point in the representation space. Detailed discussions of such vector valued representations are given in Petitot-Concorda (1985), Meunier (1991) and Eckmiller (1990). The latter author points at the importance of geometry for the study of representations in the context of neuroinformatics. He gives a detailed discussion on similarities and dissimilarities of a topological approach in contrast to the algebraic-analytical framework used in classical A.I. (knowledge based framework).

In spite of some advantages of these models (like the automatic extraction of prototypes) these systems solve only a part of the central problem of bootstrap semiogenesis. If we agree that the problems of distributed reasoning (1)-(3) are answered by these models, we also have to accept a very poor concept of agent: These simple threshold automata are connected, again, by an all-relation (1). Understanding (2) is realized by statistical learning (e.g., Hebb-rule) and conflicts are solved (3) by a collective decision procedure (STM-dynamics). In this interpretation, however, it is questionable, wether at the (low) level of a single agent the concept of representation does make any sense: each neuron "represents" only a fraction of a structure, which is only as a whole meaningful and interpretable.

Moreover, most neural network architectures need an omniscient supervisor and/or employ off-line or lab-learning. Within an auto-associator, for instance, a capacity catastrophe occurs which renders output unreliable, if no external instance is present, which stops the never-ending time series of input patterns. An external advisor is needed, who shuts off the plasticity of the LTM-traces and switches the system from a learning to a non-learning mode.

3.1.4 Adaptive Resonance Theory

An interesting alternative to the supervised learning procedures is the Adaptive Resonance theory developed by Steven Grossberg (Carpenter & Grossberg, 1987). It is based on extensive considerations on the cognitive process of classification. In this model an internal pattern $x^{(i)}$ caused by the excitation of neurons at level F^1 is sent to a higher level F^2 with suitable filtration and evokes an already learned pattern $y^{(j)}$, which feedbacks to F^1 as expectation. Both patterns are matched due to 'adaptive resonance'. In particular, a top-down critical feature pattern can prime a lower level to get ready for an exemplar from an expected class of input-patterns. This top-down expectation can also attenuate processing of unexpected inputs through a mismatch between bottom-up input and top-down expectation, which enables this architecture to function like an intentional machine that generates an active focus of attention. Roughly, the system performs:

- Hypothesis testing, data search and classification.
- Stable self-organization of pattern recognition codes. This self-organization implies that the prototypes (classes) are represented in an arbitrary form, which, nevertheless, exhibits the statistical properties of the corresponding input-pattern at a given time.
- Self-adjusting parallel memory search and global energy landscape upheaval. Due to this property these arbitrary prototype representations are updated such that new classes are generated or old ones are combined. These situations may occur quite frequently in on-line learning situations: At time t the distribution function of the environment $P_U(t)$ may be different from the one at time $t+n$. Moreover, since every physical system is limited in its memory, the network has to classify according to this restriction. It is not possible to represent the environment in a too fined grained way, i.e., sometimes a fusion of classes is afforded.

Taken together, the classical neural networks discussed above are based on architectures with numerous simple threshold automata interacting by low-level signal flows. They perform well in difficult classification tasks, separating objects from the background. These systems are default tolerant but more or less restricted to the lab world.

In ART, operations in real time and non-stationary environments are supported. This architecture may survive in the 'blooming buzzing confusion' of every day and hence in a "strange world"-situation (since for an untrained system there is no difference anyway).

However, up to now only on-line learning properties of one system have been described. As has been mentioned above the representation of classes is done *arbitrarily* - due to previous experience, random influences, and capacity. This issue leads back the problem of understanding, i.e., the communication of compressed class-representations.

4. Actor networks

4.1 The concept of classification couple

This point can be illustrated by the concept of classification couple, which, again, is borrowed from neurobiology (Edelman, 1987).

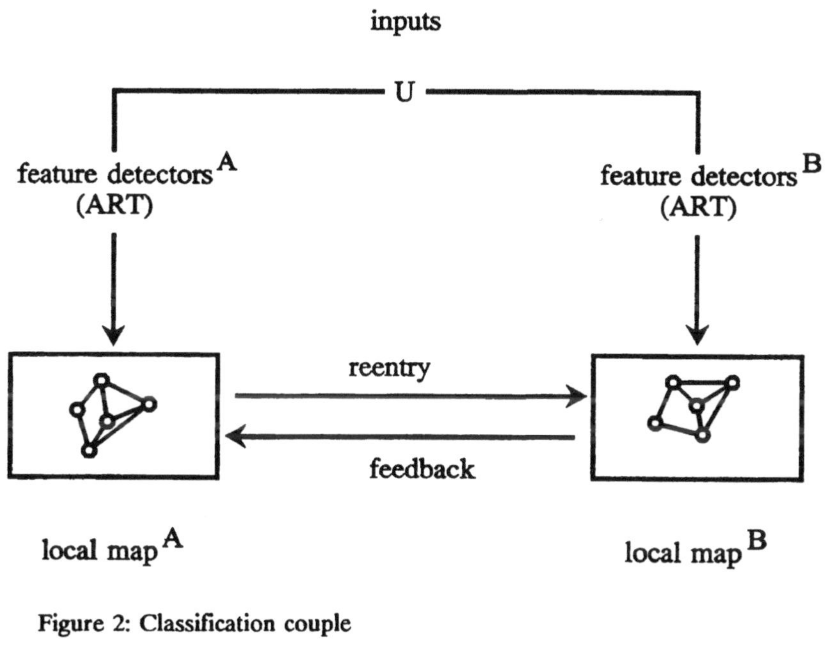

Figure 2: Classification couple

Such couple consists of two subsystems (figure 2), each of which is capable of an independent sampling of an input domain and its representation in a local map, a local representation R as discussed above[3].

Now a coordinated adjustment of these local maps, which contain spatially separated populations of feature detecting neurons (e.g., colour, texture, orientation, velocity) is needed. The coordination of isofunctional but polystructural classification systems (classification couples) is done by reentry. This self-modulating lateral feedback provides an abstract or higher-order linkage of their representations.

This means, two systems (two actors) generate a compressed representation of different aspects of an input domain (e.g., by adaptive resonance). Now they have to develop a coordinated adjustment about their representations by self modulating circular-relational feedback. In contrast to the 'classical' concept of feedback in cybernetics a dynamic modulation of the related transformers is needed.

Although it is still unknown how information from different cortical maps is integrated into coherent percepts, a lot of empirical evidences exists about a dynamic circular-relational process, which synchronizes geographically remote cortex positions by appropriate global stimulus features. This synchronization can occur on a very small time scale and allows either the establishment of fast but "crude sketches" of association codes or the formation of complex and sophisticated codes in iteration steps (repetitive internally generated synchronization; e.g., in area A17 and A18, cf. Gray et al., 1989; Aiple & Krüger, 1990).

4.2 Morphological restrictions and information processing

The module concept of the brain exhibits another fact, which is important both for the understanding of brain functions and technical applications. A communication topology (question (1)) as discussed in the previous sections (complete graph) is intractable in the general case and neurobiologically implausible. A complete linkage between all neurons or processors is out of question, since the number of connections is rapidly growing. Classical topologies for massively parallel processes like the connectionist machine (arrays, N-cubes) are far from being sufficient (not to speak about older topologies such as buses, rings, crossbars and stars).

Unfortunately, the suggested optimal graphs, i.e., densest possible graphs given a fixed number of nodes, degree and diameter, are hard to handle. In figure 3 the optimal 10-node (degree 3, diameter 2) Peterson graph is shown.

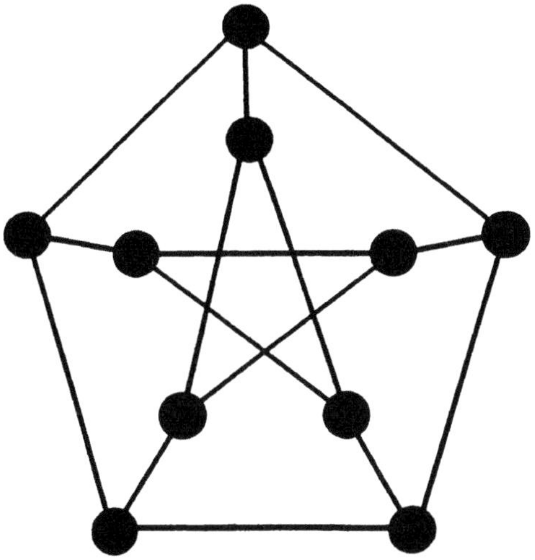

Figure 3: Optimal communication topology

However, even the 3250-node (57,2) optimal Singleton graph is proven to exist but yet not discovered. Since in technical applications much more processes are involved, locally dense graphs with logarithmically reduced fan-in fan-out are suggested as an alternative (detailed discussions of these topics are given in Uhr, 1986).

In any way, the crucial question, how to communicate representations under the conditions:

- modular structures
- only locally dense systems (fanned in and out logarithmically), which implies
- restricted channels

leads to some semiotically interesting considerations and higher-order properties.

Solution 1: Given these ubiquitous morphological restrictions both in artificial systems and in the brain (the number of synapses pro neuron is about 10^4 with 10^{10} neurons in the cortex), one possible solution is to consider the whole system (both actors) as a single (homogeneous) network with locally dense clusters and single neurons as gate-keepers. In this case, the connections between the gate-keeper neurons can be formed by classical Hebbian learning (figure 4).

This method, however, leads to a suboptimal performance and adds no new semiotic qualities. Since each of such gate-keeper neurons represents only a fraction of the whole representation, the signal flow remains a low-level one.

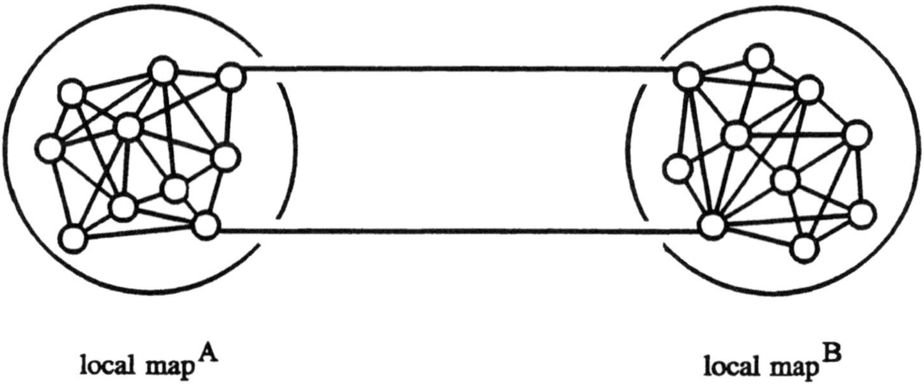

Figure 4: Simple Hebbian learning in homogeneous actor networks

Solution 2: A second possibility is the introduction of a specialized communication system within each actor. This means, that the internal structure of each independently operating network possesses "social components", i.e., special communication modules.

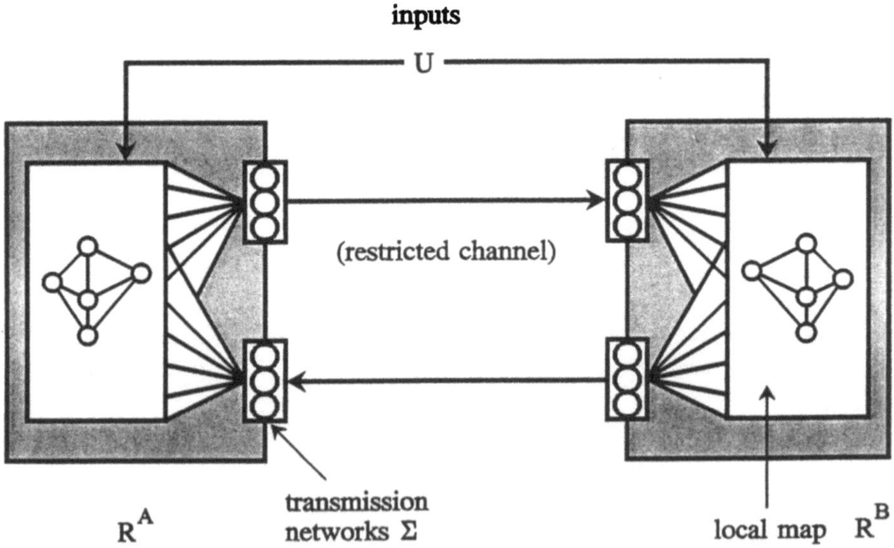

Figure 5: Representation- and transmission-subsystems in actor networks

In this case, the representation of each actor is further compressed by a transformation network. The activations of the neurons in this network denote the representation of the stimuli in a compressed form. Hence this compressed representation can be transmitted through a restricted channel to the other actor(s) as *signal patterns*, which have to be able to translate the compressed information (figure 5).

A signal, now an activation pattern, denotes a stimulus-representation of the "speaker". It should cause a representation in the receiver, which is identical to the representation caused by the related input or acts at least as a prime (Morris-condition, see table I).

	Units	Connections	Inputs	Representations	Signals/signs
Neural networks	threshold automata	LTM-traces	single elements in the input	activation of single neurons	activation of single neurons (signals)
Actor-networks	neural networks	transmission networks	input-pattern	patterns of neurons in local maps	patterns of neurons in transmission-networks (signs)

Table I: Actor networks and neural networks

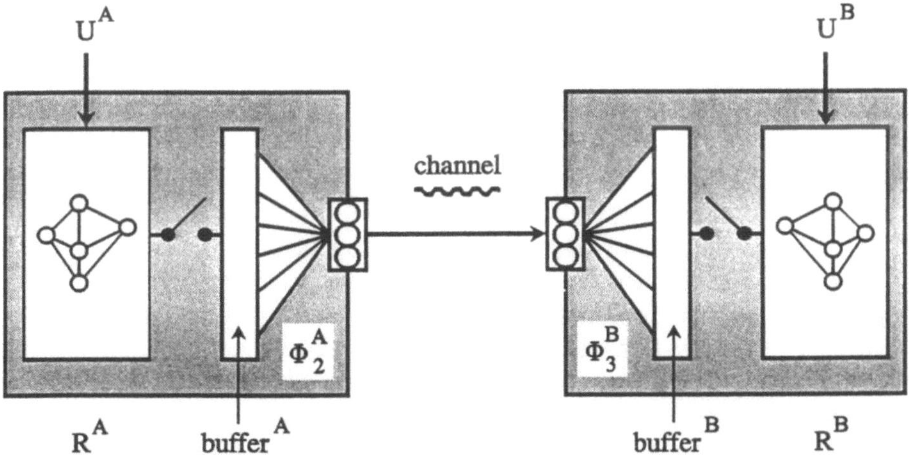

Figure 6: Transmission of a code through a reduced channel

The formation of this communication structure can be reduced to the solution of the well known encoder problem, which can be achieved by backpropagation-training of the connections between the neurons in the local maps (buffer A and B), with the transmission networks as hidden units Σ. In this case a common code is established, which transforms each representation r^A to a signal σ^{A-B}, transmitted through a (logarithmically) reduced channel and to a representation r^B (cf. figure 6). The gates are opened if the internal subsystems R have finished processing (each neuron in the buffer is connected with a corresponding neuron in R).

It is easy to generalize this model to N actors (cf. figure 7). Thus a training algorithm for modular systems (actor networks) is given, which allows the communication of signal pattern under morphological restrictions. In table 1 some consequences are summarized. We are now confronted with networks containing networks as nodes and not simple threshold automata.

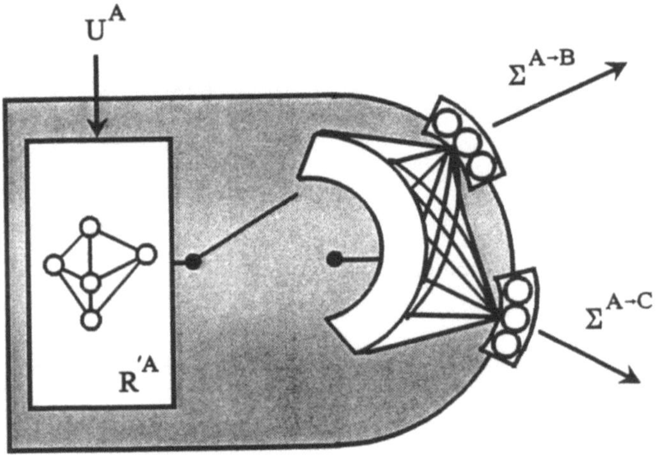

Figure 7: Actor networks

Although actor networks exhibit some new interesting semiotic features, they do not fulfil the conditions of a bootstrap semiogenesis. On that planet, there is no external teacher present, which has access to the internal states of these systems. Moreover, as discussed in section 3, backpropagation training is lab-learning and can not cope with non-stationary environments.

5. The dynamic semiotic system

5.1 Some definitions

Now more detailed semiotic explanations are in order. Let us express our classification couple in the form of figure 8, where R denotes the representation space for system A or B, respectively, and U (environment) is distributed on U^A and U^B.

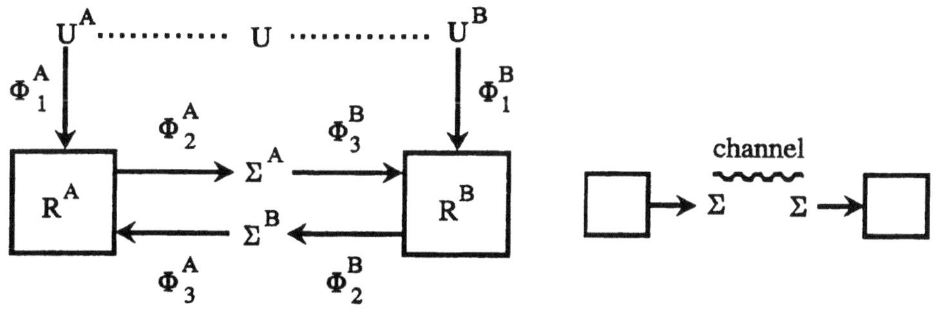

Figure 8: General structure of the model

It is possible, that $U^A \cap U^B = \emptyset$, i.e., the systems may sample completely different aspects of the input domain. It is only assumed that the systems and the input-pattern have a common time scale. Σ is called the signal space (the set of all possible signals, the potential vocabulary) but it can firstly be interpreted just as a set of physical objects or events $\sigma \in \Sigma$ where $\sigma = (\sigma_1 ... \sigma_i ... \sigma_M)$ with σ_i one of the M features of this object. A σ is transmitted by a channel k (right part of the figure; no system-index means, that the expression holds interchangeably). We define a code $C_U = \{\phi 2, \phi 3, \Sigma\}$, where $\phi 3$ is called interpretation function (operator) and $\phi 2$: designation function. The condition of mutual understanding can now be stated in the MORRIS-form (Müller, 1989):

$$(U^A \rightarrow R^A \rightarrow \Sigma^A \rightarrow R^B) \leftrightarrow (U^B \rightarrow R^B) \qquad (8)$$

for B respectively. This means, each u^A has to be transmitted by A such that it causes a state in the receiver B, which would have been caused by the corresponding u^B.

The central task for agents, who have to perform a bootstrap semiogenesis can now be posed as follows:

Find a C_U such that the Morris-condition (8) is fulfilled.

According to the restriction, the number of neurons in the Σ-network as well as the number of links to the internal representations $r \in R$ are smaller than the ones for the corresponding internal parameters.
In order to emphasize the dynamic nature of a semiogenesis, let

> $\Sigma_{+\Delta t}$ be the sign space (the vocabulary actually used by the agents) at a given time interval Δt and $\Sigma_{\cdot\Delta t}$ the space of mutually understood signs at Δt (Note, that there is always a function from the time to Σ, R, and U). It is assumed, that only Σ does not vary on an actual genetic time scale.

Since

$$\Sigma_{\cdot\Delta t} \subseteq \Sigma_{+\Delta t} \subseteq \Sigma$$

the agents have to solve a selection problem. Moreover, it is possible that some (Gaussian or white) noise is present in the channel k. Therefore all mappings ϕ are modeled as classification operators as discussed in section 3.

5.2 Architecture

There are three internal representations within each actor, comparable to those used in the backpropagation-trained actor network discussed above (cf. figure 9).

The information flow of the system is realized by the four operators ϕ:

ϕ_{1S}: $U \rightarrow R_1$, R_1: self-representation [circle]
ϕ_{1F}: $U \rightarrow R_3$, R_3: other-representation [rectangle]
ϕ_2: $\Sigma \rightarrow R_2$, R_2: sign-representation [double rectangle]
ϕ_3: $R_3 \rightarrow \Sigma$

Actor A receives an input pattern u^A and a sign σ^B from B and sends in turn a sign σ^A to B and vice versa (circular-relational structure). The set of environmental inputs is presented several times. Each presentation of u has a duration τ, which allows reentry feedback cycles, i.e., a communication about u (a vivid illustration of this procedure can be found in Müller & Strack (1992) where this model has been realized as an experimental device).

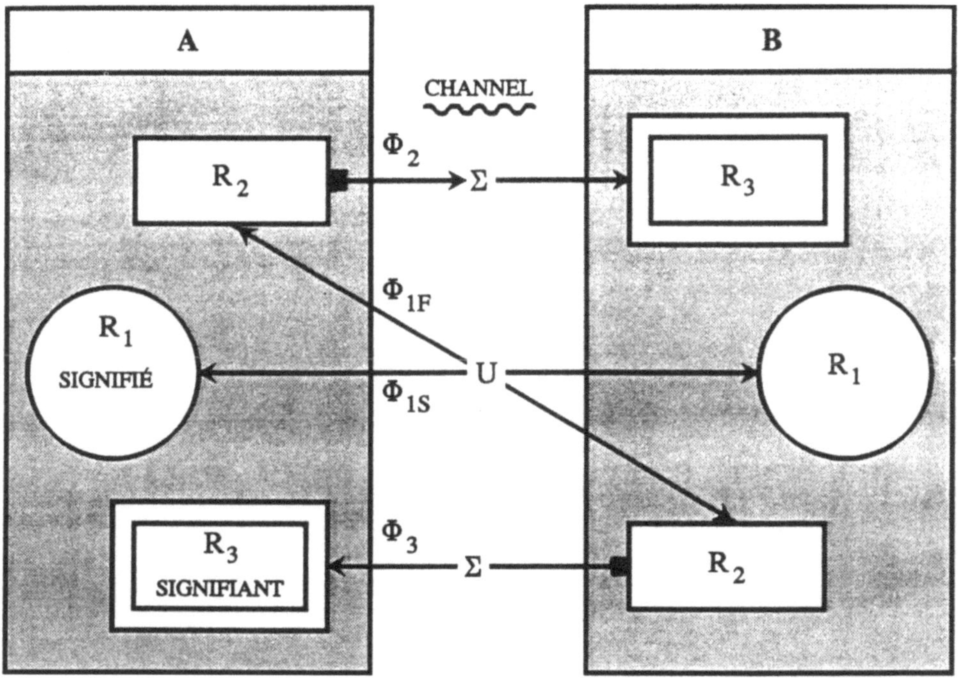

Figure 9: The DSS-model (Müller, 1989)

The actions of each system are governed by a coordination heuristic (action-protocol) $H : R \rightarrow A$ where A is a set of actions with $A = \{S, M\}$, $S = \{\text{true, false}\}$ (send) and $M = (\uparrow, \downarrow, m, r)$ (modify), with $\uparrow$: positive reinforcement, $\downarrow$: negative reinforcement, m : include noise, r : repeat until criterion is reached or new external input is received (cf. table II)

Note, that $\uparrow$, $\downarrow$ and m may be realized by any search strategy. In the first version (Müller, 1989) the four operators ϕ are changed by a genetic algorithm, which employs mutation and selection of these rules according to their equilibrium or harmony which is given by the degree of coherence between the three internal representations (figure 10).

The neural networks serve as preprocessors, which eliminate noise and extract classes from the input-sources as discussed in section 3. M is given by the classical operations of genetic algorithms (fitness $\uparrow$, $\downarrow$, mutation (e.g., cross over), reproduction). If, for instance, one actor is in an internal (local) equilibrium those rules (operators), which lead to this equilibrium are strengthened. If, on the other hand, the internal states diverge, the degree of equilibrium is lower and the probability that these rules are employed in the next cycles decreases[4].

	ϕ_{1S}	ϕ_{1F}	ϕ_2	ϕ_3	send
$R_1 = R_2 = R_3$	↑	↑	↑	↑	true
$R_1 \neq R_2 \neq R_3$	↓	↓	↓, m	↓	true
$R_1 = R_2 \neq R_3$	-	-	-	↓, m ,r	false
$R_1 = R_3 \neq R_2$	-	↓, m ,r	-	-	false
$R_2 = R_3 \neq R_1$	↓, m ,r	-	-	-	false

Table II: Coordination heuristic H

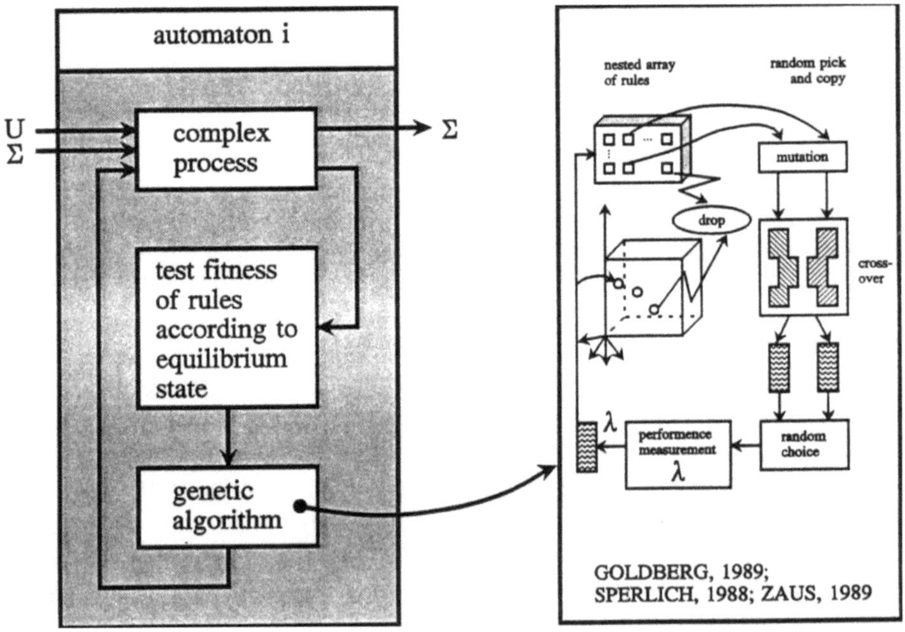

Figure 10: Mesostructure of the DSS-model (Müller, 1989)

5.3 Performance

It is not possible to discuss the various aspects of the model in this place (cf. Müller, 1989). Probably the most surprising result is that C can be generated even in the case of a bootstrap semiogenesis, a situation which is simulated by a random initialization of the operators at the beginning of the "language game."

C is a global attractor, a final state, where a) reentry feedback has generated equilibrium states for the two actors and b) the input cycle remains constant, i.e., no new environmental patterns are added. Simulations show that the Morris-condition is approximated by the two actors with a relatively high degree of accuracy (around 80 % of the input pattern). This is not too surprising since the algorithm awards a prize for rules generating a C which is associated with states of high harmony for both actors (global equilibrium).

All simulations show how the signal space is narrowed, i.e., that a semiogenesis in a "two strangers in a strange world" situation is basically a selection process. From all possible elements of Σ more and more are excluded and finally only a few are actually used (Σ_+). These signs are formed as different as possible, seemingly in order to avoid that they can be confused.

The signs used were sometimes redundant (one automaton used different signs for the same object u); different languages occurred (different signs used by the two agents for the same object). Nevertheless, both systems managed communication, i.e., the Morris-condition was fulfilled. This was also true in some situations where different representations occurred: Although both actors mapped the environment by using very different internal labels, they communicated successfully.

Adding new input pattern caused confusion if they could not be integrated immediately. Sometimes it took a while until it was noted that a discrepancy was present.

5.4 Some semiotic implications

1. As a model of communication and semiosis the Dynamic Semiotic System is comparable to models like the one of Cherry (1957). However, it additionally tries to give a computational framework for individual information processing and emphasizes the generation of the semiotic functions. The concept of sign is a dynamic one: signs emerge as results of circular-relational feedback loops from randomly generated signals. This point can be illustrated by an approach of Quine:

> ...consider the case where we teach the infant a word by reinforcing his random babbling on some appropriate occasion. His chance utterance bears a chance resemblance to a word appropriate to the occasion, and we reward him. The occasion must be some object or some stimulus source that we as well as the child are in a position to notice. Furthermore, we must be in a position to notice it...the fixed points are just the shared stimulus and the word...the occasions that make the sentence true are going to have to be intersubjectively recognizable (Quine, 1969, p. 28/81).

In Müller (1991, in prep) this asymmetric variant is discussed. In this case it is assumed that the teacher has a different coordination heuristic and does not change his/her own operators. In the symmetric "two stranger"-situation it is not necessary to know those stimuli, which have a reward-character. The reward is, generally, the coexistence of identical self- and sign-representations within an actor. In both cases, it is of crucial importance that there is a referential communication. This important demand can now be stated more detailed: a temporally coherent, but not necessarily spatially identical environment is needed in order to generate a common code. Important is neither the content of the representation nor the one of the signs. The physical form of signs, representations, and the two input domains are arbitrary. A semiogenesis affords the generation of structural connections between them, which implies that the agents operate on a common time scale and that the two input domains co-vary systematically. If the degree of covariance is low, there will be only a small number of signs and vice versa.

Furthermore, it has already been reported that a semiogenesis is a selection process. This contraction of the signal space has interesting correspondences both in biocommunication (signal matching, cf. Hultsch & Todt (1986)) and human conversation (Müller & Strack, 1992).

2. In order to reach a common code a differentiation between self-/other- and sign-representations is necessary. In other words, it is assumed that an actor is able to notice a difference between its representation of the world and the point of view of another agent, which is given by the interpretation of its sign. This leads to the question, how in the "two strangers"-situation an actor manages to detect a world-agent difference. The environment-agent differentiation is computationally tractable and can be done by recognizing events on two time scales: separation of environmental events from the background (very slow changes) and separation of signals (signs) from events, which have to change slower than the signals.

3. In addition, the internal mechanisms for a semiogenesis are specified. The actions include the following four possibilities: a) changing its self-representation (its private) processing of information about the world, b) changing the interpretation of a sign, c) changing the designation of a sign, i.e., forming or selecting new signs, and d) changing the assumption about

the processing capacity of the other system. The latter has some correspondences in the "charity principle" (cf. Davidson, 1990). Consider a listener who is assumed to have only a very coarse-grained knowledge about a domain (e.g., a child). In order to reach intelligibility it is a good strategy for a speaker, first, to transform his/her knowledge of an event (its classification to a concept) down to the assumed lower capacity of a listener, i.e., to a more coarse-grained classification. Then the second question is, to find an appropriate sign for this internally transformed concept. Hence the "rules of thumb", which guide the integration of environmental or social information have been expressed in the model in the following way: the use of the equilibrium principle and of the coordination heuristic.

To summarize: It is only assumed that the automata possess already those features which enable them to process information on their home-planets. This includes the extraction of the invariants of the world as modeled by Φ1 and those necessary for communication. Recall that the aim of this paper was not to show how these general properties may emerge phylo- or ontogenetically, but rather that it is possible to generate a (simple) language on an actual genetic time scale[5].

6. General discussion

The paper started with the question how adaptive distributed systems can communicate their knowledge. The search for the genesis of the semiotic function led to theories which emphasize that the sign-property of a physical object is given a priori to the communicants. It is embodied either by phylo- or ontogenetical mechanisms both in the speaker and listener such that mutual understanding is guaranteed. In recent philosophical positions (e.g., Davidson), however, this biologically or sociologically determined a priori synchronization is questioned. Communicants do not simply follow prepared rules of conventions - there is rather a dynamic adjustment of signs, which may lead to a convergence of the individual signal spaces in a concrete communication situation (cf. Clark & Wilkes-Gibbs, 1986). In this approach a radical scenario was given: the problem of communication in a "two strangers in a strange world"- situation, which probably marks the upper bound of this plasticity on a short, actual genetic time scale (semiogenesis).

In order to discuss this topic in a cognitive science framework, first, the concept of distributed reasoning was introduced. Since communicating machines seldom have a common phylo- or ontogenetical history, a radical scenario seems to be more appropriate in describing the coordination problems discussed in this recent field of A.I.

In knowledge based systems, too, the semiotic function comes to existence by a "baptismal act", which guarantees both internal and external consistency, while the agents are semiotically synchronized a priori. Unfortunately, in this framework neither an adaptation of individual knowledge (in the sense of world-model reorganization, McDermott & Doyle, 1980) nor of the communication structure is possible. Moreover, exactly those features and processes of a dynamic semiosis are hidden, which should be investigated. In real situations and technical applications there is no external "voice in the burning bush" which informs the agents about the proper labelling of the objects of a sometimes rapidly changing world. The conclusion therefore was, that these models can not contribute very much to the central problem. The world-mind connection was then discussed in the context of neural network theories which emphasize a geometrical approach to the notion of representation. Although these systems are able to perform pattern recognition and classification tasks, i.e., may have a sensory interface to the "real world", some serious problems were mentioned, e.g., their limited (lab-)learning capability. Moreover, the actors, the elements of these distributed systems, are extremely simple ones (threshold automata). Interesting emergent properties arise only at the global level of the whole system: one has to accept that there is only a low-level signal transmission within these systems.

A very different situation was found in actor networks. These modular systems contain subsystems each being capable of non-trivial information processing. A training algorithm was introduced, which enables these actors to communicate their representations under morphological restrictions. Unfortunately, an external supervisor is needed. However, the central problem of finding a common ground was illustrated and then a more precise formulation was found: Find a code, which satisfies the Morris-condition of mutual understanding.

The Dynamic Semiotic System, finally, may be seen as a first attempt to cope with a self-organized generation of mutually shared semiotic functions. The main features of this model exhibit some surprising self-similarities in processes of complex communicating systems. The concept of reentry feedback, borrowed from neurobiology, has correspondences in human conversation. This circular-relational process connects two systems, which contain separate representation structures. The simultaneous presence of a stimulus-representation together with an interpreted sign leads to either equilibrium or non-equilibrium states. According to these internal states a coordination heuristic is activated, such that a local harmony (within each actor) is approached. The whole system generates a set of representations with the corresponding signs even in the worst case situation. A lot of less problematic tasks such as the teacher-pupil interaction can be expressed by the model. Let me finally make two philosophical comments.

First, it may be interesting to contrast the "two strangers in a strange world"-scenario with the interaction described in Searle's "chinese room argument", which is a well known objection against the classical computational theory of mind. The artificial system inside the room passes the Turing test simply by following fixed syntactic rules, embodied a priori in the two participants of this "dialogue" (man and machine). According to Searle, the machine has no access to the meaning of the semiotic primitives since it is purely syntax driven. One is inclined to make a radical comment: it is possible that neither the machine in the room nor the man outside know the meaning of the semiotic primitives. If the human agent, too, follows a prepared and rigid schema, he is in principle in no better position than the machine and can be replaced by another syntax driven system synchronized semiotically a priori with the first one.

Does this imply, that only by a local generation of these functions intentionality and meaning emerges?

The position that intentionality and consciousness arise only in systems which are able to experience a difference between self- and other-knowledge and generate the semiotic functions themselves, has been formulated already by Mead (1909, 1910, 1913, 1934)[6] in his social theory of mind. Although this theory has been neglected completely in the traditional "monadic" cognitive science, two issues are remarkable in the context of distributed reasoning. First, recall that in the knowledge based system discussed in section 2 the notion of common knowledge plays a central role. Moreover, that what symbolic interactionists call "perspective or role taking" has a strong correspondence in the necessity of meta-knowledge within the logical axiomatization.

Second, it is less known that Mead tried to give a (neuro)biological foundation of the genesis of meaning, which include answers to the question, how a realization of such self-other difference arises in a system on all the three time scales (phylo-, onto- and actual genetically).

To conclude, it is highly probable that the recent conceptualization of the brain as "society of mind" (Minsky) or of distributed reasoning, respectively, will also point at social determinants of mind, meaning, and consciousness. The additional hypothesis that such structures are self-similar (fractal) and not limited to human interaction, i.e., that such processes appear both in neural systems within the brain and between organisms, seems only at first glance highly speculative. One should note that the search for such similarities has a strong tradition in general system theory and cybernetics. Obviously, these questions can be answered only empirically (cf. section 4)[7].

Anyway, concepts like sign and semiotic function are of central importance for the notion of distributed reasoning in A.I. and the module concept of the brain in neurobiology. In this paper, signs were conceptualized as transient states of the interfaces between complex dynamic systems which process information from other systems and the environment. Processing is done in such a way that a high degree of harmony between the individual representation of a changing world and the messages of other agents is realized. The other agents can be both a source of confirming information and disturbing elements, which force a new interpretation either of their own view of the world or of the meaning of their messages.

Interestingly, the harmony or equilibrium principle itself is a very general one and, again, points at the empirical evidence of self-similarities. As a core notion of connectionist models it is an expression of the emerging importance of concepts from physics in cognitive science (cf. section 3). Moreover, it is well known in social psychology and can be traced back to Lewin and Heider[8]. Both authors are strongly influenced by Peirce:

> Peirce did not use the word 'equilibrium' but 'harmony'. He strongly believed that there is a general harmony between the structures of the universe and our mind (C.P:, 7.438; c. 1893). That harmony makes man capable of becoming tuned with the universe through the scientific method: 'Successful research ... is conversation with nature ...'(C.P., 6.568; 1905). This harmony or equilibrium between the parts of the system (properly mind and nature) is reproduced among all parts composing mind and nature, and so on. This could involve a regress deep down to the very atoms and so forth. In each level, all the components must have that equilibrium. This harmony is not static, but dynamic. (Marostica, 1992, p. 34f)

However, such postulated harmony evokes the second philosophical question, an ontological or epistemological one. The assumed tendency to maintain balance between one's own view of the world and the co-presence of others leads to the problem of "operational closure of autopoetic systems" as radical constructivists would call it. In what sense do these systems generate a "correct" view of the environment? Is communication and even semiogenesis between operational closed monads possible at all? In this approach a common code is a compromise between the maintenance of operational closure and the co-presence of others. However, it is not difficult to show that without a common reference frame provided by the environment no convergence and no code would emerge. Even in the radical constructivist theories of communication it has been realized that external objects are needed as reference points (Ziemke, 1990). This necessity is also emphasized by Davidson:

> The idea that the propositional content of observation sentences is (in most cases) determined by what is common and salient to both speaker and interpreter is a direct correlate of the common-sense view of learning. It has profound consequences for the relation between thought and meaning, and for our view of the role of truth, for it not only ensures that there is a ground level on which speakers share views, but also that what they share is a largely correct picture of a common world. The ultimate source of both objectivity and communication is the triangle that, by relating speaker, interpreter, and the world, determines the contents of thought and speech. Given this source, there is no room for a relativized concept of truth. (Davidson, 1990, p. 325)

The question, however, what "correct view of the world" means, cannot be discussed here. In the model, processes of sign interpretation and conflict resolution operate simultaneously yielding a common classification schema of the environment at a given time - at least in the long run. Marostica (1991) has given a detailed interpretation of this aspect of the model and of this ontological and epistemological issue in the context of the semiotics of Peirce.

Let me finish with Steven Grossberg's words:

> It remains to be seen how the several scientific communities now converging with enthusiasm but vastly different training and goals upon the interdisciplinary study of mind and brain will assimilate the noisy and unexpected constraints imposed by each other's existence, notably by the fact that, despite the extra burden of difficult sociological conditions, relevant theories of mind and brain have been developing rapidly during the past few decades. (Grossberg, 1988, p. 21)

Notes

1. I thank A. Marostica for this hint.

2. I thank J. Brunning for her remarks on the connection between the work of Davidson and this approach.

3. In this part R is used instead of X in the former chapter.

4. A more detailed description of this procedure and the combination between neural networks and genetic algorithms is given by Müller (1989, 1991).

5. Müller (1991b, in prep.) and Kree & Müller (1992) give a discussion on recent development like an extension to N systems, the integration of meta-signs (modifiers), and to a formal language.

6. I thank P. Fassheber for this hint.

7. In Müller & Wolf (1992) some of these issues are discussed in the context of neurosemiotics.

8. Some relations between consistency theories and connectionist models are discussed in Müller (1991a, 1992b).

References

Aiple, F. & Krüger, J. (1990). Correlated rhythmic activity of neurons in monkey visual cortex. In: Eckmiller, R., Hartmann, G. & Hauske, G. (Eds.). *Parallel Processing in neural systems and computers*. Amsterdam; Elsevier (97-100).

Ashcroft, E.A. & Jagannathan, R. (1985). Operator nets. *Proceedings of IFIP TC-10 Working Conference on Fifth-Generation Computer Architectures*. North Holland.

Carpenter, G.A. & Grossberg, S. (1987). A massively parallel architecture for a self-organizing neural pattern machine, *Computer Vision, Graphics and Image Processing, 37*, 54-115.

Cherry, C. (1957). *On human communication*. New York; John Wiley.

Clark, H.H. & Wilkes-Gibbs, D. (1986). Referring as a collaborative process, *Cognition, 22*, 1-39.

Cohen, M.A. & Grossberg, S. (1983). Absolute stability of global pattern formation and parallel memory storage by competitive neural networks, *IEEE Transactions SMC-13*, 815-826.

Davidson, D. (1989). A nice derangement of epitaphs, in: E. Lepport (Ed.). *Truth and interpretation: Perspectives on the philosophy of Donald Davidson*. Oxford Blackwell; London.

Davidson, D. (1990). The structure of content and truth, *The Journal of Philosophy*, Vol. 87, No. 6, 279-328.

McDermott, D. & Doyle, J. (1980). Non-Monotonic Logic I, *Artificial Intelligence 13*, 41-72.

Eckmiller, R. (1990). Concerning the emerging role of geometry in neuroinformatics. In: Eckmiller, R., Hartmann, G. & Hauske, G. (Eds.). *Parallel Processing in neural systems and computers*. Amsterdam; Elsevier (5-9).

Edelmann, G.E. (1987). *Neural Darwinism - the theory of neural group selection*. New York; Basic Books.

Fagin, R. & Halpern, J.Y. (1988). Belief, awareness, and limited reasoning, *Artificial Intelligence, 34*, 39-76.

Fodor, J.A. & Pylyshyn, Z.W. (1988). Connectionism and cognitive architecture: A critical analysis, *Cognition, 28*, (1-2), 3-71.

Goldschlager, L. (1982). A unified approach to models of synchronous parallel machines, *J. ACM, 29*, 1073-1086.

Goschke, T. (1990). Wissen ohne Symbole. Das Programm des Neuen Konnektionismus, *Zeitschrift für Semiotik, Band 12, Heft 1-2*, 25-45.

Gray, C.M., König, P., Engel, A.K. & Singer, W. (1989). Oscillatory responses in cat visual cortex exhibit inter-columnar synchronization which - reflects global stimulus properties, *Nature, 338*, 334-337.

Grossberg, S. (1988). Nonlinear neural networks: Principles, Mechanisms, and Architectures, *Neural Networks, Vol.1*, 17-63.

Halpern, J.Y. & Fagin, R. (1988). Knowledge and action in distributed systems, *Distributed Computing, 3*, 159-178.

Halpern, J.Y. & Moses, Y. (1984). Knowledge and common knowledge in a distributed environment. *Proceedings of 3rd ACM Symposium on Principles of Distributed Computing*, 224-236.

Halpern, J.Y. & Moses, Y. (1985). A guide to the modal logics of knowledge and beliefs. *9th Joint Conference on Artificial Intelligence.* (IJAI-85), 480-490.

Hewes, G.W. (1977). Language origin theories. In: Rumbaugh, D.M. (Ed.). *Language learning by a chimpanzee. The LANA project.* New York; Academic Press.

Hultsch, H. & Todt, D. (1986). Signal matching: Zeichenbildung durch mustergleiches Antworten, *Zeitschrift für Semiotik, 8*, 233-244.

Jorna, R.J. (1990). Wissensrepräsentation in künstlichen Intelligenzen. Zeichentheorie und Kognitionsforschung, *Zeitschrift für Semiotik, Band 12, Heft 1-2*, 9-23.

Kree, R. & Müller, A. (1992). Classification properties of communicating neural networks. In: Opyitz, H. (Ed.). *Information and classification.* Berlin; Springer (to appear).

Lamport, L. (1984). Paradigms for distributed computing. In: Paul, M. & Siegert, H.J. (Eds.). *Methods and tools for specification, an advanced course.* Berlin; Springer (19-30, 454-468).

Levesque, H. (1984). A logic of implicit and explicit belief. *Proc Nat Conf on Artificial Intelligence* (AAAI-84), 198-202.

Machlup, F. & Manfred, U. (Eds.) (1983). *The study of information: Interdisciplinary messages.* New York: John Wiley.

Marostica, A. (1991). The semiotic and the semantic conceptions of truth. In: *Proceedings of the 1st Conference on Perspectives of Analytical Philosophy*, Saarbrücken.

Marostica, A. (1992). A nonmonotonic approach to Tychist logic. To appear in: Houser, et al. (Eds.). *Studies in the logic of Charles Sanders Peirce.* Bloomington; Indiana University Press.

Marty, R. (1990). The category of relational structure as foundation of Peirce's phenomenology and semiotic. *Manuscript: University of Perpignan*: France.

Marty, R. (1991). *L'algèbre des signes. Foundations of Semiotics.* Amsterdam; John Benjamins.

Mead, G.H. (1909). Social psychology as counterpart of physiological psychology, *Psychological Bulletin, 9*, 401-418.

Mead, G.H. (1910). Social consciousness and the consciousness of meaning, *Psychological Bulletin, 10*, 401-408.

Mead, G.H. (1913). The social self, *Journal of Philosophy, 10*, 374-380.

Mead, G.H. (1934). *Mind, self and society. From the standpoint of a social behaviourist.* Chicago; University of Chicago Press.

Meunier, J.G. (1991). Semiotic primitives and the symbolic machines. Cahiers recherches et théories, *Collections systèmes et cognition, No. Y5.* Montréal; Université du Québec.

Moses, Y. (1988). Resource-bounded knowledge. In: Vardi, M.Y. (Ed.). *2nd Conference on Theoretical Aspects of Reasoning about knowledge.* San Mateo; Morgan Kaufmann (261-276).

Moses, Y., Dolev, D. & Halpern, J.Y. (1986). Cheating husbands and other stories: a case study of knowledge, action, and communication, *Distributed Computing, 1*, 167-176.

Müller, A. (1989). Signal systems as emergent properties of interacting processes: Signs and meaning in artificial intelligence. In: *Proceedings of the IV congress of the International Association for Semiotic Studies.* Barcelona-Perpignan.

Müller, A. (1991a). Ansätze zu einer systemtheoretischen Formulierung von sozialen Repräsentationen im Rahmen von Interaktionen. in press. Göttingen.

Müller, A. (1991b). Zeichenvermittelt kooperierende Automaten. *Kolloquium Theoretische Physik*, Universität Göttingen, 12.6.1991.

Müller, A. (1992). *Interaktionsforschung im Rahmen der Cognitive Sciences: Modelle und Ergebnisse* (in prep.).

Müller, A. & Neumann, J. (1990). Classification with neural networks. In: Bock, H.H. & Ihm, P. (Eds.). *Classification, data analysis and knowledge organization.* Berlin; Springer.

Müller, A. & Strack, M. (1990). Ein automatentheoretisches Modell zur Semiogenese und seine empirische Umsetzung. *6. Internationaler Kongreß der Deutschen Gesellschaft für Semiotik*, Passau.

Müller, A. & Strack, M. (1992). Interactive concept- and sign-formation: an experimental realization of the Dynamic Semiotic System. In: Slikkerveer, L.J., Van Heusden, B., Jorna, R.J. & G. Van den Broek (Eds.). *The expert sign - semiotics of culture and expertise.* Leiden; University Press.

Müller, A. & Wolff, J.R. (1992). Semiotische Aspekte der Neurophysiologie: Neurosemiotik. In: Posner, R., Robering, K. & Sebeok, T.A. (Eds.):

Semiotik: Ein Handbuch zu den zeichentheoretischen Grundlagen von Natur und Kultur. Berlin; W. de Gruyter.

Petitot-Concorda, J. (1985). *Morphogénèse du sens I*. Paris; Presses universitaire de France.

Quine, W.V.O. (1969). *Ontological Relativity*. New York.

Sebeok, T.A. (1968). Goals and limitations of the study of animal communication. In: Sebeok, T. A. (Ed.). *Animal communication*. Bloomington: Indiana University Press (3-14).

Sejnowski, T.J. & Rosenberg, C.R. (1986). *NETtalk: A parallel network that learns to read aloud*. John Hopkins University: MD.

Smolensky, P. (1988). On the proper treatment of connectionism, *The Behavioral and Brain Sciences, 11*, no. 2, 1-74.

Uhr, L. (1986). Massively Parallel Multi-Computer Hardware=Software Structures for Learning. In: Haken, H. (Ed.). *Complex Systems - Operational Approaches*. Berlin; Springer (212-225).

Vishkin, U. (1983). Implementation of simultaneous memory access in models that forbid it, *J. Algorithms, 4*, 45-50.

Ziemke, A. (1990). Zur Differenz der Begriffe "Strukturdeterminiertheit" und "operationale Geschlossenheit", *Humankybernetik, 31*, 2, 59-63.

Implementing a sense of time in intelligent systems

J.A. MICHON (Groningen)

1. Introduction

In a quite wonderful short novel *The living end*, the American author Stanley Elkin (1979) tells the tragic story of the owner of a liquor store who gets killed in an armed robbery in his shop. More or less unjustified he finds himself in hell, rather than heaven, although there is little he has done to deserve such a fate. In Hell, he meets an interesting guy, Lesefario. In Hell as you would expect, there are billions of sinners - all being dead under the most unpleasant circumstances you can imagine. Lesefario is one of them, seemingly insignificant: one of those to whom, as the author tells us, "life had not signified." But, in a frantic effort to signify in afterlife - which is difficult in view of the fact that being dead is utterly meaningless, Lesefario makes his mind work and in the process suddenly the Truth arises: "The meaning of death is how long it takes!" That throws a sudden light on all the senseless suffering he and all the others are undergoing. Of course there is Time in Hell - seconds, minutes, hours - lots of Time, but there is no continuity, coherence, no narrative, and therefore no ending. And so Lesefario begins to count, soon followed by all the other denizens of Hell. And, indeed as Lesefario had expected, no sooner did God in Heaven notice what was going on down below, or He realized what was happening and instantly declared Doomsday.

Let me formulate what this story is telling me. It is telling me three things:

- it is important to 'keep time,' that is, to establish and maintain a continuity, a narrative, however elementary;
- there is an essential difference between implicit, automatic timing (undergoing time) and explicit, conscious time experience (acting upon time);
- explicit time is a cognitive construction, a deliberate decision to encode the dynamic contingencies of the world around us.

Here we have three fundamental presuppositions underlying the question how we can implement a sense of time in an (artificially) intelligent system.

Together these presuppositions are characteristic for the cognitive view of (human) time experience which has been summarized quite elegantly as follows:

> Time is not a condition, but rather a simple product of consciousness. It is not an *a priori* form that we impose on events. Time as I see it, is nothing but a kind of systematic tendency, an organization of mental representations (*images*). And memory is nothing but the art of evoking and organizing these representations.

This statement represents very much a point of view that is characteristic for cognitive psychologists in the 1990's. Actually, we find it in an essay on the origin of the human idea of time written, more than a century ago by the French philosopher Jean-Marie Guyau (1890; reprinted and translated in Michon, Pouthas & Jackson, 1988). Guyau was mostly a moralist and social philosopher, but his only digression into theoretical psychology has given us one of the most interesting opinions on the psychology of time, on a par with the famous chapter by William James (1890/1950), and Bergson's dissertation (Bergson, 1889/1950)

2. Questions

The question contained in both Lesefario's revelation and Guyau's statement pertains to the processes and strategies people use to organize their experiences so that they can act upon and influence the dynamic properties of their environment in a systematic way. In other words, the conclusion that time is a cognitive construction and, therefore, not just a property of nature, turns time into a genuine psychological problem. This, then, immediately leads to several psychological questions, three of which I will briefly consider:

- What is the discriminative stimulus for time?
- What is the function of a *sense of time*?
- What processes are involved?

Let me add, in passing, that there is also a fourth, equally important but much more difficult question, not to be addressed in this paper: How do these processes generate conscious time experience?

What is the discriminative stimulus for time? If time is a construction of the mind, there must nevertheless be some input from outside because we can not otherwise attribute temporality to the external world. There is, however, not terribly much in physical reality that can support our perception and cognition of time, however. Physicists have realized this for quite some time and, as a matter of fact, they have been quite effective in explaining time away. The physicist Szamosi (forthcoming), quoting Newton as claiming that

> Absolute, true and mathematical time, of itself, and from its own nature, flows equably without relation to anything external... (Newton, 1726)

has pointed out that each of the three major theories of modern physics has succeeded in eliminating one of the fundamental characteristics of the classical, Newtonian concept of metric time. The theory of special relativity has shown that there is no constant rate, no 'equable' flow (in fact it all depends on the perspective of the observer). Similarly, the theory of general relativity has forced us to abandon the idea that time could flow by itself, without relation to anything external (in fact the flow of time is changed by gravity) and, finally, quantum mechanics has shown that the assumption of continuity is not just untenable, but utterly meaningless (in fact it is meaningless to speak of arbitrarily small time intervals).

Even the stronghold of a temporal view of time, thermodynamics and its modern descendants, the far-from-equilibrium dynamic systems studied by Prigogine and his associates have not escaped occasional attacks from those who wanted to eliminate the arrow of time from physical theory (Prigogine, 1980).

The correct answer to the question if duration as such is represented in nature, seems to be 'Hardly.' Apparently we build the entire rich phenomenology of our experience of time on the basis of pretty little external information. What can that information be?

From the point of view of the human observer (or for that matter any system with the capability of retaining past experiences and matching these with present inputs) the discriminative stimulus for time appears to derive from the possibility of determining order in an absolute sense. One perceptual event can always be located with respect to another event on the basis of presence in memory. If an event A is identified as taking place whilst event B is remembered - that is, if B is part of the context of awareness within which A is taking place - then A is judged to be taking place *after* B (Tzeng, Lee, & Wetzel, 1979; Jackson, 1986). In the human organism such judgments, as so many other human judgments, are not infallible. There are many empirical studies showing that the perceptual order of events may be affected simply by manipulating their sensory qualities, such as intensity (masking; Olzak & Thomas, 1986; Scharf & Buus, 1986), or their structural coherence (Leeuwenberg & Buffart, 1979; Pomerantz & Kubovy, 1986). Also memories for past events may shift along the subjective time axis (Michon, 1967) and thereby become 'forgotten,' that is, inaccessible for retrieval (Estes, 1972, 1985). Despite these flaws, perceived sequential order seems to be one, and perhaps the only, fundamental sense-datum provided as the basic building block from which people manage to construct their experience of time.

What is the functional significance of a "time sense"? The preceding considerations lead me to the next question: what is the functional role of what we sometimes conveniently call the *time sense*? The answer seems to be simply that it enables an organism to stay tuned to its environment (Michon, 1985). The dynamic contingencies of nature are such that early in evolution life forms have found it advantageous to develop mechanisms, that allowed them to adapt to changes in their environment. This has, among many other useful things like skins and closed circulatory systems, resulted in two types of temporal mechanisms. The first type includes the biological rhythms allowing the organism to follow the course of a number of natural cycles, especially day, month, and year, and some shorter periodicities in the range of one or several hours. The other type comprises what we may call switches; generically switches operate in a one-shot manner if and only if certain preconditions are fulfilled, immediately or perhaps with a delay. The circadian rhythm to which all living organisms have been genetically tuned is the prime example of the first type, the classic reflex arc represents the prototypical organic switch.

The various instances of these two mechanisms - clocks and switches - have enabled organisms to become more and more independent of their environment, and we can easily appreciate their tremendous survival value if we try to imagine the fate of a species of tigers that would have a constant 10 millisecond delay in its hunting reactions. Similarly we can see that the internal representation of periodicities and intervals does a great deal to minimize the information load on the organism; what if tennis champions would have to continuously track and check the path of every ball coming their way?

What processes are involved and how can they account for the phenomenology of time? Let me give a working hypothesis of what time is. Elsewhere I have argued in favour of the following definition:

> Time is the conscious experiential product of the processes which allow the (human) organism to adaptively organize itself so that its behavior remains tuned to the sequential (order) relations in its environment. (Michon, 1985, p. 20)

In slightly more pragmatic terms: time is the ensemble of processes and strategies that allow people (and animals) to construct the variety of representations that they - sometimes, and not necessarily successfully - apply to remain in phase with their dynamic physical and social environment. In the remainder of this paper I'll first briefly review these processes and strategies (metaprocesses). Next I will give an example of tuning as it is required in an application, an intelligent support system that helps its user, an automobile driver, to cope with the dynamic contingencies of road traffic in real time.

2. Processes

Temporal information processing can be looked at from at least two different perspectives: Architecture and Function (Michon, 1985).

Architecture: clocks and switches. At the level of architecture we are essentially dealing with the clocks and switches mentioned before. Let me refer to these mechanisms simply as *clocks*. It has been shown that the (human) organism embodies a very large number of such clocks, perhaps several hundreds or even thousands. Fortunately it is possible to classify them into a small number of distinct categories, on the basis of their physiological or psychological nature (Richelle & Lejeune, 1980):

- neural (limbic system, cerebellum, cortical activity)
- physiological (respiration, digestion)
- biomechanical (mass-spring properties, muscle tension)
- cognitive (counting, reaction)
- collateral behaviour (pacing, scratching)

Here each type is exemplified by two or three examples of actual structures or processes to illustrate the kind of mechanism we are talking about. A considerable body of experimental and theoretical work has been carried out by physiologists and psychologists to relate these clocks and switches to particular mechanisms as summed up in the list (Gibbon & Allan, 1984; Richelle & Lejeune, 1980).

Whilst it is clear that the major periodicities such as the circadian and the circalunar cycles do indeed intrinsically time our behaviour in very predictable and replicable ways (e.g., Moore-Ede, Sulzman, & Fuller, 1983), in many cases it has been established that the human timing system is highly 'opportunistic' (Richelle & Lejeune, 1980). Depending on the nature of the task, the prevailing circumstances, and the state of the organism, one or the other suitable combination of mechanisms is apparently selected that is capable of supporting the temporal structure of the organism's behaviour. This selection may even change, as a result of fatigue, learning, motivation, time of day, or just for no apparent reason at all. This is, incidentally, one of the principal reasons why, for instance interactions that require precise real time synchronization between artificial and human intelligences are - thus far - so terribly limited and clumsy. More importantly, however, the temporal opportunism of the human being rules out an exhaustive explanation of timing in terms of these clock and switch mechanisms. We cannot avoid the introduction of the next level of discourse, the Functional level.

Function: Time as information.

> [Time] ... appears as a 'property' of patterns of information in the real world, which we call objects and events. There is no useful way for distinguishing between this latter aspect and the other properties of information, such as size, intensity or locus (Michon, 1972, p. 247).

This Equivalence Postulate of temporal information states that time intervals and other temporal relations can and do influence the behaviour of organisms. It is possible to train carps, pigeons, rats, and human infants on the basis of stimuli that only differ in their duration or their position relative to other stimuli. A great deal of effort has gone into determining what stimulus characteristics do affect the perception and judgment of time (Fraisse, 1957; Gibbon, Allan, 1984; Michon & Jackson, 1985; Block, 1990). These studies have essentially confirmed the list of temporal stimulus features provided by (Guyau, 1890; reprinted and translated in Michon, Pouthas, & Jackson, 1988). This list specifies the amount of information as well as a rudimentary syntax of temporal information.

Some information processing takes place automatically; it tends to be fast, parallel, and inaccessible to conscious monitoring and control. Deliberate information processing on the other hand is relatively slow, sequential, but accessible for control. There has been a considerable argument regarding the degree to which temporal information is processed automatically (Hasher & Zacks, 1979, Jackson, 1986). As a result it has become clear that timing (implicit processing) and time experience (explicit processing) should be clearly distinguished (Michon, 1989; 1990).

The idea behind implicit timing is that the human organism is intrinsically very well equipped with mechanisms allowing it to stay tuned to its environment without having to represent time in an explicit way. It may be said that the organism does, under many circumstances, simply express time (for an external observer). This can only be the case, as has been argued convincingly by Freyd (e.g., Freyd, 1987; forthcoming), if there are many mechanisms that can cope with the dynamic affordances of the environment. Freyd has been able to identify a number of such mechanisms which she prefers to identify as "an emergent property of processes unfolding over time." She illustrates her point of view with several impressive phenomena: representational momentum, the perception of apparent motion of the human body, and a well-known example of 'naive physics' the curvilinear momentum. To explain these phenomena she adopts a biological point of view: temporal affordances to which humans (and perhaps animals) can tune are not physical but species-specific and geared to the social context in which humans (and animals) are living. This may seem a far-fetched position, yet it conforms with earlier ideas about the 'Umwelt' and more generally with Gibsonian ideas about ecological psychology and the nature of affordances, and it provides a concrete insight in what we could possibly mean by 'implicit representation' of time.

These three elements of implicit time: dynamic representation, anticipatory present, and implied movement, return at the cognitive level, the level of explicit, conscious time experience. Functionally, whenever implicit timing fails, the organism will switch to the explicit constructive mechanism discussed in the beginning of this paper. This is the domain of time experience proper and it is, for instance the Time to which Guyau referred when, he called time, as we saw, "not a condition, but rather a simple product of consciousness." Elsewhere (Michon, 1990) I have distinguished three groups of cognitive structures to characterize the ways in which humans construct their representations of time. The first group belongs to what is known in the literature as episodes or scripts (Schank & Abelson, 1977; 1982). Composed of (quasi-)natural or verisimilar event sequences, located in space and time, they are intrinsically realistic templates for a variety of concrete behaviours. The second category consists of figural or metaphorical structures: *Time is Money* being a good example. Temporal relations are apparently so complex such that metaphors are frequently needed to encode them properly and to allow all kinds of unusual manipulations. Time is money, for example provides the terminology and perhaps the actual implications as well, of saving, wasting, or borrowing time. Thirdly, occasionally a metaphor may be found to be so powerful that a formal representation of temporal relations can be derived from it. Examples are, in the first place, the classical concept of metric time, the modern concept of space-time, and also several forms of modal logic (Van Benthem, 1983) and measurement theory (Michon, 1986).

3. An illustration: the case of GIDS[1]

Being interested in how people construct their representations of time is not exclusively a matter of intellectual curiosity. The ultimate motivating force is, perhaps, the fact that for the first time in its history, the human race must face the prospect of coping with other literate intelligences. This will sound as an exaggeration, but that is the case only because we find it difficult to project our ideas about intelligence onto the crude and stupid robots and so-called 'intelligent architectures' that are currently surrounding us. The time will come, however, that these systems will evolve, and prudence demands that we define the terms of communication before they do it! Would anyone hire a silicon nanny for their children if she would be able to hit them with arbitrary speed and precision and giving the little bastards no chance to duck and evade the blow? What would that do to the failure-driven learning that is so central to human intelligence?

To cut a long story short: it is necessary to make a time sense! Very frequently intelligent behaviour is not a matter of *what* to do, but of *when* to do it (Michon, 1966). That is what real time performance is all about.

3.1 The GIDS system

Let me present first present you with a bird's eye view of a particular real time system I have been working at during the last two years. This system is called GIDS, which stands for Generic Intelligent Driver Support (Michon, forthcoming) It is an appropriate context for my arguments because it is specifically designed as a real time support system. That is, it must cope with an environment in a way that does full justice to the anthropomorphic ways of dealing with the outside world. In other words, it must 'understand' its driver and it must rely on representations of the world and the task that are more or less isomorphic.

A co-driver is a system - human or artificial - that will provide a vehicle operator with information in the form of warning, advice, instruction, or even active intervention. Driver support systems should enable drivers to cope with the driving task more easily, safely and efficiently (and, indirectly, at less cost to the environment).

Co-driver systems derive their usefulness to a large extent from the fact that vehicle operators must cope with a growing amount of information of an increasingly complicated nature. This is caused by several factors, including the increasing traffic intensity, an increasing number of on-board and roadside sources of information and, not in the last place, by the increasing amount of additional in-vehicle equipment, such as hi-fi audio installations, car telephones and fax machines. This avalanche of information is likely to have an impact on almost every aspect of the driving task. It will affect route planning as well as navigation, manoeuvring, or elementary vehicle control. Unless action is taken this information would eventually be presented to the driver in an essentially incoherent fashion, irrespective of meaning or urgency. An important function of a co-driver, is to protect the driver from such uncoordinated, and under circumstances perhaps contradictory, information.

As part of the EEC DRIVE Program a Generic Intelligent Driver Support (GIDS) system has been conceived and implemented. The overall objective of the GIDS project has been to determine requirements and design standards for an intelligent driver support system that is maximally consistent with the information requirements and performance capabilities of the human driver. The project provides recommendations for such systems, and a (limited) operational prototype demonstrating the essential features of the GIDS concept, both under simulated and real world traffic conditions. The prototype GIDS system is presently being tested under real world conditions on the road and under simulated conditions.

The important innovative feature of GIDS is that it is the first system ever to take into account, in an adaptive fashion, (some of) the intentions, capabilities, and limitations of the individual driver. For this purpose GIDS incorporates not only a knowledge base containing detailed scenarios for driving manoeuvres such as overtaking, negotiating intersections, or merging into a traffic stream, but also a knowledge base containing information about the characteristics and behavioural history of individual drivers.

The driving task is conventionally divided into three major task levels: planning, manoeuvring and control. The GIDS system incorporates support functions at each of these levels and, in addition, provides instructional support to novice drivers. A small but realistic set of driving (sub) tasks has been selected for in-depth study, including lane following, merging into a traffic stream, and overtaking. Driving takes place in a complex dynamic environment, the road system, under a set of fairly well-defined operating constraints. The GIDS project provides recommendations for driver support in a wide variety of driving circumstances. The driver can interact with the GIDS system by means of a variety of displays and controls, including voice communication, a video-display and a special purpose keyboard. GIDS also includes two active, intelligent controls, the accelerator pedal and the steering wheel.

Ideally GIDS should cover all of driver behaviour under all conceivable circumstances. Since this is, at present, far beyond reasonable bounds, only a limited set of conditions is actually studied without, however, giving up the intended level of generality of the approach. This policy has resulted in the Small World paradigm which restricts the number of external conditions and driving manoeuvres to which the GIDS system is responsive.

The functional architecture of GIDS includes a script-based analyst/planner which accepts information from dedicated input systems (such as the speedometer, the car radio, or the on-board navigation system) and a

Dialogue Controller that regulates the communication between the driver and the GIDS system.

The structure of the intelligence as embodied in the Analyst/Planner of the GIDS system in its present state can be described as follows. GIDS knows about the world, or more specifically, GIDS has stored a representation of every world situation and of every type of event that can take place in the world. Each representation consist of a vector of variables (numerical and binary truth values) that unambiguously identify each event. These are actually the variables that GIDS will sample through its sensors, input/output devices and applications. Associated with each vector element is a range of acceptable values. As long as the driver's behaviour remains within this range jointly for all variables, there should be no output and the driver will seemingly be operating in an open loop fashion. At all times, however, the driver may actively request information from the system, in which case the system will generally answer the request.

As soon as one or more observed variables fall outside its acceptable range, GIDS will recognize this discrepancy. Every such critical situation is associated unambiguously with one or a series of messages. Here the term message is used in a generic sense: it may refer to a system-induced change in gas pedal response, a beep, a spoken phrase or a more or less complicated visual signal, a blinking light, a pictogram or a written message. Once the message has been passed on to the driver, the GIDS system will continue operating according to its overall way of operating: if the driver recovers from the critical situation (or if the problem goes away as is fortunately frequently the case in traffic) the system will stop delivering messages until the next critical situation emerges.

3.2 Dialogue management

Once a message has been determined, the problem is how it ought to be exchanged with the driver. In GIDS this problem is tackled by the Dialogue Controller. A first problem this system component must be able to face is the possibility that several critical events occur at the same time or so close in time that a *priority conflict* will arise. The second, related problem pertains to the *driver workload* created by the situation and by the message structure. And finally there is the problem of *allocation of messages* to the various interfaces of the GIDS system, in such a way that the driver is not confused or overloaded simply by the communication with the system as such.

The general issue is one of scheduling. Given an event or event sequence, the performance of the driver will depend on when and how to process the relevant information: how long does it take to read a road sign, and how long to notice that a child is standing at the kerb, waiting to cross? How long does it take to reach a decision to shift gears and how long to activate a brake? What is the range of these values in young and aged drivers, in novice drivers, handicapped drivers...? Many of these basic performance data are known, or presently being collected. What has not been studied, however, is how these elementary performance operations fit together into integrated manoeuvres such as merging into a traffic stream or during an overtaking manoeuvre. In GIDS this problem is tackled by means of a method of determining the time and resource allocation for each separate action unit - turning right, changing lane, braking to a halt at a traffic light, or, for that matter, dialing a number on the car phone - in a particular manoeuvre. A similar analysis is made for each message that may be passed to the driver and for every message that the driver may pass to the GIDS system. These allocation patterns are stored and eventually retrieved together with the various situation and event representations.

4. Temporal issues in GIDS real time performance

Now, what sort of temporal issues do we face in our development of GIDS? First of all there is the operation of the Analyst/Planner component. As indicated before, this component is essentially a script- or case-based planner. It is based on a very detailed task analysis, and it embodies the more and less likely event histories that can be encountered in the context of a (thus far quite limited) set of events. In principle it should be able to cope with the Cartesian product of situations x manoeuvres x driver actions but, to be frank, currently it is much more restricted than that. Over the range of events for which it can provide the driver with support, the scripts in the Analyst/Planner have default values for certain inputs which the system derives from its sensors and its functional goal is to minimize, under all circumstances, the work load imposed on the driver when performing safely and effectively.

As an example consider the following situation:

Function:	approach *intersection*
	to *turn right* [R at -3; slot -5/-1]]
Function:	approach *pedestrian crossing*
	[no message -4/0]
Conclude:	[R at -5]

In plain terms this just means the following: the system detects that its vehicle is approaching an intersection. It knows that, in order for the driver to reach her destination, a right turn must be made at this intersection. It knows - as is indicated in the bracketed expressions - that the supporting message for a right turn (R) must be delivered between 5 and 1 seconds before reaching the intersection, preferably at 3 seconds. Next the system detects it is approaching a pedestrian crossing located immediately before the intersection. This state of nature requires it to refrain from giving any message (except top priority warnings, that overrule any other function) between -4 seconds and the instant at which the crossing is reached. The system then reaches the decision to present the message for the right turn at -5 seconds before reaching the intersection. A considerable part of the activities of the Analyst/Planner consists of organizing the temporal pattern of support messages in such a way that normal, humanly acceptable sequencing is guaranteed for the range of situations the GIDS system can cope with.

Once the system has decided what messages to deliver and when is the time to do so, the Dialogue Controller takes over. Having a message and the situation to which it applies, given the current goal of the driver, understanding that message plus determining and organizing all related actions impose a certain workload on the driver. In other words, there is a certain time requirement for understanding the message and translating it into proper action. The Dialogue Controller takes care of this fine-tuning of the messages delivered by the GIDS system by means of a series of procedures. The function of the Dialogue Controller is to schedule the actions and messages of the GIDS system in such a way that for every conceivable event or combination of events a non-conflicting interfacing with the driver is maintained. The operational basis for these procedures derives from the Model Human Processor (MHP) or Goals, Operators, Methods, and Selection (GOMS) concepts, which are crucial to much of Allen Newell's work on task analysis and intelligent architectures (Card, Moran, & Newell, 1983; Newell, 1990; 1992). These concept are closely related to classical ideas about time and motion studies on the one hand, and those of critical path analysis as it is applied in industrial management on the other. MHP and GOMS are assumed to model the information processing activity of humans. This assumption also lies at the root of the GIDS system: the control of the dialogue between the driver and the system exercised by the GIDS system is indeed based on an elementary version of the MHP. That is, the GIDS system operates on a realistic representation of its driver to the extent that the MHP is indeed a realistic model of human information processing. On the basis of explicit estimates about the time it takes to detect and discriminate the relevant stimuli, to perform a relevant cognitive operation, or to execute a relevant elementary motor act during the execution of a given task - such as driving - a critical path analysis is made. This means that an optimal trajectory is determined for sequencing the required operations so as to impose minimal information load on the operator.

An interesting but taxing complication in this set-up is that the GIDS dialogue control requires scheduling for *uncertain* events in real time, meaning that there is no room for 'what if' strategies for finding optimal schedules. A simple but effective partial solution for this problem has been adopted: events and messages are also assigned a priority value which allows an urgent, potentially life-saving message to overrule schedules of lower priority order.

5. Conclusion

To claim that with the GIDS project we have succeeded in creating a time sense for artificial intelligences would be an exaggeration. What I have tried to show, though, is that it is possible to implement in such artificial intelligences a set of real time constraints that on the one hand make it possible to structure the internal representation of the dynamics of external events, and on the other hand can keep track of the internal requirements of human information processing capabilities and limitations. Both aspects belong to the most fundamental aspects of a genuine time sense, and their joint implementation in an operational driver support system proves that this allows such a system to take an active and somewhat independent role in the dynamic interaction between natural and artificial intelligence.

Note

1 The research reported in this and the following section was carried out under contract DRIVE V1041 of the European Community, in which the Traffic Research Centre, University of Groningen (NL) acts as Prime Contractor and Delft University of Technology (NL), INRETS-LEN (F), Philips Research Laboratories (NL), Saab-Scania (S), TNO Institute for Perception (NL), YARD Ltd (GB), MRC Applied Psychology Unit (GB), Tregie Groupe Renault (F), VTI (S), BMW AG (D), Universität der Bundeswehr (D), and University College Dublin (EI) are represented as partners. The opinions, findings, and conclusions expressed in this report are those of the author alone and do not necessarily reflect those of the EC or any other organization involved in this project.

References

Bergson, H. (1889). *Essai sur les données immédiates de la conscience* [Time and free will]. Paris; Félix Alcan.

Block, R. A. (Ed.). (1990). *Cognitive models of psychological time.* Hillsdale, NJ; Erlbaum.

Card, S. K., Moran, T. P., & Newell, A. (1983). *The psychology of human-computer interaction.* Hillsdale, NJ; Erlbaum.

Elkin, S. (1979). *The living end: A triptych.* New York; Dutton.

Estes, W. K. (1972). An associative basis for coding and organization in memory. In: A. W. Melton & E. Martin (Eds.). *Coding processes in human memory* (pp. 161-190). Washington, DC; Winston.

Estes, W. K. (1985). Memory for temporal information. In: J. A. Michon & J. L. Jackson (Eds.). *Time, mind, and behavior* (p. 151-168). Berlin; Springer-Verlag.

Fraisse, P. (1957). *Psychologie du temps* [Psychology of time]. Paris; Presses Universitaires de France.

Freyd, J. J. (forthcoming). Dynamic representations guiding adaptive behavior. In: V. Pouthas, F. Macar, & W. J. Friedman (Eds.). *Time, Action and Cognition.* London; Plenum Press.

Freyd, J. J. (1987). Dynamic mental representations, *Psychological Review, 94*, 427-438.

Gibbon, J., & Allan, L. (Eds.). (1984). Timing and time perception. *Annals of the New York Academy of Sciences, 423.*

Guyau, J. -M. (1890). *La genèse de l'idée de temps* [The origin of the idea of time]. Paris; Félix Alcan.

Hasher, L., & Zacks, R. T. (1979). Automatic and effortful processes in memory, *Journal of Experimental Psychology: General, 108*, 356-388.

Jackson, J. L. (1986). *The processing of temporal information* [University of Groningen, The Netherlands]

James, W. (1950/1890). *The principles of psychology* (Vol. 1, pp. 604-642). New York; Dover.

Leeuwenberg, E. L. L., & Buffart, H. F. J. M. (Eds.). (1979). *Formal theories of visual perception.* New York; Wiley.

Michon, J. A. (1966). The problem of perceptual motor load. In: Anon. (Ed.). *Studies in perception dedicated to M.A. Bouman* (pp. 79-91). Soesterberg, The Netherlands; Institute for Perception TNO.

Michon, J. A. (1972). Processing of temporal information and the cognitive theory of time experience. In: J. T. Fraser, F. C. Haber, & G. H. Müller (Eds.). *The study of time* (Vol. 1, pp. 242-258). Berlin; Springer-Verlag.

Michon, J. A. (1985). The complete time experiencer. In: J. A. Michon & J. L. Jackson (Eds.). *Time, mind, and behavior* (pp. 20-52). Berlin; Springer-Verlag.

Michon, J. A. (1986). J.T. Fraser's 'levels of temporality' as cognitive representations. In: J. T. Fraser & N. Lawrence (Eds.). *The study of time* (Vol. 5, pp. 114-146). Amherst, MA; University of Massachusetts Press.

Michon, J. A. (1989). Timing your mind and minding your time. In: J. T. Fraser (Ed.), *The study of time* (Vol. 6, pp. 17-39). Madison, CT; International Universities Press.

Michon, J. A. (1990). Implicit and explicit representations of time. In: R. A. Block (Ed.). *Cognitive models of psychological time* (pp. 37-58). Hillsdale, NJ; Erlbaum.

Michon, J. A. (Ed.). (forthcoming). *GIDS: Generic intelligent driver support*. London; Taylor and Francis.

Michon, J. A., & Jackson, J. L. (Eds.). (1985). *Time, mind, and behavior.* Berlin; Springer-Verlag.

Michon, J. A., Pouthas, V., & Jackson, J. L. (Eds.). (1988). *Guyau and the idea of time*. Amsterdam; North-Holland.

Moore-Ede, M. C., Sulzman, F. M., & Fuller, C. A. (1983). *The clocks that time us*. Cambridge, MA; Harvard University Press.

Newell, A. (1990). *Unified theories of cognition*. Cambridge, MA; Harvard University Press.

Newell, A. (1992). Unified theories of cognition: The role of Soar. In: J.A. Michon, & A. Akyürek (Eds.). *Soar: An intelligent architecture in perspective*. Dordrecht, The Netherlands; Kluwer.

Olzak, L. A., & Thomas, J. P. (1986). Seeing spatial patterns. In: K. R. Boff, L. Kaufman, & J. P. Thomas (Eds.). *Handbook of perception and human performance, volume I: Sensory processes and perception* (Chap. 7, pp. 1-56). New York; Wiley.

Pomerantz, J. R., & Kubovy, M. (1986). Theoretical approaches to perceptual organization: Simplicity and likelihood principles. In: K. R. Boff, L. Kaufman, & J. P. Thomas (Eds.). *Handbook of perception and human performance, volume II: Cognitive processes and performance* (Chap. 36, pp. 1-40). New York; Wiley.

Prigogine, I. (1980). *From being to becoming: Time and complexity in the physical sciences*. San Francisco; Freeman.

Richelle, M., & Lejeune, H. (1980). *Time in animal behavior.* Oxford; Pergamon Press.

Schank, R. C. (1982). *Dynamic memory: A theory of learning in computers and people*. Cambridge; Cambridge University Press.

Schank, R. C., & Abelson, R. P. (1977). *Scripts, plans, goals, and understanding: An inquiry into human knowledge structures*. Hillsdale, NJ; Erlbaum.

Scharf, B., & Buus, S. (1986). Audition I: Stimulus, physiology, thresholds. In: K. R. Boff, L. Kaufman, & J. P. Thomas (Eds.). *Handbook of perception and human performance, volume I: Sensory processes and perception* (Chap. 14, pp. 1-71). New York; Wiley.

Szamosi, G. (forthcoming). The short life of metric time. In: F. Macar, V. Pouthas, & W. J. Friedman (Eds.). *Time, action and cognition*. London; Plenum Press.

Tzeng, O. J. L., Lee, A. T., & Wetzel, C. D. (1979). Temporal coding in verbal information processing, *Journal of Experimental Psychology: Human Learning and Memory, 5*, 52-64.

Van Benthem, J. F. A. K. (1983). *The logic of time*. Dordrecht, The Netherlands; Reidel.

Towards an evaluation tool for Natural Language Interfaces

Y. VOGELENZANG & J. DE VUYST (Groningen)

0. Abstract

In the last few years there has been much commercial interest in the development of Natural Language Interfaces (NLIs). But the developments are slow. Obviously, developing NLIs is hard work. This paper addresses the question of why that should be the case, and tries to take some first steps towards formulating independent criteria for the relative performance of NLIs, involving parameters such as adaptability, system, language use, etc.

1. Introduction

Natural Language Processing is becoming more and more important in the field of Artificial Intelligence, especially in the design of Natural Language Interfaces (NLIs), programs that should enable communication between humans and computers in some kind of "natural" language rather than a computer language. Computers provide efficient means for storing data, which explains the growing interest in efficient ways to retrieve information once it has been stored in a database. Until recently, there were basically two ways of accessing a database: 1. a menu presentation to form questions, a rather slow and inflexible method; 2. a database query language, the main disadvantage there being of course the need to learn a special language. Evidently, for most people it would be easier if they could address the computer in their own language. What we need for that purpose is a sort of translator or interpreter that will intermediate between humans and computers: a Natural Language Interface.

In the past two decades various attempts have been made to build such interfaces. Some of these programs can be called successful, but the ideal situation, i.e., a computer that understands an arbitrary piece of human language, is still far from being realized. Of course one of the main problems in developing NLIs is the fact that natural language tends to be highly ambiguous. There is no single successful implementation technique for the construction of an NLI, neither is there any single linguistic theory that will guarantee successful communication via an NLI. However this does not mean there has been no progress in the development of such interfaces.

In what follows we will first consider the various attempts and products that have been put forward, then we will undertake a classification of the linguistic formalisms used and discuss some of the practical linguistic problems that arise in an attempt to build an NLI. Finally, we will try and make an inventory of the criteria that must play a role in an evaluation procedure for NLIs.

2. Natural Language Interfaces

2.1 History

In the late forties and early fifties, after people had started exploring symbol processing possibilities, the first natural language processing projects were started in the form of machine translation. At first, there was much optimism about the intricacies to be solved. After having tried to translate sentences by word-for-word substitution, however, it soon became clear that this method was only appropriate for simple examples and that machine translation would not really be possible without actually understanding text (see De Vuyst, 1990).

From 1960 onwards, there was a growing interest in natural language understanding. People from different disciplines (linguistics, psychology, computer science, semiotics, mathematics) concerned themselves with the problem of how to make computers understand natural language. Some first attempts were made in the form of key-word systems and translation of English into a formal system. The former system tried to match keywords (or lists of words) in the input-string, with words in the database. This method was used in ELIZA (a program simulating a psychiatrist, written by Weizenbaum (1966) who, incidentally, meant it to be a hoax) and PARRY (simulation of a paranoid person, described in Colby, 1974). Of course these two programs do not understand any of the input language, but they can simulate understanding language so well, that cases are known of people having had long discussions with these programs without ever realizing they were talking to a computer (cf. also Boden, 1977). An example of the method of translating English into a formal system is the STUDENT-program (Bobrow, 1968), which translates algebra word problems into a set of linear equations that could be solved by a special mathematical program. This idea of translating English into a formal language is used in many of the current generation natural-language interfaces.

Around 1970 several natural-language programs were written, amongst which the well-known program SHRDLU (Winograd, 1972). SHRDLU's domain was a world of blocks in different colours and sizes. The system contained a robot arm that could pick up and move these blocks. Commands to SHRDLU could be given in natural language and, within its restricted domain, the system handled language quite well, including phenomena such as quantification, negation and some kinds of pronouns. SHRDLU was able to update its database, to search it for an answer and to execute goals set by the user. Furthermore, it kept track of its own actions and was able to explain them to the user.

Another technique was exploited in Woods' LUNAR system (Woods, 1977), which was an interface for a data base containing moon rock sample analyses. Woods used an ATN (Augmented Transition Network grammar) to parse the input sentence and heuristics to select the most probable representation of an input sentence. A semantic interpreter based on pattern-action rules that produced a logical form was directly executed on the database using a procedural semantics. Just like SHRDLU, LUNAR could process relatively unconstrained language as long as it concerned the very narrow domain of the database. Both systems proved to work very well within their own worlds but were not portable and could not be extended outside their domain.

Also around 1970 Schank put forward his ideas on Conceptual Dependency (Schank, 1972). This CD-theory was used in Schank's NLP systems, like MARGIE, SAM and PAM. The input sentences are translated into structures containing primitives, which describe actions, for instance MTRANS (TRANSfer of Mental information) and ATRANS (TRANSfer of Abstract relationship, e.g., possession). These CD-primitives are used to represent the meanings of sentences in a kind of semantic network. MARGIE (Schank, Goldman, Rieger & Riesbeck, 1973), a program based on CD-theory, could accept simple texts and answer questions about them. Given a text, MARGIE could also generate all kinds of plausible inferences based on the input.

During the 1970s various other NLIs were marketed, such as LIFER (Hendrix, Sacerdoti, Sagalowicz & Slocum, 1978), ROBOT (Harris, 1977), and REQUEST (Plath, 1976).

2.2 The current situation

The first commercially successful interface was INTELLECT, developed from 1975 onwards by the Artificial Intelligence Corporation. In 1981 the first version of INTELLECT (a sequel to the ROBOT program) came on the market and since then it is the most widely used mainframe interface product. It provides an interface to all the most popular IBM and independent data base management systems (DBMS). The system contains a basic lexicon of 400 words. A special vocabulary and semantics of the user's domain of interest have to be added, but according to Larry Harris (president of the A.I. Corporation) ordinary technicians can do the job and can do it quickly (Harris, 1984).

Just like Woods' LUNAR, the parsing system of INTELLECT is based on an ATN. Input sentences need not be complete, INTELLECT also accepts fragments. If the system encounters ambiguity which it cannot resolve itself, it asks the user for an explanation. Accepted queries are echoed to the user as a formalized restatement of what the user intended.

Around 1984 several other natural-language front ends appeared on the market, amongst which RAMIS II ENGLISH from the Mathematica Product Group. This system was originally built for the RAMIS II DBMS and it translates natural language queries into semantic primitives corresponding to the semantics of Reporter, the RAMIS II 4th generation query language. For this translation the system uses pattern-matching techniques. The input to the interface can be a question in natural language as well as in the Reporter-language. Ambiguity cannot be dissolved by the system, but the solution has to come from the user.

Two more recently developed natural language interfaces are TEAM (Grosz et al., 1986) from SRI International and IRUS from BBN (Bolt, Beranek & Newman) [Johnson, 1985 calls them a new generation of database interface systems]. Although developed at different companies, these two systems work in much the same way (the researchers of the projects were in close contact with each other). TEAM transforms the input sentence into a logical form, using a bottom-up parser based on PSG (Phrase Structure Grammar). It uses heuristics to get the most likely representation of the sentence. The parse tree is converted into a Prolog clause and then translated into the query language for the database. All parts of the system are domain independent, but some modules require domain-specific knowledge for specific applications.

IRUS is based upon a mainly top-down ATN parser, which combines syntactic processing and semantic interpretation. It uses semantic knowledge to decide between alternative syntactic parses and to prevent ambiguity.

IRUS contains a module for acquiring domain-dependent semantic knowledge, which can construct semantic rules without being tied to a database structure. Systems such as TEAM and IRUS have some advantages in comparison with the earlier mentioned systems: they have wider linguistic coverage, increased semantic power, portability between domain, facilities for knowledge acquisition from non-specialists and independence of the underlying database structure.
Another recently developed natural language interface is CHAT-80 (Warren & Pereira, 1981), which uses the programming language Prolog for all phases of the analysis. After the input sentence has been parsed, the syntactic structure is transformed to a logical form on which a quantifier scoping algorithm is applied using simple heuristics. The final result is a logical form expressed in a notation called Definite Closed World (DCW) clauses. With the input sentence in this logical form the database can be searched for an answer to the user's question.

So far we have just listed some of the more salient systems, but in fact a classification of the various systems is possible along different parameters. We will skip parameters like price, memory-use, implementation issues, etc., and concentrate on linguistic performance.

2.3 Classification of linguistic formalisms

Since many natural language interfaces have been or are being developed, it might be useful to classify them according to the linguistic formalism used. Different theories have been exploited, the most important of which are:

- *Pattern Matching (e.g., in ELIZA and PARRY).* Pattern matching attempts to recognize input utterances as a whole, trying to match structures in the input against (patterns of) keywords to form an interpretation of the utterance. For instance the ELIZA program takes an input sentence like: "Why are you looking at me?" and tries to match the components of this sentence with keywords in the database. For the word "are" there is the following pattern in the database: "X are you Y?" which causes the output "Would you prefer it if I weren't Y?". Furthermore ELIZA would replace "me" with "you", so that the response to the sentence would become: "Would you prefer it if I weren't looking at you?". Even for restricted domains the number of required patterns of words can soon become too large.
- *Syntactically-driven parsing (e.g., Augmented Transition Networks, applied in LUNAR en INTELLECT).* In contrast to pattern

matching, which tries to interpret the input as a whole, syntactically-driven parsing is constructive. It builds up the interpretation of an input sentence out of the interpretation of its constituents (e.g., NP, VP). There are a lot of different parsing strategies, e.g., ATN, DCG, LFG, GPSG, that concentrate purely on syntax. To illustrate these techniques we will give an example of a simple transition net:

Figure 1: A very simple transition network

This example gives a description of a well formed sentence, namely starting with an NP between position S and S1, followed by a verb between S1 and S2. Pure syntactically driven parsing first creates a complete syntactic analysis of a sentence, without being concerned about an internal representation or interpretation. This is a rather inefficient method, because most sentences can have a large number of different syntactic analyses, when not taking the interpretation of the sentence into account. Therefore, more recent approaches have been made to intermix syntactically driven parsing and interpretation, for instance in semantic grammars.

- *Semantic grammars (in NATURALLINK and SAVVY)*. Semantic grammars are a useful technique for applied natural language parsing. In these grammars the grammatical categories have semantic definitions in addition to their syntactic information. The semantic definition puts constraints on the contents of the syntactic categories to avoid meaningless parses (e.g., sentences that are syntactically correct but make no sense). For instance a semantic grammar will have separate rules for each semantic verb class:
  RES-VP <-- RESERVING RES-MODS (specifying the complements allowed for verbs like "to book")
  DEP-VP <-- DEPARTING DEP-MODS (for verbs like "to leave" and their allowed complements)
  This technique is only efficient for restricted domains, because the number of rules will grow rapidly when extending the grammar.

- *Case grammars often combined with Conceptual Dependency techniques (e.g., PLUME).* Case grammar supplies a way of including semantics in the parsing of sentences. Sentences are parsed into a case frame, consisting of a head concept and a set of subsidiary roles associated with the head. The head concept is usually the action that is referred to in a sentence (usually identified by main verb) and the case frames are filled with the agent of the action, the object acted upon, the location of the action, the instrument used in the action, etc. For every case frame it is defined which cases have to be filled, which are optional and which are forbidden.
  (agent buy-1 jack-1) : jack did the buying
  The big advantage of case grammar is that it combines bottom-up parsing (constituent recognition) and top-down parsing (predicting and forbidding cases).
- *Logic representation (combined with some of the above techniques in IRUS, TEAM (Grosz et al., 1986) and also in CHAT-80 (described in Allen, 1987)).* This method translates sentences into their logical form, which can be represented in a sort of predicate logic clause or even a Prolog clause (e.g., in CHAT-80). The logical form produced is then being translated into a query in the database query language the system uses. For example TEAM will translate the question "Show each continent's highest peak" into a logical form like:
  for every continent
  for the unique peak
  such that the peak is the highest peak such that
  the continent is continent of the peak
  you show speaker the peak
  The big advantage of this method is that the underlying logical form is independent of the database. Therefore an NLI using this technique can be adapted to new databases by the user of the system.

One may well wonder, however, if the specific linguistic theory that is being followed is a dependable indication of the user-friendliness or suitability of the actual interface.

3. An evaluation tool for Natural Language Interfaces

3.1 How to judge NLIs?

How can one recognize a good natural language interface? It is not enough to know which linguistic method was used in designing the interface. There are a lot of important requirements a solid interface should fulfil. How can, for instance, a company that is considering to buy an NLI know which one to buy. Of course the companies that sell the NLIs all claim to have the perfect product that can handle all natural language input. However, since they have their own commercial interests at heart it might not be safe to rely purely on those claims. Of course, a demonstration of the program can shed some light on its quality, but still not all the problems that can occur will reveal themselves in just one demonstration session. Therefore, it seems important to develop a way of testing NLIs by a series of benchmarks.

3.2 Special purpose versus general purpose

There is an important distinction between special purpose and general purpose systems. All commercially developed systems are special purpose systems, since they were developed for applications in a specific, restricted domain. Therefore they only need to have knowledge of this low-level domain, trying to match input structures against keywords in the domain. Their linguistic methods usually resemble semantic grammars and since pragmatics is being restricted to only one specific domain, they function reasonably well within this domain. Whereas these special purpose systems may be commercially interesting in the short run, the development of general purpose systems is much more interesting for the future. Special purpose systems are only useful within their own domain and could never be adapted for applications within other domains. Furthermore, they perform hardly any genuine processing of the natural language input (mostly not much more than pattern matching). Obviously, when a system must understand all natural language input, it needs more than just pattern matching or other simple NLP techniques. It is clear that a lot of research has to be put into the creation of a system that fully understands natural language. However, since the development of such systems is such a time-consuming and thus expensive job, the commercial market has relatively little interest in the research for general purpose systems.

A similar phenomenon can be seen in the commercial development of expert systems: on one hand there is the search for general problem solvers, while on the other hand ad hoc systems for special problem areas are being developed. This resulted in the so-called expert system shells, which have a certain amount of general problem-solving techniques at their disposal that still need to be filled for a special purpose (see Walker et al., 1987). Similar developments are emerging in natural language processing, with programs like Plume (developed by the Carnegie Group) which is not a ready-made interface, but a software tool for building a purpose-specific interface (see Johnson, 1985).

The distinction between special purpose and general purpose systems is of course crucial for the assessment of natural language interfaces. Apart from testing how well a system works within its own restricted domain, we also like to know its performance in general natural language processing, concluding therefrom how well it could be adapted for applications in other domains. In fact what should be tested in evaluating interfaces is not only their performance, but also their deficiency in natural language processing.

3.3 Linguistic problems an NLI should be able to handle

In section 2.3. we gave a list of the linguistic formalisms most widely used in the development of NLIs. The use of one of these techniques (or any other for that matter) does not guarantee the construction of an effective, efficient NLI. A good NLI has to be able to handle a number of practical linguistic problems. It seems useful to form a list of criteria for NLIs, containing the linguistic problems that will occur frequently when one is using such an interface (cf. e.g., Winograd, 1983).

- *Grammaticality checking*

  For practical NLP systems, it is not vital that they should only accept syntactically well-formed strings. As a matter of fact a system that accepts ill-formed sentences as well as correct ones would even be better. It would be rather tedious to have an interface rejecting every not absolutely correct question that it is asked. On the other hand, we should set bounds to what a system is allowed to accept. Flickinger et al. (1987) for instance point out that when we allow a system to neglect agreement between subject and verb we might get into trouble in those cases where the agreement accounts for a difference in meaning, as in the following two sentences:

  "Is there a newsman with Iranian contacts who works for the CIA?"
  "Is there a newsman with Iranian contacts who work for the CIA?"
  It is clear that we have to be careful when letting the system allow a certain amount of ill-formed input, in order not to loose differences in meaning.

- *Complex clause embedding*

  Should a system be able to accept complex embedded sentences like "List all the ships the cargo of which include only what the chief officer authorized the loading of?" This example sentence is of course extremely complex, but it is our opinion that to a certain extent the system should be able to handle clause embedding. We do not want the system to reject every embedded sentence demanding the user give a series of simpler sentences in their place.

- *Complex noun phrases*

  Just like complex clauses, noun phrases can have an intricate syntactic structure, including quantification and numeration. An example of such a sentence is: "All but seven programmers were hired". A good NLI should be able to parse such complex structures.

- *Phrases and idioms*

  In natural language we use some standard phrases that an NLI can not understand by just analyzing their structure. A good example here is a question that starts with the phrase: "Could you please tell me...". A purely syntactic analysis of this sentence will not arrive at the intended goal of the user, being that the system answers the question. Therefore it seems a good solution to give the system a stock of such often used sentences and a representation of their meaning.

- *Conjunction, ellipses and comparatives*

  The problem with these three phenomena is that they allow gaps to occur in a sentence, like for instance "Devito works for and with Chiang". Gapping constructions present one of the main problems in parsing and there has not as yet appeared a sound solution of how to tackle this problem. However since people tend to use such constructions when communicating with natural language systems, those systems should at least be able to handle some standard cases.

- *Anaphoric reference and inference*

  - Anaphoric reference (e.g., discourse anaphora)

    Cf. "The conference was a big success. The profits will go to..." (where one is to conclude that "the profits" are the profits of the conference).

  - Inference

    Can the user ask a question like: "Have any new books appeared?" or does he have to ask the following: "Give me a list of books that appeared in ...", "Give me a list of books that appeared in ...", "Give me the list of books that are on the second but not on the first list.".

- *Quantification*

  Compare for instance: "Did every employee hand in the declaration?" (many declarations) with "Did every employee inform the management?" (one management).

An interface has to handle all these phenomena, because people often use them in conversation. For instance, it has to be possible to refer to something mentioned earlier in the conversation, without having to describe explicitly what is meant, thus using reference.

3.4 An evaluation tool for NLIs

What we would like to have is a methodology to judge natural language interfaces by their linguistic performance and their practical applicability, meaning the effectiveness of a dialogue between the system and a user. With respect to "natural language" we can make the following remark: Human dialogue-partners share a vast amount of world-knowledge and are able to constantly adjust aspects of that knowledge during a conversation, depending on the knowledge of the speech-partner. For many reasons computer programs are not able to do this. However, for some applications of human-machine communication such adjustment is not necessary. It seems that the adaptability of the human partner to the computer suffices to make effective communication possible. A distinction can be made between (Woods, 1984):

- natural language communication, i.e., between humans
- natural communication, i.e., between humans and machines with adaptation of the human partner
- user-friendly interfaces

An evaluation tool for the linguistic performance of natural language interfaces should be restricted to aspects of "natural communication". The evaluation tool has to test an interface on how well it can handle the syntactic problems, described in section 3.3. Flickinger et al. (1987) have built a test case of sentences to test their own NLI. It seems indeed useful to make an evaluation tool, containing a list of sentences the system should analyze or reject. Of course, because the tool has to test various interfaces, such a suite of sentences has to be adjusted according to the domain of the interface. However there is a certain basic vocabulary that every good system should include (prepositions, quantifiers, pronomina, etc.). Therefore, a good method for building an evaluation tool is by forming a list of test sentences, made up of this basic vocabulary and of a second, special domain lexicon (containing specific nouns, adjectives, verbs, etc.) which varies for each interface.

4. Conclusion

This paper mainly presents a method for testing the linguistic capabilities of a Natural Language Interface. To judge an NLI on its efficiency it should be subjected to some sort of test. Here a proposal was made on how to test an interface with respect to its linguistic behaviour. Such a test may not only be useful to judge existing interfaces, but it may also be used when designing such an interface. In the latter case it can give a good insight on where the deficiencies of the system lie and what thus remains to be done. Surely robustness of the system should be tested as well before we can conclude how efficient the system is. It should have a large degree of robustness, i.e., it should only rarely fail to interpret a phrase. Therefore it is very important that the system can accept the most common misspellings, abbreviated forms of language, interceptions, interruptions, etc. The program should thus be as liberal as possible, because its goal is to understand people and not to judge their way of expressing themselves.

Furthermore, for a program to be cooperative, it has to include pragmatics. A good NLI should understand the user's intentions and answer according to them. An example often quoted (e.g., Johnson, 1985) is for an automated airline agent. If asked "Does American Airlines have a night flight to Dallas?" it would be irritating if it responded "No, but they do have one to Miami." It has to know enough about people and travel to answer "No, but United does."

Bates and Sidner (1983) set forth a case study of a methodology for determining what capacities an NLI must have in order to be effective. They propose to test an NLI by analyzing sessions between several users and the system. Of course this method gives a good insight in where the actual problems and misunderstandings between the user and the machine occur. It might therefore be a very helpful method for testing NLIs, especially on the subject of pragmatics.

The evaluation tool described here is by far not the only test case for an interface. The system should be tested as well on its pragmatic capacities and its user-friendliness. However, a test on its linguistic capabilities is a step in the right direction. A good natural language interface should be as cooperative as possible and in fact this research in progress concentrates on this very aspect.

References

Allen, J. (1987). *Natural language understanding*. Benjamin/Cummins: Menlo Park.

Bates, M., & Sidner, C.L. (1983). A case study of a method for determining the necessary characteristics of a Natural Language Interface. In: Degano, P & E. Sandewall (eds.), *Integrated interactive computing systems*. Amsterdam: North Holland.

Bates, M., & Bobrow, R.J. (1984). Natural Language Interfaces: What's here, what's coming, and who needs it. In: Reitman, W. (ed.), *Artificial Intelligence applications for business*, Ablex Publ. Co., 179-194.
Bobrow, D.C. (1968). NL input for a computer problem-solving system. In: Minsky, M.L. (ed.), *Semantic information processing.* Cambridge, Mass.: MIT Press.
Boden, M. (1977). *Artificial Intelligence and Natural Man*. Harvester Press.
Charniak, E., & McDermott, D. (1985). *Introduction to Artificial Intelligence*. Wokingham: Addison-Wesley.
Colby, K.M., Faught, B., & Parkinson, R. (1974). Pattern matching rules of the recognition of natural language dialogue expressions. Stanford AI Lab, Memo AIM-234.
Copeland, J.E. (ed.) (1984). *New directions in linguistics and semiotics*. Amsterdam: John Benjamins Publ. Co.
Flickinger, D., Nerbonne, J., Sag, I., & Wasow, T. (1987). Toward evaluation of NLP systems. Hewlett Packard Laboratories, Palo Alto.
Gazdar, G., & Mellish, C. (1989). *Natural language processing in Prolog*. Wokingham: Addison-Wesley.
Grosz, B.L., Jones, K.S. & Webeer, R.L. (Eds.). *Readings in Natural Language Processing*. Los Altos, CA: Kaufmann.
Harris, L.R. (1977). User-oriented database queries with the ROBOT natural language query system, *International Journal of Man-Machine Studies 9*, 697-713.
Harris, L.R. (1984). Natural Language Front Ends. In: Winston & Prendergast (eds.), *The AI Bussiness.* Cambridge, Mass.: MIT Press.
Hendrix, G.G., Sacerdoti, E., Sagalowicz, D., & Slocum, J. (1978). Developing a Natural Language Interface to complex data, *ACM Transactions on DB systems 3(2)*, 105-147.
Johnson, T. (1985). *Natural language computing: the commercial applications*. London: Ovum.
Lehnert, W.G., & Ringle, M.H. (1982). *Strategies for natural language processing*. Hillsdale: Lawrence Erlbaum Ass.
Plath, W. (1976). Request: a natural language question-answering system, *IBM journal of research and development* 20:4, 326-335.
Schank, R.C. (1972). Conceptual dependency: a theory of NL understanding, *Cognitive Psychology* 3:4, 552-631.
Schank, R.C., Goldman, N., Rieger, C., & Riesbeck, C. (1973). MARGIE: Memory, Analysis, Response, Generation, and Inference on English. In: *Proceedings of the 3rd International Joint Conference on AI*, August, Stanford, 255-261.
Selles, P. (1985). *Lectures on contemporary syntactic theories.* CSLI, Stanford.

Shapiro, S.C. (ed.) (1987). *Encyclopedia of Artificial Intelligence*. Wiley and Sons.

Thompson, H. (1983). Natural language processing: a critical analysis of the field, with some implications for parsing. In: Sparck Jones & Wilks (eds.), *Automatic natural language parsing*. Ellis Horwood.

Vuyst, J. de (1990). Knowledge representation in text interpretation. In: *Literary and linguistic computing* vol. 5, forthcoming. Oxford: Oxford Univ. Press.

Walker, A., et al. (Eds.) (1987). *Knowledge systems and Prolog: a logical approach to Expert Systems and natural language processing*. Wokingham: Addison-Wesley.

Warren, D.H.D., & Pereira, F.C.N. (1981). *An efficient easily adaptable system for interpreting NL queries*. University of Edinburgh.

Weizenbaum, J. (1966). Eliza - A computer program for the study of NL communication between man and machine, *Comm. ACM* 10:8, 474-480.

Winograd, T. (1972). *Understanding natural language*. New York: Academic Press.

Winograd, T. (1983). *Language as a cognitive process*. Chapter 7. Addison-Wesley.

Woods, W.A. (1977). Lunar rocks in natural English. In: Zampoli, A. (ed.), *Linguistic structures processing*. New York: Elsevier, North Holland.

Woods, W.A. (1984). Natural language communications with machines: an ongoing goal. In: Reitman, W. (ed.), *Artificial Intelligence applications for business*. Ablex Publ. Co., 195-209.

The linguistic analysis of expert texts

F. RASTIER (Paris)

"Notitia linguarum est prima porta sapientiae"
Roger Bacon

1. Introduction

In this introductory study, we shall illustrate the subject under consideration from a linguistic semantics angle by looking at two themes. First, we shall outline what we mean by ergonomic linguistics: we need to specify what this involves and overcome the reluctance of linguists themselves towards an as yet unfamiliar application of their field of study. We shall then, in the second part of our study, look at some examples of expert discourse analysis to help us to gain an initial idea of what methods to adopt, and attempt to set out research guidelines. It is important to note that all examples quoted are either translated directly from the French original or, where detailed questions of syntax are concerned, given in French with their corresponding translation in English in brackets.

2. Towards linguistic ergonomics

Although, to our knowledge, no term has yet been coined for linguistic ergonomics, the need for an ergonomic approach is becoming more and more evident, especially with the development of man-machine communication and, in a more general sense, semiotic technologies.

Without anticipating the likely outcome of the debate currently being held within the French research community, ergonomics seems to have acquired the status of an applied field of study. Unlike a science, it does not define itself with respect to an object, but rather with respect to its objectives. This is precisely why it is able to call on various fields, which it then uses as required to pursue its concrete objectives. Its very real ability to move between different fields of study is not to be confused with the multidisciplinarity of scientific fields, such as cognitive research, for example. Ergonomics does, however, take advantage of such multidisciplinarity, as theoretical relations obviously encourage practical collaboration: the new links being established between psychology and linguistics is a case in point that will most probably lead to new applications for ergonomics in the near future.

We are nevertheless forced to admit that the foremost linguistic theories have yet to fulfil the expectations. The proliferation of universal grammars and, in a wider sense, of formal linguistics has certainly made it easier to process language automatically; but the fact remains that they have concentrated on an idealized image of language (Mehler, J. & Dupoux, E., 1987, p. 84: "Linguistics restricts its attention to an idealized speaker, speaking a perfect language"). This language in fact boils down to a few hundred examples, usually concocted by linguists themselves, that are completely out of context and therefore extremely difficult to interpret. It is therefore a long way from the actual rich variety of genuine texts.

We can thus assume that the development of ergonomic linguistics depends mainly on the progress achieved in descriptive linguistics and, more especially, descriptive semantics (Rastier, 1987). It is based on the following principles:

genuine texts produced in real-life conditions of communication are the empirical object of linguistics;

such texts are produced and interpreted within the framework of established social practices;

each type of social practice has its corresponding type of discourse (e.g., political, technical, literary);

each discourse can be subdivided into types (e.g., in medical discourse, a scientific article, an abstract or a letter to a colleague);

all texts can be ascribed to a type and therefore linked to a discourse and social practice.

If we agree on these basic principles, we can admit that the prescriptive rules and licences of such types reflect the constraints imposed by situations on linguistic exchanges. These prescriptive rules of course seem less strict than actual linguistic rules, but they have a considerable influence on their application for all that. Vocabulary, syntax and even phonetics vary from type to type. We only have to remind ourselves of the considerable differences between oral and written language types. We therefore have to go beyond an approach to linguistics that is restricted to the functional system of language. We need to describe how this system interacts with the other social norms that are the type norms at work in any text.

All this means that we have to adopt a global approach to each social practice we study. In social practice, as in all cultural phenomena, it is the global that determines the local. A global approach to the task thus makes for more accurate analysis. Without going into more detail here (cf. the author, 1991, for a more in-depth analysis), we can say that all social practices develop within three spheres:

> a physical sphere in which material interactions take place;
>
> a semiotic sphere made up of signs (symbols, icons and signals) that are exchanged or brought into play;
>
> a sphere of mental representations specific to agents and which are usually highly socialized.

As we can see, we are moving away from the dualism of traditional cognitivism, which only recognizes two fields of objectivity - the physical and the symbolical - thus reducing the symbolical to the representational. These three spheres are governed by different laws and norms, and constitute different fields of objectivity. Social practices are quite naturally meant to be in constant interaction. The semiotic sphere usually fulfils a mediating role between physical factors and representations, especially where the categorization of objects and events is concerned.

In information systems, data processing representations "replace", so to speak, mental representations. This is why we often refer to knowledge representation on the one hand, and simulation on the other; these terms are certainly rather loosely used, as data processing representations are in fact only partial transcriptions, into other semiotic codes, of the semiotic exchanges at work within the social practices in which they occur. But no matter, as the mediating function of the semiotic sphere is no less important, even if it is made more complex.

In short, whenever linguistic exchanges are involved, a detailed linguistic analysis of such exchanges is a useful (and profitable) first step prior to implementation in a data processing environment. This analysis must, however, keep to certain "ecological" conditions, that is the corpus of data to be collected must carefully exclude any artefacts. In many cases, the mere presence of a researcher can alter the data he/she is aiming to collect. We therefore have to stick closely to real communication conditions. We cannot, for example, transpose the characteristics of communication between humans to man-machine communication, for the simple reason that users adapt their language accordingly from the outset. Anne-Marie Morel and her fellow researchers compared two corpora from the same speakers. In the first, they asked an SNCF (French Railways) employee to fill in a questionnaire; in the second, the same questions were given to a (simulated) machine: the differences are edifying (Morel, 1988). Basing his work on the second corpus, Daniel Luzzati developed a deliberately rudimentary data processing system, but which obtains very satisfactory results, simply because the task has been thoroughly analyzed from a linguistic point of view (Luzatti, 1987).

Apart from these "ecological" conditions, linguistic analysis must comply with the objectives of the required application, and therefore provide a way of systematically eliminating all elements that are not relevant to the task, however interesting they may be from a purely linguistic point of view.

3. The problems of expert text analysis

We shall limit our analysis here to oral corpora collected in an interview situation and then transcribed. Collecting data from experts is not an artificial situation, but quite simply a new social practice, where linguistic exchanges are coded into a type (which remains to be defined as such). We shall not deal with the problems posed by the collection and transcription of the corpus, although the valuable experience acquired by linguists working in the field may prove useful to us. We should also be careful not to ignore the problems specific to the syntactic description of spoken language: it discourages the use of the usual methods, which are all based on a standard written language; repetitions and reformulations in particular are transcribed by "listing-type structures" like "the bloke, the person" (DR, 5), which do not fit into the neat little syntax trees familiar to linguists (Blanche-Benveniste, 1990).

So let us turn straight to the semantic analysis of interviews recorded, each one of which is to be considered as a single text, as the words of the "cognitician" and those of the expert cannot be separated. Our examples are taken from two interviews conducted during the SNCF's Socrates project, and kindly passed on to us by Cisi-Ingéniérie. Extracts are marked by the expert's initials, followed by the page or "verse" number.

3.1 Two strategies

The ultimate aim of semantic analysis is to identify "objects" and "processes" to be modelled by the information system. These entities are in fact linguistic constructs determined by the analyst from the linguistic signifieds of the text, in particular by breaking it down into equivalence classes, paraphrases, etc. Seen like this, the "knowledge" handled is simply a set of standardized linguistic signifieds.

To identify which signifieds are relevant, two strategies can be adopted: either compile an inventory of the linguistic signs indicating the required objects and processes or conduct a structural analysis of the semantic components of the text.

The first strategy consists in breaking structures down into units and soon leads to a dead-end. A language cannot be viewed as a nomenclature, and a text cannot be reduced to a mere sequence of words. The analyst can certainly reach conclusions such as: *So* ("*Donc*") at the start of a period does not introduce the next step in an argument, but rather a summary of the preceding step; it indicates repetition. *That's what...*("*Voilà*") usually introduces a change of theme. *Then* ("*Alors*") usually introduces a solution. Exact dates and proper nouns introduce examples or anecdotes. But, however useful these observations may be for encoding, they are no substitute for an overall analysis of the text. Quite the opposite, in fact, as they presuppose it. Furthermore, a series of signs does not help us to construct a real interpretative strategy. Finally, the trickiest problems, such as the distinction to be made between an example and an anecdote, cannot be dealt with on the strength of this type of signs.

For us, then, the global analysis strategy would seem to be the best solution. It consists in describing the semantic components of the text and how they are interrelated. We have singled out four different components (Rastier, 1989a):

> *Thematics* accounts for signifieds within their syntactic context and their paradigmatic structures.
>
> *Dialectics* accounts for time intervals, the succession of states between these intervals and the progression of processes with regard to aspect during these intervals. Interactions between actors fall under this heading.
>
> *Dialogics* accounts for modality and, consequently, for the speech-act represented.
>
> *Tactics* accounts for the linearity of the signified, and therefore for the order in which the semantic units at all levels are produced and interpreted.

No given directions are fixed for this heterarchical system, where each component interacts simultaneously with the others. On a semantic level, a type is defined as a typical interaction between components.

Only the thematic and dialectic components are retained in full for the purposes of expert knowledge extraction: we can say to simplify that the study of the thematic component makes it possible to identify objects and how they interrelate within the field of study represented, and that the dialectic component enables us to identify the processes associated with those objects.

In the dialogic component, anything concerning the represented speech-act and clauses contrary to fact is eliminated, leaving only conditional clauses (of the type "anybody who asks for a place all to himself in a second-class carriage is going to be disappointed", DR, p.7).

In the tactical component, only the positions indicating temporal succession or causal relationships, and which therefore play the role of interpretative signs used to identify dialectic units, are retained.

3.2 The example of the example

To give us an idea of this method, let us consider the example. This type of explanation poses some tricky problems: how do we identify it and how do we interpret the data it conveys, which obviously cannot be coded as it stands? Let us look first at a few striking cases, after which we shall attempt to establish a typology.

In the corpus from MG, we read, talking about the TGV (French high-speed train):

> "Well, I've always thought of it as a bit like a racing car. For people who like cars, you've got Ferraris, Testa Rossas, cars that are made to be driven on the motorway and not on little country B roads. It's the same sort of thing with the TGV really" (v. 11).

This comparison uses analogy to illustrate a contradiction between possible speed and actual speed. Thematically, it underlines the positive view of the TGV and the negative view of its operating conditions (cf. supra: "I think the TGV has been (...) well, handicapped"). It therefore indirectly introduces a suggestion of optimization. However, in the field of dialogics, optimization belongs to the world of that which is contrary to fact. As the application to be constructed must only contain currently applied rules, this passage cannot be kept.

> A TGV gets up to a speed of 270 km/h between the branch at Combes la Ville, which is at the start of the high-speed line, and Lyons, then drops down into the Rhone Valley after Lyon at a speed of 140, 160 (...) Then you get onto lines where for example, for those who know a bit about the geography of the railways, on the Paris-Berne or Lausanne run up to around the halfway point on the high-speed line, at Passilly, it gets up to 270 km/h, then it leaves the high-speed line between Aisy and Dijon,

> slowing down to 140 or 150 km/h at certain points. Between Dijon and Dôle it stays at 140 km/h, then it keeps on going towards Switzerland, that's to say Vallorbe on the border, then its on to Mouchard and after that it can pick up speed again, 60, 70, 80 km/h through to Lausanne. Once the train gets into Lausanne it stops there. (v.23-25).

These two successive examples are a further illustration of the contradiction between possible speed and operating conditions, and between operating schedules and maintenance. For the same reasons as above, they should not be retained as they do not reflect current regulations. They have a polemical function, as can be seen from their thematic and strategic structure: a fortiori reasoning (slower and slower: 140-160, then 140-150, then 60-80) and grouping into threes, as encountered in conventional rhetoric (three being the number best representing totality according to Indo-European tradition).

3.2.1 Types of utterance

The role and structure of examples can only be described in the light of their context. In the first place, they vary according to discourse and type. In philosophical discourse, they seem to play a problem-posing role; in scientific discourse, they serve to objectify, and in technical discourse to typify. Expert text certainly falls within the scope of technical discourse, but its examples have more than just a didactic function. As we have seen, they can also assume a polemical function.

Secondly, their meaning is conditioned by the utterances (or, in spoken language, periods) around them. We therefore have to identify different types of utterance. An analysis of the corpus shows the following:

1. *Legal utterances*, used to express valid norms. Example: "At the present time, there are two services at the SNCF - summer service and winter service" (MG, v.26). Such utterances are generally gnomic, using the so-called habitual present tense (imperfective aspect) and shifted out speech (impersonal markers like *you* ("*on*") or *There is/are* ("*il y a*"). It may be necessary to refer to technical documents to be more explicit: "I said that if you want any further details I'll have to go and get my book, then we'll look at it together".

2. *Predictable cases* describe an ordinary application of the norm. Example: "We call that an organizational meeting, which is held quite some time before the new service starts. To give you an example, the organizational meeting for the summer service in 1990 was held about a fortnight ago" (MG, v.34). Here the speech bears clear personal marks, and near future tenses expressing habit also appear. At each dialectic interval, the next

interval is in fact predictable, as in: "If you want me to explain further, when my colleague selects his trains and matches them with the right times, he'll leave out anything that's not for first-classers so that means I'll end up with first-classers" (DR p.8).

3. *Standard specific cases* correspond to examples of the application of a norm, or in other words to the leaves of a decision tree. Example: "These are the sort of trains I like, you see. The 21, for example, the daily Paris-Lausanne, which runs every day of the year. It's called the "Lutétia" (MG v.53). The imperfective present is still there, as are the personal figures of speech, but maximum determinations can also be seen (proper names, figures).

4. *Non-standard specific cases* represent situations considered to be abnormal. Utterances are thus in the perfective past tenses, especially the perfect tense (as the historic past has no currency in the spoken corpora). On top of that, there are personal figures of speech and maximum determination (dates, proper nouns), as in: "We had a problem that came up on 13 July to do with Cuneo in Italy....There's nothing but problems on the run from Marseille to Cuneo via Ventimiglia. I had a long chat about it with the bloke who does the programming this morning, and he told me he just couldn't figure it out at all, so I'm damned if I know!" (DR p.24).

5. *Anecdotal utterances*, of which there are three sorts:
Some describe a situation that is no longer covered by regulations. For example: "In 1981, we were on the Paris-Lyon, Paris-Genève, Paris-Dijon and Paris-Saint Etienne runs, on high-speed trains" (MG v.18). Such utterances give explanations (cf. ibid: "The reason for that's very simple"). They could be used in information systems where more than a simple description of the status quo is required.

Others stem from enterprise culture, and no doubt serve only to keep up a type of connivance with the cognitician, as in: "The orange TGVs have two locomotives and 8 carriages in the middle and are 400 metres long, except for one, that is. One's a bit longer, 'cause we took it out on the high-speed run one day and stretched it by a few millimetres. That's all history now" (MG v.61).

The last type illustrates personal maxims, like: "There's always somebody who wakes up at the last moment in our company. We were in an organizational meeting once, I remember, where I'd prepared a certain amount of documents, and there's this guy who says: "But last year we had a summer service from such and such a date to such and such a date. This year, why don't we have it from such and such a date to such and such a date". So I had to completely re-do all the documents I'd already prepared, just because that guy wanted to change a date" (MG v.43).

3.2.2 Conclusions

The conclusions to be drawn are:
a) The utterances we have studied can be grouped into three levels of generality: universal utterances (1), general or habitual utterances (2) and specific utterances (3, 4, 5). Types 2, 3 and 4 can be considered to be examples. Their value in terms of knowledge depends on their relation to utterances of the first type. Only types 2 and 3 can be retained for normal knowledge extraction. Types 4 and 5 in fact relate to past (invalidated) or unvalidated norms (statements of fact).
b) The *explanation cycle* proceeds as follows:
■ The initial phrase indicates a move away from the immediately higher level of generality. The word *example* is used both for examples and anecdotes. Other expressions, such as *I take* ("*je prends*") or quite simply *like* ("*comme*" - "a train like the 21") are also used.
■ The example taken as a whole describes a process, which may be specified by conditions (usually introduced by *if* ("*si*")) that generate variants (usually introduced by *when* ("*quand*")).
■ Working back from an example to the general locates it with respect to normative, more general utterances (cf. phrases such as *if all trains were like that* or *we won't go into detail*). On the other hand, working back from anecdotes locates them not with respect to normative utterances, but rather with respect to the speech-act represented (justificatory phrases such as *that'll have a considerable influence on...* or *that's what makes me say that...*).
c) To sum up the linguistic marks present:
■ On the first two levels of generality, the aspect of the processes is imperfective, but the degree of determination is not the same and is higher than on the second level. We only find a final aspect on the third level, in examples of illegitimate processes, or in the last two types of anecdote, for which the perfect tense is used. On the other hand, the present tense is used in the first two levels of generality, and the near future is reserved for the second.
■ As for the person, *you*, *we* or *they* ("*on*") are used for the first two degrees of generality and *you* ("*vous*") is reserved for the second. Only *I* ("*je*") appears in anomalies and the last two types of anecdote.
■ Determination increases progressively from the first to the fifth type of utterance. A close relationship emerges between the perfective aspect and indefinite (or inclusive) personal pronouns, and between the perfective aspect and definite first person personal pronouns. This relationship is based on semantic connections that we shall not go into here.

Finally, if the word *example* indicates both examples and anecdotes, the word *anecdote* refers to anecdotes only.

The above observations cannot, of course, be transposed as such into a language other than French. Though the method looked at here is based on a general semantic theory, its descriptive scope is nonetheless restricted to the specific nature of each language being analyzed.

3.3 The communication represented

Generally speaking, the methods used for "knowledge extraction" do not systematically take into account how a speech-act is represented in the text. The expert's attitude towards the interviewer, and towards his/her own words, is seemingly thought to be negligible. This stems from a conception of language as a mere representational instrument, supposedly capable of representing reality and conveying knowledge that can be extracted simply by using the appropriate methods. This conception dates back a long way in the philosophy of language and has recently been given a new lease of life by so-called classical cognitivism. While it has without doubt the advantage of being simple, it is also rather simplistic. It is indeed true that language can, in certain conditions that are more complex than first thought, be a means of communicating information in the non-technical sense of the word; but it can never be reduced to just that: any linguistic exchange involves various emotive factors (play, passion, phatic factors, etc.); this comes across clearly in oral texts such as those with which we are concerned. Classical cognitivist theories of language are losing ground fast, due precisely to their failure to address these factors.

A global linguistic analysis has to take such factors into account, if only to identify their effects and then to eliminate them if required for the application in question. To illustrate this, let us consider what we mean by an "interlocutory contract" when dealing with the dialogic component of a text.

3.3.1 An interlocutory contract

One of the functions of language is its phatic function, which consists in making and maintaining contact between people taking part in a linguistic exchange. This function is particularly noticeable in oral exchanges. It covers not only interpolated clauses like *vous me suivez* (do you see (what I mean)), which indicate that the speaker is sensitive to the listener's attitude, but also whole interlocutory strategies.

The relation between speaker and listener needs to be studied in detail. We need to dispel the illusion that "expert analysis extraction" is based on neutral and purely informative communication. The human factors involved in the relation between speaker and listener have a considerable effect on the quality of data collected.

3.3.2 Value judgments and optimizations

Apart from speech-acts represented in the text, which are based on interlocutory contracts, the dialogic component also covers modal expressions conveying value judgments. Such expressions situate objects on scales of acceptability, which vary depending on the people involved.

Expert texts are full of value judgments and it could be possible to define an expert's skill with respect to his/her ability to make judgments considered to be relevant. In the satellite launching field, for example, it is vital to define what the expert means by *une mesure foireuse* (a duff measurement -cf. "in the type of launch we're looking at here [...], if you compute the orbit using duff measurements, you might well find that you can't get rid of them and you end up with huge residuals all over the place", CNES document (Rastier, 1991). The aesthetic nature of value judgments is not at all surprising: once we get past a certain level of understanding, the expert uses aesthetic vocabulary (e.g., "it makes a lovely sound") not only because he/she can't find any other words to express the idea, but also as a result of the pleasure gained from the task (without which he/she would never have reached such a degree of excellence).

Apart from the parameters specific to tasks, value judgments also affect tasks themselves. These value judgments may indirectly question standards applied within a company, for example: "We've got to a stage where it's so complicated that the whole system would have to be revamped to try to make things clearer and get started again on a sounder basis. We can always touch it up of course, as they say, but that's just papering over the cracks as far as I'm concerned..."(v. 75). But information systems usually describe currently applied standards. However, when those standards are called into question by the expert, he/she is in fact suggesting how they might best be optimized. Optimization may be either local (cf. "touch it up, as they say", i.e., "papering over the cracks" for the speaker) or global ("My idea was very simple: it would have meant running them on the passenger lines and as they run practically all day, from 5 o'clock to 11 o'clock at night, we would have carried out maintenance between 11 o'clock at night and 5 in the morning. But then we don't work at night" (v. 15-16).

From a semantic point of view, local optimizations are within the realm of possibility for the speaker. On the other hand, global optimizations are within a realm that is contrary to this (cf. "my idea was", and "but then", both stressing the realm of the unreal).

Whatever the purpose of the application required and - behind that - company policy was, we can see that the semantic analysis of expert texts cannot ignore such phenomena.

3.4 Future research guidelines

Without going into further detail, it would seem that the linguistic analysis of expert texts is justified, provided that it concentrates on semantics. Naturally, a practical analytical method that could be used by cogniticians remains to be developed. Such a method is no substitute for KADS, KOD, NIAM or REX-type methods, for which it serves as an initial foundation.

An interdisciplinary study of expert texts also needs to be undertaken. This would involve the cooperation of linguists, psychologists and computer scientists within the scope of an ergonomic research programme. Expert systems are semiotic machines, and only a semiotic theory is capable of defining these interdisciplinary relations.

References

Blanche-Benveniste, C. (1990). *Le français parlé*. Paris: Editions du CNRS.

Luzzati, D. (1987). Incidence de la machine sur le comportement langagier, *DRLAV* 36-37, 183-197.

Mehler, J., Dupoux, E. (1987). De la psychologie à la science cognitive, *Le débat* 47, 65-87.

Morel, A.-M. (1988). *Dialogue homme-machine: analyse linguistique d'un corpus*. Paris: Publications de la Sorbonne nouvelle.

Rastier, F. (1987). *Sémantique interprétative*. Paris: PUF.

Rastier, F. (1989a). La sémantique descriptive unifiée. In: *Modèles sémantiques pour les traitements automatiques des langues naturelles*, Nanterre: EC2.

Rastier, F. (1989b). *Sens et textualité*. Paris: Hachette.

Rastier, F. (1991). *Sémantique et recherches cognitives*. Paris: PUF.

Visetti, Y.-M. (1991). Des systèmes experts aux systèmes à bases de connaissances: à la recherche d'un nouveau schéma régulateur, *Intellectica* Nr. 12.

Vogel, C. (1988a). *Génie cognitif*. Paris: Masson.

Vogel, C. (1988b). Les systèmes experts dans le domaine spatial: l'innovation experte. In: *Technospace symposium*, Bordeaux.

Cooperative human-machine reasoning: Communication through the user interface

M.H. CHIGNELL (Toronto)

0. Abstract

This chapter discusses the communication processes that occur between humans and machines in software applications. This work was originally motivated by the problem of developing more effective user interfaces for expert systems. However, many of the issues in expert system interface design follow from general issues in user interface design. Thus our discussion here will focus more broadly on communication in user interfaces in general. The major assumption that we will make here is that in non-trivial applications, the user interface is a communication channel for coordinating human and machine intelligence within a cooperative reasoning system. We then develop a model of the user interface as a hierarchy consisting of physical, conceptual, and task layers, and discuss the problem of making communication through the user interface more naturalistic, with particular emphasis on the design and use of icons.

1. Introduction

Coordination of human-intelligence in cooperative reasoning systems requires overcoming intrinsic problems in human-machine communication. These problems stem from discrepancies in knowledge representation and language usage between humans and machines or software. Coordinated human and machine intelligence raises problems in allocating reasoning tasks between humans and machines (Hancock and Chignell, 1987), and in developing intelligent interfaces (Chignell and Hancock, 1988) that promote effective communication between human and machine.

User interfaces for applications such as expert systems should be explicitly modeled in terms of communication between intelligent agents. Such communication imposes a heavy burden on the conceptual portion of the user interface. While there is no theory to guide the development of conceptual interfaces for applications, we shall highlight some of the relevant issues in this chapter.

2. Communication between intelligent agents

More and more tasks are being performed by human machine systems. Such tasks require cooperative reasoning and communication between humans and machines. We may define cooperative reasoning systems as:

> Systems of one or more humans and one or more machines that work together to solve problems and carry out tasks using the shared reasoning capabilities of human and machine.

Cooperation between intelligent agents in cooperative reasoning systems requires coordination of activity, and hence, communication. Successful communication implies a shared language, with each agent having an adequate model of the other agent's intentions and goals. In the case of computer software, styles of communication have typically been very restricted. An application has a set of tasks that it can perform, and it is up to the user to generate the appropriate commands and button presses at the appropriate times. This can be seen, for example, in a word processor, where at any point in the interaction there may be scores of options that the user can choose from, but there is no sense in which the software "understands" or is even aware of, the intentions or goals of the user.

Thus word processors, and most other applications, follow the directions of the user slavishly, rather than cooperatively. This is possible because the user is creatively involved in creating the text document, spreadsheet, or database, and knows the form and content of the evolving artifact fairly intimately. However, there are also situations where the user may have only part of the necessary knowledge, and here some type of intelligent assistant is very helpful. One of the classic examples of this type of situation is information retrieval. Given the limitations of human learning and memory there is no way that a single person can keep track of the many thousands of documents that are written about a particular topic.

Thus extremely large text databases have become a supplement to human memory. The problem is, of course, that it is much easier to store documents into these large databases than it is to retrieve them at the appropriate time. Human search intermediaries (e.g., reference librarians) sometimes help in facilitating communication between a user and an information retrieval system. They can help because they have specialized knowledge about the querying languages and indexing policies of the information retrieval systems.

The information retrieval intermediary is an example of an (intelligent) interface that serves as a communication vehicle between two agents that need to work together on a task in spite of having fundamentally different languages and world views (Chignell, Hancock, Smith & Shute, 1986). Like any interpreter, the intermediary must understand the languages of both agents, and needs some knowledge of the task that they are trying to perform. Figure 1 shows the role of the intermediary as a channel of communication between user and database.

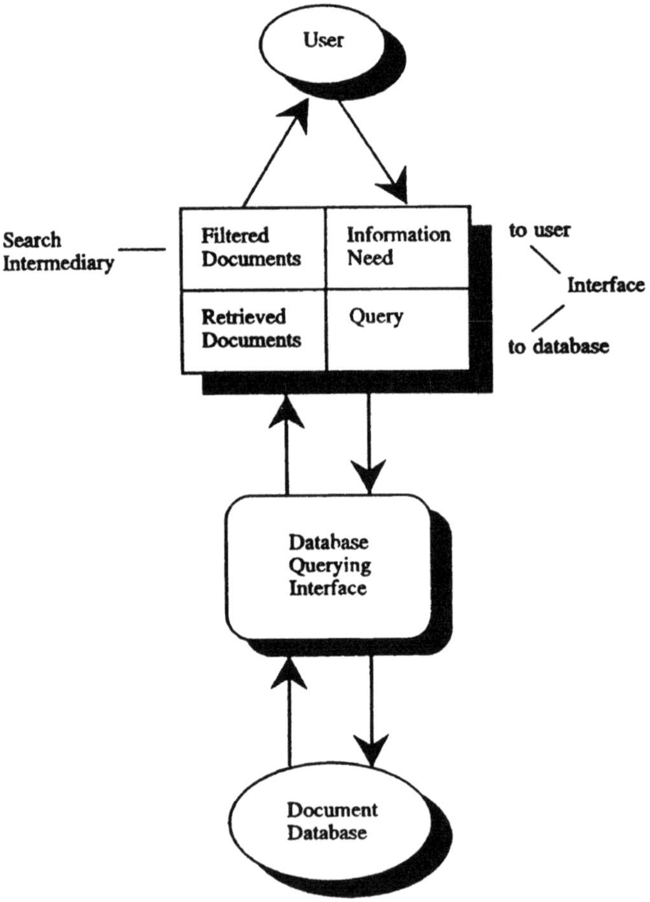

Figure 1: The role of the intermediary as an interface between user and database

Information retrieval is a more difficult interfacing task than desktop computing applications precisely because the "knowledge" is distributed between different agents in the human-machine system. These difficulties are compounded in systems where human and machine agents are involved in shared reasoning tasks. Given the inherent difficulties of communicating effectively during shared reasoning there has been a tendency to assign one or other of the agents the dominant role in reasoning so as to restrict the interface task to passing of short information messages and control instructions. This has certainly been true of early expert systems, where the machine has been assigned the dominant reasoning role, and the user has been responsible for collecting information and inputting data. Not surprisingly, perhaps, most people are uncomfortable with a role where the machine does the reasoning and they simply wait for the results. There is a natural tendency to question the results of inscrutable reasoning processes and this has led to the development of explanation systems that explain how and why expert systems reason as they do. In our view, the need for explanation in expert systems, and the difficulty of providing adequate explanation may be symptoms of inadequate communication through the user interface. Before considering the nature of communication of the user interface we will first need to define at least a minimal model of the user interface that lies at the heart of this discussion.

3. A model of the user interface

Chignell (1990) developed a simple model of the interface in terms of seven components (actions, behaviours, contexts, displays, effects, forms, and goals) that we will describe briefly in this section.

The *actions* of the computer application consist of the computational or processing functions that are performed, such as:

Computation
Storage
Retrieval
Operation of Peripheral Devices

The *behaviours* of the user when communicating through the interface are a little bit more difficult to characterize. The listing of behaviours given below emphasizes traditional concerns in human-computer interaction about the problems of navigation, information seeking, interaction styles, and input devices. Of these four problems, the issue of user navigation is probably the least understood. User navigation can be characterized as the way in which the user moves around the conceptual structure of the interface. In practice, there is a high degree of overlap between user navigation and interaction styles, since the intentions of the user during navigation will have to be communicated to the interface via some style of interaction. Thus a preliminary taxonomy of user interface behaviour is:

User Navigation
- Selection from map or display
- Move to more general command or concept
- Move to more detailed command or concept
- Move to associated concept or command
- Switch between modes, windows or environments
- Ask for Help
- Move through a sequence of commands or information

Interaction Styles
- Direct Manipulation
- CommandDriven
- FormFilling
- Menus
- Conversational
- Graphical Structures

Input Devices
- DataEntry (e.g., keyboard or function keys)
- Pointing Devices (e.g., mouse, joystick, or trackball)
- Speech Recognition

The next category in the model is concerned with the types of *contexts* that user behaviours can occur in. Some of the contexts that seem to have a strong effect on performance include task complexity, tempo constraints, hardware or software malfunctions, and knowledge of results.

The category of *displays* is becoming more complex as recent technological advances have made it possible to combine information from a number of different media and to compose it so the screen and the associated auditory space can become a collage of information from different sources. The category of displays can be divided into topics such as: multimedia, screen design, display composition, and sensory coding of information and visual cues.

The distinction between displays and *effects* in our model reflects the difference between information presented for its own sake and feedback about the operations of the application in response to user behaviours. Many of the details about effects will be application specific, so our description here will list only a few effects that generally occur across applications. Such effects include response time and error effects (e.g., error messages) and error prevention tools such as dialogue boxes.

Forms are the models in which actions, effects, and displays are embedded. The role of visual metaphors and spatial models as types of form seems obvious. The spreadsheet, for instance, has proved to be a particularly effective form for certain classes of computer application. Visualizing information has also been included as a form because it deals with the task of making the user understand the structure and gross features of information rather than the details of the information. This is consistent with the general role of forms which is to assist the user in forming an accurate conceptual model of how the interface, and the information and functions that it contains is structured.

Non-Spatial Metaphors
- Books
- Cards
- Files
- People and Situations
- Desktops

Spatial Models
- Maps
- Rooms
- Freeways
- Three-Dimensional Spaces

Visualizing Information
- Automatic Icons
- Simulations and Artificial Realities

The final category considered in our model is concerned with goals. *Goals* represent the motivating forces for human-computer action and for task performance in general. Task analysis is the process by which a task is decomposed into sequences of goals and subgoals. It is typically a normative process based on a rational model of the task. In contrast, goal identification is a descriptive process that infers goals on the basis of user behaviour while performing the task. Methods for goal identification include verbal protocol analysis, interviewing, error and critical incident analysis, and response time studies, where goals are inferred on the basis of preparatory pauses in transaction logs.

4. Metaphors and user interfaces

Approaches to modelling and implementing user interfaces are currently dominated by two main metaphors. We will review these metaphors and their impact on the design of physical interfaces before discussing how they may be supplemented with models of the conceptual user interface.

Metaphors provide a useful framework for building communication paradigms for computer interfaces. One approach to human-computer interaction is referred to as direct manipulation (Shneiderman, 1983). Here the metaphor is of a world of physical objects that are represented on the computer screen. Tasks can be performed by manipulating these objects using a pointing device such as a mouse or trackball. An alternative metaphor is the agent metaphor. In this model the computer and the user are seen as two agents that communicate with each other through the language of the user interface. In terms of the model world of the application, the agent metaphor replaces direct manipulation of the model world by the user with indirect manipulation of the model world via the agent.

Direct manipulation and indirect manipulation via a software agent are the two predominant computer interface communication paradigms. The direct manipulation style of interface has been particularly effective in tasks such as drafting, drawing, and designing where the emphasis is on creating and manipulating graphical objects (e.g., Myers, 1990).

The simplest form of a software agent is a command language interface where the user issues commands to the software which then manipulates the model world accordingly. Command language interfaces have often been used in more abstract tasks such as statistical analysis and database management.

Form-filling interfaces fall somewhere between the agent and direct manipulation metaphors. Here the model world is restricted to forms or documents that can be filled in various ways (e.g., the QBE method of database querying, Zloof, 1977). Many expert system interfaces (particularly those involved with diagnosis and classification) can be characterised as types of form-filling interface, with adaptable forms. Here the user is asked a series of questions (later questions will be chosen based on the answers to earlier questions) and reasoning is carried out as the implicit form is being filled in.

The direct manipulation approach to cooperative reasoning is appealing, but limited to only the grosser aspects of the physical interface, since many abstract concepts and functions cannot be conveniently described as objects and operations on objects. The agent style of interface is intrinsically better suited to the task of cooperative human-machine reasoning because in such situations the software is no longer a presentation of some model world that the user is manipulating, but rather an agent that is working cooperatively with the user to solve a problem. It is conceivable that user interfaces may ultimately profit by having a judicious mixture of direct manipulation and conversational dialogue, although we are presently a long way off understanding how such a hybrid paradigm should be formulated and used.

5. Levels of behaviour and layers within the user interface

There is in fact no single user interface. Previous models of the user interface have tended to focus on what we understand best, i.e, the physical interface, including the "look and feel" of a software application. However, once we get beyond this basic look and feel, each interface is a complex communication process consisting of several layered protocols (Taylor, 1988) where each layer has its own coders and decoders (Figure 2).

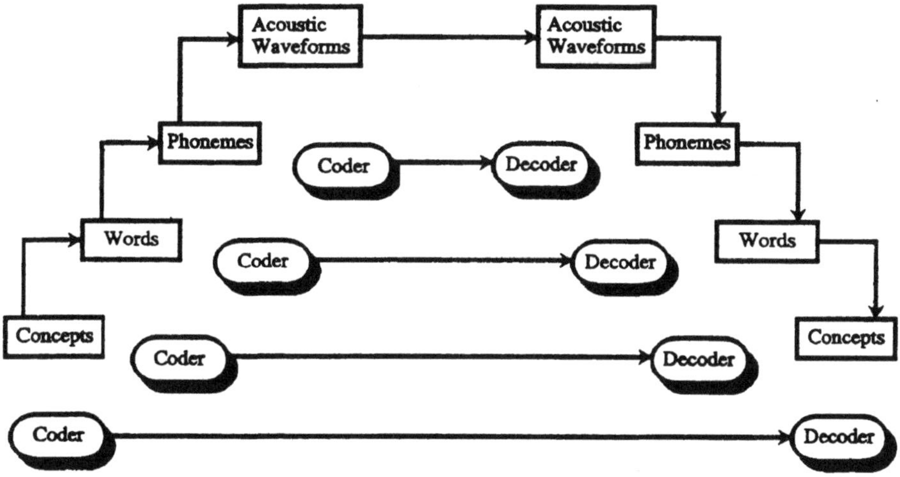

Figure 2: The layered protocol of a model of speech communication

In conversation, for instance, there is one layer for coding and decoding acoustic waveforms, another layer for coding and decoding words, and a third level for coding and decoding concepts (within which the other two protocol layers are nested). Each of these protocol layers communicates at a different level of human information processing. From a linguistic perspective, we may distinguish physical, lexical, syntactic, semantic, and pragmatic levels of the interface as we transition from the physical to conceptual aspects of communication (Figure 3).

Perhaps the most basic distinction, however, is between the physical (physical, lexical) and conceptual (semantic, pragmatic) aspects of the interface. The physical interface is the "obvious" part of an interface, and it is probably for this reason that it has received more attention in the past.

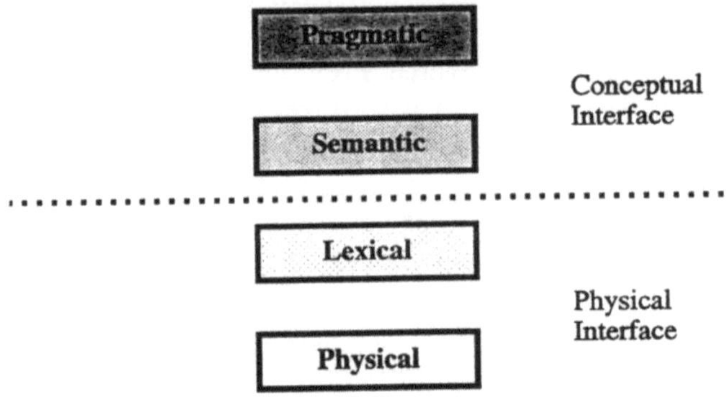

Figure 3: Levels of the user interface

While emphasis on the physical interface has not solved fundamental communication problems, it has led to impressive achievements. Most importantly, the development of what is referred to as the WIMP interface. The majority of existing visual interfaces are characterized by windows, icons, menus and pointing (or in some formulations, windows, icons, mice and pull-down menus), and hence are called WIMP interfaces.

6. The physical interface: the WIMP model

The desktop metaphor (i.e., a metaphor where files are stored in folders and deleted by throwing them into a trash can) and the WIMP interface can both be traced to the Xerox Star computer (Smith et al. 1982) developed at Xerox PARC. WIMP interfaces have the advantage of implementing basic look and feel functionality in a consistent way (but see Grudin, 1989 for arguments against user interface consistency). However, WIMP interfaces do not address the fundamental issues of communication in the computer interface. Like a chess game, the user and the system alternate moves, but the physical interface is like a description of the positions of the pieces, rather than an analysis of the goals and resources of each player.

The WIMP model of interaction provides a set of tools for constructing the user interface. Windows, Icons, and Menus, are entities within the visual display that the user can interact with, while the Pointing device is the physical mechanism through which interaction is achieved. One of the fundamental features of WIMP interaction is a point and shoot style of selection of objects and commands, and a direct manipulation style of interaction where objects may be moved around on the screen to carry out certain operations (Singh and Chignell, 1990).

Windows are portions (usually rectangular) of the screen that can overlap and be resized. Use of windows allows different applications or data to be visually separated on the screen. Thus windows provide physical separation or compartmentalization of screen objects that corresponds to different activity contexts, modes, and tasks. For instance, in a word processor, two files may be viewed at the same time, where each file is positioned in a separate window. Windows also allow efficient use of screen real estate by allowing these different activity contexts to be readily available even when there is not enough room for all of them to be on the screen at the same time. This is achieved by allowing screen real estate to be effectively shared between activity contexts through techniques such as overlapping, stacking. and resizing. Windows typically share a common set of features (Billingsley, 1988) such as scroll bars (which allow the cursor or pointer to be moved within the data set represented in the window), handles (which allow the window to be "grabbed" and moved), and close boxes (which close the window when clicked on).

The second main element of the WIMP interface is the icon. Icons serve as visual landmarks within the user interface (Glenn and Chignell 1992) . Since the Xerox Star, icons have been an essential part of the WIMP model. However, icon design remains more of an art than a science. Icons are used to represent manipulable objects within the interface as well as functions such as cutting and pasting. Icons also serve as a bridge between the physical and the conceptual interface. From the physical standpoint, the icon is a sign, a somewhat abbreviated representation of the object or function that it represents. However, an icon may also be thought of as a symbol within the conceptual interface.

Menus allow users to select what they want from a set of choices rather than having to remember what the available choices are and their explicit names. Of course, menus were in use in restaurants well before the development of WIMP interfaces. The usefulness of menus stems from the fact that they don't require people to remember or recall what the available actions or choices are. In return for this reduction in "cognitive load" users must be able to select from appropriate menus and be able to "navigate" to the submenus that hold their choices, since menus are frequently nested. Menus may also be presented in a number of different visual formats such as a menu bar, and pull-down, pop-up, and pie menus. Menu selections are frequently "guarded" by dialogue boxes to ensure that the user does not make a menu selection in error. For instance, in most Macintosh applications, when one attempts to save a new file with the same name as a file that already exists in the directory, then a dialogue box will appear to ask the user whether or not they really want to overwrite the old file.

The fourth and final main element of the WIMP model is the pointing device (often a mouse or tablet). The pointing device allows the user to move to a region in the workspace and then select it. The pointing device is extremely important in the point and shoot style of navigation. In addition to selecting an object so that it is highlighted, the pointing device can also activate the object (if it is an icon representing an application, it may then be highlighted for instance) or move it (often called "dragging"). Fortunately, pointing devices such as the mouse have been shown to work extremely well in tasks such as pointing (Card, English, and Burr, 1978) and dragging (MacKenzie, Sellen, and Buxton, 1991).

Since its development in the 1970s, the WIMP model has become the predominant style of physical user interface. It was first popularized in the Apple Macintosh after its development at the Xerox Palo Alto Research Center (PARC) and since then has moved into both the PC (e.g., Microsoft Windows) and workstation environments (e.g., X-Windows, Motif). In contrast, the technology for representing and building the conceptual aspect of user interfaces is much less well developed.

7. The conceptual interface: the NERD model

The conceptual interface is non-obvious and is also more task dependent. Thus a chess-playing program and a spreadsheet may both use a WIMP style of physical interface while having very different conceptual interfaces. But what is the conceptual interface? Like minds, conceptual interfaces exist even though it seems impossible to show what they look like or how they work. The conceptual interface may be thought of as the meeting place of the human mind and the software machine. In many instances it is difficult to maintain a clear distinction between the physical and conceptual interfaces. For instance, icons, which are a major part of the WIMP approach to physical interfaces are simultaneously major components of the conceptual interface, often representing conceptual entities and relations.

The user interface is a hierarchy of layers, each satisfying a different type (or level) of task- related goal. The physical (WIMP) interface provides a lower level of detailed physical activity and manipulation of objects within the user interface metaphor. At the next level the NERD interface (defined below) handles conceptual subgoals within the task. At a higher level still are the overall task strategies, many of which will be idiosyncratic for the current task. Thus we can imagine a hierarchy of interfaces as shown in Figure 4.

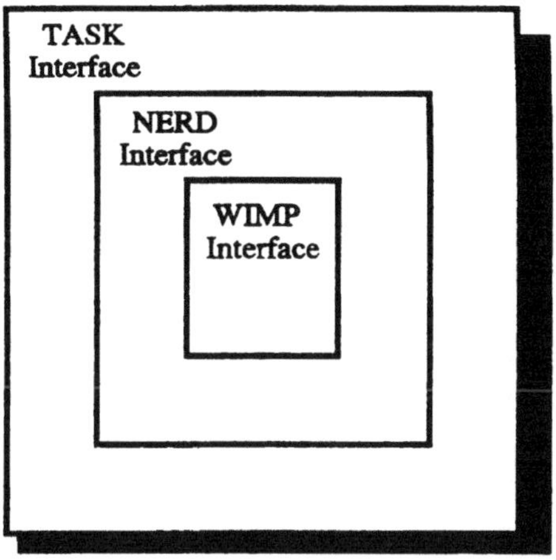

Figure 4: A hierarchical model of the user interface

The base of the hierarchy is the WIMP interface. The next level of the hierarchy is the NERD interface. At the top level of the interface is the TASK interface consisting of idiosyncratic components that represent the unique features of the current task.

The NERD model was first described by Chignell and Waterworth (1991), and it was designed to represent the conceptual interface in similar fashion to the way that the WIMP model represents the physical interface. The elements making up the NERD interface are:

Navigation
Evaluation
Refinement
Demonstration.

The first element of the NERD interface is Navigation. A central problem of the user is that of mapping their mental model of the task onto the system's representation (Norman, 1986). In the NERD model of the cognitive interface, navigation is the mechanism by which cognitive compatibility is achieved. The strategy is to present the structure of the system's model of the task to users directly, thereby encouraging them to incorporate the system's view of the task into their own models.

Navigation is the process by which the user moves through the conceptual structure of the interface. This structure may be represented by a set of hierarchically ordered menus, by a network of information, by a set of windows that open and close in different task contexts, and so on. Whatever this structure is, however, the NERD model requires that it be made available to the user, i.e., that navigability is enhanced.

While navigation emphasizes the input from user to system, evaluation deals with the output from the conceptual interface. Broadly speaking, evaluation is concerned with conveying information about task performance to the user and in assessing the user's understanding of updates to the current task status as represented in the interface.

Refinement is the process through which the output of the cognitive interface is modified to correct the user's perception of task status. Refinement implies an ability on the part of the system to recognize discrepancies in the user's cognitive model. Thus refinement is a desirable function to be included in future NERD models rather than a process that can be implemented immediately (Chignell and Waterworth, 1991). The particular implementation of refinement will depend on the type of task being carried out since higher levels of the interface will generally achieve consistency at a more abstract level (i.e., NERD interfaces will include a refinement component, but the precise way in which refinement is carried out will vary from application to application).

The final component of the NERD model is demonstration. This is the mechanism by which users are able to customize the conceptual interface to conform more closely to their conceptual models. Like refinement, demonstration is a fairly high level concept that may be achieved in a number of different ways. The basic idea of demonstration is that the user can define an operation from his mental model of the task directly onto the conceptual interface. This modification of the conceptual interface through demonstration is somewhat related to the notion of visual programming, of macro definition, and similar capabilities. For instance, some software packages have a type of "watch me" capability where the user can carry out a series of actions and then have them saved as a single operation.

Thus, the NERD model is concerned with specifying a core set of functions that enhance the compatibility between the conceptual interface of software and the mental model of the user. Navigation increases cognitive compatibility by making the structure of the conceptual interface obvious to the user, who may then operate on that structure directly. Demonstration increases cognitive compatibility by allowing the user to customize the behaviour of the conceptual interface so that it conforms more closely to his mental model. Refinement increases cognitive compatibility through modification of the conceptual interface by the system. Thus demonstration and refinement both attempt to improve cognitive compatibility through modification of the conceptual interface, but demonstration does this on the initiative of the user, while refinement does this on the initiative of the system. Finally evaluation is the process by which the error signal (i.e., lack of cognitive compatibility) is assessed. Evaluation forms the basis for refinement, and may also be used for requesting the user to customize by demonstration, in cases of low cognitive compatibility, where refinement is either unavailable or insufficient. Figure 5 provides a schematic representation of the WIMP, NERD, and TASK interfaces.

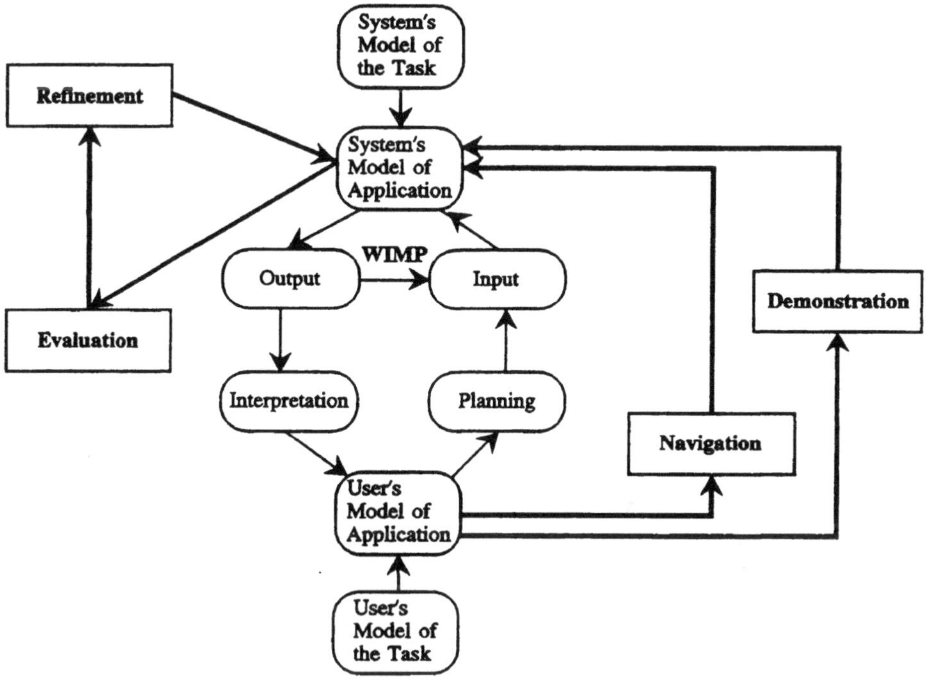

Figure 5: A schematic representation of the user interface, showing the elements of the NERD model highlighted

The WIMP interface consists of the input (e.g., mouse and keyboard) and output of the physical interface. In contrast, the NERD interface deals with the conceptual interface between the system's model of the application and the user's mental model of the application. Meanwhile the task interface connects the system's task model and the user's task model. In any human-computer interaction, communication will be occurring through all three layers of this interface hierarchy in similar fashion to the way in which layered protocols are handled in speech communication (Figure 2). However, the implementations of each user interface layer should be designed to encourage a natural and effective form of communication and we address this concern in the following section.

8. Naturalistic and non-naturalistic communication

Coordination of human-machine intelligence at the computer interface requires overcoming intrinsic problems in human-machine communication stemming from discrepancies in knowledge representation and language usage of different agents. Development of agent-like user interfaces requires specification of the relative roles of the human and machine, a shared language, and a set of suitable rules that map dialogues onto task contexts.

Disciplines such as linguistics have typically looked to natural language (spoken or written) for clues about how meaning is embedded in symbols. However, language is but one way in which we communicate. Another "naturalistic" form of communication is non-verbal, as in body language, which can be highly revealing even when unintentionally so. But what about new technologies where the rules of communication have to be rewritten anew? This is essentially the problem that confronts the user interface designer. In this "invented" or non-naturalistic situation the user interface is in fact a formalism that creates the communication channel between user and computer (e.g., Jacob, 1983; Olsen, 1990). There are few naturalistic rules that guide the design of this communication channel. In the following section we will focus on an aspect of human-computer communication that has become prominent in the WIMP model, but is also of concern to communication across the conceptual interface, i.e., naturalistic design of icons.

9. Visual semiotics and naturalistic design of icons

At present the communication issues relating to the user interface receive less attention than issues such as graphical design of the computer screen and how to design physical input devices. This is not surprising, since the communication issues are subtle, while the physical interface (e.g., screen and keyboard) is obvious. Thus legal arguments about the ownership of user interfaces have focused on the issue of look and feel (Samuelson and Glushko, 1990) rather than on communication style and language. However, one issue where appearance and meaning converge is in the design of icons.

Icons are simultaneously signs at the level of the physical interface, and symbols at the level of the conceptual interface.

In semiotics, the distinction between signs and symbols is a complex topic that is addressed in other chapters of this book. Here we will simply be contented to maintain the distinction between signs and symbols described by Jung (1964, pp. 3, 4, 41):

> Man uses the spoken or written word to express the meaning of what he wants to convey. His language is full of symbols, but he also often employs signs or images that are not strictly descriptive. Some are mere abbreviations or strings of initials, such as UN, UNICEF, or UNESCO; others are familiar trade marks, the names of patent medicines, badges, or insignia. Although these are meaningless in themselves, they have acquired a recognizable meaning through common usage or deliberate intent. Such things are not symbols. They are signs, and they do no more than denote the objects to which they are attached.
>
> What we call a symbol is a term, a name. or even a picture that may be familiar in daily life, yet that possesses specific connotations in addition to its conventional and obvious meaning. It implies something vague, unknown, or hidden from us....take the case of the Indian who, after a visit to England. told his friends at home that the English worship animals, because he had found eagles, lions, and oxen in old churches. He was not aware (nor are many Christians) that these animals are symbols of the Evangelists and are derived from the vision of Ezekiel, and that this in turn has an analogy to the Egyptian sun god Horus and his four sons. Thus a word or an image is symbolic when it implies something more than its obvious and immediate meaning. It has a wider "unconscious" aspect that is never precisely defined or fully explained.
>
> ...The sign is always less than the concept it represents. while a symbol always stands for something more than its obvious and immediate meaning. Symbols, moreover. are natural and spontaneous products. No genius has ever sat down with a pen or a brush in his hand and said: "Now I am going to invent a symbol." No one can take a more or less rational thought, reached as a logical conclusion or by deliberate intent, and then give it "symbolic" form. No matter what fantastic trappings one may put upon an idea of this kind, it will still remain a sign, linked to the conscious thought behind it, not a symbol that hints at something not yet known.

Icons and overlapping windows play an important role in making the desktop metaphor work on current computers. The issue of what makes a good icon or visual symbol with appropriate visual semantics (see Saint-Martin, 1990, for a relevant discussion, cited in the review by Sonesson, 1990) is still unresolved in spite of the ability of graphic designers to produce usable icons. The interesting feature of Jung's view on symbols is that it suggests that unlike iconic signs, iconic symbols can not be designed but have to arise in some way out of usage stemming from their role in some collective unconscious. At first glance, this role of the collective unconscious as a progenitor for iconic symbols may seem incongruous in the high technology world of user interface design, yet the whole point of icons is that they be intuitive and that they denote something more than a sign-like representation of the underlying object or function. The requirements that icons be obvious, and intuitive across a range of cultures and experiences almost requires that they be so basic as to be innately recognized or part of some collective unconscious. Is it not conceivable that the almost visceral satisfaction that some people get in terms of manipulating icons in a graphical user interface may not in some way stem from their symbolic connotations? Take for instance, the trashcan that is used to delete files or remove disks in the Macintosh operating system and Microsoft Windows (and its closely related cousin, the black hole in the NEXT interface). While the particular nature of the symbology in question could be debated (e.g., is the symbol some type of anima, or return to the womb, or banishment of an enemy?), there seems no doubt that the effectiveness of the trashcan stems from its properties as a symbol.

In applications like international road signs where some users rely completely on the pictorial content of the icon in order to determine the meaning, the symbolic aspects of the icon become paramount. While one might not be able to design a good symbol from scratch (if we are to believe Jung in this regard), it should still be possible to recognize an effective icon in terms of its usability, i.e., the ability of people to recognize the object or function that it represents. The sign-like properties of an icon can be measured in how well it represents what it purports to represent, while the symbol-like properties will be reflected both in the universality of that recognition and in the satisfaction or involvement that people have in using the icon.

Most of the icons that are available as of now seem to fall far short of the goal of universal recognizability. Empirical studies of icons indicate that they do not guarantee instant understandability across or between cultures (Barnard and Marcel, 1984). Thus design of effective icons is an iterative process that should be directed according to the measured usability of icon prototypes.

10. Usability analysis as a guide to design of icons

The development of cooperative reasoning interfaces is a difficult problem, but it should be tackled from the perspective of shared communication rather than shared intelligence. Design of icons seems to be a particularly important part of both the conceptual and physical interface. Thus effective icons are likely to be a prerequisite to effect human-machine communication across the user interface. In the absence of guiding theory about what makes a good symbol, or how an icon should be designed, it is still possible to identify which icons tend to work better in practice. Usability analysis is an empirical tool that measures how easy a user interface is to use (i.e., using the philosophy that "the proof of the pudding is in the eating"). The essence of the usability approach is to create different versions of the user interface and see which version leads to the best performance. In the case of icons, alternative designs for an icon may be tested to see which version tends to work better.

Glenn and Chignell (1992) described the iconary approach to assess icon understanding and design quality. In this approach a set of icons is obtained (either by selecting icons already in existence or by asking a group of designers to create icons that correspond to various objects or functions). A panel of judges is then asked to match the icons to a set of corresponding objects or functions. Statistical measures are then used to assess how good each icon designer is (e.g., based on the proportion of times the intended meaning of their icon was recognized) and how good the judges are at icon recognition (e.g., the proportion of times that each judge was "correct").

Waterworth, Chignell, and Zhai (1991) used the iconary method to investigate which icons were more effective with respect to hypermedia functionality. In their study, nine different subjects constructed a total of 363 different icons. Each subject then assigned each icon constructed by the other eight subjects to one of 61 categories representing functions or actions within a hypermedia interface. Overall, 61.2% of the icon presentations were correctly recognized using this procedure. The best recognized icons tended to be concrete objects existing in daily life, or geometric or spatial concepts, or standard representations that were already familiar within the culture (e.g., video play buttons). While we are a long way from having a theory of what makes a good icon, we do at least have measures of icon usability that can be used to guide icon design.

11. Conclusions

This chapter has focused on the user interface issues associated with human-machine communication. This topic poses a challenge for user interface design which has so far had its major respect in handling look and feel issues (the physical interface). User interface design is inherently difficult, and much of what is currently known about user interfaces may not be appropriate for the problem of communication in applications that require cooperative reasoning.

Given the fundamental, and perhaps universal issues that the user interface problem raises, insights about naturalistic communication may be helpful in telling us how to "invent" user interfaces for human-machine cooperative reasoning. The layered protocol approach to interface design emphasizes the two-way aspect of man-communication, and the need to decode the utterances or inputs of the other agent. Most human-human communication is cooperative in the sense that the two agents negotiate meaning, correct misinterpretations, and so on. NERD interfaces may provide the assist the development of communication through the conceptual interface. However, there are still many unanswered questions about when and how NERD interface development strategies should be used. In the meantime, the task of icon design is an important and tractable task that lies at the heart of human machine communication processes where icons play a large role in the visual appearance of physical interfaces.

Acknowledgments

I would like to thank René Jorna for his encouragement in the preparation of his chapter. I would also like to acknowledge the contribution that discussion with Bernice Glenn, Kamran Parsaye, and John Waterworth have made to my thinking on this topic.

References

Barnard, P., Marcel, A. (1984). Representation and understanding in the use of symbols and pictograms. In: R. Easterby and H. Zwaga (eds.), *Information Design*. N.Y.: Wiley.

Billingsley, P. (1988). Taking panes with windows. In: M. Helander, *Handbook of Human-Computer Interaction*. N.Y.: North-Holland.

Card, S.K., English, W.K., and Burr, B.J. (1978). Evaluation of mouse, rate-controlled isometric joystick, step keys, and text keys for text selection on a CRT, *Ergonomics* 21, 601-613.

Chignell, M.H. (1990). A taxonomy of user interface terminology, *SIGCHI Bulletin* 21:4, 27-34.

Chignell, M.H. (1991). Communication and meaning at the computer interface: WIMPs, NERDs, and non-naturalistic invention, *International Semiotic Spectrum*, Toronto Semiotic Circle, Nr. 15.

Chignell, M.H., Hancock, P.A. (1988). Intelligent Interfaces. In: M. Helander (ed.), *Handbook of Human Computer Interaction*. North Holland, 969-995.

Chignell, M.H., Hancock P.A., Smith, P.J., & Shute, S.J. (1986). Information Retrieval: An Intelligent Interface Perspective. In: *Proceedings of the IEEE International conference on Systems, Man, and Cybernetics*, Atlanta, Georgia, 372-377.

Chignell, M.H., Waterworth, J.A. (1991). WIMPs and NERDs: An extended view of the user interface, *ACM SIGCHI Bulletin 23:2.*

Glenn, B., Chignell, M.H. (1992). Hypermedia: Design for browsing. In: R. Hartson and D. Hix (eds.), *Advances in Human Computer Interaction*, Vol. 3, Norwood, NJ: Ablex.

Grudin, J. (1989). The case against user interface consistency, *Communications of the ACM* 32:10, 164-173.

Hancock, P.A., Chignell, M.H. (1987). Adaptive control in Human-machine systems. In: P.A. Hancock (ed.) *Human Factors Psychology*, Amsterdam: North-Holland.

Jacob, R.J.K. (1983). Using formal specifications in the design of a human-computer interface, *Communications of the ACM*.

Jung, C.G. (ed.) (1964). *Man and his Symbols*. London: Aldus Books.

MacKenzie, I.S., Sellen, A., and Buxton, W. (1991). A comparison of input devices in elemental pointing and dragging tasks. In: *CHI '91 Conference Proceedings*, N.Y.: Association for Computing Machinery, 161-167.

Myers, B. (1990). Creating user interfaces using programming by example, visual programming, and constraints, *ACM Transactions on Programming Languages and Systems* 12:2, 143-177.

Norman, D.A. (1986). Cognitive engineering. In: D.A. Norman and S. Draper (eds.), *User Centered System Design*, Hillsdale, NJ: Erlbaum.

Olsen, D.R. (1990). Propositional production systems for dialogue description. In: *CHI '90 Proceedings*, 57-63.

Saint-Martin, F. (1990). *Semiotics of Visual Language*. Bloomington, Indiana: Indiana University Press.

Samuelson, P., Glushko, R. (1990). Survey on the look and feel lawsuits, *Communications of the ACM*, Nr. 33, 483.

Shneiderman. B. (1983). Direct manipulation: A step beyond programming languages, *IEEE Computer* 16:8, 57-69.

Singh, G., Chignell, M.H. (1990). *Components of the visual computer: A review of relevant technologies*. Technical Report TR90-46-0, Institute of Systems Science, National University of Singapore.

Smith, D.C., Irby, C., Kimball, R., Verplank, B., and Harslem, E. (1982). Designing the Star user interface, *BYTE* 7:4, 242-282.

Sonesson. G. (1990). The challenge of visual semiotics, *The Semiotic Review of Books* 1:2, 6-8.

Taylor, M.M. (1988). Layered protocols for computer-human dialogue. I: Principles, *International Journal of Man-Machine Studies.*

Waterworth, J.A., Chignell, M.H., and Zhai, S. (1991). *From icons to interface designs: Hypermedia documents and information tools.* Unpublished manuscript, Institute of Systems Science, National University of Singapore.

Zloof, M.M. (1977). Query-by-example: A database language, *IBM Systems Journal, 16*, 324-343.

Name index

Subject index

Addresses of the authors

Prof. Dr. E.M. Barth, Kamperfoelieweg 16, 9765 HK Paterswolde, The Netherlands.

Prof. Dr. M. Chignell, Department of Industrial Engineering, 4 Taddle Creek Road, University of Toronto, Toronto, M5S 1A4 Canada.

Dr. R. J. Jorna, Faculty for Management and Organization, University of Groningen, P.O. Box 800, 9700 AV, Groningen, The Netherlands.

Dr. B. van Heusden, Institute for General and Comparative Literature, Faculty of Arts, University of Groningen, The Netherlands.

Dr. J. van der Lubbe, Department of Electrical Engineering, Delft University of Technology, P.O. Box 5031, 2500 GA Delft, The Netherlands.

Prof. Dr. G. Luger, Department of Computer Science, University of New Mexico, Albuquerque, New Mexico, 87131, U.S.A.

Prof. Dr. A. Marostica, Department of Philosophy, California State University, 5151 State University Drive, Los Angeles, California, 90032, U.S.A.

Prof. Dr. J.G. Meunier, Centre d'ATO, Université du Quebec à Montréal, C.P. 8888, Succ. A, Montréal H3C 3P8 Canada.

Prof. Dr. J.A. Michon, Rijksstraatweg 251, 9752 CB Haren, The Netherlands.

Dr. A. Müller, Institut für Wirtschaft und Sozial Psychologie, University of Göttingen, Gosslerstrasse 14, D-W-3400 Göttingen, Deutschland.

Prof. Dr. J. Pelc, Department of Logical Semiotics, Warsaw University, Krakowskie Przedmiescie Street 3, Pl 00-927 Warsaw 64, Poland.

Dr. M. Peschl, Department for Philosophy of Science, University of Vienna, Sensengasse 8/9, A-1090, Vienna, Austria.

Prof. Dr. R. Posner, Arbeitsstelle für Semiotik, Technische Universität Berlin, Ernst Reuter Platz 7, D-1000 Berlin, Deutschland.

Prof. Dr. F. Rastier, 57 Rue de Paris, 94340 Joinville, France.

Prof. Dr. M. Santaella Braga, Pontificia Universidade Catolica de Sao Paolo, Sao Paolo, Brazil.

Prof. Dr. Silverman, Institute for Artificial Intelligence, George Washington University, 2021 K Street NW, Washington D.C. 20006 U.S.A.

Prof. Dr. H. Visser, Faculteit der Wijsbegeerte, Katholieke Universiteit Brabant, Postbus 90153 5000 LE Tilburg, The Netherlands.

Dr. Y. Vogelenzang, R. Biermanpad 1, 2331 KK Leiden, The Netherlands.

Bei Fragen zur Produktsicherheit wenden Sie sich bitte an:
If you have any questions regarding product safety,
please contact:

Walter de Gruyter GmbH
Genthiner Straße 13
10785 Berlin
productsafety@degruyterbrill.com